MW00581277

Ivan the Terrible

RUSSIAN AND EAST EUROPEAN STUDIES

JONATHAN HARRIS, EDITOR

IVAN
THE TERRIBLE

FREE TO REWARD & FREE TO PUNISH

CHARLES J. HALPERIN

UNIVERSITY OF PITTSBURGH PRESS

Published by the University of Pittsburgh Press, Pittsburgh, Pa., 15260
Copyright © 2019, University of Pittsburgh Press
All rights reserved
Manufactured in the United States of America
Printed on acid-free paper
10 9 8 7 6 5 4 3 2 1

Cataloging-in-Publication data is available from the Library of Congress

ISBN 13: 978-0-8229-4591-8
ISBN 10: 0-8229-4591-6

Cover art: Mikhail Gerasimov's forensic facial reconstruction and bust of Ivan
the Terrible, 1953.
Cover design: Alex Wolfe

In Loving Memory of My Mother and My Aunts

Yvette Rudick Halperin
Dorothy Rudick Lipton
Rose Rudick Schielmann

Three sisters—together again.

Each man is three men:
who he thinks he is,
who others think he is,
and who he really is.

— **Anonymous**

Contents

Part IV. Ivan and Muscovy during and after the Oprichnina

Russia and Poland-Lithuania in the mid-sixteenth century. Map by Bill Nelson.

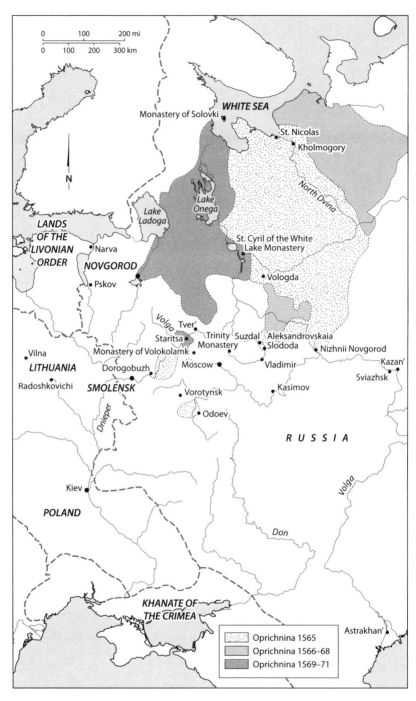

Areas incorporated into the *oprichnina*. Map by Bill Nelson.

Preface & Acknowledgments

This book could not have been written without the assistance of the Slavic Reference Service, University of Illinois at Urbana-Champaign Library, and Inter-Library Loan, Document Delivery Service, Herman B Wells Library, Indiana University, Bloomington.

I wish to thank all of my colleagues who have listened to, commented on, or responded to my convention and conference papers on Ivan IV, and endured endless conversations with me on the subject; Maria Arel, Daniel Kaiser, and Russell Martin, for copies of unpublished conference papers or essays and permission to cite them; Isaiah Gruber, for a copy of an inaccessible article; the referees of all my articles on Ivan IV; the late Norman Ingham and Ann Kleimola, for inviting me to do presentations at the Midwest Medieval Slavic Workshop at the University of Chicago and the Early Russian History Workshop at the Summer Research Laboratory of the University of Illinois at Urbana-Champaign, respectively; Donald Ostrowski, for invitations to address the Harvard Early Slavists Seminar; Jennifer Spock and Barbara Skinner, for arranging campus visits to Eastern Kentucky University and Indiana State University, respectively; and Dr. Predrag Matejic, for an invitation to deliver the Second Annual Hilandar Public Lecture, sponsored by the Hilandar Research Library and the Resource Center for Medieval Slavic Studies at The Ohio State University. I also wish to express my gratitude to the Gang of Four and all of my thirteen benefactors for their generosity in a project unrelated to Ivan the Terrible.

Barbara Skinner and Robert O. Crummey read earlier drafts of this book. I cannot thank them enough for their assistance. I also wish to thank Peter Kracht, director of the University of Pittsburgh Press, Professor Jonathan Harris, editor of its Russian and East European Studies series, and the two anonymous readers for the University of Pittsburgh Press. All remaining errors are my responsibility alone.

I use the Library of Congress system for transliterating Russian. Russian words appear in the text without diacritical marks at the end of words, except for Rus', which refers to the medieval East Slavs.

Muscovy utilized the Byzantine calendar from the Creation of the World, circa 5508 BCE, in which the year began on September 1. When we know the Byzantine year of an event but not the month, it is impossible to be certain of the CE calendar year, because September to December were one year earlier than January through August. In such cases the convention is to put a slash between the years: 1555/1556 means in either 1555 or 1556, depending upon the month; 1555–1556, with a dash, means from 1555 to 1556.

The field of Ivan the Terrible studies has flourished in recent years, and some sources have been issued in new editions. I have cited only the edition I have used.

In the sixteenth century foreigners called the country Ivan ruled "Muscovy" and its inhabitants "Muscovites." Ivan's subjects referred to themselves as "Russian" or "Rus'," the same term used by the East Slavs as early as the tenth century. I find the modern connotations of the word "Russia" misleading in reference to sixteenth-century history, so I prefer to use "Muscovy" instead.

For reasons of space, it is impossible for me to cite, let alone engage, all of the scholarly works I have consulted. For the same reason, I cannot point out all factual errors in those works.

Ivan the Terrible

Introduction

On August 12, 1976, a situation comedy about an irascible paterfamilias and his household of colorful denizens debuted as a summer replacement on the CBS television network. It was not very funny and went off the air just a month later. The series was set in Moscow, its protagonist was named Ivan, and it was called *Ivan the Terrible*.[1] Television network programming executives have never been accused of exaggerating the historical knowledge of their viewing audience. Therefore, we may assume that they correctly expected the public to recognize the name *Ivan the Terrible*. Tsar Ivan IV (1533–1584), commonly called Ivan "the Terrible" (in Russian, "Groznyi"), is an icon of Western civilization and a card-carrying member of the Historical Hall of Shame—a dubious pantheon of mostly rulers, infamous primarily for their vices, that includes Nero, Caligula, Attila the Hun, Chinggis (Genghis) Khan, Vlad the Impaler (Dracula), Caesare Borgia, and the Marquis de Sade (who was not a ruler).[2] Ivan's celebrity status explains how inmates of a Nazi concentration camp could label a sadistic Ukrainian guard named Ivan "Ivan the Terrible" and how American media could dub a 2004 hurricane named Ivan "Ivan the Terrible."

Ivan's evil reputation precedes him, prejudices scholarship, and distorts history. Russians writing about Ivan have to contend with the sheer weight of his negative image in Russian culture.³ During Ivan's lifetime to be styled "Groznyi" would have carried positive connotations, meaning "awe-inspiring," "formidable," or "dread," but in fact no one called Ivan "Groznyi" in his lifetime. The epithet did not become pejorative until the eighteenth century.⁴ Nowadays Ivan is so universally and uniquely known as Ivan Groznyi that in Russian "Groznyi" alone means Ivan IV. The historian Anna Khoroshkevich even created neologisms for "historians who study Ivan IV's reign" (*groznovedy*) and for "the study of Ivan IV's reign" (*groznovedenie*) from that epithet.⁵

During his lifetime Ivan was both idealized *and* demonized. Domestic sources extolled him as the God-chosen, pious tsar. This positive image of Ivan infused literary texts such as the *Book of Degrees of Imperial Genealogy*, a thematic history of Ivan's dynasty from Kievan times (starting in the ninth century and ending in the middle of the thirteenth century) to 1563, and artistic works such as the icon *Blessed Is the Host of the Heavenly Tsar* (often called the Church Militant), which most scholars believe depicts Ivan's conquest of the Tatar khanate of Kazan, and works created under the supervision of state or church authorities. One contemporary Muscovite, boyar Prince Andrei Kurbskii, produced perhaps the most influential negative image of Ivan, but only from the safety of exile in the Grand Duchy of Lithuania. Kurbskii wrote several letters and a *History of the Grand Prince of Moscow* denouncing Ivan.⁶ Numerous foreigners, some of whom served Ivan and then wrote scathing attacks on him after they left Muscovy and even others who had never been there, wrote sensationalist anti-Muscovite propaganda for Moscow's enemies during the Livonian War (1558–1581). Muscovy lacked an effective printing industry that could respond to the massive pamphlet literature denouncing Ivan, so the vicious portrayals of Ivan by his enemies went largely unanswered.⁷ The satanic image of Ivan propagated by such publications created the still pervasive negative myth of Ivan.

This foreign satanic image was largely borrowed. Foreigners lifted images of Ivan's "tyranny" verbatim from texts about other "monstrous" rulers from antiquity on. Many authors appropriated stories from literature about the Ottomans, which demonized the Ottoman sultan.⁸ These, in turn, had already been applied to the Ottomans' enemy, Vlad the Impaler (Tsepesh), in the second half of the fifteenth century the ruler of Wallachia in modern-day Romania, the original Dracula. As a result, Ivan appeared on gravures and woodcuts wearing a turban. Universal folkloric motifs were also applied to Ivan. The story that Tsepesh nailed an ambassador's hat to his head when he refused to take it off in the ruler's presence was applied to Ivan simply by changing Tsepesh's name to Ivan's.[9] Similarly, fantastic legends that Ivan blinded the architect of St. Basil's Cathedral so that he could not duplicate his feat, ordered the execution of an elephant that refused to bow to him, or "punished" a bell that spooked his horse also reflect Ivan's imputed reputation, not his actual actions.[10]

Contemporary foreign writings also presented Ivan as a typical "Muscovite barbarian." Ethnic origin was used to explain the "Eastern" tyranny of Ivan and the Ottoman sultan but not the "Western" tyranny of "civilized" Romans such as Nero or Caligula.[11] Ivan became the personification of what modern scholars call Russian exceptionalism, the theory that Russia's history differed significantly from that of "Europe," for the worse. Ivan was uniquely worse than any non-Russian ruler, because Russians were uniquely worse than any other people. Such stereotyping must be rejected. Other sixteenth-century monarchs also took a cavalier attitude toward the lives of their subjects. If Ivan was no worse than his contemporaries, neither was he any better. He resembled his contemporaries among foreign rulers more than he did his Muscovite predecessors or successors.

It is no exaggeration to say that everything significant about Ivan's life is contested among historians, from his parentage to his cause of death. His reign was politicized in his own time and has remained so ever since.[12] In 1891 Nikolai Mikhailovskii blamed Ivan's contradictory reign for disorienting even experienced historians to the point that they disregarded the sources and indulged in fantasy.[13] Whether a particular explanation is best understood as an analysis of existing sources, an extrapolation from available evidence, an inference based upon a reliable foundation, a baseless speculation, or an ignorant, worthless fantasy often depends upon the point of view of the critic. When it comes to interpreting Ivan, all theories can be described as controversial; so describing any given theory as controversial says nothing.

While the negative image of Ivan remained constant outside of Muscovy after his death in 1584, the positive image within Muscovy did not. Especially during the chaotic "Time of Troubles" at the turn of the seventeenth century, Muscovites were able to express not only positive but also more ambivalent, and even critical, opinions about Ivan. This ambivalence continued throughout the seventeenth century, epitomized, on the one hand, by false claims by the Romanov dynasty, beginning in 1613 with Tsar Mikhail Romanov, that they were descended from Ivan (they were actually descended from the family of Ivan's first wife, Anastasiia Romanovna), and, on the other, by Tsar Aleksei Mikhailovich's "apology" to the relics of Saint Metropolitan Filipp for the saint's murder at the order of his "ancestor," Ivan.[14]

Modern historical studies about Ivan began to appear in Russia in the middle of the eighteenth century, but Russian opinion about Ivan remained divided. The aristocrat Prince Mikhail Shcherbatov excoriated Ivan for attacking the aristocracy. The early nineteenth-century court historiographer Nikolai Karamzin praised the "good" Ivan of the 1550s and denounced the "bad" Ivan of the *oprichnina*, Ivan's infamous instrument of mass terror,[15] a separate domain within Muscovy within which Ivan had unlimited authority, staffed by *oprichniki*. (The words "oprichnina" and "oprichniki" are untranslatable.)[16]

Karamzin's paradigm of the two periods of Ivan's reign dominated nineteenth- and early twentieth-century Russian historiography. Late Imperial Russian historiography began to produce serious scholarly works of lasting value about Ivan. Despite detours such as Stalin's "cult" of Ivan, such work continues down to the present in Russia.[17] Scholarship about Ivan increased significantly in Russia after the Communist Party rejection of Stalinism in 1956, and even more so after the fall of the Soviet Union in 1991. The removal of censorship in Russia after 1991 permitted Russians to express all shades of opinion about Ivan. Defending Ivan against "foreign" slander became a cause célèbre of Russian chauvinists. Monarchists and extreme Russian Orthodox devotees urged the Russian Orthodox Church to canonize Ivan, an effort that ultimately failed.[18] The same, often anti-Semitic, milieu continues to inspire apologias for Ivan. Nevertheless, Russians in Russia can now elect to categorize Ivan as a sadistic, immoral tyrant and totalitarian "Asiatic" despot, and some do. The anachronistic "deadly parallel" to Stalin, never far below the surface in the Soviet Union, has now risen to the full light of day.[19] At the same time, the views of amateurs clutter the bookshelves, radio and television broadcasts, movies, and Internet, creating a cacophony of interpretations of little or no scholarly value.[20] Even a broad overview of all professional historical scholarship on Ivan would require too much space to be included here.[21] Suffice it say that Ivan and his reign remain lively and contentious subjects of study in his homeland.

Since the Second World War, Western scholarship on Ivan has also grown significantly. The fragmentary nature of the extant documentation makes it impossible to write a conventional biography of Ivan. No personal documents from Ivan survive, no diaries, no private correspondence, no memoires, autobiographies, or diaries from Ivan's intimates. We have no insight into Ivan's character away from the public eye.[22] It is impossible even to construct a reliable chronology of his life. The refractory sources at our disposal—chronicles (narratives that organize events by years), other narrative tales, saints' lives, law codes, sermons, charters, cadastres, foreign policy memos and negotiation accounts, registers of military and civilian service, and so forth—cannot answer some of the key questions we would like to pose about events during Ivan's time, such as identifying his personal role in policy formation. We have no minutes of meetings of the Royal Council or draft legislation or memoranda to show us who initiated a policy, how it evolved, or who expressed alternative opinions. Narrative sources, following literary etiquette, presented events as they "should have" taken place. In the chronicles, political actors played cliché roles.[23] Given these inherent limitations of the sources, even writing a purely political biography of Ivan remains impossible. So-called biographies of Ivan are actually books about Ivan and his reign, as is this volume.

To blame Ivan's actions upon his insanity, as many have done, divorces Ivan from that context; to assert that sixteenth-century Muscovite history resulted only from long-term processes unaffected by Ivan's "excesses" marginalizes Ivan from that context. The latter is not a fault only of Soviet Marxist scholarship; it can be found in Vasilii Kliuchevskii, perhaps the greatest Imperial Russian historian, who wrote that the Muscovite order would have turned out the same, with less difficulty, without Ivan.[24]

The problems created by the nature of the sources for writing about Ivan and his reign have sometimes been misconstrued. The contrast in terms of reliability between narrative sources, such as chronicles, and documentary sources, such as registers and charters, has sometimes been exaggerated.[25] Dissimilar genres of sources filter reality differently, but from an underlying common mentality. The greatest source problem in studying Ivan's reign is the 1567 termination of the all-encompassing Moscow chronicle tradition, the continuation of the Nikon Chronicle, which provided a basic narrative of events. There is no consensus on the identity of the authors/compilers of the chronicle or their institutional sponsor, but whoever wrote these narratives had superb access to both state and church archives.[26] Despite the bias of these writers and omissions from the chronicle, it is invaluable. We have no idea why this particular chronicle tradition came to a dead stop in 1567, nor can we connect its termination to any event in that year. Chronicle writing did not completely cease in Muscovy in 1567, but the local, monastic, and private chronicles that persisted cannot compensate for the loss of the "central" chronicle. So midway through the crucial oprichnina years, historians must shift from relying upon the Muscovite chronicle to using foreign accounts, many of them deliberately tilted against Ivan, and laconic documentary sources. Our knowledge of Ivan's reign from 1567 to 1584 suffers enormously from that change.

Specialists on Ivan's reign disagree about which sources are reliable, contemporary, or even authentic. As a result, it is virtually guaranteed that they will disagree about what happened and why. Therefore, definitive and broadly accepted conclusions about Ivan's reign hardly exist among scholars. Because historians disagree about which sources are "reliable," writing an account of Ivan based only upon "reliable" sources is impossible. Some historians doubt the authenticity of all literary works attributed to Ivan and Prince Andrei Kurbskii, a skeptical school "founded" by Edward Keenan. I find his conclusions unconvincing. More recently Brian Boeck has tried to impugn the authenticity of Kurbskii's *History*. I do not find his arguments persuasive. Because I have concluded that these works are authentic, I will not qualify my references to them below. However, it should be noted that although authentic, I consider these works mendacious; they are reliable as to Ivan's or Kurbskii's point of view or at least propaganda, but not always reliable in their factual content.[27] All sources, indeed all types of sources, may contain reliable and unreliable information; blanket rejection of any source, or type of source, in toto is therefore unwarranted.

Historians have traditionally divided Ivan's reign into four periods: 1) Ivan's minority, from his accession at an extremely young age in 1533 to his coronation and marriage in 1547, during which he did not have much influence upon the actions of the Muscovite government but during which the violent atmosphere of court politics and the boyars' neglect of his needs are supposed to have greatly influenced his character and determined his later attitude toward the boyars; 2) the period of reforms, the "long" 1550s, from Ivan's coronation and marriage until the eve of the creation of the oprichnina in December 1564, a period of major domestic political and religious reform, exciting cultural productivity, and foreign policy success, including the conquest of the Tatar khanate of Kazan and the initial victories in the war against Livionia to secure Baltic Sea ports, during which Ivan's role remains contested among historians; 3) the oprichnina, from January 1565 until some time in early 1572, when Ivan's security apparatus, the black-robed oprichniki, with dogs' heads and brooms on their horses' necks, committed brutal mass murder and atrocities upon the Muscovite population, for which a "paranoid" and "sadistic" Ivan has been given sole responsibility; and 4) the rest of Ivan's reign, from the abolition of the oprichnina to Ivan's death in 1584. Of course each period has continuities and discontinuities with its predecessor and/or successor.[28] Most books on Ivan's reign present uninterrupted narratives, but whether they acknowledge this four-part periodization or not,[29] somehow chapter breaks seem to coincide with the ends of the first three.

Because Ivan of necessity makes almost no appearance in events of his minority and his role during the reforms remains a matter of conjecture, Ivan perforce disappears, entirely or partially, from half of a straight narrative history of his reign. Therefore, instead, I have adopted a mixed chronological and thematic structure. Part I describes the rise of Muscovy and the nature of the Muscovite state and society at the time of Ivan's accession. Part II focuses on Ivan's life from 1533 to December 1564, the first two periods of the traditional periodization. With this background in hand, we can better evaluate Ivan's role in events in Muscovy during that time, the subject of part III. Because Ivan's responsibility for what happened in his realm during and after the oprichnina is not disputed, part IV examines together the oprichnina and Ivan's life for the remaining two periods of the traditional periodization. The conclusion presents a brief characterization of Ivan's contribution to Muscovite history.

In this book I have tried to avoid exclusivist paradigms and monocausal explanations of Ivan's actions. For example, at some times the Muscovite state did dominate society, but at other times it did not. Sometimes the government pursued centralization of authority and power, and sometimes it sought to achieve its goals by decentralized means.

Although all of Ivan's life and Muscovite history during his reign are connected, it is impossible to discuss everything at once. Any text or event referred to but not explained at first mention will be described in full elsewhere. I have chosen not to burden the text with innumerable cross references to "see below" or "see above"; the index and glossary should ameliorate this problem.

I have reached three general conclusions about Ivan. First, while there is considerable continuity between Ivan and his predecessors, Ivan was also unique in key respects, and he cannot be called a typical Muscovite ruler. No Muscovite ruler before or after Ivan, no Imperial Russian ruler, and no Soviet ruler save Stalin ever used mass terror as a political instrument.[30] Ivan was neither all "good" nor all "bad" nor did he shift from all one to all the other. At all times Ivan was a human being, a paradoxical human being to be sure but not simply the monster of legend.

Second, to understand Ivan's actions, they must be placed within the context of Muscovite history during the sixteenth century. To blame Ivan's actions solely upon his mental state divorces him from that context. Ivan's behavior is far too complex to be reduced a single all-encompassing theory, a "magic bullet," that will "explain" Ivan. To attribute Ivan's torture and execution of seemingly innocent members of the elite and the population at large to his insanity, or to the fact that he was was a tyrant, explains nothing, in part because it avoids questions of why no one stopped him and why various members of the elite assisted him.To assert that the shape of sixteenth-century Muscovite history resulted from long-term processes unaffected by Ivan's "excesses" marginalizes him from that context. For this reason, in order to analyze Ivan, the historian must address all aspects of Muscovite history during his reign, because Muscovite political, social, economic, and cultural history were all related to Ivan and to each other. The economic prosperity of the 1530s to 1550s was essential to the growth of local self-government, domestic administrative and religious reform, foreign expansion, and cultural flourishing, all reflective of an optimistic, self-assured state and society. I interpret the oprichnina as the result of the interaction between Ivan and Muscovite society. On the one hand, Ivan was dealing with the multiple ideological stresses imposed upon him as he tried to live like a good Orthodox Christian but rule ruthlessly to defend the realm. On the other hand, a century of Muscovite expansion, necessitating mobilization of existing social resources and the creation of new social classes to serve government needs, had created significant social tensions. Social innovation produced a degree of upward and downward social mobility beyond the limits of Muscovy's traditional society. Ivan created the oprichnina to escape his moral dilemma as ruler, but in doing so he created a medium through which these accumulated social tensions could express themselves violently. The result was social pathology, certainly not what Ivan intended. Of course it would be foolish to expect any Muscovite source from Ivan's reign to explain the oprichnina that way; my interpretation is an extrapolation that tries to do justice to what the sources do tell us.

Third, Ivan not only made an impression on contemporaries and posterity but also had a real impact.[31] Some of the institutions established during Ivan's reign survived one, two, or three centuries after his death. Kazan remains part of the Russian Federation to the present. At the very least, Ivan did not prevent these reforms or sabotage these accomplishments.[32] While it is often impossible to determine how much responsibility Ivan bears for specific policies, he certainly initiated enough atrocities to merit condemnation and enough successful policies to deserve praise.

Ivan's contradictory legacy reflects his contradictory, if always charismatic, character and rule. Ivan made a difference in Muscovite history, a difference as contradictory as he was.

PART I

Muscovy in the Sixteenth Century

Muscovy in 1533

When his father, Grand Prince Vasilii III, died in 1533, Ivan, then three years old, became Grand Prince of Moscow and All Rus'. Muscovy's domestic institutions and international situation determined how the Muscovite elite dealt with a minor ruler. These factors also influenced how the adult Ivan would relate to the elite, to the Muscovite governmental apparatus, and to Muscovite society. This chapter first examines the rise of Muscovy before 1533 and the uncertainties affecting dynastic succession, then it explores some of the major characteristics of the Muscovite polity and society: Muscovy's political structure and political culture, the development of a bureaucracy and an administrative apparatus, the concept of centralization, and the reciprocal relationship between the government and society.

The Muscovite principality arose at the turn of the fourteenth century, when the Mongols still ruled the land. By the middle of the fourteenth century it had become a grand principality. As a result of continued expansion during the fifteenth and early sixteenth centuries, by the time of Ivan's accession it encompassed all the formerly independent Russian principalities of the northeast, including Tver and Riazan, as well as the formerly independent city-states of the northwest, Lord Novgorod the Great and Pskov.

Muscovy had even conquered the city of Smolensk from the Grand Duchy of Lithuania and extended Muscovite rule into the former heartland of the ancestor of all three East Slavic peoples (Russians, Ukrainians, and Belarusians) of Kievan (Kyivan) Rus', the Dnieper (Dnipro) River valley, by taking the city of Chernigov (Chernihiv). Although Muscovy did not try to conquer the city of Kiev itself, the Muscovite elite remained fully conscious of Muscovy's Kievan roots.

Muscovy had become more powerful than its long-time regional rival, the Grand Duchy of Lithuania, which included considerable East Slavic territories populated by Ukrainians and Belarusians. Poland also included East Slavic lands, and the elected king of Poland after 1506 automatically became Grand Duke of Lithuania. Polish and Latin sources called East Slavs living under Polish and Lithuanian rule "Ruthenians." I refer to "Poland-Lithuania" as one country, although they were separate states with the same ruler until 1569, when they formally united in the Polish-Lithuanian Commonwealth. Lithuania was not reconciled to losing East Slavic territory, such as Smolensk, to Muscovite expansion and particularly coveted Novgorod and Pskov, which it had never ruled.

The territorial boundaries of Muscovy to the west reached the state created by the crusading Livonian Knights on the Baltic Sea, called Livonia, which monopolized Muscovite-Baltic trade. Muscovy also bordered Finland, then part of Sweden; Sweden and Muscovy competed for influence over the Lapp population of the Arctic Circle. Sweden, Denmark, and Poland-Lithuania all had territorial designs on Livonia, which became especially prominent after war erupted between Muscovy and Livonia in 1558. The Livonian War lasted twenty-five years, and Muscovy lost.

The Juchid *ulus*, commonly and anachronistically called the Golden Horde in scholarship, the Mongol successor state of the Mongol Empire that had conquered Rus' in the thirteenth century, had disappeared by the time Ivan came to the throne. The Juchid ulus derived its name from Juchi, Chinggis Khan's eldest son, to whom Chinggis left the western lands conquered by the Mongols, and the Turkic word "ulus," meaning a polity. In the middle of the sixteenth century a Muscovite writer gave the Juchid ulus the name "the Golden Horde" (*Zolotaia orda*).[1] However, its successor states, the khanates of Kazan, Astrakhan, Crimea, and Sibir (western Siberia), and the nomadic Nogai hordes, still threatened Muscovy's southern and southeastern borders with slave raids. Under Ivan's grandfather, Ivan

III, Muscovy had begun encroaching down the Volga River to influence Kazan. Ivan completed the process by conquering Kazan and Astrakhan in 1552 and 1556. The Crimeans retaliated by burning Moscow in 1571. Crimea had more military resources than Kazan. Muscovy and Poland-Lithuania engaged in a bidding war to bribe the Crimeans to attack the other, and both lost. The Crimeans raided the Ukrainian and southern Polish regions as well as Muscovite territory. Therefore, the ruler of Moscow always faced the risk of a two-front war, on the south and southeast with Muslim Tatar states and on the west and northwest with Christian states.

Until 1453, when Constantinople fell to the Ottomans, the Patriarch of Constantinople appointed the Metropolitan of All Rus', the head of the Rus' Orthodox Church, usually a Greek, originally one metropolitan in Kiev. In the fourteenth century the metropolitan moved to Moscow. In 1453 the Muscovite Church became autocephalous, although after 1458 a rival Metropolitan of All Rus' was established in Halych for East Slavs under Polish and Lithuanian sovereignty. We are interested only in the metropolitan in Moscow. Historians disagree as to how much control the grand prince of Moscow exercised over the autocephalous Russian Church and the selection of its metropolitan. The Russian church continued to show due respect to the Greek Patriarch of Constantinople, who was also the recipient of royal philanthropy. Some historians assert that it was the triangular relationship among the grand prince of Moscow, the Metropolitan of Moscow, and the Patriarch of Constantinople, and not just relations between the grand prince and the metropolitan, that created political tensions in Moscow.

Both the Habsburg Holy Roman emperor and the pope knew about Muscovy. Imperial envoys had visited Muscovy during the reign of Ivan III, in part because Muscovy and the empire had a common enemy in Poland-Lithuania and in part because the emperors, like the popes, never ceased hoping for Muscovite aid against the Ottomans. Indeed, the Ottoman threat played a role in the papacy's intervention as matchmaker in arranging Ivan III's marriage to Sophia Palaiologa, the niece of the last Byzantine emperor. The pope wanted Muscovy to expel the Turks from Constantinople. Muscovite rulers knew that Muscovy lacked the military capacity to accomplish such a goal. Moscow assiduously courted the sultan's approval, in part because of the profitable oriental trade and in part in hopes, no more fulfilled than those of the Holy Roman emperor or pope for a Muscovite crusade, that the sultan would restrain the ruler he treated as his vassal, the Crimean khan, from raiding Muscovite territory.

Therefore, Muscovite expansion before Ivan's accession left in its wake potential problems in dealing with Moscow's neighbors, the Tatars, Livonians, and Lithuanians.

DYNASTIC SUCCESSION

At home, in the middle of the fifteenth century, Muscovy endured a long dynastic war over succession. Vasilii II claimed the throne by direct succession from his father, Vasilii I. Vasilii I's brothers and nephews asserted a counterclaim by collateral succession, from brother to brother. Vasilii II won. Brothers and nephews of the grand prince of Moscow became holders of appanages, hereditary semiautonomous domains with their own institutions. In the absence of a direct heir, an appanage prince could still claim the throne. Before Vasilii III had an heir, his eldest brother, Prince Iurii Ivanovich, had been heir apparent, and his younger brother, Prince Andrei Ivanovich, next in line. When Ivan ascended the throne as a minor, his appanage princely uncles became a problem. Muscovy lacked a fixed law of succession, so the ambiguity of direct or collateral succession could only be resolved by politics, a very problematic process sometimes, as the crisis of 1553, when it was expected that Ivan was fatally ill, demonstrated all too clearly.

MUSCOVY'S POLITICAL STRUCTURE AND POLITICAL CULTURE

In the absence of a mentally and physically competent adult male grand prince after Ivan's accession as a boy, someone else had to fill the vacuum at the center of political authority. Muscovy's political structure and culture determined how the elite would respond to this situation.

Muscovy's political culture rested upon tradition (*starina*) and custom (*obychai*), not codified laws. No fundamental law regulated dynastic succession or political decision making. Muscovy lacked Renaissance abstract political theory, however marginal such theorizing was to political reality in contemporary states.[2] The absence of constitutional legislation gave the Muscovite political elite a certain degree of flexibility in adapting to changing circumstances. Nothing prevented Muscovites from declaring innovations in administration to be the restoration of tradition, which they did. Failure to deal with political problems cannot be blamed on the customary nature of the Muscovite government.

The Royal Council (Duma) stood at the apex of the administrative structure. It was more than an ad hoc meeting of whichever councillors the ruler (or whoever acted in his name) decided to summon at the moment; it was an institution. Muscovite diplomatic sources beginning in 1536 referred to gentry who lived "in the Royal Council." (In the sixteenth century the word "*dvoriane*" referred to members of the royal court or household [*dvor*], literally "courtiers," who included boyars, gentry, and others; it was only in the seventeenth century that it acquired the meaning of "gentry." In this study I translate *deti boiarskie / deti boiarstvo* as "gentry" and dvoriane, except when dealing with conciliar gentry, as "courtiers" or "members of the court.") Beginning in 1555, the sources referred to the Privy Council (Blizhnaia duma), not just to "privy councillors."[3] While the relationship of the Privy Council to the Royal Council remains obscure, nevertheless these references demonstrate that the Muscovite political structure recognized the existence of functioning permanent political bodies. At Ivan's ascension only boyars and associate boyars (*okol'nichie*) belonged to the Royal Council. The boyars, from approximately twenty to forty families, constituted the upper elite (gentry and some bureaucrats formed the lower elite). They filled the major civilian and military leadership posts. Judging by boyar testaments, land purchases and donations, and cadastres, they owned large amounts of land, the major form of wealth in Muscovy, as patrimonies (*votchiny*). However, the Royal Council was a state, not a class, organ. Modern historians invented the term "Boyar Council" (Boiarskaia duma).

Later in Ivan's reign, without impugning boyar preeminence, Ivan appointed members of two additional classes to the Royal Council: conciliar gentry (*dumnye dvoriane*, the only case during the sixteenth century in which *dvoriane* meant "gentry") and conciliar state secretaries (*dumnye d'iaki*). "State secretaries" refers to clerks who worked for the central government, as opposed to those who worked for individuals, other institutions, or freelanced. The highest level of state secretary was conciliar state secretary. The gentry had begun assuming more prominence in Muscovite service after the Muscovite annexation of Novgorod, when Ivan III initiated a program of assigning conditional land grants (*pomest'ia*) to gentry military servitors as a reward for service. (Boyars accepted conditional land grants as well.) By Ivan IV's reign, gentry who held conditional land grants and did not serve could forfeit those grants. Gentry cavalry archers constituted the core of the Muscovite army and occupied lower administrative offices than did boyars. Although state secretaries and almost all treasurers (*kaznachei*) were nonaristocratic bureaucrats, the office of majordomo (*dvoretskoi*), an official in charge of the ruler's personal properties, could be a boyar or an associate boyar. Only one treasurer ever rose to boyar rank. The majordomos and treasurers of boyar rank who helped set policy acted not as boyars or members of the Royal Council but as officials. The state secretaries were the highest-ranking professional bureaucrats in Muscovy. They headed the most important administrative bureaus. State secretaries served on "boyar" diplomatic negotiating teams.[4] Historians have paid much attention to how the boyars reacted to the promotion of gentry and state secretaries to positions of influence in the Muscovite governmental apparatus because much of traditional historiography assumes that rulers sought to offset aristocratic influence by relying upon gentry and non-noble bureaucrats. In this study "nobles" or "the nobility" refers to the Muscovite boyars (aristocracy) and gentry combined.[5]

Officially, the ruler decided who acquired the status of boyar. He did so primarily but not exclusively on the basis of genealogical seniority within the clans customarily entitled to supply members.[6] The word "boyars" often encompassed associate boyars as well. Unofficial texts also employed the word "magnates" (*vel'mozhi*).[7] The ruler could not dispense with the leadership of the boyars, who commanded his armies, administered the most important provinces and cities, advised him in council, and who alone had the experience to perform these services.

Why the Royal Council could not prevent Ivan from committing atrocities is a question that has dominated modern historiography.[8] Legal historians in particular have blamed this failure on the absence of boyar constitutional and political rights that would have enabled them to stand up to Ivan the way the English barons stood up to King John, producing the Magna Carta in 1215. (Such historians would do well to remember that later King John in effect tore up the charter.) Such a rigid approach to political history underestimates the Muscovite ability to manipulate their customary institutions.[9] No law regulated the competence of the Royal Council or how the ruler selected its members. Legislation could become law without its approval, as was also true of the English Parliament.[10] In all likelihood the boyars arrived at decisions by consensus, not voting, but because no minutes of the council's proceedings survive, this inference cannot be tested. In any event the Royal Council presented all its decisions as unanimous. It is likely that all boyars belonged to the Royal Council but unlikely that all boyars actually attended any given session, because some were always out of town with field armies, in various cities as governors, on leave, sick, or in disgrace ("disgrace" officially deprived a courtier out of favor of the tsar's physical presence; the nature and duration of the punishment depended entirely upon the ruler's discretion).[11]

Muscovy lacked any concept that the Royal Council should oppose the ruler. No law defined the rights of the Royal Council, but no law defined the rights of the ruler either. Custom dictated that no member of the Royal Council could be punished without trial by the grand prince or the boyars, but political reality permitted exceptions.[12] Tradition expected the ruler and his boyars to cooperate, rendering the distinction between the Royal Council's legislative and consultative authority moot. The ruler should consult his subjects, especially his elite; if he did not, he was a bad ruler. Literary texts, icons and frescoes, palace and church architecture, and ritual and ceremony—in a word, image and performance—articulated this same harmonious conception of politics. A grand prince without a royal council would have been as unthinkable as a royal council without a grand prince.[13] Muscovite political culture did not share the assumption of many historians that conflict should and did govern the relationship between the ruler and the boyars.

Boyar dominance of Muscovite politics depended in part upon the boyars' relationship to members of other social groups active in administration. Unfortunately, we know only enough about patronage-client relationships among the elite to conclude that they existed.[14] Theoretically, boyars could patronize other boyars, gentry, or officials. In addition, non-boyar members of the elite such as appanage and serving princes (southwest border princes who retained some regalian rights when they switched loyalty from the Grand Duchy of Lithuania to Muscovy), as well as bishops and monasteries, had their own clients. Therefore, as in France, nobles could choose to act on the basis of kinship or patronage. Loyalty to one set of ties might entail disloyalty to another.[15] Of course, the boyar clans played politics among themselves, most of all via marital alliances. Kinship politics among boyars did not exclude non-kinship political relationships among boyars or between boyars and non-boyars.

Who initiated policy cannot be established.[16] The ruler (if not a minor), the boyars, the metropolitan, leading clerics, and even state officials—state secretaries, majordomos, and treasurers—could all contribute to policy formulation, formally or informally.[17] State officials were not just flunkies who took orders. State secretaries wrote and presented "position papers" to the Royal Council. If it approved them, they became decrees or decisions. If it rejected them, most likely the paper on which they were written was discarded. Without an adult ruler the Royal Council had to play a stronger role in government, unless someone else successfully acted in the name of the ruler, as Ivan's mother did for a time.

During Ivan's minority changes in bureaucratic personnel did not reflect changes in the boyar clans dominating the Royal Council. No boyar faction constituted a "government" in the modern sense of controlling the entire administrative apparatus of state. Consequently, continuity in government operation resulted from cooperation. It was not a case of just the leading boyar clans playing musical chairs at the top. The entire elite, including the gentry and highest apolitical professional bureaucrats, had to work together. Only such cooperation explains Muscovy's ability to defend its borders and even to innovate in domestic policy during Ivan's minority. Preserving the dynasty constituted the number one priority of the elite as a whole, and in this it succeeded: Ivan lived to adulthood. However, chaos at the top did permit greater abuse of authority in the provinces.[18]

THE BUREAUS AND BUREAUCRACY

Historians have long considered the development of a bureaucracy, a professional administrative apparatus, as a hallmark of the new, modern monarchies of the sixteenth century. A bureaucracy freed the monarch from dependence upon the "feudal" aristocracy, and provided an instrument for the implementation of royal policy. Ivan's Muscovy certainly had officials, but whether it had a bureaucracy depends upon one's definition of the word. Max Weber defined a bureaucracy as a completely meritocratic, rational, efficient administration independent of outside interests. Because this sociological "ideal type" exists only in theory, Muscovy could hardly have a Weberian bureaucracy. Whether Tudor England had a Weberian bureaucracy remains disputed. As in Muscovy, results, personality, and power mattered more than abstract, rational principles or plans. It is more productive to look at bureaucracy not as an institution but as a process.[19]

Counterintuitively, Muscovy had bureaucrats before it had bureaus (*prikazy*). By the beginning of the sixteenth century state secretaries conducted administrative business according to standardized procedures and wrote administrative documents in professional jargon. The government apparatus evolved out of the household of the ruler, the Royal Council, or the treasury.[20] Because departments were not established by decree, we know only the date of the first reference to a department, not necessarily its date of creation. Most departments appear first as "huts" (singular, *izba*) and did not acquire the designation "bureau" (*prikaz*) before the 1560s. Even after that, either designation could apply.[21] Some bureaus utilized names without either "bureau" or "hut," such as the Treasury (Kazna) and the Register (Razriad), which could also appear as the Registry Bureau (Razriadnyi prikaz). To further complicate matters, sources refer to state secretaries as bureau secretaries earlier than the first reference to the bureau itself. Allusions to "registry secretaries" (*razriadnye d'iaki*) predate the first reference to the Registry. Therefore when the Law Code of 1550 referred to "bureau people" (*prikaznye liudi*), it did not mean "people who work in bureaus" but "people (civilian officials) who take orders." "To work in a 'bureau'" (*v prikaze*) meant to work under someone's supervision.[22] During Ivan's reign Muscovy never developed a "bureau system" in which all bureaucratic institutions became "bureaus," although more bureaus existed by the 1570s than earlier.

Muscovy's administrative structure remained "unsystematic," not only in its terminology but also in its functionality. Even bureaus differed in the type of activity they performed. Some served a single function everywhere, while others served multiple functions in a single territory.[23] The dvor sometimes served as the household, headed by a majordomo, which administered all estates owned by the dynasty and supplied the ruler and his royal family with necessities, and sometimes as the court, which included boyars, gentry, the armorer, the master of the bedroom, and the keeper-of-the-seal. (I say "the ruler's household" or "the household of the ruler" or "royal household" to refer to Ivan's royal household; "household" by itself refers to someone else's household.) The court served governmental functions and included the Royal Council. Muscovites did not perceive a distinction between public and private bureaus. The two functions varied in other countries too, and at different times in the same country.The tsar served as head of the two highest-ranking bureaus, the Ambassadorial Bureau and the Registry.[24] The Law Code of 1550, unlike the preceding Law Code of 1497, made mention of the majordomos as well as the treasurer, demonstrating that state law drew no distinction between the ruler's household and other elements of the state administrative apparatus.[25]

During Ivan's reign, Muscovite administration became less "personal" and more "institutional." At the beginning of Ivan's reign documents from an office did not even carry the office's name. Scribes wrote documents in Ivan's name. If necessary, the documents would refer recipients to a specific official or boyar in Moscow, not to an office. Early but inconsistent references to the Anti-Brigandage Bureau constitute the exception. Gradually the concept of "institution" took hold. A 1577 report to the Royal Council recounted cooperation by the Conditional Land Bureau (Pomestnyi prikaz), the Registry, and Major Revenue (Bol'shoi prikhod, also known as the Bureau of Major Revenue) by name in sending cash to gentry without conditional estates in frontier districts.[26]

Muscovy was underadministered in terms of the number of officials per capita. However, enough officials already resided in Moscow to merit special attention by the 1551 Church Council of One Hundred Chapters (Stoglav). The Council authorized early and late masses in Moscow's churches to accommodate officials' work schedules.[27] Therefore, scribes and state secretaries staffing government offices had a tangible social presence in the capital.

CENTRALIZATION

In traditional historiography bureaucratization usually goes hand in hand with centralization, but neither the Muscovite state nor Ivan articulated any such concept.[28] Centralization is a matter of degree.[29] No sixteenth-century state possessed the kind of central administration, civil service, standing army, countrywide treasury, or uniform tax system that the concept of centralization evokes. In Muscovy, as elsewhere, the central authorities lacked the wherewithal to impose homogeneity.

The Muscovite government had a mixed record on centralization issues. Territorial unification certainly "centralized" political authority in Moscow.

Regulatory charters (*ustavnye gramoty*) strengthened central control over the provinces by defining very precisely how much a governor (*namestnik*) or county administrator (*volostel*, from *volost*, "county") could collect as taxes, fees, and customs, when he could do so, and how many people (who had to be housed and fed) could accompany him when he visited localities. Local representatives had to witness his court proceedings.[30]

However, the government continued to issue fiscal and judicial immunities. Judicial immunities exempted laymen or ecclesiastical institutions from the jurisdiction of governors by placing them under the direct jurisdiction of the grand prince and later of the tsar. Fiscal immunities exempted them from taxes, which depleted central revenue. One motive need not explain the issuance of all immunity charters. Administrative routine, soliciting political support, or, for immunities to monasteries, religious piety might all have inspired charters.[31] The central government had trouble just keeping track of what immunities it had already issued. In 1551 the government performed the most extensive review of immunity charters of any year of Ivan's reign. It renewed, modified, or issued 170 charters. Although judicial immunities underwent greater modification than fiscal immunities, on the whole immunities decreased. Moscow adjusted ecclesiastical judicial immunities to fit the provisions of the Council of One Hundred Chapters.

Moreover, Moscow had no monopoly on issuing immunity charters. Appanage princes could also issue them, and Moscow made no attempt to abolish the appanage system. The government abolished the Staritskii appanage more than once, but then restored it, until the cadet branch of the royal line died out naturally. Ivan gave an appanage to a refugee Wallachian voivode. Ivan offered appanages to any children he would sire with Englishwoman Mary Hastings. In his testament he left the throne to his elder son, Tsarevich Ivan, but an appanage to his younger son, Tsarevich Fedor.[32] Holders of such appanages could no longer issue coinage or conduct foreign policy, but they still retained administrative autonomy.[33] The perpetuation of the appanage system attests that either Moscow, or later Ivan himself, did not favor centralization, or that neither the government nor Ivan thought appanages threatened centralization. Inconsistently, however, Moscow did gradually abolish the regalian rights of serving princes, much as the Tudors treated English marcher lords.[34]

Despite what some contemporary foreigners wrote, Muscovy conspicuously lacked uniformity. Muscovy had multiple currencies (Novgorodian and Muscovite), systems of weights and measures (the "share" [*vyt*] or "units" [*obzhy*], the "plow" [*sokha*] or the "quarter" [*chetvert, chet*]), legal systems (state law, canon law, Shari'a), tax systems, faiths (Orthodox Christianity, Catholicism, Protestantism, Islam, animism), and languages (Russian, Tatar, and many more). Such heterogeneity was endemic in contemporary states.[35] Muscovite heterogeneity set limits to Muscovite centralization.

Moscow, like London and Paris, did centralize political and administrative decision making. In 1553 the English had to wait on their ship on the White Sea while the local authorities sent to Moscow for instructions. Muscovy, England, and France, although they did not have identical political structures, differed in this respect from a federal state like the Holy Roman Empire, or composite states, in which previously separate polities retained their autonomous institutions and customs when they united, such as Spain or Poland-Lithuania.[36] Muscovy was not a composite state. Its annexed territories, whatever their regionalism, did not retain their political structures, princely lines, or legal systems and did not support separatism.

Therefore, the Muscovite government pursued centralization only partially. Centralization, in Muscovy and in some other countries, was a negotiated and inconsistent process. Moreover, the ostensibly centralized Muscovite state, like other supposedly centralized states, often utilized decentralized mechanisms, such as local self-government, to achieve its goals.

STATE AND SOCIETY

Traditional historiography argues that the Muscovite government dominated society, that all social groups lacked autonomy and meekly served the state; this is the hypertrophic school conception of the relationship of state and society.[37] Recent scholarship has contested that paradigm by arguing that the boyars ran the government collegially and by consensus; this is the consensus and collegial school perception of the relationship between the state and society.[38] The relationship between the state and society in Muscovy cannot be reduced to a single formula, however. Neither interpretation adequately explains all of Ivan's reign. We do not know who initiated, let alone who influenced, policy decisions.[39] Sometimes "autocracy," the theory of unlimited royal authority, was a facade, but at other times the consensus of the boyars was also a facade. In any event the significance of the theory of autocracy for Ivan's ideology has been exaggerated.[40] As elsewhere, centralization and negotiated contractual modes of rule might go hand in hand. Ivan's minority fits neither paradigm.[41]

In practice the state knew that its administrative reach exceeded its grasp. The government acknowledged that its ability to control its dispersed population was limited. It delegated authority to its officials and local social groups and admitted its own lack of omniscience. Ivan, like other contemporary rulers, had great difficulty getting his officials to carry out his orders.[42] The ruler called his boyars his "slaves," and boyars called themselves "slaves" of the ruler, but a boyar who petitioned Ivan as his "slave" enhanced, not demeaned, his own status.[43] Boyars knew that they could sell their slaves, but the tsar could not sell his boyars. Ivan considered Muscovy his patrimony (*votchina*), which he could bequeath to his heir, but he could not sell it as a boyar could sell his patrimony.

The ideal that the ruler should consult (*sovetovati*) his advisors, shared even by Niccolò Machiavelli,[44] should not be confused with reality. During his minority, Ivan "consulted" his mother; as an adult, he "consulted" his brother, Prince Iurii, considered by many historians to have been a deaf-mute, although the matter is not so simple.[45] The appearance of consultation had genuine meaning to the Muscovite court, but it should not automatically be taken literally. It is impossible to correlate Ivan's proclivity for "consultation" and his supposedly "autocratic" aspirations.[46]

Muscovites distinguished the ruler from both society and the state. Narratives and documents refer to "the land's and the sovereign's business" (*zemkoe i gosudarskoe delo*), separating the affairs of the "land" (*zemlia*) from those of the ruler.[47] The "land" could be society or the state in this passage. In 1536 Muscovite negotiators informed Lithuanian representatives that although Ivan was young, his *gosudarstvo* was "mature." Usually "gosudarstvo" meant "reign," how long a ruler had been "sovereign" (*gosudar*), but this reference indicates duration from before Ivan's time, an abstraction, the "state."[48] State secretary Fedor Karpov, who was familiar with some of Aristotle's works, wrote of the "general good" and the "common good" (*delo narodnoe, obshchee chelovecheskoe delo*), but no other writer used these concepts. One could compare these phrases to the Latin res publica/publicae or Polish Rzeczpospolita (the name of the Polish-Lithuanian Commonwealth).[49]

Historians cite Ivan's increasing reliance upon political surety (loyalty) oaths by boyars as evidence of state domination of society.[50] Whether contemporary states employed similar oaths to prevent defection seems unclear.[51] Such sureties reflect the increasing political tension between Ivan and his elite. However, we do not know if the guarantors supported the man for whom they stood surety, and therefore opposed Ivan's policies, or, to the contrary, whether they served the government loyally as unpaid surveillance officers.[52] After Ivan's reign, sureties for princes and boyars disappeared, but late in Ivan's reign the surety practice spread throughout the Muscovite administrative apparatus as a means of insuring job performance. The need for political sureties may attest to the weakness of the social bond between the state and its subjects rather than the strength of state domination over society. The Muscovite government apparently used collective responsibility, a group guarantee of service performance or obligation fulfillment, like surety, more often and at higher levels of society than contemporary states because of Muscovy's underadministration.[53]

Muscovy's customary political structure and culture underwent considerable change during the sixteenth century. Muscovites camouflaged innovation as a return to custom. The ruler and his elite either consulted or pretended to consult each other as the political situation warranted. Territorial expansion produced centralized political decision making in Moscow, but the locus of authority within the city of Moscow varied because of accidental factors such as the presence of a boy ruler. The personal relationship between the ruler and his subjects, especially the members of the elite, did not prevent the growth of institutional affiliations or consciousness within the administrative apparatus. The state did not unilaterally dominate society, because it lacked the resources to do so, and acknowledged that constraint upon its activity by delegating operational policy implementation to its officials on the scene outside Moscow or to local institutions. In conclusion the hypertrophic and consensual or collegial models of the relationship between the state and society are both partially correct and partially incorrect. Muscovites did not confuse unambiguous political or social ideals with ambiguous, and certainly malleable, political and social reality.

2

The Young Ivan's World

Examination of several issues pertinent to the history of Ivan's family and the Muscovite court during Ivan's minority provides a fuller background for understanding how events then may have influenced Ivan.

Vasilii III had long been married to Solomoniia Saburova, but she had not produced an heir. He wanted at all costs not to leave his throne to his brother, Prince Iurii Ivanovich, heir-presumptive.[1] Under Russian Orthodox canon law, Vasilii III could not divorce Solomoniia because she was barren. To solve the problem, Solomoniia had to take the veil. Sources disagree as to whether she became a nun voluntarily to free her husband to remarry or if she had to be coerced. Only Sigismund von Herberstein, envoy of the Holy Roman emperor to Vasilii III, reported a rumor that Solomoniia had given birth to a son, Iurii (Georgii), after she entered a convent. Herberstein immediately discounted the veracity of this story, which has not impeded its propagation.[2] Vasilii III then married the much younger Elena Glinskaia, who gave birth to the requisite heir, Ivan, the future Ivan IV, in 1530, and then to a second son, Iurii, in 1532.

Vasilii III's testament, which did not survive, would have made arrangements for Ivan's minority. Presumably Vasilii named Ivan's mother as his guardian. The assumption in traditional historiography was that Vasilii appointed her uncle, Prince Mikhail Glinskii, Ivan (Shigon) Podzhogin, and Mikhail Zakhar'in to a "regency council" to rule in Ivan's name. Mikhail Krom disproved that theory. Muscovy lacked legal precedents for a regency council. A true regent would have had the power to issue decrees in his own name, which Glinskii and associates could not do. Rather, the triumvirate served as the executors of Vasilii III's testament, a legitimate role in Muscovite private law but one that circumscribed their political authority. Worse yet the executors Vasilii III chose lacked the political clout to take charge of the situation. Glinskii did not hold boyar rank. According to some chronicles, on his deathbed Vasilii III emphasized Glinskii's loyalty, even though he was a "newcomer" (*priezzhii*), from a family of relatively recent immigrants from the Grand Duchy of Lithuania. Vasilii obviously tried to preempt opposition to assigning Glinskii a prominent political role. As a blood relative of the grand princess, Glinskii could not only leapfrog boyars, whose clans had served the ruler of Moscow far longer, but he could also acquire far more power than other boyars could tolerate.[3] In a move that would probably have surprised Vasilii, Elena herself took over. She removed the triumvirate from power and disposed permanently of Ivan's uncles, the appanage princes Iurii Ivanovich of Dmitrov and Andrei Ivanovich of Staritsa. In 1538 Elena died. At that point Ivan was still only eight years old, so the Royal Council had to assume a more influential role.

Historians sometimes describe Elena unflatteringly as cold, calculating, ruthless, and dissolute, if also effective. She not only had her uncle arrested but also, with boyar support, masterminded the arrests of Vasilii III's brothers, Iurii of Dmitrov and Andrei of Staritsa, who died in prison, probably from starvation. Ivan later saw to it that his mother escaped blame for the deaths of her brothers-in-law. Catherine de Médicis, Queen Mother of France, failed to escape similar blame for political murders, even when she was blameless.[4] Prince Ivan Fedorovich Telepnev Obolenskii Ovchin (Obolenskii for short) became Elena's closest associate and, some said, her lover. Indeed, some historians assert that Obolenskii became her lover during Vasilii III's lifetime, and that Obolenskii, not Vasilii III, fathered Elena's children. Elena supposedly removed her uncle from power because he criticized her scandalous love life. However, the structure of Kremlin life precluded Elena from imitating the adulteries of Lucrezia Borgia, sister of the infamous Cesare Borgia, in Italy. No sexual dalliance could have escaped notice in the *terem*, the women's quarters in the Kremlin, before or after Vasilii III's death. The sixteenth-century Muscovite court conspicuously lacked the sexual improprieties, royal mistresses, and bastards endemic to contemporary courts.[5] Later allusions to Ivan as illegitimate—his evil birth "explained" his misdeeds—did not refer to the identity of Ivan's biological father but to Vasilii's "uncanonical," because coerced, divorce.[6] Elena's reputation should not be sullied by unreliable court gossip.

Obolenskii had more than enough influence to arouse jealousy among other boyars, but he did not govern. Obolenskii's sister Agrafena Cheliadnina became Ivan's nurse, although historians disagree about whether she got the job because of her brother or whether he became the royal favorite because of her proximity to the young grand prince. After Elena's death the boyars ordered Obolenskii's immediate execution and exiled his sister to a convent.[7] Like all royal favorites, Obolenskii lacked an independent political base to enable him to survive his patron's disappearance from the scene.

Elena ran the government and took care of her sons. According to the chronicles and other sources, "Grand Princess Elena and her son Grand Prince Ivan" made many political decisions. When a royal spy who had worked for Vasilii III fell on hard times and found himself in prison, he petitioned Ivan and Elena for mercy. Nogai Tatar *mirzas* (nobles) addressed diplomatic correspondence to Elena and Ivan.[8] She revised the currency to end counterfeiting, introducing the coin later known as the kopeck. She firmly repulsed diplomatic attempts by the Crimean khan, the king of Poland/grand duke of Lithuania, and a Nogai Tatar prince to take advantage of Ivan's youth.[9] Muscovy lost the Belarusian city and region of Gomel, recently acquired from the Grand Duchy of Lithuania, during the Starodub War, but no core Muscovite lands were lost.[10] At the same time Elena did not neglect her sons. She dined and traveled with them. Ivan, judging by Ivan's first letter to Kurbskii and his actions, always remembered her affectionately.

In 1538 Elena died young, perhaps in her late thirties. Again, only Herberstein reported without comment the rumor that someone, probably boyars, poisoned her. Because at royal banquets, or even in the women's quarters, servants served food family style, poison in Elena's food would have poisoned everyone at table, including perhaps her sons, an unacceptable risk even to homicidal-minded boyars. Unlike for England, neither Muscovite nor foreign sources mention a food taster in Moscow. Assertions based upon her autopsy that Elena died of poisoning in food or cosmetics have been contested; individuals who did not die of poisoning show the same symptoms as Elena. Ivan never accused anyone of having poisoned her, although he did voice such unproven accusations concerning two of his wives, Anastasiia and Anna Koltovskaia.[11] The only reliably attested use of poison against royals during Ivan's reign occurred at Ivan's command. In 1569 he ordered his cousin Prince Vladimir Staritskii, Staritskii's wife, and one or more of Staritskii's children, to commit suicide by swallowing poison.

Sufficient violence accompanied Elena's rise to and exercise of power to arouse considerable anxiety among the Muscovite elite. An Italian architect in Muscovite service fled to Livonia, blaming boyar oppression in Moscow on Ivan's youth. The defection to Lithuania of boyar Prince Semen Bel'skii and associate boyar Ivan Liatskoi testified to the degree of uncertainty of the time.[12] Hundreds of Muscovite gentry also fled to Lithuania. Even so, Elena at least restrained boyar feuding. Her death unleashed yet greater violence.

Chaotic political infighting seems to have broken out among boyar factional cliques after Elena's death, primarily between the princes Shuiskie, descendants of Riurik, the legendary founder of the Rus' dynasty, and the princes Glinskie, Elena's family, descended from Grand Duke Gedimin of Lithuania. By 1547 internecine violence had resulted in the murder of thirteen princes, boyars, and their gentry supporters, and the removal from office of two metropolitans, Daniil and Ioasaf.[13] Boyars accused of being too close to Ivan, meaning that they monopolized access to the grand prince and packed the Royal Council with relatives and supporters, paid with their lives for their arrogance; their associates ("advisors," *sovetniki*) suffered exile.[14] In 1542 the Shuiskie staged a military coup by invading the Kremlin. In 1543 Ivan (or, according to some chronicles, the boyars) ordered the leading boyar (*pervosovetnik*; literally, "first councilor") Prince Andrei Shuiskii seized by kennel men who, with or without orders to do so, killed him.[15] Such a high death toll among the elite, in addition to the deaths during Elena's ascendancy, testify to a genuine political crisis. In Muscovite sources written in hindsight, during the period of "boyar misrule" selfish ambition guided the actions of the aristocrats in control of the government, resulting in corruption, violence, and the weakening of the country.[16]

Ivan's minority constituted a necessary but not a sufficient cause of the political crisis.[17] Similar disorder did not characterize the minority of every ruler in similar circumstances in Muscovite history. The minorities of

Grand Prince Dmitrii Donskoi and his grandson, Grand Prince Vasilii II, in the fourteenth and early fifteenth centuries, escaped such chaos. During Donskoi's minority Metropolitan Aleksei and during Vasilii II's minority his maternal grandfather Grand Duke Vytautus of Lithuania guaranteed political stability. Perhaps if Elena had lived longer, she could have done the same in the 1530s and 1540s. Vasilii III did not select effective executors of his testament or build a consensus among the boyars to prevent such extreme political infighting after his death.

Even after Elena's death in 1538, however, the political situation in Muscovy was not entirely negative. The government could muster enough consensus among boyars and officials to defend the realm against invasion, improve the administration, and protect the minor ruler, who did, after all, live long enough to rule and not just reign. All boyars protected the integrity of the throne and the realm. Ivan may have feared for his life, but no boyar threatened it. Even while they feuded with their rivals in the "politics of status," the boyars still reached policy decisions and instituted some reforms, such as legislation to fight brigandage, which the "reformers" of the 1550s retained. The nascent bureaucracy provided administrative stability. The boyars did not just run around killing each other while waiting for the grand prince to grow up. Even while they arranged each other's untimely demises, they somehow managed to serve their country.[18] They merely disagreed over which boyars would live long enough to see Ivan become an adult. Consequently, the divide between the period of Ivan's minority and the reforms of the 1550s was not as great as polemicists in the 1550s, including Ivan, and traditional historiography contended. Ivan illogically disavowed his participation in 1550s politics in his first letter to Kurbskii in 1564 in order to blacken the reputations of his advisors during that period. Historians should not take his propaganda at face value. Nevertheless, Ivan's criticism of the abuses of his minority had some connection to reality. He declared null and void state land grants and donations made to monasteries between the death of Vasilii III and Ivan's coronation, although we do not know if this declaration was implemented.

Part II

*Ivan's Life from His Accession
to the Oprichnina*

3

Ivan's Minority

Many historians agree with William Wordsworth that the child is father to the man. They see Ivan's childhood as the key to his adult behavior, either good or bad. Ivan himself described his childhood as deprived when he sought to absolve himself of responsibility for his adult misdeeds. Some historians interpret Ivan's persecution of the boyars as just retribution for the boyars' abuse of power during his minority and their mistreatment of Ivan and his brother at that time. Other historians take the position that Ivan's childhood reading led him to believe that he, as ruler, should occupy an exalted place of authority in the realm, and thus the boyars' failure to respect his status when he was a child produced Ivan's backlash against them when he became an adult. Still other historians believe that sycophantic boyars encouraged Ivan's inherently immoral impulses toward cruelty and debauchery in order to curry favor with him. These negative qualities resurfaced during the *oprichnina*, after those who exercised restraint on their expression during the "long" 1550s—his first wife Anastasiia, Metropolitan Makarii, the Chosen Council—disappeared naturally or by Ivan's will in the early 1560s. All these theories explain Ivan's adulthood by way of his childhood, and they all misstate the evidence or exaggerate the influence of Ivan's childhood upon his adulthood. They uniformly deny Ivan the

ability to overcome his putative childhood trauma. They rely upon Ivan's
very suspect retroactive autobiographical depiction or Prince Kurbskii's
equally suspect retroactive blackwash of Ivan's childhood. Contemporary evidence of how the boyars treated Ivan during his childhood tells a
different story.

Ivan attended the funeral of his father and then ascended the throne as
Grand Prince of Moscow and All Rus' at the age of three. In England at
this time royalty, such as Henry VIII, did not witness death or attend royal
funerals. Ivan might not have remembered his father's death. He certainly
remembered his mother's funeral, which occurred when he was eight years
old.[1] How much Ivan understood those events remains unknowable.

At age thirty-four, in his first letter to Kurbskii, Ivan explained his
untoward acts against boyars by claiming that the boyars neglected him as
a child. They failed to clothe, feed, and care for him properly.[2] Ivan did not
claim that he was depraved because he had been deprived, but he did use
his deprivation as an excuse for his untoward acts. He did not specify at
what age this abuse occurred. We can rule out the period before his mother's death in 1538. Neither his father nor his mother would have tolerated
anything but the best care for their son. Ivan never accused his parents of
not nurturing him. Therefore, if Ivan's accusation carries any credibility, he
must have been referring to the time after his mother's death, when he was
eight years old, and lasting not much longer than five years, since in 1543
thirteen-year-old Ivan ordered Prince Andrei Shuiskii arrested, after which
he was killed. Boyars, servitors, or servants, if they valued their freedom,
let alone their lives, would not have failed to fulfill Ivan's personal wishes
after that episode.

Good evidence attests that after 1538 the orphan Ivan was well taken
care of. The Kremlin made child care a high priority, even if we know
little about its particulars. Contemporary chronicles demonstrate an abiding
recognition that the child Ivan (and his younger brother) required special
consideration. The Muscovite diplomatic establishment appreciated that
the boy Ivan could not preside over diplomatic banquets. Ivan began to
take some part in diplomatic receptions in 1537. As a child, Ivan performed
the ceremonial duties of office as best he could. Supposedly, he presided
over various court cases from 1536 on, including a murder trial in 1539, and
delivered a speech at the installation of Ioasaf as metropolitan of Moscow
in 1539.[3] When the Crimean Tatars threatened Moscow in 1542, the boyars

decided not to evacuate Ivan and his brother because of the problems of transporting boys aged twelve and ten. The sixteenth-century Muscovite elite knew a royal child when they saw one and knew how to take care of one.[4]

Ivan did endure traumatic experiences. In 1542 the twelve-year-old Ivan witnessed the storming of the Kremlin at night by the Shuiskie faction, who assaulted rival boyar Prince Ivan Bel'skii and roughed up Metropolitan Ioasaf. Although the rebels had no intention of doing Ivan harm, he might legitimately have feared for his well-being. In 1543 at a meeting of the Royal Council, before Ivan's eyes, many boyars attacked and nearly killed his mentor at the time, the boyar Fedor Vorontsov. Only Ivan's intercession induced these boyars to exile Vorontsov instead of ordering his execution on Red Square. Elizabeth I of England and Peter the Great in Russia experienced worse during their childhoods.[5]

Kurbskii's account of the young Ivan as already a monster-in-training lacks credibility. According to Kurbskii's *History*, as a boy Ivan threw "small animals" off the Kremlin walls for sadistic pleasure, and when slightly older, perhaps already a teenager, he led a gang of mounted hooligans through the streets of Moscow trampling people and goods alike.[6] Kurbskii wrote these passages at least twenty years after the fact, however, while in exile in the Grand Duchy of Lithuania. No evidence places him in the Kremlin when Ivan was young, so he may not have witnessed the behavior he attributed to Ivan. Ivan's nannies, tutors, and servants would have prevented the boy from walking alone on the Kremlin walls, let alone engaging in animal abuse. When he was a teenager, Ivan's bodyguards would have inhibited reckless horseback rides in the heart of Moscow on grounds of security concerns alone. No other sources confirm Kurbskii's portrait of Ivan as a juvenile delinquent. His portrayal of Ivan's misspent youth smacks of ex post facto slander. Because Karamzin accepted Kurbskii's depiction of the boy Ivan as a sadist, Karamzin's twofold periodization of Ivan's reign into the "good" Ivan of the 1550s and the "bad" Ivan of the oprichnina actually consists of three periods: it suggests that Ivan first changed from the "bad" Ivan of his minority to the "good" Ivan of the 1550s and then regressed after 1564.[7]

As an adult, Ivan became an inveterate liar who manipulated history, including his own, to serve his purposes. Ivan's plaintive complaints about his neglected childhood strain credulity. They are the self-serving excuses of an arrogant ruler rewriting history. Ivan's image of his childhood merits attention as evidence of his consummate skill as a writer, not as evidence of his difficult childhood.

Ivan's political policies, including the oprichnina and mass terror, did not constitute an attack only on the boyars. Although boyars suffered disproportionately from Ivan's repression, far larger numbers of gentry, peasants, and urban residents lost their lives. Ivan would not have needed the oprichnina with all its symbolism to take his revenge on the boyars for transgressions during his childhood. In his writings Ivan expressed an ambivalence toward boyars that mitigates against accepting the premise that Ivan directed his ire solely against them for misdeeds committed decades earlier.

As Ivan approached his middle teenage years, he performed more of the functions associated with being a monarch. In 1545, under careful boyar supervision, he undertook his first campaign, "commanding" troops sent to Kolomna. In the mid-1540s he took part in a lengthy series of pilgrimages and hunting trips that kept him away from Moscow for months at a time. Accusing him of selfishly disregarding his royal duties misses the point because these travels *were* Ivan's royal duties. By symbolically marking off the boundaries of his realm, he demonstrated to the elite and the populace at large his adult status, physical health, and commanding authority. Hunting showcased his courage, strength, and masculinity; pilgrimages, his piety.[8] Through these excursions Ivan learned more about his realm. His peripatetics continued in his adulthood. The progresses of Tudor monarchs served the same functions and earned the young Henry VIII the same criticism.[9] Contemporaries often contrasted the behavior of rulers when they were young and when they matured, not just in the case of Henry VIII but also Elizabeth I in England, Francis I in Spain, and Charles V in Habsburg Burgundy. In general the younger ruler evinced less interest in ruling; the elder ruler became more capricious and lethal.[10]

Some unedifying incidents marred Ivan's image as a maturing ideal ruler. In 1546 in Kolomna a group of Novgorod gunners (*pishchal'niki*) attempted to accost Ivan to complain of their work conditions. Ivan showed no interest in their grievances and ordered his bodyguards to disperse them. Resistance led to a skirmish with fatalities on both sides. Perhaps Ivan held some of his boyars responsible for inspiring or not preventing this confrontation. First Ivan ordered one boyar's tongue cut out for "disrespectful speech." Then he placed five others in disgrace. Months later, Ivan ordered two of the boyars and a majordomo beheaded, supposedly without benefit of confession or last rites. Later chronicles contain contradictory versions of the incident that blame either Ivan, a state secretary as provocateur, or Ivan's victims. Historians disagree about what actually happened and Ivan's role.[11]

Ivan had boyar and master of the horse (*koniushii*), at least ceremonially the most prestigious office at court after the sovereign (Boris Godunov held that office during the reign of his brother-in-law, Tsar Fedor Ivanovich), Ivan Fedorov stripped naked for not greeting him properly. Fedorov avoided execution by admitting his guilt. Ivan sent him under guard to Beloozero and confiscated his property. Just shy of his sixteenth birthday, Ivan was old enough to be held responsible for his actions. Of course we cannot be certain if someone else put Ivan up to his treatment of Fedorov.

In 1547 Pskov petitioners repeated the experience of the 1546 Novgorod gunners when they tried to complain to Ivan about their governor. Ivan poured wine on their beards and was preparing to set them on fire when the great Moscow fire distracted him. Ivan's gratuitous cruelty, recorded much later, resonates with other sensational accounts of his atrocities, which might lead us to disregard this evidence except for the fact that the chronicle containing the story also expressed pro-Ivan attitudes. Therefore we can neither dismiss this incident out of hand nor can we assign responsibility for Ivan's actions to anyone else.

Other narratives of Ivan's arbitrary or cruel treatment of his subjects lack credibility. Only post-1584 chronicles criticized Ivan's visits to Novgorod (1544) and Pskov (1548) in passages not confirmed elsewhere that probably reflect the ill will generated by Ivan's assault on those cities in 1570.[12] Still, Ivan's encounters with the Novgorod and Pskov petitioners tarnish his reputation and speak poorly of his sensitivity, solicitude toward his subjects, and tolerance.

Krom suggests that some Muscovites in their writings already took a dim view of Ivan's behavior. He concludes that a letter of consolation, written by the monk Fotii of the Iosifov Monastery to a boyar widow-nun, impugned the justice of Ivan's 1546 punishment of boyars.[13] The content of the letter permits a different interpretation, however. Fotii described Prince Ivan Kubenskii as having died a "bitter and ferocious death," but Fotii counseled Kubenskii's widow to accept God's will, as all men are sinners.[14] Fotii neither declared Kubenskii innocent nor did he accuse Ivan of being a "tormentor" (*muchitel*), the classic impious ruler in Muscovite theological and political discourse.[15] The monk Zinovii of Oten, in the northwest region, wrote letters of consolation to disgraced nobles. Without questioning the propriety of their punishment, he too urged them to reconcile themselves to their fates as God's will. Fotii's letter, like Zinovii's, avoided the question of guilt. A letter of consolation might urge a sinner to repent and save his soul, as all men are sinners, but without judging guilt; even so, Fotii would hardly try to convince a widow that her husband deserved to be beheaded. The only Muscovite standing on Muscovite soil when he accused Ivan of the murder of innocents was Metropolitan Filipp; he paid with his life for speaking up.

Other historians see generic moral exhortations to Ivan by the priest Sylvester and Maksim Grek ("the Greek"), a monk from Mount Athos sent to Muscovy as a translator under Vasilii III, as direct criticisms of Ivan for becoming too fond of women, wine, minstrels (*skomorokhi*), and homosexuals.[16] The imprisoned Maksim, convicted of heresy, humbly petitioned Ivan to let him take communion and/or return to Mount Athos; complaining about Ivan's morals would hardly have served Maksim's purpose.[17] Muscovite sins in general, not Ivan's, preoccupied Sylvester. The evidence of Ivan's putative homosexuality consists only of unsubstantiated innuendo during the oprichnina, minuscule compared to the abundant evidence of the lifestyle of James I/VI of England/Scotland or the supposedly bisexually depraved Henri III of France.[18] No reliable evidence attests to Ivan's supposed debauched lifestyle before 1547.

Historians should not assume that either all of Ivan's victims before 1547 deserved their punishments or all the punishments meted out by Ivan reflected only the excesses of royal caprice. After over a dozen years of not having a functioning ruler, some members of the elite might not have been prepared to pay Ivan due deference. As a result, Ivan may have sometimes, selectively to be sure and occasionally lethally, exceeded the usual norms governing disgrace and punishment in disciplining his obstreperous elite. Such incidents, even if Ivan and not his advisors were responsible (and he could still be responsible for letting his advisors act improperly), remained few and far between and were not the general rule. Ivan's behavior had not yet irretrievably exceeded moral limits.

4

Ivan's Coronation and First Marriage

After his sixteenth birthday Ivan was no longer a boy. His coronation and marriage marked the commencement of his rule. Of course, Ivan could not immediately take over the reins of power completely, but the boyars, the court, and the administrative apparatus had to treat him with much greater deference. Ivan's coronation illustrates the Muscovite conception of the responsibilities and obligations of the tsar, which was derived selectively from multiple ideological models. With his marriage, Ivan assumed the primary responsibility of a monarch: to produce a male heir in order to maintain the continuity of the dynastic line. How both events occurred demonstrates the extent to which Ivan had become his own man and illustrates the roles of the Russian Orthodox Church and the boyars in Muscovite politics.

CORONATION: KHAN OR *BASILEUS*

On January 16, 1547, in the Dormition (Uspenskii) Cathedral in the Moscow Kremlin, Metropolitan Makarii crowned Ivan tsar, making him the first crowned tsar in Muscovite history. The government wasted no time in using his new title, Grand Prince and Tsar, although some government clerks somehow did not get the message.[1] Muscovy became a Grand Principality

and a *tsarstvo*, which could mean "kingdom" or "empire," but in connection
with Ivan's coronation conveyed imperial connotations, elevating Ivan above
mere royal status. Who engineered this ceremony and its ideological significance remain matters of dispute. The title became the foundation stone
of Ivan's ideology. The Muscovite Ambassadorial Bureau spent the rest of
Ivan's reign trying to secure its recognition abroad, but Poland-Lithuania
never accepted the title in writing.[2]

According to the chronicles, the proposal that Ivan be crowned tsar originated with Ivan. Metropolitan Makarii and the boyars merely concurred
with his decision. This presentation adheres to the chronicles' tendency to
attribute all decisions to the ruler, no matter how young. Some historians
contend that the sixteen-year-old Ivan lacked the experience in governing
required to conceive such a bold step, no matter how much he had read
about Byzantine history. Historians have ascribed the initiative for Ivan's
coronation to his natal family, the princes Glinskie, his future in-laws (the
Iur'ev-Zakhar'ins), or to Makarii. The case for Glinskie influence rests upon
their supposed role in ordering two executions at the time. Rulers of sixteen
or seventeen did exercise authority elsewhere. In the sixteenth century King
Philip II of Spain had political input at the age of sixteen, and in the seventeenth century at the age of seventeen King Charles XII of Sweden led armies
and Peter the Great became ruler. Still, Ivan probably had help in making
the decision to be crowned tsar. The coronation ceremony took place in a
church, so Makarii must have agreed to perform it; it is likely that the idea
originated with him.[3] No source mentions anyone opposing the coronation.

No literal transcription of the ceremony survives. Nevertheless, the
description of the rite expressed Muscovite ideals.[4] Ivan's coronation rite
ultimately derived from a Byzantine model, but Muscovy imported Byzantine imperial theory only selectively. The 1498 coronation of Ivan III's
grandson, Dmitrii, as his co-ruler, served as the immediate model for the
1547 coronation, but that in turn derived from a Byzantine prototype.[5] The
Rus' translated the Byzantine title *basileus* as "tsar." The Byzantine emperor
was the icon of Christ, ruling his earthly kingdom just as Christ ruled the
heavenly kingdom. One ruler in heaven meant only one ruler—meaning
one universal, supreme ruler—on earth, the basileus. The Muscovites understood the universal aspirations of the title "basileus." As tsar, Ivan felt
himself superior to almost all contemporary rulers, especially those who
ascended the throne via election.[6]

Nevertheless, the Muscovite ceremony did not completely mimic its Byzantine prototype. No one raised Ivan on a shield, he made no profession of faith, he did not join lower clerical orders, and he did not enter the Great Entrance during the liturgy reserved only for clergy.[7] Scholars dispute whether Makarii anointed Ivan. The earlier version of the coronation mentioned Ivan's anointing, but only the later version fully described it.[8] It may be more significant that in his speeches, letters, and diplomatic communiques Ivan asserted that Makarii had anointed him, and even Kurbskii concurred. Of course Ivan could have meant a rhetorical, not physical, anointment. Later coronations always fully describe the anointing of the new tsar.[9]

According to Makarii's sermon and Ivan's speech at the coronation, state and church should act in "symphony," in complete harmony with each other. Ivan had no aspirations at this time to imitate the degree of control that King Philip II exercised over the Catholic Church in Spain, which exceeded the authority even of Protestant rulers who did not have to contend with the pope in Rome.[10]

Unlike Orthodox South Slavs, Muscovites manifested considerable reticence about pursuing the foreign policy implications of adopting the Byzantine title of basileus. When a medieval Bulgarian or Serbian ruler became tsar/basileus, he tried to conquer Constantinople, to replace the Byzantine emperor. Ivan had no such ambition. Greeks living in the Ottoman Empire dreamed of liberation at Russian hands, but Ottoman power and the distance between Moscow and Istanbul precluded the Muscovites from sharing that dream.[11]

Pskov monk Filofei's claim that Moscow had become the Third Rome played no role in Ivan's coronation. Filofei argued that the first Rome, on the Tiber, and the second Rome, Constantinople, had fallen because of religious impurity, leaving Moscow as the Third Rome. If Moscow did not protect true Orthodox Christianity, then the world would come to an end because there would be no Fourth Rome. He sought to inspire the ruler of Moscow to reform the Russian Orthodox Church, not to conquer the world. Filofei's spiritual and eschatological concerns lacked a messianic dimension. The theory of Moscow, the Third Rome, had nothing to do with the historical legacy of the Roman Empire that infused contemporary English, French, and Spanish imperial notions. Moreover, Ivan's government wanted no part of Third Rome theory.[12] The Muscovite government neither attempted to make Moscow a "new" Rome architecturally by constructing a Muscovite Appian Way, Colosseum, or Circus, nor to make Moscow a "new" Constantinople by constructing a Hippodrome. Kiev, Novgorod, and Polotsk (Polatsk, now in Belarus, temporarily under Muscovite rule during the Livonian War) had their St. Sophia cathedrals, like the Hagia Sophia in Constantinople, but not Moscow.[13] The phrase "Third Rome" did not appear in any Muscovite governmental document during Ivan's reign, and it did not appear in Ivan's writings.[14]

The word "tsar" also translated the Turkic word "khan," but the Muscovite government manifested equal reticence in invoking Mongol imperial ideology. The Mongol image of ruler did influence Rus'. The Muscovites appreciated, and in the fourteenth and fifteenth centuries sometimes exploited, Chingissid legitimacy, the doctrine that only descendants of Chinggis Khan could bear the title "khan." Some historians claim that Ivan's title "tsar" meant "khan." Ivan became a khan in order to conquer the Kazan Khanate; the conquest of Kazan constituted Ivan's "true coronation" as tsar. Ivan sought equality in status with the khans of Kazan, Astrakhan, and Crimea.[15] This interpretation misstates the Muscovite attitude toward Chingissid ideology. Even though Muscovy had conquered part of the heartland of the Juchid *ulus*, the middle Volga River valley, it respected the claim of the Crimean Khanate as successor of the Juchid ulus.[16] Ivan became khan of Kazan and khan of Astrakhan by (actual) right of conquest and (fictitious) inheritance from previous Rus' rulers, not because he had been crowned tsar. (Muscovite diplomats argued that in 1487 Kazan had submitted to Ivan III by accepting a Muscovite puppet ruler, so Ivan IV inherited sovereignty over the khanate. Kazan later repudiated that puppet khan anyway.) Ivan's 1547 coronation did not imitate the Mongol practice of throwing the new khan in the air on a rug. Moscow exploited its steppe expertise for political advantage, but Muscovy's elite did not identify Muscovy as a steppe Mongol khanate and Ivan did not perceive himself as a khan.[17]

Ivan demonstrated equal flexibility in relating his title to East Slavic history. On the one hand, he and his diplomats asserted that Kievan rulers St. Vladimir and Vladimir Monomakh had held the title "tsar."[18] In their own time, neither could possibly have thought of replacing the still powerful Byzantine Empire, and Chinggis had not yet created the Mongol Empire. On the other hand, Ivan admitted that the title had been "forgotten" until he revived it. A literary text, the so-called vita of Dmitrii Donskoi, lauded him as "tsar of the Rus' Land," a claim probably based upon the theory of the fourteenth-century Tverian monk Akindin that "the prince is tsar in his own land," the equivalent of the medieval doctrine that "the king is emperor in his own realm" (*rex imperator est in regno suo*). Ivan did not cite Akindin's theory and never claimed Donskoi as a predecessor as tsar.[19]

Ivan's coronation elevated the significance of his imperial regalia, which was, like his title itself, inspired by multiple sources.[20] Monomakh's Cap (*shapka Monomakhova*), supposedly given to Ivan's ancestor Vladimir Monomakh by the Byzantine emperor Constantine Monomachos in the twelfth century, occupied pride of place. In actual fact, Constantine and Vladimir Monomakh were not contemporaries and the "cap," actually a crown, originated in fourteenth-century Central Asia.[21] Only the later version of the coronation rite mentioned a scepter (*skipetr*), although Ivan definitely later appeared in receptions holding one.[22] Even if Ivan did not wield a physical scepter, in narrative and diplomatic sources he still held the "scepter" of the realm (*derzhava*) or the "scepter of the Russian Empire" (*rossiiskoe tsarstvo*), rhetorically or metaphorically.[23] "To hold the scepter" meant "to rule." The dying Vasilii III left Ivan his "scepter" long before Ivan's coronation. The word for "orb" (*derzhava*) also meant "realm." Ivan's silk shoulder-covering (*barma*) came from Byzantium. Ivan also had ceremonial military regalia, including a bow and arrow, spears, helmet, and armor, but unlike contemporary rulers no sword. Shields had gone out of use.[24] The quantity and diversity of Ivan's regalia paralleled that of contemporary rulers.

In 1557 Ivan sought confirmation of his imperial title from the Patriarch of Constantinople. He got less than he bargained for when the answer arrived in 1561.[25] Patriarch Ioasaph II approved the title, but because of St. Vladimir's marriage to Byzantine princess Anna Porphyrogenita, not because of Ivan's coronation. Ioasaph rejected Metropolitan Makarii's authority to perform the ceremony alone. The Muscovites altered Ioasaph's letter in translation to read that the pope or the patriarch had to approve such a coronation. Whether the patriarch thought a recoronation necessary cannot be determined.[26]

Ivan's identity as tsar, he proclaimed, made him superior to other rulers. Even after Peter the Great became "Emperor," Russian rulers remained "tsars" until 1917. Ivan's coronation as tsar became one of his longest-lasting "reforms." Ivan claimed the title neither as heir to Byzantium nor as ruler of the Third Rome nor as the successor of Chinggis Khan or the Juchid ulus

but by a genealogically correct but historically fictitious inheritance from
Kievan rulers St. Vladimir and Vladimir Monomakh. Ivan's ideology as
ruler began and ended with his title of tsar.[27]

IVAN'S FIRST MARRIAGE

In Muscovy, or any contemporary monarchy, the ruler's marriage was a
matter of state. According to the chronicle, Ivan made the decision that he
should marry, as he had made the decision that he should be crowned tsar.
It seems more likely that Ivan was the originator of the marriage project
than that he initiated his coronation. Weddings were a sacrament of the
Russian Orthodox Church. Metropolitan Makarii performed Ivan's first
two marriages and delivered appropriate sermons at both, but he played
no role in the selection of the bride. A number of elements of Ivan's wedding, such as showering the bride and groom with coins or hops, derived
from pagan fertility rites, but Makarii did not object. Such marital customs
found their way into a later version of the very Christian *Book of Household
Management* (*Domostroi*).[28] Ivan declared, so the chronicle recounts, that
differences in customs with a foreign wife would augur ill for a foreign
marriage; therefore, he had decided to marry a Russian girl. Ivan's bride,
Anastasiia Romanovna-Iur'evna, came from a respectable gentry family that
had previously held boyar rank.[29] How Ivan selected her reflected Muscovy's
court customs and social structure.

The process of selecting a royal bride entailed a "bride show." (Henry
VIII did something similar to replace Jane Seymour in 1537.) According to
the chronicle, the government summoned all the eligible maidens in the
land to appear before Ivan, who personally chose his bride. Of course, for
practical and social reasons, that romantic scenario did not take place. No
bachelor-ruler could possibly "inspect" all eligible maidens. In a hierarchical
society such as Muscovy, the ruler could not marry a bride of peasant, artisan, merchant, or clerical origin. Indeed, bride show documents attest that
the families of eligible noble brides did not always demonstrate enthusiasm
about producing their daughters for consideration as Ivan's bride.[30]

Boyars dominated the bride-selection process. They found appropriate
virgin candidates and appointed boyar women to vet them physically. The
bride show managers assumed the piety and morality of the brides but
carefully described the candidates' health. The wedding documents paid

great attention to the candidates' genealogy and relatives, probably in order to locate instances of mental or physical illness that boded ill for the bride's future fecundity. The Muscovites lacked any knowledge of genetics, but, as devout Orthodox Christians, they believed that illness signified God's disfavor. Therefore, a family with a dubious medical history lacked God's favor, and God's favor alone guaranteed a bride's ability to produce a healthy male heir.[31]

The teenage Ivan, even if he had help, still had the last word on who would be his betrothed. Ivan knew his choice of bride was political in the broadest sense. He could not have chosen a bride from a clan in disgrace, and he had to take into account boyar reactions to his future in-laws. However, a bride's age, health, and piety probably counted most. Unfortunately, we have no idea of the precise characteristics of Anastasiia that motivated Ivan's choice.

Ivan's marriage ended the worst of the feuding among boyar clans because it signaled that Ivan had become an adult, mature enough to arbitrate elite feuds. The Zakhar'in-Iur'ev clan, now Ivan's in-laws, (re)joined the boyars. The significant expansion of the Royal Council between 1547 and 1550—Ivan appointed twenty-three boyars and fifteen associate boyars—restored equilibrium.[32]

Ivan's coronation and marriage did much more than mark him as an adult. The coronation illustrates the multiple, complex sources of Muscovite imperial ideology, as well as their limitations. It legitimized Ivan's authority at an infinitely higher level.[33] The marriage process illustrates the inseparability of Ivan's personal life from his rule. Metropolitan Makarii performed both Ivan's coronation and wedding, symbolizing the role of the Church in Ivan's life and that of the court.

5

Life at Ivan's Court

Religion dominated Ivan's life, as it did the life of the Muscovite court.[1] Religious values, religious practices, religious rituals, and religious symbols infused everything Ivan did. The physical setting of the court, the Moscow Kremlin, unlike most contemporary capitals, emphasized religious, not royal, power. Cathedrals, not palaces, dominated its architecture. Foreigners, accustomed to courts where palaces outshone churches, did not always appreciate its message that God is great and man is small.[2] The government could not always convert religious belief into political policy, however. Pragmatic concerns sometimes dictated compromises that obfuscated religious preferences. Nevertheless, such instances cannot impair the fundamentally religious mentality and identity of Ivan and the court.[3]

Sacraments marked transitions in Ivan's life and the lives of the members of his court. Priests baptized them, usually giving them the names of saints,[4] married them in church, and buried them in churches or monasteries. The lay elite endowed churches in honor of their name-saints. All social classes participated in the memorial culture of donations for prayers in memory of the dead.[5] Ivan made enormous donations to monasteries of money, land, robes, vessels, icons, books, and veils.[6] Before Tsarevich Ivan's death, Ivan's largest donations occurred between 1563 and 1571, probably totaling over thirty-five thousand rubles. Many boyar clans had a special attachment to a specific monastery. Inscriptions attest that the elite owned religious books, which they donated or bequeathed to churches or monasteries.[7] Over twenty testaments allocated religious objects to heirs and monasteries, some as part of dowries.[8]

The icon and the cross played major roles in Ivan's life. The tsar crossed himself before taking a bite to eat or a sip to drink. He did not wash his hands after touching a non-Orthodox, even though foreigners criticized him by claiming that he did.[9] Ivan's personal belongings included crosses and icons. He signified his acceptance of an international treaty by "kissing the cross," a religious ceremony, although clergy neither participated nor attended.[10] Ivan's actions evidence his faith that saints performed miracles.[11] Despite years of haggling over their ransom, Ivan's government offered to exchange fifty prisoners of war from Lithuania for an icon held in Vilnius, even if the Lithuanians kept the precious stones on its cover.[12] Icons made visible the parallel between the heavenly and earthly kingdoms, the heavenly and earthly tsars, and the heavenly and earthly hosts (*voinstvo*), reinforcing the religious identity of Ivan and the lay elite every time they saw these images, let alone bowed or prayed to them.[13]

Lay elite personal religious belief found expression verbally and materially. Ivan's best military engineer, Ivan Vyrodkov, rode into battle in chain mail with the inscriptions: "Mother of God be with us" and "God is with us, who can stand against us." (God did not save him or his family from execution on Ivan's order.)[14] Bureaucrats inserted gratuitous expressions of religious sentiment into government documents. State secretaries employed scriptural citations in foreign policy negotiations and documents. Private individuals went beyond the required formulae by invoking God's guidance in legal documents.[15]

No linguistic wall separated the Slavonic of the church from the chancery Russian of the court. Texts employed mixed language. Saints' lives and chronicles in Slavonic included charters and decrees in chancery language. The state register in chancery Russian took information from chronicles written in Slavonic.[16] The difference between Slavonic and the spoken tongue matched that between Shakespeare's language and modern English.[17] Members of the court elite wrote religious texts in Slavonic. Gentry-man Vasilii Tuchkov wrote a new version of the vita of St. Mikhail Klopskii.[18]

Religion exerted a powerful influence on the quotidian life of the court elite and society at large. The tsar went to church almost every day. The ceremonial life of the court revolved around the liturgical calendar. Ivan went on frequent pilgrimages.[19] Marriages could not take place during church fasts or on Wednesdays or Fridays. Fasts determined what the elite could eat and drink, and whether they could have sex. Dates of birth suggest that the laity observed such bans on sex.[20]

Government actions appeared in religious garb. Religious motives justified political policies. In wartime Ivan sent requests to monasteries for prayers.[21] Religious ideology infused state sources concerning the 1563 conquest of Polotsk from the Grand Duchy of Lithuania.[22] The Muscovite court perceived Muscovy to be more like other Christian than steppe or Muslim countries.[23]

The criminal justice system reflected religious sensibilities. A decree banned executions in Moscow on days when the metropolitan performed the longer funeral service because public punishment drew crowds who should have been attending religious services.[24] Religion pervaded judicial procedures. Boyar and gentry witnesses testified "in God's truth" or "as is right before God." Judicial ordeals, trial by combat, even drawing lots presumed divine intervention. Litigants offered to swear on a cross to validate their testimony.[25]

Ivan might have exaggerated his knowledge of theology, but he was not theologically illiterate. He took time in 1570 to debate Jan Rokyta, a member of the Protestant Bohemian Brethren.[26] The reply to Rokyta's exposition of his Protestant faith issued in Ivan's name lacks his literary style, but the text still reflects Ivan's obligation as tsar to defend Orthodox Christianity against heresy.[27] At Ivan's request, the pope sent the Jesuit Antonio Possevino to Muscovy to arbitrate the Livonian War between Muscovy and the Polish-Lithuanian Commonwealth. Ivan had promised to engage in a theological debate with Possevino, who wanted him to recognize papal supremacy. Ivan realized that disagreement over religion might impair Possevino's mission, so at first he declined to debate at all, claiming that he could not speak of religion unless the metropolitan and all the bishops were present, and then he deliberately sabotaged the discussion by asking why the pope wore a cross below his belt and shaved. Ivan simply manipulated his promise to debate Possevino as he thought best for Muscovy's foreign policy. Despite his interest in theology, as a writer Ivan was more a political polemicist than a theologian.[28]

Ivan, the diplomatic establishment, and the court believed in Muscovy's Kievan religious inheritance.[29] In diplomatic papers Ivan repeatedly invoked his descent from St. Vladimir, who baptized the Rus' Land, which Ivan now ruled.[30] He referred to the monk prince Sviatosha of the Kievan Monastery of the Caves in his 1573 letter to the Kirillo-Beloozero Monastery. The lay elite bore the names of Rus' saints of Kievan origin, such as the princely martyrs Boris and Gleb, the first saints of Kievan Rus', more often than they did Tatar names.[31]

Muscovy could not, however, impose its religious confession upon all its residents. The entire native population of the Kazan Khanate professed faiths other than Christianity. The Tatars in Kazan and the volatile nomadic Nogai Tatar hordes adhered to Islam, and many of the Finnic and Ugric ethnic groups living along the middle Volga River practiced animism. Even the Russian Orthodox Church, for all its repeated diatribes against Islam, recognized the practical impossibility of forcibly converting this vast population to Orthodox Christianity. Attempting to do so would have exacerbated the still dangerous security problems of controlling the region. Moreover, Ivan and the court saw political advantage in tolerating Islam among its servitors and subjects. Muscovy did not want to give the sultan, the defender of the Muslim faith, an excuse to intervene in Kazan or Astrakhan or exacerbate its relations with the Nogai Tatars. Ivan invoked his benign policy toward Islam in correspondence with the Ottoman Porte and the Nogai Tatars. When addressing the sultan, Ivan could even profess agnosticism regarding which was the true faith.[32]

On the other hand, Ivan did not mention, let alone defend, his toleration of Islam in his dealings with Christian states. Instead, to them he claimed that the conquest of Kazan constituted a Christian victory over Islam. Although he assiduously avoided military confrontation with the Ottomans and curried friendship with Istanbul, Ivan invoked the Ottoman threat in diplomacy with the Holy Roman emperor and the pope. Moreover, no pragmatic considerations could diminish his religious animosity toward Jews. When a Muscovite army conquered Polotsk, he ordered the drowning of all Jews who refused to convert. Whatever contribution the Jewish population of Polotsk made to its economy was outweighed by Ivan's anti-Semitism.

In the sixteenth century ethnic and religious identity often overlapped, not only in Muscovy but also elsewhere, as was the case with Calvinism in the Netherlands, Anglicanism in England, and Catholicism in Poland

and Ireland.[33] Circumstances, not religious indifference, dictated the 1556 Peace of Augsburg between Protestants and Catholics in the Holy Roman Empire and the 1555 truce between the Sunni Ottoman and Shiite Safavid empires, just as they compelled Muscovy to tolerate Islam.[34] The sixteenth century was a confessional age, the age of the Reformation and Counter-Reformation (or Catholic Reformation). The religious element of royal life at the time belies labeling royal courts "secular" even if, unlike Muscovy, they patronized Renaissance art and culture.[35] Necessity, not choice, drove religious toleration; when circumstances permitted, Catholic, Protestant, Orthodox, Sunni, and Shiite regimes persecuted "heretics."

Muscovite textual, visual, and behavioral sources ascribed a religious raison d'être to the state to facilitate the salvation of the Russian people and a political function to the church to assist the state to succeed. The behavior of Ivan and his court demonstrate that church and state in Muscovy were united in ideology, mentality, and identity.

ELITE LITERACY

To appreciate the religious content that saturated their lives, the court elite had to be literate. Visual images alone could not adequately convey Orthodox Christian theology. Murals, icons, and frescoes would have made no sense to servitors without a proper religious background that could only come from reading scripture or understanding scripture read aloud in the liturgy. Images were not "books for the illiterate."[36] The literacy of the bureaucratic class can be assumed. The literacy of the peasants, who constituted the great bulk of the population, lies outside the scope of this study. Here our interest is in the literacy of the lay landowning class.[37] Most Western historians estimate its literacy rate as exceedingly low, although historians in Russia usually disagree.[38] Given their linguistic proximity, anyone able to read chancery Russian could read or understand Slavonic at some level. Literacy did not need to entail the ability to compose theological works in Slavonic.[39] Members of the lay elite who read chancery Russian had access to the basic religious content of the liturgy and other prayers, of icons and frescoes, and of religious rites and ceremonies. Evidence attests to fairly extensive functional literacy among the elite, comparable to that of other contemporary elites.[40]

Church and state assumed that some members of the lay elite were literate but that others were not. Therefore, they regulated procedures for probating testaments without signatures and specified that literate gentry serve as anti-brigandage elders respectively.[41] Literacy greatly facilitated land-ownership because all land transactions required written documentation.[42]

Visual and textual evidence confirms elite literacy.[43] Consider, for example, the miniature in the *Illustrated Chronicle Compilation* showing Prince Mikhail Temriukovich, Ivan's brother-in-law, learning "letters" (*gramota*) in order to convert to Christianity, which posed him sitting next to a piece of paper with the first four letters of the alphabet. Possevino wrote from personal experience that Muscovite ambassadors, boyars, as well as secretaries, read their opening statements in diplomatic negotiations aloud from scrolls. Tax collectors from the gentry, who were not professional scribes, wrote receipts.[44] Seven gentry envoys and couriers sent to Nogai Tatar nobles deep in the steppe dispatched written memos back to Moscow, although there is no mention in the records that scribes accompanied them.[45] Vasilii Griaznoi, a gentry *oprichnik*, described himself as using paper and quill to write a quite literary letter to Ivan. A boyar or gentry governor in the provinces had to keep up with a daunting quantity of government correspondence, instructions, and requests for information. An illiterate governor would have spent an inordinate amount of time listening to his scribe read such memos aloud and then also reading aloud the replies he dictated or that the scribe wrote on his behalf in order to confirm their contents.[46] Even a field general, who presumably had a secretary, had to be able to read to keep in touch with his superiors. Commander Prince Vasilii Khilkov's "field archive" in 1580 contained twenty-seven dispatches sent to him by Moscow bureaus between May and September 1580 alone. When an officer in a field army "wrote" a petition to the ruler for redress, he must actually have written it because the petitions did not mention that anyone else wrote them.[47] Therefore, historians need to reconsider whether the Muscovite administrative apparatus could have functioned with illiterate boyars and gentry occupying so many central and provincial administrative offices.

Counting signatures remains the standard method of determining literacy.[48] In Muscovy witnesses to a legal act "affixed their hands" (*ruku prilozhil*) to the document.[49] Those who did not "know letters" (*gramota umeet*) could not "affix their hands." Of eighteen boyars and associate boyars at the 1566 Assembly of the Land, only two "did not know letters." In the functional educational curriculum of Muscovy (which had no formal

schools) and elsewhere, students learned writing only after learning reading. Therefore, anyone who could write could read. Under Elizabeth I of
England one peer was supposedly so close to illiterate that he could barely
scratch out his signature.[50] However, no one in sixteenth-century Muscovy
"signed" documents by making a "mark" or an "X." Witnesses in legal
proceedings testified that they recognized signatures. Numerous public
documents specify that only literate litigants and witnesses would affix their
hands, while the presumably literate priests of the illiterate signed for them.[51]

Charters often explained why someone could not affix his hand: because
he was not present, had a physical injury or illness, his hands had been
amputated, he was physically incapable of writing, he was too young to have
learned to write, or he had started learning reading and writing but had
not yet finished.[52] Drafting a legal document in chancery Russian required
more skill than signing one's name. Men not identified as scribes wrote over
a hundred charters.[53] In another hundred-plus cases, one of the parties to a
document, rather than a secretary, wrote the charter himself, "in my own
hand."[54] Several dozen boyars or gentry, who may themselves have been
literate, chose to employ "men," meaning servants, servitors, or slaves, not
described as professional scribes, to write documents for them.[55]

The functional literacy of a great many members of the lay elite helps
explain the influence of Orthodox Christianity upon their daily lives. Anyone who could read, let alone write, chancery Russian knew the Cyrillic
alphabet and could read Slavonic. Listening to the liturgy or scripture read
aloud in Slavonic could have provided the lay elite with the background
information they needed to understand the frescoes, murals, icons, rituals,
and ceremonies they saw, but it is more likely that at some time, somehow,
they became familiar with Christian theology via reading. In Ivan's case we
can judge his reading by the quotations in his writing. For the overwhelming majority of the court elite who practiced Orthodox Christianity the
same way Ivan did, save Kurbskii, we lack such evidence.

6

The Dynastic Crisis of 1553

After his coronation and marriage Ivan went from success to success. In 1550 he issued a new law code to improve government efficiency and adapt the law to changes in Muscovite society. In 1551 he summoned a church council to improve the functioning of the Russian Orthodox Church and the piety of the Russian people. In 1552 he personally led the Muscovite army that conquered the Muslim Tatar khanate of Kazan. However, in 1553 Ivan became so ill that Muscovites considered his death imminent. The question of dynastic succession revealed a deep rift within the Muscovite elite. Unfortunately, the surviving sources about that crisis obscure what actually happened.

The contemporary chronicle reports that in March 1553 Ivan "was sick." This is the only time the chronicle mentions his health.[1] From the exceptional nature of the allusion we may infer that Ivan suffered a particularly severe illness, but no further details are provided. Interpolations in the *Tsar's Book* (*Tsarstvennaia kniga*), a segment of the *Illustrated Chronicle Compilation* written much later, tell a much longer story.[2] Ivan and his wife Anastasiia had one infant son, Tsarevich Dmitrii. Princess Evfrosiniia Staritskaia, the villainess of Sergei Eisenstein's classic film *Ivan the Terrible*, began politicking for the selection of her son, Prince Vladimir Staritskii,

Ivan's first cousin, as Ivan's heir, rather than Tsarevich Dmitrii. Evaluations of Staritskii's abilities vary.[3] Unfortunately, the sources convey nothing about his personality or capacities. Ivan suffered such delirium that he could not recognize people, but supposedly he debated the merits of the two choices of successor with the boyars summoned to his bed to swear loyalty to Tsarevich Dmitrii as heir apparent. Ivan's preference elicited concern and disagreement among the boyars.

Associate boyar Fedor Adashev, father of Aleksei Adashev, traditionally considered a leader of the reform party supposedly dubbed the Chosen Council by Kurbskii, purportedly said that he would willingly swear loyalty to Tsarevich Dmitrii, but Tsarevich Dmitrii's minority would be dominated by the Zakhar'iny-Iur'evy, Anastasiia's family, and chaos would reign. Another boyar insisted that the full-grown Prince Vladimir Staritskii would do a better job as tsar than an infant still in swaddling clothes. Still other boyars objected to swearing loyalty to Tsarevich Dmitrii on procedural grounds because Ivan had not yet died or because such an oath should be taken in the throne room, not in Ivan's private quarters.

Ivan advised the boyars who supported Tsarevich Dmitrii to flee the country to save the lives of his widow and son. He warned the Zakhar'iny that they had better defend his son because they would not survive a Staritskii accession, echoing Vasilii III's dying words to Prince Mikhail Glinskii to protect his widow, Elena Glinskaia, and her sons.[4]

When Prince Vladimir Staritskii attempted to see Ivan on his sickbed, boyars objected, but the priest Sylvester, also considered a member of the Chosen Council, excoriated the boyars for interfering in a proper act of familial sympathy. The interpolations imputed enormous influence to the priest Sylvester, who putatively ruled church and state, dictated policy to the metropolitan and bishops, and controlled all government appointments. The interpolations described Sylvester as a great friend of the Staritskie who had secured their release from prison. Sylvester's actions, the interpolations concluded, created enmity between himself and the boyars. Even in his 1564 first letter to Kurbskii and in his 1573 letter to the Kirillo-Beloozero Monastery, written when Sylvester had become a monk in the Solovetskii Monastery and no longer had any influence at court, Ivan presented Sylvester as very influential but not this powerful.[5]

The bureaucrat Ivan Viskovatyi loyally insisted upon the propriety of the loyalty oath to Tsarevich Dmitrii. Some boyars swore immediately, but two did not show up on grounds of illness. They did not take the oath until after the boyar "revolt" (*miatezh*) had ended. In order to induce Prince Vladimir Staritskii to swear loyalty to Tsarevich Dmitrii as heir, loyal boyars threatened to kill him. They also importuned Princess Evfrosiniia Staritskaia in her household three times before she swore loyalty to Tsarevich Dmitrii, all the while complaining about the worthlessness of a coerced oath. Ivan instructed those boyars who had taken the oath not to let Tsarevich Dmitrii fall into the hands of "the boyars." Intra-boyar animosity became heated, and boyars called each other traitors or impugned the loyalty of their fathers.

In the end all this political maneuvering counted for naught because Ivan recovered and his heir did not need to ascend the throne. In fact Tsarevich Dmitrii never succeeded his father. He died three months later, according to early seventeenth-century chronicles, when his nurse accidentally dropped him in a river as Ivan and family traveled on a pilgrimage to celebrate Ivan's recovery.[6]

A story related to the death of Tsarevich Dmitrii and later recounted by Kurbskii provides additional hindsight evidence about who had influence at Ivan's court in 1553. Supposedly Maksim Grek, then confined to the Trinity Monastery because of his earlier conviction for heresy, delegated Kurbskii, Aleksei Adashev, and others to convey a warning to Ivan not to go on that pilgrimage because Tsarevich Dmitrii would die.[7] He urged Ivan instead to see to the welfare of the troops who had fought at Kazan and to their widows and orphans. An imprisoned monk was in no position to prophesy the demise of the heir apparent, unless he wanted to be burned alive for witchcraft. However, whoever made up this story did not choose Maksim's designated emissaries accidentally.[8]

To complicate matters even further, interpolations in the Synodal manuscript of the *Illustrated Chronicle Compilation* offer a competing narrative. After Ivan's recovery, border guards supposedly caught boyar Prince Nikita Lobanov-Rostovskii trying to flee to Lithuania. He confessed that many boyars and gentry had discussed replacing Tsarevich Dmitrii on the throne with Prince Vladimir Staritskii. Lobanov-Rostovskii objected to Ivan's marriage to a daughter of a boyar, so that now the boyars had to serve their "sister," as if they were her slaves. Ivan appointed men from the Royal Council to investigate Lobanov-Rostovskii's confession. This group included individuals who had, according to the interpolations in the *Tsar's Book*, resisted swearing loyalty to Tsarevich Dmitrii.

If the interpolations in the *Tsar's Book* and in the Synodal manuscript both accurately reported the course of events during Ivan's illness, then Ivan either had a short memory or he did not bear a grudge. Ivan's actions toward the elite after 1553 corroborate the latter possibility. He promoted those who had dissented from his son's succession. Fedor Adashev rose from associate boyar to boyar, and Aleksei Adashev rose to associate boyar. Ivan punished only Lobanov-Rostovskii and his associates.[9]

It is self-evident that no one could have written either interpolated account before the *Illustrated Chronicle Compilation* itself had been compiled; a text must exist before anyone can add an interpolation. Unfortunately, historians disagree about the dating of the *Illustrated Chronicle Compilation*. The identity of the authors and the purpose of the interpolations remain unknown. Many historians assert that, at Ivan's order, someone composed the *Tsar's Book* interpolations in 1569 to justify the murders of Princess Evfrosiniia and Prince Vladimir Staritskii and his family. In 1569, however, Ivan fabricated a different excuse to dispose of his aunt and cousin—their fictitious plot to assassinate him—and he did not mention their actions during the succession crisis. Historians have proposed different men as authors of the *Tsar's Book* interpolations, but none has done so convincingly.[10] Some historians fall back upon the conclusion that the interpolations reflected Ivan's views, even if we do not know who wrote them or when.[11] Even this assertion depends upon the dubious assumption that the chronicles constituted "official" texts.[12]

Historians should devote more attention to the omissions, errors, and contradictions in the interpolations. Three names are notably absent from the interpolations: Kurbskii, Prince Iurii Vasil'evich, and Metropolitan Makarii. Ivan later accused Kurbskii of favoring Vladimir Staritskii's accession in 1553, which Kurbskii denied. No one proposed Ivan's twenty-one-year-old brother Prince Iurii Vasil'evich as an alternative candidate to Tsarevich Dmitrii, or even asked him to take a loyalty oath to Ivan's choice of heir, his own nephew.[13] Finally, Makarii's absence makes absolutely no sense because he bore the responsibility of crowning Ivan's successor. No theory satisfactorily explains his nonparticipation.[14]

Sylvester probably had not yet arrived in Moscow when the boy Ivan supposedly pardoned Princess Evfrosiniia and Prince Vladimir Staritskie, so his role in that event may be fictitious.[15] Despite Sylvester's putative influence, the boyars refused to heed his advice to let Staritskii enter Ivan's bedroom. Ivan warned the Zakhar'iny to protect his son from "the boyars," yet the boyars became hostile toward Sylvester, in opposition to his intercession on Staritskii's behalf and therefore ostensibly in defense of Tsarevich Dmitrii's accession.[16] The Synodal manuscript interpolations misrepresent the status of Anastasiia's family. Her father became a boyar *after* her selection as Ivan's bride, and all boyars were "slaves" of the tsar, not the tsaritsa.

On the other hand, dismissing the interpolations as late, embellished, and unreliable in their entirety is not justified. The absence of the "long" story of the dynastic crisis of 1553 from the contemporary chronicle does not prove that no succession crisis occurred. Absence of evidence is not evidence of absence. The *Tsar's Book* interpolations contain some very plausible political analysis. The Zakhar'iny would have dominated a Tsarevich Dmitrii minority, and oaths to the tsar's successor administered in the tsar's private quarters before he died did violate custom and decorum. The interpolations recount that Tsar Ivan told associate boyar Lev Saltykov that Prince Dmitrii Nomovo had told him while crossing Red Square that the boyars did not wish to serve the young Tsarevich Dmitrii, preferring the older Prince Vladimir Staritskii. Only a court insider had access to such hearsay. Unfortunately, the interpolations would have served entirely different political purposes in the 1560s, the 1570s, the early 1580s, or after Ivan's death. Without a plausible dating, establishing a credible political context for the writing of the interpolations remains elusive.

If both interpolations contain even a grain of truth, then they attest to serious divisions among the boyars and to Ivan's misreading of the situation. Some boyars might genuinely have feared that the political ascendance of the unpopular Zakhar'iny would result in disorders comparable to those during 1538–1542. Ivan later frequently and vehemently criticized boyar abuses during his childhood, but he remained deaf to concerns that Tsarevich Dmitrii's succession as a child would unleash comparable improprieties. Ivan myopically focused exclusively on the succession and safety of his son. At the same time many historians exaggerate the degree of boyar dissent in 1553. Even if some boyars talked about favoring Prince Vladimir Staritskii as heir, they did not replay the 1542 Shuiskii coup. Staritskii supporters did not storm the Kremlin. Boyar action confined itself to politicking.[17]

Ivan's relations with Vladimir and Evfrosiniia Staritskie after the crisis suggest that Ivan took their behavior seriously. He ordered Prince Vladimir to reside in Moscow and limited the size of Staritskii's household to 108 people, perhaps to restrict the resources at his command. After his recovery Ivan imposed new loyalty oaths on Staritskii. Vladimir promised not to seek the throne. He also obligated himself to inform on his mother if she said anything seditious or if he heard of any nefarious scheme she was concocting. Ivan imposed restrictions on where Staritskii could buy land, which servitors he could accept into his service, and how he could treat servitors who left his service.[18] Ivan certainly did not go out of his way to respect the memory of his uncles, including Prince Andrei Staritskii, husband of Evfrosiniia and father of Vladimir Staritskii. The 1557 special commemorative list Ivan sent to the Patriarch of Constantinople omitted their names. Contemporary royalty habitually distrusted their kin, as the relationship between Mary Tudor and her half-sister Elizabeth I dramatically attests. Ivan's actions toward Staritskii do not bespeak any great amity between Ivan and his cousin.[19]

Evfrosiniia's rejoinder took artistic form. Her workshop embroidered a shroud that cast her son as Boris or Gleb, the innocent martyred Kievan princes, which implicitly assigned to Ivan the role of Sviatopolk "the Accursed," the prince who martyred them.[20]

The events of 1553 did not produce a major turnover in Royal Council membership.[21] Aleksei Adashev and the priest Sylvester lost favor only seven years later. Evfrosiniia and Vladimir Staritskii lost their lives sixteen years later. Whether Ivan chose his victims because of their actions in 1553, or whether someone later attributed such actions to people after they became Ivan's victims, cannot be resolved.

Whether the succession crisis of 1553 took place as described in the interpolations of the *Tsar's Book* and the Synodal manuscript remains unknowable, but their story illustrates the primacy of dynastic concerns in Muscovite politics. Whoever wrote them knew that disagreements over dynastic succession, procedures, propriety, and custom could produce fierce political conflicts.

7

The Prehistory of the Oprichnina

From 1553 until 1560 Ivan's reign seemed to go on as if the dynastic crisis of 1553 had never happened. His behavior did not display any drastic change. Beginning in 1560, however, Ivan reportedly began to demonstrate the immorality and cruelty that he had earlier manifested before his coronation and marriage and that achieved fruition in the terror of the *oprichnina*. In his correspondence with Kurbskii, initiated by Kurbskii in 1564, Ivan articulated the ideology of unlimited rule that he sought to actualize in the oprichnina. Thus, in traditional historiography, Ivan's actions between 1560 and December 1564 constitute the pivotal transition point in his reign. Nevertheless, even if Ivan's punishment of misbehaving boyars grew significantly harsher and he expressed his concept of divine royal rule in no uncertain terms, neither of these developments necessarily presaged the oprichnina.

IVAN'S TURN TO THE DARK SIDE

As the people who purportedly had restrained Ivan's sadistic impulses passed from the scene between 1560 and 1564, at least according to Kurbskii and many historians since, he is believed to have changed from the "good" Ivan

into the "bad" Ivan. Ivan's religious fervor of the 1550s petered out to the
degree that he resumed hunting and perhaps playing chess, both criticized
by the 1550 church council.[1] However, the traditional paradigm of Ivan's
transition rests upon ambiguous or unreliable sources.

In 1560 Anastasiia died, probably worn out by pregnancies and pilgrimages. Beginning with the late eighteenth- and early nineteenth-century
historian Nikolai Karamzin, historians have bemoaned the loss of her
moderating influence on Ivan. Skeptics relegate Ivan's romantic attachment to Anastasiia to myth. Before her death, Ivan and Anastasiia lodged
at Kolomenskoe, a vacation retreat outside Moscow. Ivan left her there to
return to the city to combat a serious fire. His departure does not prove
his emotional detachment from his dying wife. Rather, it demonstrates
Ivan's devotion to duty. He could hardly have forgotten the Moscow fire of
1547. After Anastasiia's death, of course, propriety dictated that Ivan make
donations to monasteries in her memory, but he donated more cash for her
than for some of his later wives. Ivan referred to Anastasiia fondly for the
rest of his life.[2]

Despite Karamzin, no contemporary source attributes Ivan's good
behavior between 1547 and 1560 to Anastasiia's benign influence or his
increasingly bad behavior after 1560, such as the oprichnina and Ivan's
supposed murder of his son Tsarevich Ivan, to her absence. Only Jerome
Horsey, an English traveler who wrote his account after Ivan's death, the
1617 Muscovite world chronicle, and other late sources did so.[3] These ex post
facto rationalizations tell us nothing about Ivan's emotional state in 1560.

On August 6, 1560, the day before Anastasiia died and probably in anticipation of that eventuality, Ivan ordered special residences built quickly
for the Tsareviches Ivan and Fedor, aged six and three, respectively. Ivan
assigned a separate court (household) to his brother, Prince Iurii, twen-
ty-eight years old and married but still living in Ivan's quarters.[4] Ivan also
arranged a fourth, separate court for his ward, the converted Tatar Tsarevich
Aleksandr Safakireevich, the last khan of independent Kazan, baptized after
the Muscovite conquest. Tsarevich Aleksandr died at age seventeen in 1567,
so he must have been about ten in 1560.

Ivan did not evict these people from his royal household so that upon
Anastasiia's death he could embark upon a life of sexual degradation. A
seventeenth-century Muscovite chronicle was the only account that accused
Ivan of engaging in sexual promiscuity after Anastasiia's death.[5] One can

only guess Ivan's motive. Certainly Anastasiia was primary caretaker for her sons and probably for Aleksandr Safakireevich. Conceivably, Ivan was making sure that after her passing his sons and ward would each receive proper care in fully staffed, separate households, and he now trusted his sister-in-law to take proper care of his brother.

On August 14, one week after Anastasiia's death, Metropolitan Makarii requested that Ivan set aside his grief and remarry. At age thirty, Ivan was still too young, Makarii declared, to live in the world without a spouse. To avoid sin, he should marry as soon as possible. The haste with which Makarii proffered this request might appear unseemly to us, but it was completely canonical. Ivan could have even remarried during the initial forty-day period of mourning for Anastasiia. Diplomatic correspondence to Lithuania inquiring about King Sigismund Augustus's sisters Anna and Ekaterina as potential brides attributed this same argument to Metropolitan Makarii. Makarii's logic in favor of Ivan's remarriage seems quite transparent.[6]

Two days after hearing Makarii's request, Ivan summoned Makarii, clergy, and boyars to his presence to inform them that "due to the age of his children, he had thought not to remarry," but if Makarii and everyone else so wished, he would comply. Ivan implausibly implied that his children were old enough not to need maternal care. Even if Ivan had no desire to remain single, voluntarily acceding to Makarii's request was the proper response of an Orthodox tsar to a request by an Orthodox metropolitan. Ivan declared that he would search for a bride in foreign lands, in Lithuania, Sweden, and Kabarda (Circassia). Ivan had obviously overcome his 1547 aversion to a foreign bride. The choice of prospective brides reflected foreign policy considerations: a Polish or Lithuanian wife might bring a Livonian dowry, while a Circassian wife would cement Muscovy's flank against the Crimeans. The likelihood of a Polish or Swedish match cannot have been very high. Poland and Sweden each wanted all of Livonia, although they eventually settled for less. Moscow's insistence that the prospective bride convert to Orthodox Christianity precluded any Polish or Swedish marriage. Ivan's Circassian bride did convert.

Despite the speed with which Metropolitan Makarii asked Ivan to remarry in 1560, Ivan's remarriage to Kuchenei (Altynjan), baptized as Mariia Cherkasskaia, did not take place until September 21, 1561, a one-year interval after Anastasiia's death. By contrast, King Henry VIII of England became engaged to Jane Seymour the day after he had his previous wife, Anne

Boleyn, executed on trumped-up charges of incest with her brother and adultery with four other men. Henry married Seymour ten days later.[7]

Foreign policy toward Crimea dictated an alliance with the North Caucasus Circassian Kabardinians. Unfortunately, the "subjects" of Cher-kasskaia's father, Temriuk, expelled him from the region. Only Muscovite military assistance restored his lands to him. However, the Kabardinians controlled the main highway across the Caucasus, and Ivan's in-laws supplied troops against Crimea and Livonia.[8]

The chronicle recounted that upon first seeing Kuchenei in 1561, Ivan "fell in love with her" (*poliubil*). Of course Muscovy lacked the modern conception of romantic love. The word denoted a spiritual, not a physical, attraction. Muscovite sources applied it to other royal betrothals.[9] After Ivan's remarriage, he, his young wife, his sons by his first wife, and his brother Prince Iurii went off together on a family outing to the Trinity-Sergius Monastery. Then Ivan sent the tsareviches and Iurii back to Moscow, while he and his bride spent two months together traveling, before themselves returning to the capital. Ivan's lust played no role in his remarriage.[10]

After 1560, by his own choice, Ivan dispensed with the services of Aleksei Adashev and the priest Sylvester. Historians disagree on the reasons for their loss of influence.

Ivan lost his brother, Prince Iurii Vasil'evich, in November 1563.[11] We know nothing of Ivan's emotional attachment to Iurii, but, whatever his younger brother's limitations, Ivan had always taken care of him.

Metropolitan Makarii could not perform Prince Iurii's funeral because he lay dying himself. In December 1563 he passed away. Makarii lasted in office longer than any other metropolitan during Ivan's reign. Ivan must have respected him, but we know nothing of their personal relationship.[12]

Ivan's treatment of his elite became harsher, but his punishment of Prince Dmitrii Bel'skii in 1562 for attempting to flee Muscovy did not exceed the "normal" limits in such cases. Bel'skii suffered disgrace, imprisonment, and confiscation of his property. The man who convinced him to attempt to defect lost his tongue. Bel'skii's other associates endured knouting and prison.[13] However, Ivan's punishment of the Vorotynskie serving princes for unspecified treason exceeded what was usual. Ivan not only confiscated their properties but also ordered both brothers, Aleksandr and Mikhail, imprisoned with their wives. Ivan had never previously taken such action against the wife of a boyar. Ivan ordered disgraced Prince Dmitrii

Kurliatev and his son shorn, which removed them from court permanently. Ivan had never imposed that penalty before either. He also decreed that Kurliatev's wife and daughters take the veil, terminating even the family's female line, another punishment that Ivan had not previously used.[14] New but unspecified charges of treason against the Staritskie clan resulted in the reassignment of the personnel of Prince Vladimir's appanage and a restructuring of its territory. Although Ivan later visited Prince Vladimir and joined him in a feast, ostensibly a friendly gesture, Princess Evfrosiniia "requested" permission to become a nun. She might have had help making her request. Still, Ivan permitted her son, Prince Vladimir Staritskii, to make financial arrangements at his own expense to ensure Evfrosiniia's comfort at the Goritskii Convent. Evfrosiniia remained a member of the royal family, so propriety dictated that she live in the style to which she was accustomed. Ivan symbolically but ungenerously scheduled her vows on her late husband's birthday.[15] Prince Vladimir had to sign new loyalty oaths. Ivan had significantly escalated his repressive measures, but he had not yet irrevocably crossed the line.

When Ivan dropped Adashev and Sylvester, he did not dispense with all advisors. He found new confidants as quickly as he fell out with old ones. Kurbskii tried to impugn Ivan's judgment in choosing advisors. According to Kurbskii, former bishop Vassian Toporkov whispered in Ivan's ear: "If you wish to be an autocrat, do not keep beside you a single counselor wiser than yourself. . . . If you keep near you men wiser than yourself, then perforce you will be subject to them."[16] Toporkov's supposed advice derives from Kurbskii's preface in *Novyi Margarit* (New Pearl), a compilation of translations of the works of St. John Chrysostom.[17] Ivan's reported conversation with Toporkov sounds like court gossip, which Kurbskii might have heard before or after he defected rather than invented himself. Possevino wrote that Ivan strove to cut short the career of any individual who was "regarded as more learned or wiser" than himself.[18] That tyrants feared advisors wiser than themselves was a political cliché.

Ivan's increasingly severe repression remained selective. It did not approach the mass terror promulgated by the oprichnina. Nothing connects Ivan's actions before December 1564 to the black-robed *oprichniki* on black horses with dogs' heads and brooms. A world of difference separates his behavior before the oprichnina from that during the oprichnina. The period from 1560 to 1564 did not mark a rapid decline into insanity and tyranny.

It did witness a changing of the guard in the Kremlin as Ivan's relatives, supporters, and enemies died or defected, but no one observing Ivan during these years could have anticipated the oprichnina.

Ivan had ample opportunities to react to the loss of those he valued before 1560. He lost his mother at age eight and his children in infancy between 1553 and 1560. To infer that the loss of his first wife, brother, and trusted advisor Metropolitan Makarii so traumatized Ivan that he lost control of himself and then of his country gives him too little credit for resilience. If it took another straw to break the camel's back, though, that straw might have been the defection of Prince Andrei Kurbskii in 1564.

THE KURBSKII-IVAN CORRESPONDENCE AND MUSCOVITE POLITICAL IDEOLOGY

Historians cite the correspondence between Ivan and boyar Prince Andrei Kurbskii more frequently than any other source when discussing sixteenth-century Muscovite political ideology. Kurbskii's criticism of Ivan and Ivan's replies articulate their respective interpretations of Ivan's behavior and authority. Ivan's letters often also serve as the foundation for analysis of Ivan's personality. Other works by the two men also speak to these questions.

Kurbskii, commander-in-chief of all Muscovite armies in Livonia, defected to Poland-Lithuania in 1564. He later claimed that, after recent military reverses, he had feared for his life. He brought twelve retainers with him, but left his wife and property behind.[19] His defection created a major scandal in Muscovite eyes. For the remainder of Kurbskii's life, Muscovite envoys to Poland-Lithuania repeatedly demanded his extradition.[20] In negotiations for a Muscovite candidacy to the Polish-Lithuanian throne, Muscovite diplomats offered to drop demands for Kurbskii's extradition as though it were a significant concession. Even in 1582 Muscovite negotiators sought confirmation of an untrue rumor of Kurbskii's death.[21] Because of the symbolic value of Kurbskii's defection, the king of Poland would never agree to repatriate him. King Sigismund II Augustus arranged for Kurbskii to be present at his court when Muscovite ambassadors arrived, just to rub their noses in the matter.[22] Following precedent set during the 1530s, the Ambassadorial Bureau instructed Muscovite envoys to refuse to attend diplomatic functions in Kurbskii's presence. Ivan complained vehemently to Stefan Batory (Bathory), the former Transylvanian prince elected king of Poland and grand duke of Lithuania after the termination of the Jagiellonian dynasty, about Kurbskii's advice on Poland-Lithuania's Muscovite policy. Even the Crimeans knew about Kurbskii's defection.[23] Kurbskii's importance to Poland-Lithuania as a symbol far outweighed his value as an advisor or as a military commander against Muscovy.[24] Kurbskii's denunciation of Ivan only enhanced Kurbskii's value to Poland-Lithuania and exacerbated Muscovy's obsessive attempts to get its hands on him.

Any interpretation of Ivan's first letter to Kurbskii must begin with the realization that he and his government, like other contemporary rulers and governments (such as the French government in defending the St. Bartholomew's Day massacre), habitually lied.[25] It would be naive to expect political polemicists to tell the truth. In 1558 Ivan's emissary lied to the Patriarch of Alexandria by claiming that Ivan did not permit Muslims or Armenians to have dwellings in Muscovy. In 1563 Ivan blamed bad relations between Muscovy and Crimea on three of his officials whom he said he had removed. One had died, and Ivan had not removed the other two.[26] Beginning in 1566 the Ambassadorial Bureau instructed Muscovite diplomatic personnel in Poland-Lithuania to deny that the oprichnina existed. Letters to Sigismund and Lithuanian officials written in the names of boyars included this denial. In 1570 a Lithuanian delegation doubted that Ivan's absence from Moscow had delayed its negotiations with him, so the Ambassadorial Bureau informed them of the precise time that Ivan would pass by the Lithuanian compound upon his return from Aleksandrovskaia Sloboda. Presumably black-robed oprichniki carrying dogs' heads and brooms on their saddles accompanied him. Once home, the Lithuanians reported that oprichniki, not the usual musketeers, forced them to dismount en route to their reception. Obviously, Lithuanian diplomatic personnel knew oprichniki on sight.[27] After the 1571 Crimean raid on Moscow Ivan requested that Crimean Khan Devlet Girei release two of his former brothers-in-law, who had been captured during that raid. The khan replied that such a request made no sense coming from someone who had just executed yet another brother from the same family, Prince Mikhail Cherkasskii. Ivan blithely lied that he bore no responsibility for Cherkasskii's death, although Ivan later included Cherkasskii's name in the memorial lists of his victims. In 1583 the Ambassadorial Bureau instructed a liaison assigned to escort a Lithuanian delegation to Moscow to claim that all of Kazan had been converted to

Christianity and the region pacified, both lies.[28] Honesty took second place to opportunism in communications from Ivan and his government.

When defending his treason in his writings, Kurbskii hardly respected the truth more than Ivan.[29] He admitted that in writing his *History* he relied upon faulty memory and incomplete or contradictory rumors that reached him abroad. Perhaps this explains Kurbskii's description of the trial of Aleksei Adashev and Sylvester for heresy in absentia, lest their presence permit them to bewitch Ivan. No evidence corroborates that such a trial took place.[30] To take Kurbskii at his word, that he could not write his name in Cyrillic or that he had learned enough Latin to translate Latin texts into Slavonic, does not seem prudent.[31] Kurbskii probably had a reason other than illiteracy not to sign his name in Cyrillic rather than in Latin letters and "patronized" the translations from Latin credited to him.

Kurbskii's first letter to Ivan excoriated Ivan as a cruel ruler who had violated the dictates of Christian behavior.[32] Kurbskii's accusations undermined Ivan's identity as an Orthodox Christian tsar. If Ivan were not a true tsar, then he must be a "tormentor" (*muchitel*), which meant the same thing in the sixteenth century as "tyrant," who had to be disobeyed if his orders violated Christian conscience.[33] According to Kurbskii, Ivan already served Satan. Kurbskii made these charges while safely abroad. Some of Henry VIII's subjects committed treason by labeling him a "tyrant" during his lifetime in his own realm.[34] Kurbskii criticized Ivan on political and religious grounds simultaneously. He accused Ivan of abandoning good advisors for evil servants of the devil.[35] Ivan previously ruled properly, but now he had a minion of the Antichrist as his main advisor. Kurbskii pilloried Ivan as the "helper of the first beast and of the great serpent itself." Because Ivan executed worthy servitors, Muscovy suffered defeats in war. If Ivan did not repent and mend his ways, then he would be held answerable on the Day of Judgment when he met his maker.[36] Kurbskii presumed the innocence of all of Ivan's victims, portraying them in his *History* as saints. He spared no prose in recounting Ivan's atrocities, but the rumors upon which he relied, not surprisingly, contained much erroneous information. Historians cannot confirm much of his unique "information."

Kurbskii's contradictory comments on political issues complicate his simple moral condemnation of Ivan.[37] He advised Ivan to consult everyone, even the low-born. In his letter to the monastic elder Vassian Muromtsev of the Pskov Caves Monastery, Kurbskii painted a dismal picture of corruption and oppression in Muscovy, where peasants had to sell their children into slavery, merchants and peasants paid exorbitant taxes, cowardly clerics kept silent, and greedy monks accumulated wealth.[38] Simultaneously, he accused Ivan of relying too much upon upstart low-born bureaucrats, who insulted the well-born by giving them orders. Fellow émigré gentry-man Timofei Teterin shared Kurbskii's animus toward Ivan's bureaucrats. Like any aristocrat anywhere, anytime, Kurbskii thought that the well-born made the best advisors.[39] At the same time Kurbskii, often portrayed as the spokesman for the conservative, if not reactionary, boyars, criticized Ivan's "quarrelsome boyars," obviously a reference to those boyars of whom Kurbskii disapproved. In this case Kurbskii admitted that Ivan's advisors included boyars. Kurbskii stood up only for "good" boyar advisors. He blamed Ivan for his own participation in Polish-Lithuanian campaigns against Muscovy. He disingenuously claimed that he tried to prevent Lithuanian Muslim Tatars and Christian heretics under his command from burning Muscovite Orthodox churches.[40] Kurbskii criticized Ivan for arbitrarily violating the law and indulging in excessive violence against the innocent, but he omitted from his *History* the unedifying details of his own personal life in exile in Volynia, a part of the Grand Duchy of Lithuania. Kurbskii broke the law, conducted violent feuds with his neighbors, and ordered his officials to torture Jews with whom he had a financial conflict by incarcerating them in a flooded dungeon.[41]

Kurbskii's religious argumentation resonated with his role as defender of Orthodox Christianity against Protestant and Catholic assault. His preface in *Novyi Margarit* regurgitated the same accusations against Ivan and apologias for his own defection.[42]

What Kurbskii did not write in his works sheds light on his views. He did not diagnose Ivan as insane. He did not accuse Ivan of being the Antichrist, nor were his references to the apocalypse more than clichés.[43] He did not defend any specific boyar rights or privileges, nor did he ever mention the 1566 Assembly of the Land. He neither hinted that he preferred the Polish-Lithuanian constitutional system of an elected monarch to Muscovy's political system nor that Muscovite boyars should envy the class privileges of the Polish-Lithuanian gentry (*szlachta*).[44] In his *History* he lambasted the Polish gentry as lazy, immoral cowards who did not fight invading Crimean Tatars, hardly a model worth emulating. In his first letter to Ivan, he did not

specifically defend Adashev or the priest Sylvester, his putative collaborators
in the "Chosen Council." By 1564 both had been removed from power, and
Adashev was dead.[45] He did not even use the expression "Chosen Council"
in his letters; it occurs only in his *History*.

Ivan responded to Kurbskii's first letter with a lengthy diatribe.[46] Struc-
turally, his verbose and bombastic first letter to Kurbskii replied point-by-
point to Kurbskii's accusations, but it indulged in long digressions over-
flowing with inaccurate scriptural and patristic quotations and snippets of
biblical, Byzantine, and Rus' history.[47] Ivan committed numerous historical
and factual errors, contradicted himself, and perpetrated illogical arguments
in sometimes unintelligible prose.[48] Stylistically, Ivan wrote with more
emotion than lucidity. His allusions to the apocalypse were as generic as
Kurbskii's.[49] Ivan did not draw upon books that should have been available
to him from his legendary classical library of Hebrew, Greek, and Latin
texts because that library never existed, but he did own some books, such
as, later, the famous Ostroh Bible published by Ivan Fedorov.[50] The sudden
shifts in theme, eclectic literary style, and lack of discipline characteristic
of Ivan's first letter matched his mercurial character.[51]

Substantively, Ivan monotonously insisted that everyone he had executed was guilty—and even if some were not, he was only human, so he
could not be held responsible if he made mistakes. As tsar he answered
only to God, not to his subjects, who were obligated to follow his orders
without question. Similar letters written in the name of the boyars to
King Sigismund Augustus and Hetman of Lithuania Jan Chodkiewicz
contended that the boyars happily served him without complaints; from
their shared template, scholars believe Ivan ghostwrote these letters.[52] Ivan
claimed that Adashev and Sylvester had told him what to do politically
and personally. A tsar who did what his subjects told him to do was not a
tsar, and certainly unworthy to be a tsar, he wrote, echoing the "Valaam
Discourse," a text that criticized monastic involvement in politics. Ivan's
famous insulting remark about Aleksei Adashev, that Ivan had raised him
from a dung-heap, was a lie, echoing scriptural language. The Adashev
family belonged to the respectable gentry. Aleksei's father had the rank
of associate boyar when Ivan began favoring him.[53] History showed that
states whose rulers listened to their subjects perished, Ivan declared, sec-
onding the views of Ivan Peresvetov, a Ruthenian immigrant and author.
Besides, the boyars had abused their prerogatives during Ivan's minority and

mistreated him. Such self-serving, circular apologias for his behavior abound in Ivan's letters.

Ivan formulated his theory of rule succinctly: he was "free to reward our slaves . . . and also free to punish them" (*a zhalovati esmia svoikh kholopei vol'ny . . . a i kazniti vol'ny zhe*). Ivan did not invent this dictum—Grand Prince Boris Aleksandrovich of Tver used the same formula in 1427—but his diplomatic establishment assiduously promulgated it. Previous Muscovite rulers had been "free to reward and to punish their subjects." Ivan's merciless enemies had separated him from his first wife, Anastasiia. If they had not done so, there would have been no executions, which cannot apply to executions before 1561. Ivan implicitly deflected blame from himself by arguing that his enemies were responsible for his actions. A long description of negotiations with Lithuania in 1563 in the diplomatic papers, incoherent enough to have been composed by Ivan but not usually attributed to him, claimed that "our sovereign is free to punish and reward his slaves" and later quoted Ivan as saying, "in truth we are free to punish or reward our slaves." In 1567 the Ambassadorial Bureau instructed Muscovite negotiators to insist that Ivan was "free to reward the good and punish the bad." The 1567 letter to Hetman Chodkiewicz attributed to Prince Vorotynskii opined that the true Orthodox Christian Ivan "gave his beneficence to the good, and punished the evil." Instructions for negotiating with Poland-Lithuania repeated the same refrain in 1578.[54]

While intellectually Ivan's first letter to Kurbskii had firm roots in writings available during the 1550s, including the "Tale of Dracula," the works of state secretary Fedor Karpov and Peresvetov, and the "Valaam Discourse,"[55] an even stronger link bound Ivan's writings to his personality and life. Dmitrii Likhachev linked Ivan's role-playing in his writings to his role-playing in his life: his use of pseudonyms, such as writing a canon to the Archangel Michael under the nom de plume of Parfenii Iurdovii (Ivan's authorship of the canon is less convincing than Likhachev's other examples) and ghostwriting replies by boyars to invitations by the king of Poland to commit treason; his self-deprecation in his testament and petition to Simeon Bekbulatovich; his "abdications" in 1564, which led to the oprichnina, and in 1575, which led to the installation of Simeon Bekbulatovich on the throne; and his performance as the poverty-stricken ruler toward the envoy of the Crimean khan after the burning of Moscow in 1571. Role-playing came naturally to sixteenth-century monarchs and the members of their courts. Sigurd Shmidt observed that Ivan was as unrestrained in writing as he was in action. Ivan badly needed a copy editor, but he refused to permit anyone to serve that function. Vasilii Kalugin wrote that in literature as in life, Ivan thought that everything was permitted to him and to him alone.[56] Ivan's inimitable literary persona reflected his behavior and character.

Kurbskii criticized Ivan's lengthy reply to his previous letter by denigrating Ivan's skill as a writer, accusing him of verboseness and crudity in prose.[57] Kurbskii and Ivan did not debate literary style over a cup of tea at a café. Kurbskii lampooned Ivan's style to undermine his credibility. Kurbskii and Ivan took their correspondence personally.[58] Kurbskii wrote his first letter to Ivan from the city of Wolmar in the Grand Duchy of Lithuania (now the Latvian city of Valmiera). When the Muscovites took the city, Ivan taunted Kurbskii by writing his second letter to Kurbskii from Wolmar. Kurbskii had the last laugh, because Batory retook Wolmar.

In his first letter to Kurbskii Ivan disavowed responsibility for the reforms of the 1550s that many historians consider the greatest achievements of his reign. To do so he exaggerated the influence of Aleksei Adashev and Sylvester. No reform could have been instituted over Ivan's vigorous objections, so at the very least Ivan did not prevent the reforms. Ivan's retrospective judgment of his role in the reforms should be discarded as history and treated as propaganda.[59] It should not be utilized to justify the argument that Ivan played no role in the reforms of the 1550s.

Ivan insulted fellow rulers as easily as he did Kurbskii, although contemporary rulers also believed that their power derived from God and did not shy away from insulting each other.[60] In his diplomatic correspondence Ivan dismissed the Swedish Vasa dynasty as parvenus because their ancestor engaged in trade. The Vasa family actually derived from the gentry. Ivan called the Danish king the ruler of "water and salt." Neither could legitimately call himself Ivan's brother; that is, his equal. Ivan criticized Queen Elizabeth I of England for letting merchants tell her what policies to follow. Such behavior was beneath the dignity of a ruler. Elected monarchs such as the kings of Poland or Sweden or even the Holy Roman emperors ranked lower than hereditary monarchs like Ivan. Elizabeth I also asserted her superiority as a hereditary monarch to the elected king of Poland. Muscovite genealogies maligned the social origins of the Lithuanian royal line as slaves, servants, or, at best, the heirs of minor Riurikid princes.[61] Ivan responded to Batory's successful invasion of Muscovite territory with a letter insulting Batory's unknown origins, Muslim taint, heretical subjects, elected throne, barbarous desecration of the corpses of Muscovite soldiers, arrogant mistreatment of Muscovite envoys, and unworthy rhetoric. Ivan sounded like an arrogant bully who has been called out and petulantly whines at his humiliation, but of course he was bluffing. Batory sent an equally insulting reply and challenged Ivan to a duel to satisfy his honor. Holy Roman Emperor Charles V at least twice made the same offer to King Francis I of France. Ivan, like Francis I, did not accept the challenge.

When reality compelled him, however, Ivan tempered his arrogance. He never insulted the Crimean khan or the Ottoman sultan; they were far too dangerous. In 1562, because he needed the Danish fleet in the Livonian War, he treated the king of Denmark as an equal and concluded with Denmark Muscovy's first bilateral treaty. When convenient Muscovite diplomats could laud the "elected" Holy Roman emperor as superior to the king of Poland.[62]

Ivan used his sarcastic, sardonic wit, his vicious sense of parody, and his creative invective not just to display his virtuosity as a writer and his erudition, although he was a show-off, but also to overwhelm, humiliate, dismiss, or trick his opponents, including Kurbskii.[63] Although no Muscovite official or writer used insults better than Ivan, they sometimes tried.[64] Whether Ivan's prose expressed arrogance or humility, an authoritarian attitude toward his addressee or a conciliatory one, his letters always sought to gain an advantage. Ivan wrote letters the way he played politics, to win.[65]

Ivan's ambiguous treatment of the boyars precludes characterizing his ideology as anti-boyar. Ivan did not condemn *all* boyars. In his first letter to Kurbskii he did castigate "you boyars," including Kurbskii, and berate "the boyars" for undermining his policies and threatening his life, but he vented most of his anger against two individuals, the priest Sylvester and associate boyar Aleksei Adashev, not the boyars as a class. Ivan did defend the boyars who had stood up for him during his minority. "How many boyars and well-wishers of our father and commanders did they [the "bad" boyars] not massacre?" Ivan defended Prince Ivan Bel'skii, one of the prime boyar-intriguers during his minority, no doubt because other boyars murdered him. Ivan accused the Shuiskie of trying to murder his boyar and protector Fedor Vorontsov and blamed his enemies, the "treacherous boyars," for the death of boyar and relative Prince Iurii Glinskii at the hands of the Moscow mob in 1547. Ivan accused "bad" boyars of treasonously wanting him and his family dead in order to rule themselves. He seemingly contended that all boyars were bad, except those he liked. He even defended individuals whom he later executed, such as Vorontsov and the treasurer Nikita Funikov. We have no way of knowing if Ivan only criticized boyars who agreed with Kurbskii—or whom Ivan suspected of agreeing with him—because many incidents took place long before Kurbskii achieved any prominence. Earlier Ivan had defended the nobility of the boyars he appointed as governors of Novgorod to Swedish envoys, so as to sweeten the pill that the envoys had to swallow by dealing with the governors instead of with him.[66]

Ivan wrote so much about the boyars because within Muscovite political discourse the boyars mattered most. They constituted the most influential, highest-status class, and there was more to be gained by criticizing or praising them than any other class. In Ivan's rhetoric Adashev and Sylvester became leaders of the boyars. Ivan, in Daniil Al'shits's neologism, turned all his enemies into boyars (*oboiarival*).[67] Some historians take this rhetorical ploy as gospel truth and accuse Sylvester and Aleksei Adashev of serving boyar interests, despite the comment of the interpolations in the *Tsar's Book* about enmity between Sylvester and the boyars.

Historians should not believe either Kurbskii or Ivan about the guilt or innocence of all of Ivan's victims. References to Ivan's "real and imaginary" enemies do not change our inability to determine who was in each category. Even if Ivan was so suspicious, if not paranoid, that he could not tell the difference between actual and fictitious foes, historians must move beyond his limitations. Muscovites had a conception of insanity, which Ivan did not fit, so they did not diagnose Ivan as insane.[68] Ivan accused anyone he wanted to punish of treasonous intentions because treason encompassed virtually all political crimes within Muscovite discourse, from trying to emigrate to plotting to assassinate Ivan. No evidence confirms even one conspiracy to kill Ivan.

Ivan knew that he did not *exercise* unlimited authority. Otherwise he could not have complained about violations of his authority by his advisors or sabotage of his policies by his officials and generals. Ivan's actions demonstrate his perception of the difference between the theory of unlimited rule and reality, as well as his understanding of the impracticality of implementing his theory. Ruslan Skrynnikov observed that Ivan's first letter to Kurbskii has fooled historians into thinking that Ivan possessed the unlimited power he claimed he was entitled to. Time and again Ivan had to adjust his policies because of resistance by powerful classes such as the boyars and powerful institutions such as the Russian Orthodox Church.[69] More broadly, the Muscovite government under Ivan knew that its apparatus possessed neither omniscience nor omnipotence. The central administration repeatedly delegated authority to its officials in order that they might use their own judgment about how to apply centrally dictated policies. Ivan never dispensed with advisors entirely, probably because he realized that he could not rule Muscovy without them. He needed advisors simply to stay informed of what was going on. In any type of government whoever supplies information also shapes policy by doing so. Ivan ruled at different times for opposing parties in a lawsuit over market rights because he had no sources of information of his own to contradict either side's assertions.[70]

The necessity of consulting the boyars did not hamstring Ivan or impede him from conducting political affairs in person. As a rule Ivan did not negotiate privately with foreign ambassadors, not to prevent him from making anti-boyar deals behind their backs but to protect his dignity.[71] By not getting involved, he gave himself and his diplomatic representatives more flexibility. The Muscovite negotiating team could reject or stall any proposal by insisting that it had to consult Ivan. Ivan could then act magnanimously by acceding to proposals that his negotiators could not. As early as 1549 he accepted a compromise on his title in the truce with Poland-Lithuania: the Muscovite copy of the truce referred to him as "tsar," but the Polish copy did not, an arrangement his boyars had indignantly rejected but then accepted as Ivan's generous concession. At one point in negotiations to end the Livonian War the Muscovite envoys informed their Polish counterparts that if they allowed the Poles to keep the fortress of Velizh, Ivan would execute them.[72] Perhaps with Ivan's blessing, and certainly with his indulgence, the Muscovite representatives utilized Ivan's reputation for cruelty as a bargaining chip. Ivan could and did negotiate personally in private as well as in public, and this did not constitute meddling in matters beyond his competence or authority. Ivan's tirade on English-Muscovite relations confirms his expertise.[73] The ideas Ivan expressed in his correspondence with Kurbskii and elsewhere should be appreciated as Ivan's ideal, not his political program. Proclaiming unlimited rule in theory enabled him to achieve more influence in practice.

When Metropolitan Makarii crowned Ivan and performed his wedding ceremony, Ivan was sixteen. He was thirty-four when he left Moscow in

December 1564 on the path that led to the establishment of the oprichnina. By then Ivan had probably gained maturity from experience.[74] It would be foolish to equate a man in his early thirties with a teenager or a man in his early twenties. Likewise, to conclude that Ivan had no role in developments in Muscovy during the "long" 1550s because all reform activity ceased after he established the oprichnina rests upon a false premise—Ivan not only did *not* undo previous reforms, he also instituted new reforms, such as the creation of the Assembly of the Land. Ivan's role during the reforms should not be discounted.

Part III

*Muscovy from Ivan's Accession
to the Oprichnina*

8

Domestic Political Reform

Having traced Ivan's growth from a boy to a teenager to a young man, we are in a better position to explore which developments in Muscovite history from 1533 to 1564 he might have influenced.

Political reform began before Ivan reached maturity. Despite lethal political rivalries among the boyars, the government dealt creatively with the problem of brigandage, and its solution met with approval during the period of reform. After Ivan's coronation and marriage, the government undertook a much wider range of domestic political reform. Traditional historiography notwithstanding, no Council of Reconciliation met in 1549 and no so-called Chosen Council guided the reform process. In 1550 the government issued a new law code, the first since 1497. Procedurally, the law code updated government regulations based upon the experiences of the intervening period. The law code did not try to limit the authority of the ruler. Its revision of the procedure to pass legislation merely codified custom. New substantive provisions on dishonor and a new form of slavery reflected significant social change. The central government also applied the principle of "drafting" local resources to revise its tax collection method by creating a new institution of local government, the "land." Thus, the principle of decentralization bridged the divide between Ivan's minority and the period of reforms. Additional reforms sought to protect, mobilize, standardize, support, and regulate the elite to sustain its position in Muscovite society and the economy, so it could better serve the Muscovite government at home and abroad. Even when Ivan and the Royal Council granted the lower classes autonomy, the government still served, and expected to be served by, the elite.

POLITICAL INSTITUTIONS AND POLITICAL REFORM

Irrespective of who initiated the reforms of the 1550s—Ivan, boyars, or bureaucrats—no Muscovite had any abstract concept of "reform."[1] Here, as elsewhere at the time, the government presented all changes in administration or policy as returns to "tradition" and "antiquity." Nevertheless, the absence of a concept of reform did not preclude the practice of instituting reforms, incremental measures to improve the functioning of the administration. Ad hoc reform qualifies as reform. The government wanted a more efficient and effective administration in order to generate more resources. Although no comprehensive reform plan existed, the participants in the process did have agendas. For this reason we will use the word "reform" without the affectation of quotation marks. Sixteenth-century governments made changes to serve the elite, not, except accidentally, the masses. Like all contemporary states, Muscovy lacked the modern conception of democracy. Governments did not rate improving the life of the "people" as a priority. Changes constituted "technical reforms," which left the fundamental social and political structure of the regime unchanged.[2]

ANTI-BRIGANDAGE LEGISLATION

Although Grand Princess Elena had undertaken some reform measures, such as monetary reform, she did not address the problem of brigandage. The first anti-brigandage (*guba*) charters appeared in 1539–1541, during the period of boyar rule. Despite boyar ascendancy in Moscow, some historians still interpret the anti-brigandage reform as anti-boyar because it reduced the obligations and authority of the governors, most of whom were boyars. While boyars monopolized the major governorships, gentry held many less important gubernatorial offices. The significance of the anti-brigandage reform lies elsewhere, in the fact that this reform utilized local participation to address the brigandage problem. Local communities could create anti-brigandage institutions to perform gratis the task of catching and punishing bandits. Governors retained jurisdiction over other serious crimes. So-called absolutist regimes everywhere at the time used similar mechanisms to achieve their goals. Although this was probably an unintended effect, the anti-brigandage reform also contributed to local social cohesion. Historians need to devote more attention to regionalism in sixteenth-century Muscovy, but without misrepresenting it as political separatism.

The anti-brigandage charters adhered to a common pattern.[3] A community petitioned the central government on the grounds that banditry had become endemic and that the governors and the county administrators had proven incapable of containing the crime wave. The central government acceded to the community's request to deal with the problem on its own. Moscow gave anti-brigandage elders (*gubyne starosty*) carte blanche to summon grand juries of members of all social classes to identify "known" criminals and to impose capital punishment on the spot. The elders were initially elected locally but then ratified by Moscow, and they were later appointed from Moscow, probably with local consultation. Contemporary states did not lightly share their monopoly of capital punishment. Moreover, the draconian anti-brigandage procedures did not include trials, a sacrifice of state judicial fees. No central government official even attended the anti-brigandage grand juries.

Local discretion did not approach local vigilantism, however, because the anti-brigandage authorities proceeded according to centrally defined regulations. They reported to Moscow. The central institution to which local anti-brigandage elders reported was variously identified. Originally, elders had to forward their reports to Moscow "to the boyar in charge of anti-bandit affairs" (*boyar prikazany razboinim delam*), who was sometimes named, sometimes not, with no institutional name. Later the institution in charge of fighting bandits possessed multiple names, such as the Anti-Brigandage Hut (*gubnaia izba*), the Bandit Hut (*razboinaia izba*), or the Bandit Bureau (*razboinyi prikaz*).[4] The Anti-Brigandage Bureau qualifies as one of only a few, and perhaps the only, central government department headed by a boyar during Ivan's reign.[5] The fluidity of its nomenclature reflected the flexible development of an institution in an under-institutionalized customary state.

The chronology and scope of the anti-brigandage reform remain matters

of dispute. The earliest charters applied locally. A charter to a southern
frontier town mentioned anti-brigandage elders, although large frontier
garrisons should have obviated the need for anti-brigandage institutions.
Eventually, in theory the system became countrywide, and central orders
superseded local initiative.[6] The Law Code of 1550 assumed that anti-
brigandage elders existed everywhere, although they probably did not.

Anti-brigandage elders could be state peasants or suburban artisans,
but the government preferred gentry, whose combat skills equipped them
best to deal with violent bandits. When possible charters specified that
anti-brigandage elders should come from literate gentry so that they could
correspond with anti-brigandage officials in neighboring districts in the
pursuit of named accomplices and supervise the recording of their proceedings to be dispatched to Moscow. Sixteenth-century English gentry
not asked to serve as unpaid justices of the peace considered themselves
snubbed.[7] Muscovite gentry should not have resented acquiring a respectable
and respected service role in the local community.

The inquests to identify "known brigands" probably encouraged formation of regional collective identities. The grand juries were drawn from local
residents, regardless of class, united in a common goal of mutual self-interest. The grand juries did not completely ignore class distinction, however.
The charters stipulated that the testimony of boyars, state secretaries, and
government officials was not to be questioned. The gentry who became anti-brigandage elders had strong provincial links. The anti-banditry charters
presumed not only that local communities knew all their neighbors but also
that "outsiders" automatically became suspects.[8]

A reciprocal relationship linked these local communities to the political
center. The first petitions pertained to relatively few and distant regions.
The central authorities lacked the knowledge of local conditions necessary
to mastermind a charade of popular initiative. Local communities wanting
to institute an anti-brigandage system easily found out the "proper" way to
articulate their request. The anti-brigandage reform did not demonstrate
either excessive centralization or central government impotence but, rather,
the cooperation of center and provinces to their common benefit. The anti-
brigandage, and later the local self-government, institutions served both as
conduits for the transmission of central state policy to the provinces and as
communication channels from the provinces to the center. They integrated
local and central elites.

Problems remained. Anti-brigandage elders did not always fulfill their obligation to keep Moscow informed. They sometimes exceeded the scope of their authority to pursue criminals who were not bandits. Governors, military governors (*voevody*), and other local officials did not always work well with them. Some anti-brigandage elders shirked their duties or, worse, became bandits. In 1556 the government tried to deal with the problem of family collusion in criminal activity by tightening central control.[9] Although local communities supported the anti-brigandage institutions in theory, in practice not all community members behaved accordingly.

The timing of this reform could have resulted from a rise in brigandage because of weak central government during boyar rule or because of social instability.[10] Muscovy enjoyed prosperity during the first half of the sixteenth century, so we can rule out economic hard times as a cause. Lower local tolerance for antisocial behavior or greater central government concern for "law and order" might explain the implementation of the anti-brigandage reform. It is likely that local society and the central government jointly perceived an existing level of brigandage as an increase. Social instability increased sensitivity to disorder. Banditry everywhere reflected social tension, as late sixteenth-century English paranoia about crimes against property attests.[11] Some Muscovite gentry became bandits, so not all banditry qualifies as social protest, as some have suggested.[12]

Although the boy Ivan had no role in the formulation of anti-brigandage policy during the late 1530s and early 1540s, the anti-brigandage charters attributed to him the central government's decision to respond favorably to local initiative and the charters were issued in Ivan's name. In this way the reform projected a positive image of Ivan into the provinces.[13]

THE COUNCIL OF RECONCILIATION

In 1549, according to the traditional narrative, Ivan gave two speeches proclaiming his intention, now that he had attained adulthood, to end the disorders of his minority, restore social peace, and initiate needed reforms. In the first speech, delivered to the boyars, he declared that he would vacate all lawsuits about past boyar transgressions and take no measures against their perpetrators, *if* the boyars ceased their wrongdoing. Ivan then addressed the same message to a group of gentry and officials on Red Square, which constituted the first Assembly of the Land (*zemskii sobor*), a countrywide representative assembly, called by historians, because of Ivan's message, the Council of Reconciliation (*sobor primireniia*).[14] Ivan committed himself to justice for all.[15] He appointed Aleksei Adashev, a member of the gentry and a leading light among the Chosen Council, to the post of head of the Petitions Chancellery, with authority to adjudicate grievances.

This episode did not take place as the traditional narrative proposes. Someone in the seventeenth century fabricated Ivan's speech. No Petitions Chancellery existed in 1549.[16] No one summoned gentry and "Christians" to Moscow in 1549.[17] Ivan "spoke" to the gentry rhetorically, not in person. Nor did these events constitute Muscovy's first Assembly of the Land.

An Assembly of the Land did meet during Ivan's reign, in 1566, so the institution does belong in a history of Ivan's reign. Nineteenth-century historians invented the phrase "Assembly of the Land" for meetings of representatives of several social classes.[18] Contemporary sources do not even call the 1566 meeting a "council"; they just describe its proceedings without giving it a name. After 1584 sources refer to a "council of the entire land" (*sobor vseia zemli*). The ruler, or someone acting in his name, summoned such councils. During the Time of Troubles (Smutnoe vremia) from 1598 to 1613, "Assemblies of the Land" acquired considerable political power. The parallels with an Estates-General, Parliament, Sejm, Cortes, or Riksdag inspired inferences that Muscovy developed constitutional institutions and an "estate-representative monarchy" comparable to those of other countries.[19] Regardless of the validity of these comparisons, the history of the Muscovite Assembly of the Land did not begin in 1549.

THE CHOSEN COUNCIL

The seventeenth-century ascription of a role to Aleksei Adashev in the fictionalized account of events of 1549 resonates with the wider question of the existence of a Chosen Council (Izbrannaia rada) spearheading Muscovite reform. According to Kurbskii's *History*, after the 1547 Moscow fires the priest Sylvester bellowed at Ivan that the fires were God's punishment for his sins and that Ivan needed to repent. Kurbskii modeled his story on the Prophet Nathan's confrontation with King David in the Old Testament. Ivan took the advice to heart and made Sylvester his closest advisor. Thus supposedly arose the Chosen Council, which included the rising gentry reformer Aleksei Adashev, the priest Sylvester, perhaps Metropolitan Makarii, and a number of progressive-minded boyars, including Kurbskii.[20]

As Anthony Grobovksy and Aleksandr Filiushkin have conclusively demonstrated, however, the Chosen Council never existed. The name appears only in Kurbskii's *History*.[21] Kurbskii might have chosen the word "*rada*," the name of the Polish and Lithuanian royal councils, to accommodate the audience of his *History*, to translate the Muscovite word "*duma*" (council). The phrase "Izbrannaia duma" does not occur in Muscovite sources. Grobovsky's meticulous analysis of Kurbskii's text established that Kurbskii did not mean "*the* Chosen Council," an institution, but "chosen council," a phrase referring to selected, competent advisors, and one that Kurbskii loosely applied to any advisor executed by Ivan. Therefore, Kurbskii could not have meant the Privy Council (Blizhnaia duma), which was an institution.[22] Filiushkin showed that the career trajectories of the putative members of the Chosen Council do not correspond. Kurbskii spent most of the 1550s campaigning, not serving as a reform advocate in Moscow. No cleric, whether priest or metropolitan, could have belonged to a government council. Leading clerics belonged to the Holy or Consecrated Council (Osviashchennyi sobor), headed by the metropolitan. (In Poland-Lithuania the nobility monopolized episcopal office, so bishops sat on the Polish or Lithuanian "royal councils." In Muscovy, boyars rarely became bishops.) Unfortunately, mainstream scholarship on Ivan's reign, especially in Russia, remains committed to the Chosen Council paradigm because it provides a ready excuse not to attribute any positive role to Ivan in the institution of reforms.

Although Sylvester and Adashev could not belong to a nonexistent institution, they did enjoy proximity to the throne and did exercise concomitant influence. Letters from the imprisoned Maksim Grek to Sylvester and Adashev, asking for mercy, document that contemporaries recognized their prominence. In 1585 Polish bishop Stanislaw Karnovski, speaking to Muscovite envoy Luka Novosil'tsev, compared the influence of Boris Godunov, by then virtually running Muscovy as Tsar Fedor's brother-in-law, to that of Adashev. By the first quarter of the seventeenth century, a Muscovite chronicle asserted that Adashev coruled the "Rus' Land" with the priest Sylvester.[23] Ivan in his first letter to Kurbskii, and Kurbskii in his later letters and *History*, did not invent but only exaggerated the influence of Adashev and Sylvester. Even so, neither they nor anyone else exercised

such influence through the mythical Chosen Council. Political influence
flowed through Ivan.

THE LAW CODE OF 1550

In 1550 Ivan issued a new law code, which he promulgated with his "brothers" (his brother [*brat*] Prince Iurii Vasil'evich and his cousin [in Russian
dvoiurodnyi brat, often abbreviated simply as "brother"] Prince Vladimir
Andreevich) and the boyars.[24] The sources do not permit us to apportion responsibility for its contents among these parties. We do not know who compiled the new law code or who wrote any of its provisions. By 1550, if Ivan
seriously objected to the law code, he might have refused to issue it. Instead,
during the 1550s Ivan seems to have enforced and abided by its provisions.
We may, therefore, infer his approval of its contents. The 1550 Law Code
was procedurally conservative and substantively innovative. Approximately
two-thirds of its provisions derived from the 1497 code, modified to reflect
judicial practice during the intervening fifty-three years. New substantive
provisions reflected changing social conditions and government needs.[25]

Most of the Law Code of 1550 dealt with procedural law, with a heavy
emphasis on inhibiting corruption. All contemporary governments worried
about the honesty of their officials. Impartial justice served the state's financial and political interests. Foreigners disagreed about whether Muscovy
enforced justice too severely or too mildly, but all governments proclaimed
justice as their goal.[26] Anti-banditry reform and administrative charters
had limited or regulated the jurisdiction of the governors. Now they lost
jurisdiction over the gentry too. The gentry acquired the class privilege, and
attendant prestige, of coming under Ivan's personal jurisdiction, although
the government did not abolish the office of governor.[27]

On the whole, judges made decisions based upon evidence and testimony. Elected "sworn-men" (*tseloval'niki*), representing the community, aided
Muscovite judges in ruling impartially. Judges even articulated the reason-
ing behind their decisions (*ratio decidendi*). The law code made crimes of
false accusations (*iabednichestvo*), slander, and oath-breaking, already seen
as sins.[28] Judgment charters (*pravye gramoty*) suggest that judges utilized
common sense in reaching their verdicts.[29] They only reluctantly abdicated
human justice to divine intervention by permitting judicial duels to decide
guilt. Therefore, although the Law Code of 1550 continued to refine the law

of judicial duels and foreigners claimed to have witnessed them, judicial charters from Ivan's reign do not contain a single example of an actual judicial duel, which might have become a judicial fiction.[30] Judges exercised discretion by accepting out-of-court settlements forbidden by law, by threatening corporal punishment for crimes to which it did not apply, and by not employing torture when legislation permitted. Judges relied upon popular notions of justice and the spirit, not just the letter, of the law, as they saw fit. Even Ivan went above and beyond judicial procedure to establish the truth in one land-related case, during the *oprichnina* no less. The Law Code of 1550 fostered equal justice and fair procedural law, except, as elsewhere, in treason cases.[31]

Substantively, the Law Code of 1550 introduced a new tax measure, the "big plow" (*bol'shaia sokha*), which standardized tax rates based upon social status. State peasants paid the most, military servitors the least. The government also introduced a new countrywide dry measure of weight, the "quarter."[32] An article regulated the practice of land redemption, whereby for forty years after a sale or donation specified relatives of the vendor or donor could "redeem" it by making restitution. Parallel practices existed elsewhere. In Muscovy all classes could take advantage of redemption, but in France only the nobility could.[33] The rising volume of sales of patrimonial estates may have motivated the development of redemption law. Redemption restricted individual property rights in the interest of strengthening family or clan property rights. Clauses defining redemption became almost de rigueur in land transactions.[34] Such regulation diminished the number of lawsuits and facilitated the efficacious resolution of those that did occur. Redemption of land donated or sold to monasteries violated the supposed inalienability of ecclesiastical land, but monasteries could insist on no-redemption clauses in their bills of sale and donation charters.[35] Redemption was always for cash.

Article 98 of the Law Code of 1550 specified that the boyars had to give their assent before any new *delo* (plural *dela*) could be added to the law code. This provision neither expressed aristocratic pretensions nor limited royal prerogatives. Throughout the law code the word "delo" denoted a legal "case."[36] Boyars usually decided "cases" (sometimes gentry or state secretaries did so too), so a "case" that led to a new "decree," "order," or "decision" already had boyar (or other elite) assent. In Muscovite discourse royal actions always resulted from an agreement between the ruler and his elite: "the tsar decreed and the boyars assented" or "the tsar proposes and the boyars dispose" (*tsar' ukazal i boyare prigovorili*). No legal distinction distinguished decrees "with the boyars" from decrees "with all the boyars." In practice decrees of the tsar alone, "decisions" of the boyars alone, and "decisions" of Ivan and the boyars together carried equal legal power. Article 98 merely codified Muscovite custom.[37]

The Law Code of 1550 contained new articles on dishonor or "injured honor" (*bezchestie*).[38] The law code did not define dishonor, but ample case law demonstrates that verbal rather than physical offenses against honor predominated. Even physical insults entailed more symbolic than corporal harm, such as pulling a man's beard or touching a woman's hair. The scale of fines for dishonor offenses reflected the social hierarchy: highest for boyars and government officials, because insulting a government official insulted the tsar whom he represented, and lowest for peasants. Consequently, "honor" did not encourage individual social worth; an individual's honor derived from group membership. The Law Code of 1550 did not include a fee for dishonoring slaves per se.[39] Fines doubled for crimes dishonoring women, because an insult to a woman also insulted her father if she were single or her husband if she were married. Heightened concern for honor reflected social insecurity. Law suits over defamation increased dramatically in the second half of the sixteenth century in England, France, Italy, and Germany, so the development of dishonor law in Muscovy kept pace with that in other countries.[40]

The Law Code of 1550 also regulated a new form of limited-contract slavery (*kabal'noe kholopstvo*, via a "limited-service slavery contract" [*kabala*]). People sold themselves into slavery without any expectation that they could "repay" their purchase price and resume a life of freedom. The law code forbade gentry from selling themselves into slavery;[41] by this prohibition the government sought to protect the army. Gentry-mounted archers, usually holding conditional land grants (singular, *pomest'e*) in return for service, constituted Muscovy's primary military force.[42] Military servitors who could not afford to fulfill their military obligations tried to sell themselves into slavery to evade service. By contrast, better-off military servitors owned elite military slaves.[43] A slave emancipated with a quiver, saber, armor, horse, and saddle must have been a military slave.

Slavery can coexist with a money economy, even capitalism, as it did in the US Antebellum South, so the growth of slavery in Muscovy during

Ivan's reign does not contradict evidence of the increase in cash economic transactions. Serfdom, not present in Muscovy at the time, also coexisted with a money economy. The so-called second serfdom appeared in sixteenth-century Bohemia, Poland, and Hungary to guarantee the gentry the labor that they needed to grow grain to export for cash.[44]

The Muscovite administrative and judicial apparatus used the Law Code of 1550, and eventually every government bureau and governor had a copy. Secretaries frequently updated copies by adding subsequent legislation, although some provisions that should have been added to the Law Code of 1550 only appeared in the Compilative Law Code (Svodnyi sudebnik) of 1606.[45] Case law, instructions, and charters all cited the Law Code of 1550.[46] Foreign descriptions of Muscovy as a "lawless" society grossly misstated the situation.[47]

The compilers of the Law Code of 1550 manifested a more pragmatic attitude toward government actions during Ivan's minority than Ivan's rhetoric in his first letter to Kurbskii might suggest. The government retained Elena Glinskaia's currency reform and expanded anti-brigandage legislation. The procedural content of the Law Code of 1550 reflected continuity, while substantive innovations in redemption, dishonor, and slavery reflected discontinuity. Overall the Law Code of 1550 conservatively defended the existing social order but made incremental "liberal" legislative changes. Political reform did not stop with these measures, however, but also addressed other issues.

LOCAL GOVERNMENT REFORM

The so-called land (zemskaia, the adjective from the noun zemlia) reform of local government matched the anti-brigandage reform in structure, implementation process, and, in part, consequences.[48] Localities petitioned the central government to complain about illegal exactions by governors and county administrators, excessive fees, and gratuitously large gubernatorial entourages to be fed and housed at local expense, despite prohibitions in administrative charters. If given the authority to apportion and collect taxes themselves and to deliver the revenue to Moscow, the petitioners offered to pay double taxation. Moscow graciously acceded to these requests, granting localities the right to elect unpaid local government elders to be supervised by local sworn-men. The elders had to make up revenue shortfalls themselves. The land reform charters forbade the local government clerk (*zemskii d'iak*) from taking the documents he wrote home, lest he "revise" them. The central government implemented the local government reform in two stages: first, only volitionally in selected regions, such as among the prosperous state peasants of the north, and second, nationally by central decree. Local government reform facilitated the formation of communal identity. Historians often anachronistically apply to these local government institutions the word "*zemstvo*," the term from the Great Reforms of the 1860s, because the word derives from the same root meaning "land."[49]

The "land" local government reform never entirely replaced its predecessor. Previously, the government appointed tax collectors to a "feeding" (*kormlenie*), sometimes translated as "provender" or "prebend," because in lieu of salaries such officials "fed" off customary gratuities and fees from the people they administered. Custom defined bribery only as those gifts that sought benefits harmful to the public interest, not gift giving that incorporated the governor into the local community.[50] Returning from conquering Kazan in 1552, Ivan distributed "feedings" and other gratuities to his victorious officers. In 1558 noble Livonian German captives received "feedings." Perhaps local government institutions never reached border garrison regions. Later in Ivan's reign military commanders replaced "feedings" and "land" as local governmental institutions.[51] During the oprichnina many cities switched from "feeding" to tax farming (*otkup*).[52]

Local self-government did not apply to landed estates with fiscal and judicial immunities. Governors with "feedings" and "land" local governmental institutions could coexist in the same locations. Administrative experimentation produced an unsystematic patchwork of "feedings," elected local government elders, anti-brigandage elders, urban administrators (*gorodovye prikazshchiki*),[53] fortification stewards (*osadnye golovy*), and urban commanders. The central government never stopped experimenting with mechanisms to limit administrative abuse and increase local revenue.[54]

The local government reform primarily served fiscal needs, but it also freed elite personnel for other military and administrative functions. Would-be officials could not buy jobs in Muscovy as they could in France and elsewhere where venality of office was practiced. Boyars and gentry deprived of their jobs by the local government reform had no cause for complaint, because in 1555/1556 Ivan issued a law establishing a "feeding tax" to generate the funds needed to compensate former "feeding"-holders for lost revenue. Ivan instituted the local government reform with the approval of the boyars in the Royal Council. Clearly neither Ivan nor the boyars had any problem with depriving boyars and gentry appointed as governors and county administrators by the tsar of direct administrative responsibility for tax collection.[55]

Local communities willingly paid more for autonomy in tax administration to avoid excessive payments to governors and county administrators, as well as to emancipate themselves from aristocratic and gentry administrative fiat. The economic prosperity of the first half of Ivan's reign gave localities that choice. The local government reform cannot be described as a top-down measure of fiscal oppression, imposed upon localities by an avaricious central government. Local petitions were more than a pro forma facade to mask a tax hike and raise service obligations. Ongoing negotiation between the center and the provinces shaped the process of implementation of the reform. The local government reform, like the anti-brigandage institutions, fits the pattern of so-called absolutist states that frequently resorted to mobilizing unpaid social groups to fulfill state-dictated functions.[56]

MOBILIZATION, STANDARDIZATION, AND REGULATION OF THE ELITE

To facilitate swift mobilization of elite cadres, in 1550 the government issued the Book of the Thousand (Tysiachnaia kniga), granting graduated amounts of land in conditional tenure to selected military servitors who did not have estates within seventy kilometers of Moscow. Presumably these servitors could now reside in close proximity to the capital or could sustain households in Moscow.[57] Few gentry could afford to live in Moscow on a regular basis. Servitors living on distant estates took longer to assemble. The size of the land grants supposedly also guaranteed that the servitors had the wherewithal to serve. Historians disagree about whether the government fully implemented the reform because there was not enough available land to go around.[58] We lack definitive proof either way. The selected Thousand included only eighteen of thirty-two boyars and seven of twelve associate boyars because the remainder already possessed estates in the Moscow region. Allotment amounts depended upon social category: the largest to boyars, associate boyars, and the highest of the three "ranks" (*stat'i*) of gentry; less to the second and third gentry ranks. Bureaucrats, such as the treasurers, also received estates. Scribes did not update the Book of the Thousand to keep up with changes in the demographics of its personnel. It continued to list servitors assigned to appanages that no longer existed. Therefore its totals remained inaccurate. The Thousand overlapped the membership of the court.[59] The Thousand reform did not set a precedent for the oprichnina, nor would its total implementation have eliminated the need for the oprichnina. The men of the Thousand did not take a special oath, did not wear special dress, did not carry dogs' heads or brooms on their horses, and did not belong to a pseudo-monastic brotherhood. They lacked all the symbolic markers of oprichnina.[60]

Gentry who could not pay their debts could not afford to serve, so the government tried to deal with servitor indebtedness in 1558. A decree freed servitors from interest payments for the next five years. After that period the decree limited interest to 10 percent, half the going rate. (Loan rates in Spain rose as high as 50 percent.) The Orthodox Church enjoyed no more success in banning interest on loans on the grounds that it constituted the sin of usury than did the Catholic Church.[61] Servitors on service received payment deferments. The legislation permitted "righter" (*pravezh*) punishment for debtors proportionate to the size of the defaulted debt, one month of punishment for each one hundred rubles of debt for nonserving people but double that duration for servitors. (A debtor on "righter" suffered potentially crippling public beating on the shins daily until he paid up.[62]) Why servitors incurred a heavier penalty for debt remains unclear. One hundred rubles was an enormous sum, enough to fund daily commemorative prayers in monasteries for two deceased. The extent of gentry debt suggests economic hardship but also the prevalence of sufficient cash to be borrowed.

In order to protect the landowning economic base of the serving elite, the government limited the right of landowners to dispose of patrimonial (inherited) clan lands. A 1550 decree authorized landowners to sell, mortgage, or bequeath to monasteries purchased land in full but no more than half of patrimonial land. Violators forfeited any monies received. Landowners could not sell their land to "outsiders" (people who did not reside in the locale). They could not donate it to monasteries without a report to the crown. A 1562 decree restricted monastic acquisition of purchased land. It also forbade female inheritance, probably because upon the marriage of the inheritor the land would pass out of her natal clan. According to a donation charter, if Ivan disallowed the donation of land to a monastery and took the land for his royal household or reallocated it as a conditional land grant, the donor would compensate the monastery in cash for any resulting loss. The government did not oppose monastic landownership, but it restricted monastic land acquisition in the interest of the continuity of elite clan landownership in order to guarantee the continued military capacity of the state. Security concerns trumped religious sentiment.[63]

In order for the central government to control the elite it needed more information and a better articulated conception of the servitor corps. The Court Quire (Dvorovaia tetrad') restructured the royal household. Territorial organization gave way to class organization, centralizing the membership of the royal household. The court elite included not only boyars, associate boyars, and gentry but also state secretaries, treasurers, and other officials. Scribes amended the Court Quire for as long as a decade after its promulgation in a vain effort to keep it current. Unfortunately, only defective copies survive.[64] The significance of the gradual elimination of separate serving princely and regional princely and non-princely groupings remains under discussion. However, organizing the royal household members into ranks differentiated by status and wealth did not impair group cohesion. The Court Quire distinguished conditional landholders from patrimonial owners, but it did not segregate either group. Annotations described personnel in disgrace, captive, retired, dead, blind, or in prison; minors not yet old enough to serve; and those who were now monks or bandits. Obviously, no completely up-to-date version of the list ever existed, but the attempt to compose an authoritative definition of the royal household elite resonated with the composition in 1556 of the Sovereign's Register (Gosudarev razriad, "deployment book") of military and civilian appointments, and the Sovereign's Genealogy (Gosudarev rodoslovets), a compendium of princely and aristocratic lineages to serve as evidence in precedence suits.[65] Regulating central government money allotments to nobles might have inspired compilation of the so-called Boyar Book (*boiarskaia kniga*) of 1556. In the 1560s the government created new fiscal departments, called "quarters" (*cheti, chetverty*).[66]

DECREE ON PRECEDENCE

Precedence, the system of allocating civilian, military, or ceremonial "places," dictated that no noble could be assigned an office or a "place" at a ceremony that made him inferior to someone who ranked lower in a complicated calculation based upon seniority among clans and within a clan and all offices ever held by members of that clan. The historiography of precedence uniformly presents it as a boyar issue, but one quarter of all precedence cases and one quarter of all participants in precedence cases were members of the gentry. Consequently, precedence affected all nobles, boyar and gentry alike. Precedence inspired sometimes vehement, sometimes humorous rivalries among the nobles. Ivan might have to send officials to drag a noble to a feast because he refused to sit "lower" than a rival noble. Precedence inspired a plethora of lawsuits over dishonor that occupied not only Ivan's time but also that of the Royal Council and the Registry Bureau. The origin and uniqueness of the system remain debatable.[67]

Historians disagree about whether precedence limited royal discretion in making appointments, impeding the promotion of less well-born but more competent servitors, or facilitated royal manipulation of the elite because rival elite clans devoted their time to competing with each other rather than opposing royal authority. When no adult ruler could discipline boyar feuds over office and political favoritism during Ivan's minority, the precedence system assumed its final form.[68] Whether precedence inhibited military efficiency or helped the aristocracy maintain a monopoly of higher office remains disputed. Only rarely can historians attribute military defeats to precedence disputes.[69] Ad hoc decrees suspending precedence for particular campaigns proved insufficient to control the unintended consequences of the system. In 1552 at Kazan, Ivan intended for all his privy boyars to gather in order of worth, but the number involved dictated that precedence be lifted.[70] The government needed to take additional action.

In 1556 Ivan issued a decree on precedence. Unfortunately, the decree survives only in a confusing chronicle paraphrase. The decree concerned the relative status of commanders of the divisions (*polki*, sometimes translated as "regiments") of a Muscovite field army: main, right hand, left hand, advance guard, and rear guard.[71] Precedence never applied to commanders of the artillery and reconnaissance units, which did not stop an artillery officer from filing a precedence suit. When the tsar personally took the field, he commanded his own division, the largest in any field army, comprised of his royal household troops. Precedence did not apply to this unit, variously called the Tsar's (*tsarev*), Court (*dvorovoi*), or Big Sovereign's (*bol'shoi gosudarev*) Division.[72] The 1556 decree forbade lawsuits between commanders of the lower divisions and among second-in-commands of the Main Division.

The Decree on Precedence of 1556 did not affect the system's application to civilian appointments or ceremonial occasions, for which it could also be suspended, or appointments to offices in the tsar's court, mostly held by gentry, such as the keepers-of-the-seal (*pechatnik*) or treasurers.[73] Ivan obviously concentrated on minimizing divisive and distracting precedence lawsuits within the field army.

Based upon their class structures and social hierarchies, all military systems limit who can command. Nowhere does merit alone govern acquisition of office. In Ivan's Muscovy the tsar's choice regarding whom to appoint to a given position was limited by precedence, but precedence did not require him to appoint a specific person to any specific office or appoint a specific person to any office. The decree on precedence created a framework for the resolution of lawsuits. Jealousy, arrogance, and other personal motives inspired many disputes. Suits over who handed over dispatches, sequences of names in dispatches, or receipt of gold medals did not affect military operations, except indirectly by impinging on morale. In practice, in the absence of the tsar, precedence did not apply to command of the Main Division, so Ivan could appoint anyone of ability.[74] Appointing an exceptionally competent second-in-command or declaring a campaign "without precedence" could mitigate the potential harm created by the need to appoint an incompetent commander-in-chief based upon social status. Up to a point Ivan could manage the weaknesses of the precedence system.

Ivan responded to precedence disputes in a variety of ways. He could simply order two feuding officers separated. Ivan indulged his zealous anger to compel obedience to the decree on precedence and his decisions by cursing stubborn litigants and calling them stupid, "delirious fools," or thieves. He threatened filers of gratuitous precedence lawsuits with everything from disgrace, beating, and imprisonment to execution in order to shock them into understanding the error of their ways.[75] The ferocity with which nobles pursued precedence suits, even when ordered not to by an infuriated tsar, belies their supposed servility. The vocabulary and temperament displayed by Ivan in registers concerning precedence cases conform to Ivan's persona in his letters, his diatribes in diplomatic papers, and his depiction in sixteenth-century foreign accounts.[76] Ivan's emotional explosions over precedence had no perceptible effect upon litigious, prickly nobles.

Statistics concerning precedence cases, however imperfect, offer some interesting insights into the system. Of course, extant documentation might not include every precedence lawsuit during Ivan's reign. Moreover, the registry state secretaries probably took precedence into account in making assignments, in order to preempt precedence conflicts as much as possible. Nevertheless, the most comprehensive register of known precedence cases raises a number of questions. During the entirety of Ivan's reign, 351 precedence cases occurred, averaging about seven a year. During the seven years of the oprichnina, 36 cases occurred, slightly below the annual average. All seven years with double-digit precedence cases, from 19 to 33, occurred after the oprichnina, the highest number in 1582. Therefore, whatever else was true about the impact of the oprichnina, it did not destroy the nobility's commitment to defending its precedence status; if anything, it enhanced that procilivity.[77]

The 1550s constituted a decisive phase in the evolution of the precedence system because of the interrelated appearance of the Decree on Precedence of 1556, the Sovereign's Register in 1556, and the Sovereign's Genealogy in 1555/1556. Clearer rules, restricted applicability, and definitive documentation promised fewer and more easily resolved disputes. The authorities—whether Ivan, a boyar court, or the register bureaucrats—settled most precedence lawsuits on the basis of the law and the evidence, but political favoritism, especially during the oprichnina, tainted some decisions. Irrespective of credible evidence of impropriety, losers hurled accusations of bias to overturn negative decisions.[78]

Ivan did not try to abolish the precedence system either because he knew that he lacked the ability to do so or, more likely, because the thought never occurred to him. Ivan never challenged the legitimacy of precedence; he only attempted to ameliorate some of its consequences. Precedence did put a glass ceiling on how high low-born officers could rise, but during Ivan's reign Muscovy never lost a war because of precedence. While precedence lawsuits fractionalized the noblity, the system also facilitated a common esprit de corps that united its exclusive beneficiaries—boyars and gentry—against everyone else.[79]

DECREE ON MILITARY SERVICE

Ivan issued the Decree on Service (*ukaz o sluzhbe*) at the same time as the Decree on Precedence, in 1556. It also survives only in a chronicle paraphrase, however, in less obtuse language. The decree defined service obligations for all landowners, not just those who held conditional land grants. Every land-owner or landholder owed one mounted, armed military servitor for every 100 *chetverty* of arable (a *chetvert* equaled 1.35 acres). Such a standard may have existed previously, but now it became uniform.[80] In other countries, too, all landowners owed an obligation to serve that was proportionate to their landed wealth or they served voluntarily.[81] Service was linked either to land or to class. Ivan's decree reflected a common understanding of the relationship between land and service in contemporary states. This decree did not constitute the "enserfment" of the nobility, a precedent for the enserfment of all social classes in Muscovy. Nobles retained their privileges such as higher dishonor penalties, precedence preference, and for gentry being subordinate only to royal judicial authority.[82] The decree clearly served the interests of the Muscovite state, however, especially its armed forces.

The chronicle's exposition of this decree linked it to the abolition of the "feeding" system and the creation of anti-brigandage institutions, which violated chronology. The chronicler asserted that God loves the "magnates and the middle [level servitors] and the young [poorer, lowest status servitors] equally," a pithy expression of landowner solidarity. Mandatory service helped consolidate the aristocracy and gentry into a single class. The chronicle also contained an extensive praise of Ivan's piety, perhaps to suggest that his personal virtues matched the quality of his political leadership.[83]

Cadastres reveal that practice did not match theory. All patrimonial holders did not serve, and those who served did not all serve the tsar. The Tver cadastre contained many servitors of the bishop of Tver and of the dominant local family, the princes Mikulinskie. Fewer than half the servitors served Ivan. The Zvenigorod cadastre contained servitors of the Chingissid Semen Kasaevich, who had entered Ivan's service and converted to Christianity.[84] Cadastres demonstrate the existence of regional variations in conditional landholding and the ubiquity of the service-conditional landholding nexus.[85] The central government did not conduct a national cadastre, but a series of regional cadastres sought to stabilize land titles and hence military service assessments. The 1556 decree declared its intent to foster equity in obligations, which it did, but greater mobilization of military resources animated its issuance. No historian has demonstrated that after 1556 all landowners *did* serve. Moreover, as is obvious from the Boyar Book of 1556/1557, an account of a muster, the government frequently denied boyars and gentry their full cash allotment because they and their "people" (military slaves) did not appear with proper armor and weapons.[86] Not all landowners *could* serve, in Muscovy or elsewhere.[87] However, the service mentality of the Muscovite aristocracy and gentry did not distinguish it from its contemporary noble counterparts. Service, whether military or at court, voluntary or mandatory, everywhere led to political influence and wealth.

Despite the Decree on Service of 1556, government mobilization of land for state service had limits.[88] The government sought to prevent donation, sale, exchange, or mortgaging of conditional land without the tsar's permission. It converted much "black" (state) land into conditional land assigned to servitors, but not much royal household land. The land of "serving princes" became simple patrimonies when their holders lost their regalian rights, but the "serving princes" were already serving. The government made no systematic attempt to eliminate appanages, whose owners voluntarily supplied troops for the ruler's service. It did not challenge directly the largest type of landowning not under direct government control, church land. Ecclesiastical gentry served in state armies only with the assent of bishops and abbots. The government's ambition exceeded its capabilities, but its reach definitely increased during the reforms.

The government's attitude toward its elite appears two-sided. The government apparently did not worry that restricting the obligations of boyar and gentry as governors and county administrators in fighting banditry or collecting taxes would weaken the elite. Co-opting local social forces to accomplish these administrative tasks aided governors and county administrators in governing and freed personnel resources for military service. Ivan and the Royal Council tried to save the elite from the consequences of too much debt or of deaccessioning too much clan land. The government facilitated elite service by supplying the wherewithal for servitors to mobilize quickly. It strove to minimize distracting precedence lawsuits in the field army. It tried to rationalize the structure of the royal household. However, Ivan and the Royal Council did these things as much to help themselves as to help the elite. The government wanted the elite to be able to serve. To the government, arguably to Ivan and to the boyars in the Royal Council, as well as to the state secretaries and gentry officials, the interests of the state and the elite coincided.

Church Reform and Heresy

J ust as the government sought to improve its performance of its mission during the long 1550s, so did the Russian Orthodox Church. The church contributed to state reform efforts, and the government contributed to church reform efforts. The overlap between state and church responsibilities dictated this synchronicity, although church and state sometimes had conflicting interests concerning jurisdiction over criminal clergymen, ecclesiastical fiscal and judicial immunities, and, most of all, expansion of ecclesiastical, especially monastic, landowning. These conflicts found expression in compromises and inconsistent policies by both parties.

The church's push to standardize theology and enforce conformity resulted, with state compliance, in the persecution of dissenters and heretics, both real and imaginary. The taint of heresy even attached itself to the priest Sylvester and the state secretary Ivan Viskovatyi, despite their royal patronage. Heresy in Muscovy never rose to the level of countries affected by the Protestant Reformation, but, as in those countries, it drew some of its energy from social unrest and injustice. "Holy fools" expressed moral discontent in dramatic fashion.

The Russian Orthodox Church did not confine itself to administrative reform. It also strove to raise the religious level of its congregants. As head of the government Ivan took an active interest, and played an active role, in ecclesiastical reform activities. Whether he actually undertook all the actions attributed to him remains disputed. He patronized religious reform, persecuted heretics, and interacted with holy fools.

CHURCH REFORM AND CHURCH-STATE RELATIONS

In 1551 Ivan summoned a church council to consider reforms. Following Byzantine practice, only the tsar could summon such a council. The church had already held at least one council, in 1547, to canonize new Russian saints and to establish which saints were to be venerated countrywide and which only locally.[1] The Church Council of 1551, the Council of One Hundred Chapters (Stoglav), exceeded all previous and subsequent church councils in scope.[2] The name dates from the late sixteenth century. The document of the council's decisions prepared at the time referred to it as a "conciliar" or "new code" (*sobornoe, novoe ulozhenie*).[3]

Ivan not only presided but also addressed the council and prepared a list of questions for the assembled clerics to consider. He may have been responsible for a separate list of topics to discuss. Historians disagree about whether it was Ivan or someone else who wrote "Ivan's" questions. Whether Ivan composed or even delivered the speech to the council attributed to him also remains disputed. That speech invoked themes common in Ivan's writings; namely, his troubled childhood and boyar abuse of power during his minority. Ivan asked the Council of One Hundred Chapters to give its imprimatur to the Law Code of 1550. (Coincidentally, the Law Code of 1550 and the Church Council of 1551 both contained one hundred articles.) The scathing criticism of monasteries for laxity, greed, and impiety in Ivan's questions resonated with the contents of his 1573 letter to the Kirillo-Beloozero Monastery.[4]

Some scholars suggest that Metropolitan Makarii wrote some or all of "Ivan's" questions. Makarii had no doubts, however, about the legitimacy of monastic landowning of populated villages, and he opposed the decision of the Church Council of 1551 to set limits on the tax exemptions of ecclesiastically owned enclaves (*slobody*). Makarii would not have authored questions on these issues.

Manuscripts containing long excerpts from the church council's decisions were sent to various regional or social constituencies. These documents and contemporary decrees referring to the council's decisions definitively confirm the substance of its resolutions. Even so, only later sixteenth-century manuscripts contain the entire document.[5] Taken together, these manuscripts establish the authenticity of the Church Council of 1551 beyond reproach.

The Church Council of 1551 dealt far more with practical matters than with theology. Its rules, such as the proper way to cross oneself, became so normative that changes to them in the seventeenth century helped lead to the Russian Orthodox Church schism (Raskol). While the Church Council of 1551 set standards for icons, invoking not only Byzantine models but also the brilliant works of Andrei Rublev (medieval Russia's most famous icon painter), it did not deal with the innovative icons that bureaucrat Ivan Viskovatyi was even then criticizing. To regulate the behavior of priests, the Church Council of 1551 established a system of priestly elders elected by a city's or district's priests to supervise them, a close parallel to elected state anti-brigandage and tax-collection elders.[6] The council's regulations tried to foster better education for priests and laity alike.[7]

According to the traditional view, the Church Council of 1551 continued the Russian Orthodox Church's battle against the combination of pagan and Christian beliefs known as "dual faith" (*dvoeverie*). Historians have labeled as "pagan survivals" some elements of popular religion practiced by people who thought of themselves as Christians. The phrase "dual faith" did not refer to combining the practices of two faiths but to the combination of irreligious and religious practice. Entertainments such as fistfights, bear-baiting, minstrels, executions, and taverns constituted sinful, but not "pagan," practices. The same applied to consulting witches, sorcerers, or shamans.[8] The Russian Orthodox Church had as little success in disciplining popular entertainment as did the Tudor English government and the Anglican Church.[9]

In general the Church Council of 1551 sought to conserve episcopal authority and ecclesiastical wealth. The council declared uncanonical the state's issuance of judicial immunities to monasteries, exempting them from the authority of their bishops for non-spiritual crimes. The government only honored that prohibition some of the time.[10] The council decided that peasants, not the Russian Orthodox Church, should pay for ransoming Tatar captives, an uncharitable decision criticized by former Metropolitan Ioasaf. The council forbade laymen from judging clerics, except in cases involving

high crimes, and forbade the tsar's boyars and majordomos from judging
the metropolitan's boyars. Both measures reinforced episcopal jurisdiction.
The Church Council of 1551 could not separate government and church
justice completely, however. Although clerical courts employed canon law,
their judicial fees derived from the fee schedule in the Law Code of 1550.[11]

The Church Council of 1551's emphasis upon episcopal authority reinforced the shift in the sixteenth-century Russian Orthodox Church's
choices for sainthood from charismatic monks to bishops. Prestige now
accrued to the monastery itself as an institution, not its charismatic monks.[12]
The church had already elevated the founders of three of the four leading
Muscovite monasteries (Trinity-Sergius, Kirillo-Beloozero, and Solovetskii)
to sainthood, and, even if the church did not recognize its founder as a local
saint until 1579, the Iosifov Monastery did quite well for itself. Monastic
prestige did not decline. In 1542 Metropolitan Makarii became the first
metropolitan since 1473 chosen from among the bishops, rather than abbots.
But this did not set a precedent: Makarii's successors during Ivan's reign
included one monk, one archbishop, and three heads of monasteries.[13] The
Church Council of 1551 succeeded only partially in adjusting the balance of
prestige between bishops and monasteries in favor of the bishops.

Discussion of the issue of monastic ownership of populated villages at
the Church Council of 1551 resonates with the supposed factional divide
between the Trans-Volga Elders or Non-Possessors, followers of the ascetic monk Nil of Sora, and the Josephans, followers of Iosif, abbot of the
Volokamsk Monastery, who both lived at the turn of the sixteenth century.
The former has been said to have opposed monastic ownership of populated
villages, which the latter defended. The factions also supposedly disagreed
on the punishment of heretics. Recent scholarship has undermined this
paradigm.[14] Unquestionably, Nil and Iosif respected each other's works and
disagreed less than the paradigm implies. Nil opposed landownership by
hermitages, not by communal monasteries. The presumed Non-Possessor
Maksim Grek did not recommend confiscation of monastic lands.[15]

The Trans-Volga Elders and the Josephans did, however, differ in their
organizational and spiritual conceptions of monasticism. The Josephans
formed something similar to an old boys' club, involving only "graduates"
of the Iosifov Monastery. Although the Iosifov Monastery's abbot did not
even merit the rank of archimandrite, the monastery's monks dominated
appointments of bishops and leading abbots, particularly during the tenure

of Metropolitan Makarii, shorn at a monastery headed by a disciple of Iosif. Five of ten bishops at the Church Council of 1551 had taken their monastic vows at the Iosifov Monastery.[16] The word first appeared in Greek in 1528/1529 when Dosifei Toporkov called himself "*Iosifitis*," the "Josephan."[17]

Second-generation successors of Nil and Iosif became far more intolerant than their mentors. Josephan hostility toward any deviation from their theological views peaked in the middle of the sixteenth century. The Josephan Russian Orthodox Church turned hard right, repressing the entire Trans-Volga Elder movement as heretical. Both sides participated in this polarization. The Non-Possessor text, "Debate with Iosif," accused the Josephans of being "Judaizers" for seeking Old Testament revenge against heretics. The Josephans projected their mid-sixteenth-century extremism onto Nil and Iosif by rewriting the history of the Church Council of 1503.[18]

Whether Metropolitan Makarii adhered to the Josephan hard line remains unclear. The vita of Iosif attributed to the Serbian monk Lev Filolog, written during his tenure as metropolitan, treated both Nil and Iosif with respect. Although Makarii did not include this version of Iosif's vita in his *Great Menology*, he did include a vita of Nil's Kirillo-Beloozero disciple and literary executor Grigorii Tushin. Iosif approved the burning alive of heretics who did not repent, but Makarii did not usually follow that practice. (In 1563 the Muscovites burned alive the monk Foma, émigré follower of heretic Feodosii Kosoi, when they caught him in Polotsk.)[19] In the 1540s Josephan metropolitans pardoned two contrite, convicted heretics. Metropolitan Ioasaf released Isaac Sobaka, and may have tried to install him as archimandrite of the Moscow Simonov Monastery. Makarii appointed Sobaka archimandrite of the Kremlin Chudov Monastery. In no later than 1543 Makarii lifted the ban on communion for Maksim Grek, although he was not permitted to return to Mount Athos, either at Makarii's or the government's decision.[20] Maksim was accused of objecting to Muscovite denigration of the prerogatives of the Patriarch of Constantinople and to the Muscovite insult to Jerusalem by designating Moscow the "New Jerusalem." Makarii did include some of Maksim's works in his *Great Menology*, and eight years after Maksim's death in 1556 (and after Makarii's death in 1563), some metropolitan or Ivan ordered or approved painting Maksim's likeness on a fresco of the Kremlin Annunciation Cathedral and on an icon in the Dormition Cathedral.[21] While the Russian Orthodox Church continued to relax its position on Maksim after Makarii's death, Makarii reversed himself on Sobaka, ordering him defrocked and sent to monastic prison. The church imposed a new system of surveillance of possible heretics, leading to the 1550s heresy trials. Makarii excluded all of Nil's work from his *Great Menology*.[22] His moderation remained inconsistent.

Some historians have interpreted Ivan's question about the legitimacy of church landownership as the apex of a century-long campaign to secularize church lands that would have made Ivan the Russian Henry VIII. No direct evidence verifies that Ivan knew about the secularization of ecclesiastical land in England in 1536–1539, Sweden in 1527, or Denmark in 1536. The vehement church reaction to Ivan's question attests that it took Ivan's intentions quite seriously. Some cleric fabricated a charter (*iarlyk*) to the church attributed to the fourteenth-century Khan Uzbek of the Juchid *ulus*, granting it fiscal immunities, in order to argue that if even Muslim Mongol rulers respected the church's privileges, then Orthodox Christian rulers could do no less. The forgery was gratuitous because authentic charters from the khans to the church already granted it those same privileges. Makarii probably wrote or at least commissioned "The Reply" (*Otvet*), an uncompromising defense of ecclesiastical landownership that castigated any alienation of ecclesiastical land. The "Reply" relied for evidence upon the "Donation of Constantine," already recognized as a forgery in Renaissance Europe.[23] Makarii utilized the "Donation" selectively: for example, it advocated the superiority of the pope over the emperor, whereas, at least in theory, Makarii favored their cooperation. The Church Council of 1551 devoted the better part of nine chapters to arguing that ecclesiastical land should remain inviolable.[24] Some historians see a major defeat for Ivan in the church's successful defense of monastic landowning.

Ivan may have manipulated the Church Council of 1551 on the issue of monastic landowning. He did not propose secularization of ecclesiastical land. He confiscated some lands belonging to the bishop of Riazan, but this exceptional act seems to derive from local circumstances, the need for frontier defense, not a principled objection to ecclesiastical landownership.[25] At the council he went no further than raising the question of the legitimacy of monastic landowning. Perhaps he used the threat of confiscation as a negotiating tactic in order to gain leverage. After the Church Council of 1551 Ivan successfully had restraints on monastic acquisition of additional land and limits on ecclesiastical fiscal and judicial immunities added to its decisions.[26] He forbade monasteries to acquire property without informing the tsar. Not coincidentally, several major monasteries immediately ceased land purchases. The council did limit the growth and tax exemptions of church enclaves. Neither bishops nor monasteries could acquire patrimonies without royal permission. Monasteries had to return to their former land-holders conditional land grants that had been mortgaged to them or seized by force. Boyar donations of land to monasteries since the death of Vasilii III, in theory, became null and void. Ivan later entirely banned some sales and donations of patrimonies to monasteries to protect clan patrimonial land. Violation of these prohibitions led to the forfeiture of the land to the tsar, for which the monastery received monetary compensation. In 1578 a monastery lost a landownership dispute when the judge invoked such a prohibition.[27]

However, Ivan vitiated his own tactical victory because his religious devotion prevented him from remaining consistent on the issue. The Church Council of 1551 voided the right of redemption of land previously donated to monasteries for memorials, which guaranteed monastic retention of considerable land. Moreover, Ivan violated his own limitations on donations of land to monasteries. In 1556 he granted permission to the Trinity-Sergius Monastery to purchase land, albeit with limitations on how much money it could spend, where it could purchase land, and from whom. Although laws designed to preserve princely landowning barred sales or donations of such land to monasteries, Ivan permitted exceptions.[28] In 1580, amid economic stress and defeat in the Livonian War, a church council approved a ban on any further episcopal or monastic acquisition of lay land by purchase or donation, permitting only cash donations.[29] Even then Ivan granted an exemption to a monastery "in need."[30] Ivan never reconciled his piety and state needs concerning ecclesiastical land.

Church-state relations encompassed more than ecclesiastical landowning. The state certainly had some say in church governance. During the *oprichnina* Ivan not only removed Archbishop Pimen of Novgorod and Metropolitan Filipp from office and imprisoned them but also humiliated the former and had the latter murdered. His actions horrified Kurbskii and no doubt other Muscovites not in a position to complain. It is difficult to determine who influenced the choice of metropolitan. Bishops selected abbots of monasteries in their eparchies after consulting the monks, but the tsar had to ratify the selection, a system that encouraged considerable politicking by all parties. After 1551 Ivan could not issue new charters exempting monasteries from the authority of the bishop in whose diocese their monastery lay, but he did not always repeal earlier exemptions. Jurisdiction over clergymen who committed lay crimes remained a sensitive matter, but only abbots and bishops could judge religious misconduct. The government judged the murder of a monastic elder. Monasteries and bishops complained to the central government when provincial state officials violated their fiscal and judicial immunities.[31] Although the Law Code of 1550 recalled all "special fiscal immunity" (*tarkhan*) charters and forbade their further issuance, the Church Council of 1551, which ratified the Law Code of 1550, nevertheless referred to operative "special fiscal immunity" grants.[32] In fact the government continued to issue "special fiscal immunity" grants, as did the church. A Muscovite envoy tried to assuage English unhappiness at having to pay customs dues in 1581 and 1582 by informing Elizabeth I that even "special tax exemption-holders" contributed to the war effort.[33] Thus, the quid pro quo between church and state remained fluid.

The Muscovite state and the Russian Orthodox Church shared responsibility for maintaining social order and religious conformity. The concept of "church-state relations" implies a separation of the two institutions not maintained in practice. Both opposed injustice. Metropolitan Makarii began or supported the composition of new penitentials designed for "the powerful and grandees," meaning high government officials, which admonished them, consistent with the anticorruption provisions of the Law Code of 1550, not to betray their oaths to the sovereign, not to rule unjustly, not to take bribes, and not to acquire wealth through violence. To disobey the sovereign was to disobey God. The government legally and the church morally advocated the same behavioral standards for magnates as Christians and as state officials.[34] Under Metropolitans Daniil and Makarii the Russian Orthodox Church envisioned an ideal society—pious, close-minded, paternalistic, authoritarian, and hierarchal. Ivan and the boyars would not have disapproved.[35]

Church and state utilized the same administrative means to deal with the same administrative problems. Both lacked sufficient manpower to administer their huge domains directly. Both used immunity charters to accomplish their goals and sometimes employed their subjects as their officials. The diocesan administration employed mostly lay officials, secretaries and gentry, not priests or (as monasteries did) monks. Both church and state lacked sufficient cash to pay their employees, and instead both used conditional land grants, subject to confiscation for malfeasance. Bishops assigned "feedings" to their administrative officials.[36] Sometimes secretaries moved between episcopal and state service. The identical administrative cultures of church and state created a rarely appreciated zone of common understanding, one apart from the potentially divisive issues of priority of authority or conflicts of interest over land and jurisdiction.[37]

HERESY

Reforming the Russian Orthodox Church entailed enforcing conformity on church beliefs and practices. The church treated those who refused to comply as heretics. Muscovy during the reign of Ivan IV did not experience any mass heretical movement on the scale of the Reformation.[38] Some Orthodox monks and laymen did espouse heretical views, and the church labeled unsuccessful religious reformers as heretics too. Opponents of heresy gave the impression that heresy ran rampant, but such hysterical overreactions to "heretical" ideas were par for the course. Spanish hysteria over the Protestant Reformation far exceeded actual Reformation influence in Spain.[39] Accused heretics might admit foreign influence under torture because that was what the authorities wanted to hear, but heretics originated at home, whatever role foreign influence played.[40] Unfortunately, everything we know about the Muscovite heretics comes from trial records and denunciations written by their opponents.

In October 1553 the church accused the head of the Ambassadorial Bureau, the state secretary (*dumnyi d'iak*) Ivan Viskovatyi, of heresy for agitating for three years against the new icons and frescoes in the Kremlin Church of the Annunciation and the new murals in the Golden Hall (Zolotaia polata). Viskovatyi denounced these new religious paintings as heretical because they introduced symbolic or allegorical representations of the members of the Holy Trinity.[41] Contemporary manuscripts of the trial record survive. A church council found Viskovatyi guilty, which he admitted, and sentenced him to a mild punishment, three years of penance. The verdict emphasized Viskovatyi's humility. It might have helped that the council judging him found some of his objections valid. Virtually all scholars concur with Viskovatyi's analysis of the new icons. The icons of the Ancient of Days and Jesus with closed palms, winged or in armor, show tangible Western influence and violated traditional Russian Orthodox

Christian iconography. Obviously, Viskovatyi, who, according to the trial record, read patristic literature, had more than a passing acquaintance with theology and iconography.[42]

During the trial Viskovatyi implicated gentry-man Fedor Bashkin and the priest Sylvester.[43] The church council acquitted Sylvester but convicted Bashkin. (Suspecting a trap, the usually politically clumsy Maksim Grek adroitly declined Ivan's invitation to comment on Bashkin's heresy.) Bashkin confessed under torture to denying the sacraments and icons, as well as other proto-Protestant beliefs.[44] Unfortunately, Viskovatyi's trial created more problems than it solved.

Historians have paid too much attention to the supposed political aspects of this incident. Viskovatyi acted from religious motives, not from a desire to weaken the political influence of Metropolitan Makarii or Sylvester. Of course Ivan's patronage of Viskovatyi might explain why he did not lose his government job. Makarii, who had selected Sylvester to restore the Kremlin icons and had approved those icons, would have been more than embarrassed if he had approved heretical icons. Ivan had also approved the icons and murals, and he would have shared complicity.[45] Viskovatyi could hardly have intended to attack his own patron. Curiously enough, long after Viskovatyi's conviction the monk-author Zinovii Otenskii, a notable opponent of heresy (when he was archbishop of Novgorod, Makarii commissioned Zinovii to rewrite a vita), apparently suffered no punishment for endorsing Viskovatyi's view of the illegitimacy of the icons. No one has explained the church's apparent failure to act against Zinovii.[46]

If Makarii put Sylvester in charge of renovating a Kremlin church and palace, he must have considered Sylvester an expert in church art as well as an able project manager. Sylvester must already have enjoyed a favorable reputation as a priest and royal advisor to serve in a Kremlin church. Presumably, Sylvester wrote his letter advising the governor-designate of conquered Kazan, Prince Aleksandr Gorbatyi-Shuiskii, how to govern that region because Gorbatyi-Shuiskii, aware of Sylvester's reputation, had asked for his counsel.[47] Despite Sylvester's renown, Viskovatyi's accusations put him on the defensive.

A church council also convicted the monk Artemii of heresy. Artemii had earlier been named abbot of the Trinity-Sergius Monastery, supposedly at Ivan's instigation.[48] The monks did not take a liking to their new superior, who fled the monastery without permission. Trinity monks then accused him of heresy, for which he was tried and sentenced to imprisonment in the Solovetskii Monastery. He escaped to Lithuania where, in conjunction with émigré Muscovite printer Ivan Fedorov, he played an active role in defending Orthodoxy against the Reformation. This strongly suggests that he was framed.[49] During Artemii's tenure as abbot, the Trinity-Sergius Monastery, a large landowner, acquired no land, but his tenure there was so brief that we cannot be sure that this was because of Artemii's views of monastic landownership.[50] We do not know if the Trinity-Sergius monks expelled him because he had Non-Possessor views. Monks sometimes rejected abbots because they were too strict or because they were outsiders. Artemii got off easy. Monastic elders at the Skolova hermitage (*pustynia*) of the Most Holy Mother of God (Prechistaia Bogoroditsa) Monastery murdered their unpopular abbot.[51]

Whether Artemii opposed monastic ownership of populated villages (because monks should live by their own labor) and, further, whether he advised Ivan to confiscate all monastic landed properties (but not episcopal landed properties) or only those not properly registered with the government is not at all clear because Artemii's statements at his trial for heresy, in his letter to Ivan from Lithuanian exile, and in the "Debate with Iosif" (*Prenie s Iosifom*), which some scholars believe he authored, are not consistent. Ivan might not have cared what Artemii thought, as long as he could frighten the church by asking for opinions about the legitimacy of monastic lands. But Artemii definitely made an unwise political decision in answering Ivan's question whatever he said. Neither Nil Sorskii nor Vassian Patrikeev (a former princely boyar forced to take the cowl, who became a Non-Possessor) nor even the "authors" of the "Valaam Discourse" advocated government confiscation of monastic lands. Artemii's emphasis in another letter on noncoercive treatment of heretics appears to stand in sharp contrast to Josephan authoritarianism, but even Artemii conceded that the church could employ undefined "severity" against obvious opponents of religious truth, those who refused to conform to Orthodoxy, even after punishment. Sir Thomas More in England, hailed as a martyr to religious conscience, shared Artemii's qualified approval of the use of coercion against those he considered heretical.[52] Judged against the rigid standard of mid-sixteenth-century Josephan orthodoxy, Artemii qualified as unreliable.

The heresy of Feodosii Kosoi, known only from the antiheretical works of Zinovii and an anonymous author, appeared in the 1560s in the northwest, completely unrelated to the heretics uncovered at Viskovatyi's 1553 heresy trial. We know nothing about Zinovii's premonastic life.[53] He ascribed great popular support to Kosoi, which would suggest that Kosoi had more followers than Bashkin, but Zinovii's excited complaints may reflect nothing more than clerical paranoia.[54] Kosoi left no writing. Indeed, his opponent wrote that Kosoi opposed writing. Two sources ascribed entirely different, but both extremely radical, programs to him: one a theological rejection of virtually all Orthodox Christianity, including the divinity of Jesus, Mary, baptism, saints, icons, the liturgy, and monasticism; the other a rejection of Muscovy's social hierarchy. Kosoi's putative assertion of the equality of all religions resonated with the notion of the equality of all mankind of the "Tale of the Dispute of Death and Life," translated into Slavonic at the end of the fifteenth century and popular in Muscovy during the sixteenth.[55] One of the two anti-Kosoi sources called him a Judaizer, while the other called him a Protestant, both vacuous polemical clichés. Zinovii Ottenskii probably wrote "A Truthful Witness by the Monk Zinovii to Those Who Have Inquired Concerning the New Teaching" (*Istiny pokazanie k vosprosivshim o novom uchenii inoka Zinoviia*) in 1565–1566, which snobbishly argues that a slave could not legitimately speak truth about religion. Zinovii probably did not write the "Protracted Letter" (*Poslanie mnogoslovnoe*), which is sometimes attributed to him.[56] Scholars consider the "Protracted Letter" more reliable in its exposition of Kosoi's views than the "Truthful Witness," which weakens accusations of Kosoi's theological extremism but bolsters accusations of his social radicalism.[57] Some historians assert that Kosoi changed his views once abroad, so that each work about him reflects a different stage of his intellectual evolution. Both sources probably imputed views to him that he did not share.

A church council convicted Kosoi of heresy, but, like Artemii, he escaped to Lithuania. There Kosoi and his followers joined the most radical wing of Polish Protestantism, the Socinians and Anabaptists, who rejected the Trinity and the divinity of Christ, which lends credence to the view that Kosoi was a religious heretic.[58] Potential contradictions remain. Someone who rejected Christ might quote the Gospels or patristic authors such as John Chrysostom, but they would have to be extremely selective in doing so.[59]

Zinovii had views on a variety of religious issues, not just heresy. He defended the right of poor monasteries to own land for their own sustenance, as long as the monks avoided greed. He specifically criticized Maksim Grek and Vassian Patrikeev for hypocrisy in opposing monastic wealth while benefitting from tsarist largesse. Zinovii also accused Maksim of bias against Muscovite monasteries because of his incarceration in them, which makes it unlikely that Zinovii was Maksim's disciple.[60] Kosoi stood accused of opposing monasticism itself, not just landowning monasteries, a far more radical position than that of Maksim or Patrikeev. Zinovii did not blame Kosoi's teachings on foreign influence, nor did he share current church opinion of Maksim, nor did he mention Nil Sorskii. Zinovii's defensiveness on the issue of monastic landowning suggests that the Church Council of 1551 had not terminated debate on the subject.

Accusations of heresy reflected genuine religious ferment, which the Josephans politicized. The Josephans disregarded the distinction between heretics such as Bashkin and Kosoi and reformers such as Viskovatyi and Artemii. From the late fifteenth century on, the Josephans instituted an inquisition that rode roughshod over legality. Makarii persecuted Orthodox reformers, social dissidents, and incipient sectarians as heretics. Zinovii, on the other hand, linked Kosoi's influence to administrative abuse and social and economic problems.[61]

The Russian Orthodox Church's reformist drive toward uniformity spawned a growing intolerance toward dissent within its ranks. The Spanish Catholic Church, led by the Spanish Inquisition, became much more intransigent against Jews beginning in the second half of the fifteenth century, but in the sixteenth century, in response to the Reformation, it grew more suspicious of humanists, accusing previously respected Erasmus of heresy.[62] Needless to say, the Reformation increased religious antagonism. The papacy and Spain formulated indexes of forbidden literature. Muscovy did not experience "the" Reformation, but Russian Orthodox Church fear of Reformation theology spurred greater rigidity on its part. The Russian church had its own list of forbidden books, mostly about astrology.[63] During the late fifteenth and early sixteenth centuries manuscripts appeared in Muscovy of works of belles lettres such as the "Tale of Dracula." In the middle of the sixteenth century the church categorized these works as "not useful." As a result no one made new copies of them, with the partial exception of the "Tale of Petr and Fevroniia." New manuscripts reappeared only in the seventeenth century. This pattern reflects unique mid-sixteenth-century censorship.[64]

Russian Orthodox Church repression never found all possible victims. Zinovii escaped discipline for his views of iconography or for disagreeing with Iosif Volotskii on monastic rules. Zinovii and Sylvester wrote letters of sympathy to victims of ecclesiastical or state discipline. The letters contained cookie-cutter content—we are all, including the tsar, sons of Adam, and must all patiently suffer until we attain the bliss of Heaven. The importance of these letters lies less in their content than the fact that these clerical writers did not hesitate to write to those in disgrace in the first place. Sylvester did so from the perspective of an acquitted suspect. Nevertheless, all social reformers and social critics, clerical or lay, were at risk of accusations of heresy.[65] Those convicted of heresy may have taken comfort in the church's mixed record of keeping incarcerated heretics locked up. Two leading "heretics," Artemii and Kosoi, succeeded in escaping not only from monastic confinement but also from Muscovy entirely, which suggests less than total competence on the part of ecclesiastical and state authorities at controlling the convict population.

Accusations of heresy in mid-sixteenth-century Muscovy, valid or invalid, accurate or exaggerated, reflected intellectual and religious ferment as well as social unrest. The intellectual ferment derived from the innovation and experimentation characteristic of Muscovite culture at the time. The religious ferment derived from the very reformist impulses that inspired heightened concern with Orthodox practice and belief. The social unrest derived from massive social instability, occasioned by Muscovy's political development.

HOLY FOOLS

Holy fools were neither priests nor monks but charismatic laymen who gave voice to social and moral protest in a period of social change. Homeless holy fools went about naked or almost naked, wore chains, spoke in riddles, uttered prophesies, and committed inexplicable antisocial acts that turned out to be denunciations of the hypocritical morals of people from the ruler on down. Holy fools expressed popular piety in Muscovy and supposedly engaged in more political protest than the holy fools of Byzantium, where the practice originated. The sixteenth century witnessed the apex of Muscovite holy foolishness, possibly because there were fewer charismatic monks to compete with them. No analogies to holy fools occur in Judaism, Islam, Catholicism, or Protestantism.

Holy fools did not lack a vindictive streak. Vasilii "the Blessed" (*Blazhennyi*), who gave St. Basil's Cathedral on Red Square its name, blinded several peasant girls who mocked him and caused the death of a thief pretending to be dead to defraud him of money. He restored the sight of the contrite peasant girls, but the thief remained dead. Holy fools sought to induce fear in people. Holy foolery became so fashionable in Muscovy that hagiographers attached the label to saints whom it did not fit.[66]

Although Vasilii "the Blessed" lived during Ivan's reign and the Muscovite central government considered his death so significant that the register recorded it, Ivan's interactions with Vasilii "the Blessed" belong to legend because they were recorded only in a vita written during the 1590s and cannot be confirmed through other sources.[67] Vasilii's vita largely plagiarized the Byzantine vita of St. Theodore of Edessa. It also plagiarized the more reliable account of an encounter in Pskov during the oprichnina between Ivan and another holy fool, Nikola Salos (*salos* is Greek for "holy fool"), by having Vasilii "the Blessed" prevent the sack of Novgorod. Vasilii "the Blessed" died either in 1552 or 1557, before the 1570 sack of Novgorod. Thus, after his death Vasilii "the Blessed" became Ivan's political critic. Elsewhere in the vita Ivan honored Vasilii.[68]

Historians and contemporary foreign accounts disagree about the confrontation between Ivan and Nikola Salos. Nikola objected when Ivan and his *oprichniki* entered Pskov, intent on repressive measures.[69] In one version Nikola prophesied the death of Ivan's favorite horse should Ivan not desist. When the horse died, Ivan left Pskov. In another version Nikola offered Ivan raw meat. When Ivan objected that the church forbade eating meat during Lent, Nikola asked him why he ate the meat of his subjects. Again, the chastened Ivan left Pskov. Some foreigners thought Nikola a charlatan; others doubted that he ever met Ivan.

Ivan's reaction to Nikola Salos should not be dismissed as superstition. Genuine faith generated respect for holy men. It is entirely credible that Ivan would accept and react seriously to criticism by a holy fool.

Historians describe the sixteenth century as a confessional age. Foreign travel accounts to Muscovy emphasize the centrality of Muscovy's religious identity. During the long 1550s, the Russian Orthodox Church undertook a major reformist program to improve its operation and the level of religious observance among the laity. Religion infused the daily lives of the elite, including Ivan. The elite could not have been indifferent to the efforts of the church to standardize religious practice. If Ivan crossed himself before taking food or drink, he had to know that the Russian Orthodox Church validated how many fingers he used.

Church fear of heretical or unauthorized religious views at home and abroad transformed reform into repression. Social disorder exacerbated both social unrest, sometimes expressed in religious ways, and church intransigence toward religious change. The major social changes underway in Muscovy, some represented by new provisions of the Law Code of 1550, goaded the church into trying to impose absolute conformity by force, to convince itself that Muscovite religious purity remained unsullied. Ivan's treatment of Jews arose from the same imperative.

10

Intellectual and Cultural History

Reform initiatives by Ivan and the Muscovite government during the 1550s did not occur in an intellectual or cultural vacuum. The same Russian Orthodox Christian monarchical values and concepts that inspired government action also inspired the creation of cultural artifacts that expressed them. Court and church patronized the efflorescence of literature, art, and architecture.[1] Ritual and ceremony actualized the notion of a divinely approved monarch ruling a divinely protected realm found in Ivan's first letter to Kurbskii. The optimism and ambitiousness of Muscovite domestic reform and territorial expansion found expression in grandiose literary projects, not all of which reached completion. The cultural and political mood of Muscovy during the 1550s devolved from the notion that human activity, with God's favor, could influence the world. The political, social, religious, and cultural elites, and Ivan himself, shared this mentality.

INTELLECTUAL FERMENT

To discuss the nature of monarchical rule mid-sixteenth-century Muscovite authors could draw upon earlier Slavonic translations of three foreign texts. The sayings of the sixth-century Byzantine deacon Agapetus, a "mirror of princes," became the textual foundation for virtually all Muscovite political theory. Muscovite writers applied Agapetus's portrait of an ideal ruler to Muscovite grand princes and tsars. Defenders and critics of the ruler invoked the Agapetan precept that the tsar is "in body" like other men but "in power" like God.[2] Authors could tilt this axiom either to exalt or excoriate the tsar.

Muscovites only rarely quoted another "mirror of princes," the "Secret of Secrets" (*Secreta Secretorum, Taina tainykh*), purported to be Aristotle's advice to Alexander the Great.[3] Only a single allusion to blue-eyed men as suspicious reflects direct textual borrowing from this work.[4] Muscovite court behavior did not conform to its precepts. The "Secret of Secrets" advised rulers to seat everyone at ceremonies or in council by merit and to meet servitors between two and four times a year. In Muscovy precedence governed seating, and business meetings between the ruler and his advisors took place several times a week.[5] Nevertheless, the existence of sixteenth-century manuscripts of the "Secret of Secrets" attests that some Muscovites read it.

The "Tale of Dracula" (*Povest o Drakule*) hit much closer to home, uncomfortably so. The "Tale" argued graphically that in order to end sin and crime, a ruler needed to be "dread" (*grozen*). Ivan echoed this premise in his first letter to Kurbskii, albeit without applying to himself the word "dread." Dracula's sadistic sense of humor matched that attributed to Ivan. The story that Dracula ordered an ambassador's hat nailed to his head when he refused to doff it as a sign of respect toward him appeared in popular pamphlets of Ivan's time outside Muscovy, with Ivan as perpetrator. Such episodes reflect Ivan's image, however, not necessarily his self-image. Ivan employed Dracula's favorite means of capital punishment, impalement, but less often. Of course Dracula did not have a monopoly upon that practice. Dracula crossed the line by converting from Orthodox Christianity to Catholicism and by burning all poor people alive so that everyone in his realm would be rich. The former act sufficed by itself to arouse the moral approbation of the author of the "Tale." Ivan could not have imitated the actions of an apostate. Scribes did not copy the "Tale" during the mid-sixteenth century, but neither did they destroy earlier manuscripts, so Muscovites of Ivan's time could have read it. The "Tale" portrayed Dracula's vices too honestly for Muscovite authors to mine it on Ivan's behalf. Anti-Muscovite foreigners had no such qualms about using Dracula horror stories.[6]

While Agapetus had a major impact upon Muscovite political thought in general and the "Tale of Dracula" and the "Secret of Secrets" lurked in the background, several Muscovite writers in the 1550s dealt with monarchical reform in seminal original works: Ivan Peresvetov, the priest and later monk Ermolai-Erazm, and the anonymous author of the "Valaam Discourse."

Peresvetov

Historians have paid considerable attention to Peresvetov's literary compositions because of their supposed influence upon Muscovite reforms of the 1550s, although all surviving manuscripts date to the seventeenth century. The connections between Peresvetov's proposals and the reforms are more apparent than real. His claim to be a descendant of the Muscovite warrior-monk Peresvet, who fought the Tatars at the battle of Kulikovo Field in 1380, cannot be verified. Peresvetov certainly did not write all the works attributed to him. Nevertheless, the inventory of the Muscovite archive during Ivan's reign mentioned a manuscript of unidentified works by Peresvetov, and in his works Peresvetov supplied credible details of his career as a soldier of fortune before his arrival in Moscow. The historical verisimilitude of Peresvetov's autobiography and the inventory reference suffice as grounds to reject theories that Peresvetov was a pseudonym, whether used by Ivan or anyone else, or a seventeenth-century invention.[7]

Peresvetov's works include petitions, tales, and allegories.[8] In Tudor England, too, circumspect political criticism could take the form of allegory. Alone among sixteenth-century Muscovite authors, but like foreign contemporaries, Peresvetov portrayed the Ottoman sultan Mehmed (Magmet in Russian) the Conqueror, who took Constantinople in 1453, as the ideal ruler, a far cry from Maksim Grek's opinion of Ottoman rule. The last Byzantine emperor, weak because dominated by rich, effeminate aristocrats, served as the antithesis of the sultan. Peresvetov disliked aristocrats. He claimed that boyars persecuted him after he lost his Muscovite patron. The same motif, of rich aristocrats who made poor soldiers, occurred in the *Kazan History*, a narrative of Muscovy's conquest of Kazan, and in Kurbskii's *History*. Peresvetov advocated a wide reform program directed by a powerful ruler graced with "awe," supported by an army of loyal, low-born, salaried military servitors.[9]

Peresvetov asserted that God loves justice (*pravda*) more than faith (*vera*), his most controversial axiom. What he meant remains disputed, in part because he immediately added that Christ was true justice. Regardless of Peresvetov's adherence to Russian Orthodox Christianity, clearly he judged a state by its social justice and military strength, not its religious purity, however inseparable justice was from piety. He did not describe Muscovy as the "New Israel." In order to ameliorate Mehmed's Muslim identity, Peresvetov invented his desire to convert to Christianity, claiming that he was Christian in "all but name," and highlighted the influence of Christian books upon his behavior.[10]

The reforms of the 1550s neither resembled Peresvetov's proposals nor derived from Ottoman models.[11] The Muscovite conditional land grant for military service conveyed land, not just income, unlike the Ottoman *timar*, the Tatar *soyurghal*, or the Arabic *iqta*. The simple concept of granting land for service needed no foreign inspiration.[12] Muscovy's musketeers did not emulate the Janissaries, who were converted, celibate, enslaved foreigners.[13] Peresvetov preferred salaried warriors, but Ivan did not salary his gentry military servitors. Peresvetov opposed slave-warriors (ignoring the slave Janissaries) as poor fighters, but Ivan permitted military slaves in his armies. Peresvetov abhorred rich generals, but Ivan did not fire all his rich boyar officers. Peresvetov's proposals differ from Ivan's policies in principle, not just in degree. Even if Peresvetov did not influence the 1550s reforms, however, the "secular" and rational elements in Peresvetov's thought resonated with the works of other contemporary writers in Muscovy and with some of Ivan's ideas.

ERMOLAI-ERAZM

The compositions of Ermolai-Erazm (the priest Ermolai became the monk Erazm), whose works survive in contemporary manuscripts, unsuccessfully advocated utopian reforms, but his social criticism and mode of thought illustrate the novelty and richness of Muscovite culture during the 1550s.[14] Ermolai-Erazm condemned social injustice. He supported love and truth. Magnates insulted the poor. Government officials abused peasants. If the rich acquired gold and silver for selfishness, they were evil. Like fellow monk Maksim Grek, Ermolai-Erazm suspected immorality of anyone who put profit ahead of morality, including acquisitive monks. Christ told his disciples to abandon their material goods and follow Him. Man cannot serve God and Mammon. Ermolai-Erazm's economics derived from his theology. Goods should be purchased for their "natural price" (*cherez estestvo mnogo tseny*), a medieval scholastic notion. Like Peresvetov, Ermolai-Erazm complained that boyars persecuted him, but we have no evidence of why he became a monk.

Two of his works, very different from each other, merit individual attention. Some scholars contest the authorship and dating of the first text, the "Tale of Petr and Fevroniia," but majority opinion accepts Ermolai-Erazm as author and a mid-sixteenth-century dating. The "Tale" tells the story of a Murom prince who married a wise, lower-class maiden after she had cured him of an illness contracted from the blood of a dragon he killed. The church canonized both in 1547.[15] With its folk motifs the "Tale" hardly qualifies as a proper vita, which may have disqualified it for inclusion in Makarii's *Great Menology*. Fevroniia displays common sense, patience, and devotion, but she did not conform to the Muscovite stereotype of an ideal wife, who was submissive and obedient.[16] Ermolai-Erazm foregrounds Petr's humility and mercy and anachronistically gives him the title "autocrat," meaning a pious ruler in this case.

In one telling episode, Petr and Fevroniia become victims of social prejudice. Because of Fevroniia's social background, the animosity of the wives of the Murom boyars force her and Petr to leave Murom. Ermolai-Erazm treats the snobbishness of the boyar wives as sin. They were, after all, denigrating a saint. He espouses Christian egalitarianism because high born and low born are equal in Christ. Similarly, in his letter to the Kirillo-Beloozero Monastery Ivan preached a monastic egalitarianism, arguing that all monks should be equal regardless of their social origin. Iosif Volotskii did not want to abolish slavery, but he did want to permit slaves to join his monastery. On the Day of Judgment there would be no slaves and no freemen.[17] Feodosii Kosoi's putative heretical belief in social egalitarianism went much further. That various Muscovite writers addressed the question of social inequality in a variety of ways suggests that the issue had social relevance at the time.

Ermolai-Erazm's other work, "To the Benevolent Tsar, Rule and Land Measurement" (*Blagokhotiashchim tsarem pravitel'nitsa i zemlemerie*), urged government reform to save the farmers (the peasantry), the mainstay of society, the people who grew the grain for communion wafers. Ermolai-Erazm advocated the abolition of noble landownership and the "feeding" system.

Peasants should pay taxes or dues to their former landowners only in kind. The government should implement a new uniform tax measurement based upon Ermolai-Erazm's geometrical assessment unit, which would require a new survey of all arable land in Muscovy.

Unfortunately, despite Ermolai-Erazm's sympathy for the peasantry, his proposals were quite impractical. The government should forbid peasants to grow hops to prevent the production of alcohol, thus eliminating drunkenness; of course brewers can produce alcoholic drinks without hops. Blacksmiths should manufacture only dull knives to prevent murderous brawls. Ermolai-Erazm's uniqueness consisted in combining his morality with mathematics and uncompromising rationality. Despite strict adherence to his own logic, he expressed inconsistent ideas on a cash economy. Peasants should not pay taxes or rent in cash, but landowners should sell their land and donate the cash to monasteries because landownership distracted monks from their piety, a patristic notion shared by Nil Sorskii. Ermolai-Erazm did not ask if utilizing cash would distract monks.[18] He grappled unsuccessfully with the moral and economic implications of a money economy for monks and peasants, perhaps because a money economy was becoming more prevalent in Muscovy at the time.

Ermolai-Erazm's heartfelt protest against peasant exploitation remains significant. His depiction of the moral failings of mid-sixteenth-century Muscovite society rests upon religious belief. Unfortunately, the agrarian utopian policies he advocated would not have worked. No evidence survives that Ivan or anyone in the government ever read Ermolai-Erazm's "Rule and Land Measurement." The existence of this text does attest that clerics did not confine their reformist impulses to morals. In addition his proposals illustrate a hyperrational mathematical bent unique at the time. We know from the fact that his writings survive that, despite his complaints of persecution, neither boyars nor the government nor the church censored him.[19]

"Valaam Discourse"

The "Discourse of the Valaam Wonder-Workers Sergii and German" (*Beseda valaamskikh chudotvortsev Sergiia i Germana,* commonly called simply the "Valaam Discourse" [*Valaamskaia beseda*]) roundly criticized monastic wealth and clerical interference in the state. It attributed its authorship to monastic elders. Scholars disagree about its dating.[20] The text took positions incompatible with those of Metropolitan Makarii and the Church Council of 1551. To the "Valaam Discourse," monks were greedy parasites who could not even sing properly. A ruler must rule with "awe," not "meekness," not "simplicity" (*prostota*), not Artemii's "mildness." The ideal ruler possessed "humble imperial awe" or "humbling regal awe" (*smirennaia tsarskaia groza*),[21] which sounds like an oxymoron. Rulers did not deserve praise for giving estates to monasteries. They should give villages to military servitors, who would defend the realm. The "Valaam Discourse" did not, however, go so far as to advocate secularization of existing monastic lands.[22] Rulers should never listen to the political advice of monks, which can only ruin the state.

The reference of the "Valaam Discourse" to a "simple" ruler raises an interesting question. In safe exile Kurbskii in his *History* called Ivan's brother, Prince Iurii Vasil'evich, "without mind, memory, or speech."[23] The *Kazan History* described him as "simple" (simple-minded). Jerome Horsey described Tsar Fedor Ivanovich as "simple."[24] No one in Muscovy during Ivan's reign, or even during the reign of his physically and mentally challenged son Tsar Fedor, could have written such things. Nevertheless, if scholars could date the "Valaam Discourse" more reliably, we might discover whether its authors had a specific "simple" ruler in mind.

The attitude of the "Valaam Discourse" toward monks found assent in other sources. In his letter to the Kirillo-Beloozero Monastery Ivan criticized the failure of monks to live up to their own ideals. A petition of Moscow-region lower monastic brothers (*klyroshane*) bewailed the rich diet of archimandrites that was bankrupting monasteries and advocated that food and drink in a common-life monastery be shared on an equal basis. Zinovii Otenskii sympathized with poorer monasteries. Nevertheless, the objections of the "Valaam Discourse" to any political role for monks seem unique. Kurbskii opposed the political actions of *some* monks—Josephan supporters of Ivan's arbitrary rule—but not of all. He praised pious monks victimized by Ivan's atrocities. The interpolations in the *Tsar's Book* about the dynastic crisis of 1553 and Ivan's first letter to Kurbskii attacked the role in politics of a priest, Sylvester. Ivan ordered some monks executed but admitted some monasteries into the *oprichnina*. The "Valaam Discourse" did not oppose monasticism per se, the view ascribed to Feodosii Kosoi. The author of the "Valaam Discourse" might have been a monk who wanted to "save" monks from themselves by getting them out of the business of owning land or playing politics. In Renaissance Italy monks wrote some of the most scandalous satires of monks. However, one would not expect a monk to insult monks as "buried" or call them "corpses," descriptions that merit further study.[25] What developments inspired this passionate tirade against any monastic involvement in politics remains undetermined.

The intellectual interconnectedness of the works of Peresvetov, Ermolai-Erazm, and the anonymous author of the "Valaam Discourse" speak to a shared cultural and political atmosphere, a reason to date them all to the mid-sixteenth century, but they did not speak with one voice. Their disagreements suggest an open-mindedness and toleration of diversity that did not last beyond the 1550s. Moreover, even during the 1550s, the Josephan Russian Orthodox Church establishment had already begun attacking such freedom of expression.

LITERATURE

Three major, innovative literary monuments, and the introduction of printing, illustrate the creativity, ambitiousness, and heterogeneity of Muscovy's literary culture during Ivan's reign.

The *Great Menology*

The *Great Menology* (*Velikie Minei Chetii*), a comprehensive compendium of religious writings acceptable to the Russian Orthodox Church and organized as reading material for each day of the year, represents the impulse in mid-sixteenth-century Muscovy to regulate cultural output. Makarii compiled the first redaction of the *Great Menology* when he served as archbishop of Novgorod before his promotion to metropolitan. As metropolitan, Makarii produced a second redaction of twelve huge monthly volumes. He deposited one copy in the metropolitan's Dormition Cathedral and gave a second to Ivan. Only these three witnesses exist. Clearly Makarii did not intend the project for mass consumption or liturgical use. Who read it remains unknown. The desire for standardization motivated the enterprise. Makarii omitted literary works unacceptable from a literary or substantive point of view. The pretentious literary style of the *Great Menology* matches the ostentation of Moscow court ceremonies and the monotonous, stultifying, pompous literary style of Muscovite "monumentalism" of the period.[26]

The ambitiousness of this literary project matches the ambitiousness of Muscovite territorial expansion during the 1550s.

The *Great Menology* reflects Makarii's and the church's ambivalence about the theory of Moscow, the Third Rome. The compendium included a letter of Filofei of Pskov characterizing Moscow as the Third Rome. However, neither Makarii nor Ivan ever utilized the phrase in original writings.[27] Indeed, even Muscovite authors who quoted passages from Filofei's letters did not cite sentences that referred to the Third Rome. The *Tale of the White Cowl* (*Povest o belom klobuke*) mentioned Third Rome in its fictitious description of the migration of that sacred headdress from Rome to Novgorod, where Makarii, as archbishop, had worn it. Makarii continued to wear it when he became metropolitan. Upon his death, a church council decided that in the future all metropolitans would wear it, but in so doing it noted the absence of any written record of how the white cowl had arrived in Rus'. Therefore, the *Tale of the White Cowl* did not yet exist in 1563. The earliest reliably dated reference to Third Rome in an official source dates to 1589 in the document elevating the metropolitan of Moscow, not Novgorod, to the rank of patriarch.[28] The church treated Third Rome ideology as gingerly as did the state; presumably for the same reason: its alarming eschatological implications.

Makarii's *Great Menology* resembles the ambitiousness of Thomas Aquinas's *Summa Theologica*, even if in a different form, an encyclopedia rather than a treatise. Undertaking such a project requires the kind of confidence only a period of prosperity and optimism can generate, but it also carries a not so faint whiff of cultural complacency, the notion that authors have already expressed all valid, original ideas, so additional originality would be unwelcome. Moreover, deciding what to include in such a work also entails deciding what to exclude, such as the "useless" works. Makarii censored Muscovite Orthodox reading material.

THE *BOOK OF DEGREES*

The *Book of Degrees of Imperial Genealogy* (*Stepennaia kniga tsarskogo rodosloviia*) departed from the annalistic (year-by-year) format of Rus' and Russian chronicles to structure the first coherent, consistent history of the East Slavs, organized into seventeen "degrees" (*stepeni*). It originated in the metropolitan's chancery, and metropolitans receive due attention.[29] Scholars debate whether Metropolitan Makarii or his successor Metropolitan Afanasii, Ivan's former confessor, played a greater role in its conception and compilation.[30] The first degree treated St. Vladimir; the last, Ivan.[31] A vita of St. Vladimir's grandmother, St. Olga, sometimes unconvincingly attributed to Sylvester, served as a preface. Each degree discussed a different ancestor of Ivan. The *Book of Degrees* remained incomplete.[32] Contradictions in the text betray a lack of final editing. Degree seventeen on Ivan stopped in 1560. Isolated interpolations date to as late as 1563. The three earliest manuscripts date to the 1560s. The editor could have presented Ivan's actions from 1560 to 1563 favorably by using the same selective approach applied to the years before 1560, but he did not. Why the project came to a halt in 1560 remains a mystery.[33]

The compiler sanitized the history of the Rus'/Russian Orthodox Church and the Rus' princes. Genealogical and biblical concepts, such as the Tree of Paradise, served as literary models for his portrait of harmonious relations between church and state, the divine nature of the Russian dynasty, and God's protection of tsar and country as the Rus'/Russian people advanced toward salvation. To do so, he omitted conflicts within the church almost entirely and omitted or downplayed princely cooperation with the Tatars and unedifying instances of conflict between princes and the church.

The *Book of Degrees* accorded rulers from St. Vladimir through Ivan the title "autocrat" (*samoderzhets*). Although Makarii lauded Ivan as "autocrat" in Ivan's coronation, Makarii did not crown him as "autocrat." In the *Book of Degrees* the title denoted a pious ruler, not an independent ruler or one with unlimited authority.

The compiler could have intended the *Book of Degrees* for Ivan personally, or for him and his children, as edifying reading but hardly as an oblique criticism of the tsar's un-Orthodox Christian behavior. The inventory of the "Tsar's Archive" did not mention a copy of the *Book of Degrees*, however, and no direct evidence confirms that Ivan ever read it.[34] The text most likely served multiple functions for multiple audiences. Our ignorance of who read it, and the paucity of copies from Ivan's reign, precludes reaching definitive conclusions on this question.[35] No sixteenth-century ruler would have rejected a text combining love of God, ruler, and country.

The *Illustrated Chronicle Compilation*

If the *Book of Degrees* confined itself to Rus' history as an expression of God's will, the equally unfinished *Illustrated Chronicle Compilation* tried to examine the workings of divine providence in world history. The *Illustrated Chronicle Compilation* placed Muscovy within a grander, even cosmic, plan of history since the Creation. One statistic adequately conveys its scope: if finished, it would have included approximately sixteen thousand miniatures.[36] The work contains many blank spaces for future miniatures, as well as uncolored miniatures or mere outlines. It remains an open question whether the state or the church sponsored the work. The *Book of Degrees* served as a source for the *Illustrated Chronicle Compilation*. Indeed, one of the former's compilers may have served as one of the latter's editors. Yet the annalist chronicle structure of the *Illustrated Chronicle Compilation* took a step backward from the thematic structure of the *Book of Degrees*. Identifying the intended audience of an incomplete work of indeterminate patronage remains problematic. Scholars have not yet fully investigated its interpretation of Ivan's reign and Muscovite history.[37]

Most scholars believe work on the *Illustrated Chronicle Compilation* took place during the 1570s. Even if it could have begun earlier, it could not have been started any earlier than the date of the composition of the *Book of Degrees*. Even if the copyists and artists preparing the text lived during or after the oprichnina, the inspiration behind its creation belongs to the cultural flowering of the long 1550s. That both the *Book of Degrees* and the *Illustrated Chronicle Compilation* remained unfinished suggests that Muscovite intellectuals had exhausted the willpower and resources necessary to carry such ambitious projects to fruition. The incompleteness of the *Book of Degrees* and the *Illustrated Chronicle Compilation* might be connected to problems of scale or cost. Cultural productivity probably began to decline during the oprichnina, exacerbated further by the accompanying economic crisis. Even if Zinovii and an anonymous individual writer could still muster the energy to compose massive denunciations of Kosoi's heresy, group projects such as the *Book of Degrees* and the *Illustrated Chronicle Compilation* required not only institutional sponsorship but also social optimism. It was precisely that optimism that had declined, perhaps starting when Muscovy could not sustain its initial successes in the Livonian War, begun in 1558. On the other hand, regional, monastic, and private chronicle writing did not cease at this time, so the termination of work on the *Book of Degrees* and the *Illustrated Chronicle Compilation* cannot be explained by difficulties within the genre.

Printing

Muscovy took its first steps toward joining the "print revolution" during Ivan's reign. The first printing press in Muscovy began to function during the 1550s. Muscovites already had access to foreign printed books. The first books printed in Muscovy appeared anonymously and without dates of publication. In 1564 Ivan Fedorov and Petr Mstislavets printed the first dated book, the Acts of the Apostles.[38] Muscovy must have imported the technology, perhaps from Poland-Lithuania, although much early Muscovite printing vocabulary came from Italian. Muscovy's first paper mill may have also appeared during Ivan's reign, but it vanished without a trace.[39]

Many questions about the history of Fedorov's press remain open. Fedorov and Mstislavets published only a few religious works before they departed from Moscow. Fedorov claimed that ignorant clergy and citizens, whose motives he did not elucidate, drove them out. Even in exile he lauded the support that Ivan and Metropolitan Makarii had provided, asserting that Ivan had subsidized the press out of his own treasury. Fedorov's explanation implies that neither Ivan nor Makarii could control the people of Moscow who opposed printing. Most scholars infer that scribes feared that printing would put them out of business, but the small scale of printing in Muscovy makes that unlikely. Why the Moscow mob drove him out of town cannot be determined.[40]

Regardless of this mysterious popular opposition, printing resumed in Muscovy after 1572 at Aleksandrovskaia Sloboda. The press of Fedorov's student Andronik Nevezha also printed liturgical and religious books. Early printing everywhere lived a precarious economic life, so printers frequently moved about looking for new patrons. Fedorov eventually printed the first complete Cyrillic Bible, the famous Ostrog (Ostroh, Ostrih) Bible, for the Ukrainian Orthodox magnate Prince Constantine Ostrozky. Fedorov must have taken his tools of the trade, a press and type fonts, with him. If so, Muscovy must have replaced them. No one in Muscovy "banned" printing.[41]

Printing made censorship easier. The Muscovy Company had Fletcher's *Of the Russe Commonwealth* banned because it feared that the book would hurt their business in Muscovy. Both the preacher who preached a sermon that Elizabeth I should not marry a French Catholic and the printer who printed it lost their right hands. The government of Poland-Lithuania banned books whose negative images of Ivan threatened to impair relations with Muscovy.[42] The absence of free speech in Muscovy cannot be blamed upon the absence of printing.

Ivan's patronage of printing in Muscovy demonstrates his receptivity to technological improvement. We can only guess at his motives, but the use of the early printing presses to print ecclesiastical books suggests a religious one. The Church Council of 1551 addressed the question of accurate copies of ecclesiastical manuscripts. Printing offered a more reliable means of textual transmission than copying. Even so, printing had no impact upon Muscovy during Ivan's reign or for a long time thereafter.

RITUAL, CEREMONY, ART, AND ARCHITECTURE

The same conception of the connection of the ruler and Muscovy to God that infused literary sources from Ivan's reign also animated works of art and architecture and rituals and ceremonies.

All physical appurtenances of the ruler projected his image. The royal seal and coinage bore a rider perceived by foreigners as St. George but by Muscovites as the ruler. The seal's two-headed eagle derived from a Byzantine prototype.[43] The big state seal borrowed heraldic images from Poland, Sweden, and the Holy Roman Empire to substantiate regional subservience to Moscow. Ivan and Anastasiia donated an embroidered liturgical curtain (*katepetasma*) to the Hilandar Monastery on Mount Athos that extolled the position of the Muscovite ruler in the Orthodox Christian world.[44]

The decorum of Ivan's seating at banquets sometimes differed from practices of other rulers of the time. Ivan sometimes sat alone and sometimes at the same table as his closest relatives, the metropolitan, or the boyars. By contrast, in Spain, Burgundy, and the Holy Roman Empire the ruler always sat alone, elevated above his subjects.[45] When Ivan sat alone his spatial distance from his subjects illustrated his exalted status. When he sat beside the metropolitan his deference to a cleric illustrated his piety. When he sat with relatives or boyars his seating illustrated his generosity and the collegiality of the Muscovite elite. In all cases Ivan's seating enhanced his image.

The Palm Sunday, Epiphany, and Furnace ceremonies, mainstays of the court's calendar, had diverse origins and conveyed multiple messages. Multivalent rituals and ceremonies functioned on four levels: as performance, iconography, history, and eschatology. Muscovy's countrywide festivals resembled those in Italy, but not those in Northern Europe, where local monasteries, courts, and cities fostered their own holiday events.

The Palm Sunday ritual, of Western, Catholic origin, re-created the entrance of Jesus Christ into Jerusalem.[46] The metropolitan played the role of Jesus. The tsar led his "ass" (usually a horse with artificial ears). Historians disagree on whether Ivan's service to the metropolitan demeaned him by dramatizing the superiority of the church because Christ's authority devolved to the metropolitan, not the tsar, or enhanced him by foregrounding his humility in imitation of Christ. Both interpretations seem plausible, and they need not be mutually exclusive. After the construction of St. Basil's Cathedral, the procession wound its way to its Jerusalem chapel, proclaiming its message to Muscovites not permitted inside the Kremlin.

The Epiphany ceremony, the Blessing of the Waters, belonged primarily to the metropolitan, but the tsar and court attended. The Muscovite version differed greatly from its Byzantine prototype. The tsar stood while the metropolitan sat, but here, unlike in the Palm Sunday ritual, the metropolitan functioned as the very human head of the church, not as a surrogate for Christ. The tsar's deportment conveyed his piety and his respect for the metropolitan, not the metropolitan's superiority over the tsar.[47]

The Furnace ceremony, a re-creation of the biblical story of Shadrach, Meshach, and Abednego, resonated with ecclesiastical insistence that the ruler listen to wise advisors, presumably including bishops. It carried an apocalyptic echo because the Chaldeans served the Antichrist.[48] Royal attentiveness to clerical advisors did not entail church superiority to the state.

In these ceremonies Muscovy became the New Israel and Moscow became the New Jerusalem.[49] Muscovites experienced their identity in scriptural, not Byzantine or Roman, terms, similar to seventeenth-century New England Puritans. The concepts of the New Israel and New Jerusalem were ubiquitous in miniatures and paintings. Murals on Old Testament themes in the Golden Hall, a privileged space open only to the elite, depicted Muscovy's ruler as a new Solomon or David, God's protection of Muscovy, and the Muscovite military establishment as a parallel to the Heavenly Host and the armies of ancient Israel. Christological, apocalyptic, and salvific themes also appeared in the Golden Hall murals, along with Rus' saints and history.[50] *The Tale of the Princes of Vladimir* (*Skazanie o kniaz'iakh vladimirskikh*) was based on a legend of Byzantine imperial gifts to Kievan Grand Prince

Vladimir Monomakh, which supposedly included the Crown of Monomakh and conveyed imperial status upon the Rus' prince. Artists carved
scenes from the *Tale* around the so-called Monomakh Throne. The Tsar's
Place (*Tsarkoe mesto*), the royal pew in the Dormition Cathedral, perhaps
installed in 1551, replicated the throne of King Solomon.[51] If Muscovy had
become the New Israel, the Muscovites had become God's chosen people.

The developing concepts of Muscovy as the New Israel and the New
Jerusalem may have influenced Muscovy's changing attitude toward contemporary Jews.[52] Expressions of hostility toward Judaism, embedded in
Christianity, found voice in Kievan times. Ivan went a step further when
in 1550 he barred from Muscovy Jewish merchants from Poland-Lithuania.
In this new phase of Muscovite history, Ivan could not tolerate endangering
Muscovite religious purity as the "new" Israel by permitting descendants of
the "old" Israel to tread on its soil. In 1563, when Ivan conquered Polotsk, he
ordered the drowning of Jewish residents of the city who refused to accept
baptism.[53] Pragmatism did not moderate Ivan's bigotry toward Jews. To
remove all Jews from Polotsk was to ignore their contribution to the Belarusian economy. Even Ivan's predecessors had permitted a handful of useful
Jews, doctors and merchants, to enter Muscovy.[54] Ivan bears responsibility
for this unique massacre (probably only because no other city acquired by
Muscovy during the Livonian War had a Jewish community, so the opportunity for a repeat did not occur). Its extremism equals the worst excesses
of the Spanish Inquisition against *conversos*, Jews coerced into converting
to Christianity to avoid expulsion from Spain. The Spanish Inquisition
burned secret Jews at the stake.[55]

Other artworks also propagated Muscovite ideology. The Muscovite
army marched on Kazan under an icon of Christ. The *Blessed Is the Host of
the Heavenly Tsar* (*Blagoslovenno voiska nebesnogo tsaria*) icon, sometimes referred to as the *Church Militant* (*Voinstvuiushchaia tserkov*) may have depicted the conquest of Kazan by allegorically linking Moscow and Jerusalem
and by showing the Muscovite army under the protection of the Heavenly
Host led by the Archangel Michael. Scholars have proposed a variety of
interpretations of this striking, large, and complex icon.[56] The Muscovite
army of 1559/1560 marched behind a banner showing the Heavenly Host
headed by the Archangel Michael and the Muscovite army that marched on
Polotsk in 1563 bore a banner showing the Muscovite army led, not by the
tsar, but by Christ as a warrior, an image of apocalyptic "sacred violence."[57]

The Cathedral of the Intercession of (the Protective Veil [*Pokrov*]) of the Mother of God (Theotokos) on the Moat, now known as St. Basil's Cathedral, built outside the Kremlin on Red Square, made its message available to the entire population of Moscow, not just the elite. Not all scholars still believe that Pskov stonemasons Posnik and Barma designed it.[58] Its architecture evolved between 1552 and its consecration in 1561. The original ensemble structure metamorphosed into a single edifice. Its complex theological and allegorical meaning exceeded the simple dedication of its chapels to saints connected to events in the conquest of Kazan. St. Basil's lauded Ivan as procreator for fathering Tsarevich Ivan and Tsarevich Fedor, linking conquest and dynastic continuity. The onion domes with their multicolor painting were probably added later. Architectural historians have not identified any antecedent for its novel architecture, but its exuberance, vibrancy, and playfulness suggested that the conquest of Kazan inaugurated a new period in Muscovite history.[59]

Without "a rich knowledge of the Bible, Orthodox theology, and iconographic motifs," visual monuments such as seals, coinage, banners, icons, frescoes, murals, and church architecture or ceremonies such as Palm Sunday, the Epiphany, and the Fiery Furnace would have made little sense to the Muscovite audience.[60] Moreover, the oral element of ceremonies and liturgies was uttered in Slavonic. Fortuitously, members of the court elite by and large possessed a level of literacy in chancery Russian sufficient to give them access to Slavonic. Therefore, they possessed the religious and historical background necessary for them to appreciate these ideological messages.

11

The Economy and Economic Management

Muscovy could not have afforded its cultural flowering or territorial expansion during the 1550s unless its economy had generated a sufficient discretionary surplus to fund such activities. There is no doubt that Muscovy prospered economically more before the *oprichnina* than during and after it. Why the shift occurred, and whether the Muscovite economy changed, remain open questions.[1] This chapter discusses theories of Muscovite economic development during Ivan's reign, inspects evidence of cash flow, and considers a sterling expression of Muscovite elite attitudes toward economic activity conducive to profitable enterprise, the *Book of Household Management.*

THE ECONOMY

Daniil Makovskii made the case that the pre-1564 Muscovite economy was developing on capitalist lines, by which he meant not only the use of cash but also capitalist ways of using cash.[2] He cited separation of handicrafts from agriculture; opposition to the spread of slavery; division of labor in manufacturing; regional specialization in agriculture; increasing sale of food and cash crops such as hemp, flax, and hops; expansion of the money economy; conversion of natural or labor rents to money; moneylending; increased use of hired labor, especially in transportation, metallurgy, construction, and also in agriculture; increasing urbanization, both in the growth of existing towns and in the creation of new towns; rising prices; and the elimination of internal trade barriers.[3] Even peasants sold grain. Hired labor became sufficiently widespread that the Law Code of 1550 mandated that an employer owed his employee double pay if he failed to pay the agreed upon wages in full.[4] As Makovskii saw it, the economy displayed the capital accumulation and economic differentiation necessary for capitalist development. Government and church construction projects, legal protection for enterprises, construction of safe roads, and expanding domestic and foreign markets all fueled capitalism. Tragically, Ivan's oprichnina destroyed any prospects for further prosperity or economic progress, perverted the legal structure of the reforms, and initiated a spiral of economic regression.[5]

The Muscovite cash economy developed unevenly. The north, populated by peasants and monks, not boyars or gentry, became the most cash dependent. The Solovetskii Monastery even allowed its monks, who had taken vows of poverty, to keep cash in their cells. (Iosif Volotskii's Extended Rule allowed monks to keep money in their cells only with the superior's permission.) In a nonagricultural region, everyone had to purchase food. Residents of other regions also had ready access to cash. Even during the economic downturn, some peasants managed to pay rising rents and taxes with money.[6]

The concepts of private property and contract law penetrated deeply into Muscovite society. State confiscation of land for treason or eminent domain did not impugn private ownership of property. Sales of land and civil litigation over land ownership presupposed private property. Land registration developed to mitigate litigation. Foreigners trusted in the validity of business deals enough to make loans to natives. The use of promissory notes, payment in advance to deliver goods, assumed enforceable contracts.[7] Aside from their ability to act collectively, northern peasants working as artisans, hunters, fishermen, traders, and trappers also had a strong sense of individual private property, including shares of saltworks or fisheries. Contracts figured very prominently in their economic activities.[8] A peasant could contract his labor in a written "agreement charter" (*poriadnaia gramota*) that clearly defined his obligations. Some "agreement charters" look like labor contracts, but others resemble leases. Cash penalties applied for contract violations.[9] The oprichnina did not abolish the concept of private property or the use of such contracts.

Some trends identified by Makovskii need not be seen as evidence of capitalist development. Landlords shifted back and forth between money rent and rent-in-kind or labor, depending upon their profitability. When the price of grain or cash crops rose, landlords switched to labor dues to exploit their demesnes. Therefore, a rise in money rent does not demonstrate a trend toward a cash economy. Opposition to slavery did not preclude the spread of the new form of limited-contract slavery, but in any event slavery can coexist with capitalism.[10] Ivan exempted ecclesiastical institutions from internal customs, but he did not abolish them completely. Land constituted the only permanent form of wealth in sixteenth-century Muscovy, so disposable income, including that of merchants, went mostly into purchasing land, not into commerce or industry, as was also the case in most contemporary countries.[11]

Excessive government regulation did not inhibit economic development in Muscovy as compared to England. English aristocrats favored government regulation as a break against social mobility and to protect England's security and economic self-sufficiency. Except when fiscal necessity or patronage dictated otherwise, the English court agreed.[12]

Blame for the economic contrast between the first and second halves of Ivan's reign does not rest solely upon the oprichnina. Grain prices rose after, not during, the oprichnina.[13] Ivan bears the responsibility for the economic hardship of the oprichnina as well as the Livonian War. He did not cause crop failures or epidemics, but he can be held responsible for the failure of famine relief or the inability to impose effective quarantines. Nevertheless, the Muscovy Company and the Stroganovs did very well for themselves during the 1560s by joining the oprichnina. The authority vested in the Stroganovs recalls that of the Dutch and English West and East Indies Companies. While forced loans from monasteries in the 1580s suggest government revenue shortfall, Ivan's cash donations to monasteries and the continuing commercial market for land indicate a still positive economy. Monasteries, prime economic entrepreneurs, expanded their landowning by leaps and bounds during the oprichnina through donations, purchases, and foreclosures. The peasantry, however, suffered considerably.[14]

Makovskii's analysis erroneously treated natural and money economies as mutually exclusive successive stages of economic development.[15] The value of Makovskii's conclusions lies in their focus on Muscovite economic behavior in practice, not theoretical *oberta dicta* about the deleterious consequences of Muscovy's lack of capitalist institutions such as banks, letters of credit, and joint-stock companies. As elsewhere, kinship and personal networks compensated for the absence of modern capitalist institutions and procedures.[16] The flourishing Muscovite economy of the 1550s showed no signs of backwardness.

CASH FLOW IN MUSCOVY

Makovskii included use of cash among his indicators of Muscovy's economic development. Historians cannot measure the percentage of the economy that functioned on a natural basis, but we can extract data on who had cash, especially among the elite, and how much cash they had, from bills of sale for land and registers of donations to monasteries. Coin hordes started to increase in Muscovy during the 1540s and continued to do so throughout the rest of Ivan's reign.[17] Documentary evidence demonstrates conclusively that some elite Muscovites disposed of considerable cash.

As some contemporary foreigners and all Muscovites realized, sixteenth-century Muscovy possessed no gold or silver mines.[18] During Ivan's reign, Muscovites could not yet mine Siberian gold. Therefore, whatever gold or silver Muscovites possessed must have been imported from the New World, the Old World, or the Orient.[19] The Muscovite government never borrowed money abroad. Muscovy obtained cash via a favorable balance of trade or, specifically, a favorable balance of payments. Muscovy's trading partners knew that Muscovy imported specie. Even the strict mercantilist Elizabeth I had to permit English export of specie to Muscovy.[20] Allowing for fluctuations and regional differences, on the whole prices generally rose during Ivan's reign, a development usually attributed to the Price Revolution of the sixteenth century. Muscovy may have been peripheral to Immanuel Wallerstein's European world-economy of the sixteenth century, but profits from foreign trade had a profound impact on the Muscovite economy.[21]

Muscovy's elite needed cash. Furs did not suffice as a substitute for currency. The need to regulate punishment for debt in multiples of one hundred rubles testifies to the volume of borrowing. Some boyars, let alone gentry, lacked cash, fell deeply in debt, and even went bankrupt. A testator allowed his executor to donate a hamlet to a monastery if his estate could not muster the ten rubles he hoped to donate in cash. Ivan had to lend a boyar's wife a gown for her daughter's wedding because her husband had pawned her wardrobe to pay his debts. Gentry failed to raise the necessary cash to redeem sold or donated estates.[22] Partible inheritance cannot be blamed for such elite poverty because Muscovite boyars and gentry constantly received additional lands for service.[23] But elite debt and bankruptcy do not tell the entire story.

Not all boyars or gentry lived in poverty. Some elite landowners had ample cash.[24] A boyar testament abounds in cash transactions of many types (dowries, loans, contracts, and purchases), involving hundreds of rubles. Borrowers also served as lenders. A testator opined that if the tsar disallowed a land donation to a monastery, then his executor should compensate the monastery with forty rubles in cash. In the cadastres of the Tver region landowners frequently validated their rights to land ownership by citing bills of sale.[25] Lay landowners bought land for cash. Bills of sale and other land transaction documents specify how many rubles lay elite members paid for landed estates. A 1565–1568 census details an active real estate market in Kazan. Analysis of these cash sales shows little decline in quantity of sales or volume of cash during or after the oprichnina.

Some boyars, of course, controlled fabulous wealth. Prince Mikhail Glinskii spent over 1,000 rubles on land purchases in 1535/1536. Prince Andrei Shuiskii purchased a village for 900 rubles.[26] Lay landowners donated large amounts of cash to monasteries and churches.[27] Individual cash donation charters and composite monastic records, such as registers and accounting books, demonstrate lay monetary largess to ecclesiastical institutions. A nun donated 9,024 rubles to the Trinity-Sergius Monastery, topping Ivan's donation of 5,500 rubles in memory of his son Tsarevich Ivan.[28] Absence of cash did not necessarily motivate land donations to monasteries.[29] The same people made donations of both kinds. We do not know how they decided in which form to make a donation. Cash donations to monasteries rose in importance in sixteenth-century Muscovy relative to donations of land or in kind.[30]

The ruble was only a unit of account; there was no ruble coin in sixteenth-century Muscovy. A ruble contained 100 Novgorod dengi or 200 Muscovite dengi. Paying 1,000 rubles in coin meant transmitting 100,000 or 200,000 tiny silver coins. Historians and numismatists need to investigate the logistics of doing so, which required a great deal of counting, not to mention the ability to transport a large weight of silver.

Of course land purchasers did not imitate modern real-estate developers. Some men purchased land to donate to monasteries, which avoided depleting clan land. Something other than profit motivated a boyar to sell an estate to a monastery for its original purchase price.[31] Moreover, men and women "invested" their money in the hereafter by donating it to monasteries and churches or paying for memorial prayers for themselves and their loved ones. Such pious usage of cash, while not without nonreligious aspects, such as status and prestige, does not qualify as "capitalistic."

Muscovites with ample capital in cash utilized it for a variety of purposes, not just for land purchases or cash donations to monasteries. Merchants, bureaucrats, boyars, and gentry all lent money. A Smolensk merchant lent English merchants 6,200 rubles. A state secretary and Anfim, son of the priest Sylvester, lent Lithuanian merchants 1,210 rubles. An Englishman owed seventeen Muscovite merchants a whopping 23,343 rubles. English complaints of nonpayment of loans attest that no economic, cultural, or legal barriers prevented extensive English-Muscovite financial transactions. Muscovites gave out money in return for limited-service slavery contracts. A gentry-man who "lived in the Royal Council" at the time of his death in 1541 was owed 119 rubles by nine people, held limited-service slavery contracts on ten people worth 262 rubles and fifty pieces of gold, and left six hundred pieces of gold to Ivan, 50 rubles to his wife, and a total of 338 rubles to thirteen monasteries. The average number of debtors named per testament in Muscovy peaked in the first quarter of the sixteenth century. The average number of creditors reached its apex in the second half of the sixteenth century. The average total ruble debt in the second quarter of the sixteenth century climbed to an impressive 50 rubles per testament before falling in the second half of the century.[32] Money from dowries redeemed donated or sold land and financed mortgages.[33]

Investment of cash in land purchases did not take that cash out of circulation, because the vendor presumably spent it or lent it. If the vendor donated cash to a monastery, the monastery could spend it or lend it out. Only specie turned into sacred or secular objets d'art went out of circulation; what percentage of circulating cash did so cannot be determined. How imported specie wound up in the hands of boyars and gentry for them to spend cannot be ascertained, but it was certainly not as state salaries for military service, which were paid intermittently at best and almost never in full. These aspects of sixteenth-century Muscovite economic history require further study.

Although the tsar had the most cash at his disposal, all classes used cash. Peasants and artisans, especially in the north, needed cash to pay some of their rents and taxes. Peasants, artisans, and slaves could only have acquired even petty amounts of cash by selling something or receiving wages in cash. Merchants spent, borrowed, and lent cash. Bishops and abbots acquired and spent cash. State secretaries and musketeers received cash allotments. Boyars and gentry spent, borrowed, donated, and lent cash, no matter how much dues in kind or labor dues they received. The percentages of noncash transactions varied from class to class, region to region, and time to time, but the money economy flourished right alongside Muscovy's natural economy.[34]

THE *BOOK OF HOUSEHOLD MANAGEMENT*

The *Book of Household Management* (*Household Management* for short) sheds light on many aspects of Muscovite life,[35] but here we will focus on its economic philosophy. Like any advice book, *Household Management* represents an ideal, not reality. Historians cannot safely presume that Muscovites did everything *Household Management* prescribed or avoided doing anything it proscribed. Nevertheless, ideals play a significant role in actual practice.[36]

Household management books proliferated in the sixteenth century. They originated to the west of Muscovy and made their way eastward via translations. Logically, one would therefore expect the Muscovite version of *Household Management* to be a translation, but no one has located an original. A translator would have had to adapt an existing book to the Russian Orthodox Church calendar and the Muscovite diet. Moreover, unlike texts such as Castiglione's *Book of the Courtier* or Erasmus's *A Handbook of Good Manners for Children*, *Household Management* did not address the problem of civility per se. It subsumed manners under morals.[37] Similarities between *Household Management* and other household management manuals derive from shared religious sources. The appearance of such a text in Muscovy does not represent foreign influence but rather parallel social development.

Household Management described the ideal religious practice, family deportment, and economic management of a midsized, fairly well-off "household" (*dvor*), a fenced-in compound of living quarters and storage rooms that defined a distinct private sphere.[38] We do not know who composed the original text, to what social class he belonged, or when he wrote. Unlike some Italian treatises, *Household Management* did not extol the country life.

Its precepts applied primarily, but not exclusively, to an urban milieu. The priest Sylvester not only had a copy but also wrote a conspectus in the form of a letter to his son Anfim.[39] The text preaches the rational allocation of resources, which, by definition, presumes the existence of discretionary resources. Only a prosperous economy affords the well-to-do the opportunity to make economic decisions.

The question of who read *Household Management* during Ivan's reign cannot be answered. A gentry-man who could write a bill of sale or a donation charter to a monastery could read *Household Management*. Different sections of the text appear to address urban merchants and artisans, rural gentry military servitors, senior clerks and bureaucrats, and the milieu in which Sylvester lived—elite, married, urban parish clergy. On economic grounds only the wealthiest peasants could have belonged to its audience. Most peasants did not have discretionary income to manage. Social grounds exclude boyars. To maintain their status boyars needed to demonstrate their wealth, not manage it. A secluded royal or aristocratic wife might have "run" the women's quarters, but she would have had great difficulty running the entire household, including its male servants. Had he followed the dictates of *Household Management*, Ivan himself could hardly entertain lavishly, as he did. *Household Management* addressed the middling segment of society, not society as a whole.[40] The generation of several versions of the text in the sixteenth century demonstrates that some literate men not only read the text but also engaged its substance.

The mentality of *Household Management* qualifies as bourgeois, neither because it treated the concept of profit positively nor because it linked piety to prosperity but because it combined profit, piety, and propriety in the quintessentially middle-class ethic.[41] It was not only laity or priests such as Sylvester who associated prosperity with a near-Puritan work ethic. The Solovetskii Monastery shared a belief in their connection. Monks could laud economic success, if such success did not involve the vice of greed.[42] *Household Management* espoused bourgeois values: proper performance of religious ritual, without much concern for theology; strict family hierarchy (its limited advocacy of beating wives and children did not exceed the norms in contemporary societies); rigorous adherence to social hierarchy, requiring both deference to betters and modesty toward inferiors; lack of waste in time and goods, thrift (*not* miserliness), a rare virtue in Old Rus' texts; lack of ostentation; cleanliness; considerable concern for social reputation; and moderation in all things. Scholars have not addressed the extraordinary novelty of a Rus' or Muscovite text valuing cleanliness. Earlier literature insisted only on ritual cleanliness. In Renaissance Italy, Italians praised cleanliness and thought themselves cleaner than "filthy" barbarian Germans. Physical cleanliness became identified with moral cleanliness.[43] *Household Management* reflects the same new bourgeois economic and social ethos that had appeared outside Muscovy.

Household Management encapsulated its philosophy in two related Russian phrases, "according to one's strength" (*po sile*) and "as much as you have the strength [to do]" (*eliko tvoia sila*).[44] The text advised its reader to give alms "in accord with one's means"; to invite priests and monks into the home, "as many as [you] can afford"; to invite priests into the home of the sick, "as many as [you] can afford"; to donate alms, "as much as you can afford"; to pray "according to your strength"; to make offerings to priests, "as much as you can spare"; to live "according to [your] means"; to spend only "according to your means"; to keep only as many slaves "as you can afford," and to emancipate, not sell, those "you cannot afford" to retain. In his letter to his son Anfim, Sylvester regurgitated the advice to bring clerics and the poor into your house "according to your means," to give charity "as much as possible," and to give alms "according to your means." Sylvester claimed that he had bought prisoners out of jail and debtors out of debt "according to my means" and fed the hungry "according to my means." He admonished his son yet again to take care of the poor and needy "according to your means."[45]

Other texts also used these phrases. The Church Council of 1551 advised giving charity "according to one's ability." Penitentials declared it sinful *not* to give charity according to one's means. From the fifteenth century on, the government admonished lords not to impose taxes and quitrents beyond the ability of peasants to pay. The government expected peasants to pay according to their ability.[46] However, to the author of *Household Management* giving excessive charity constituted just as serious a sin as not giving at all. Only this text transformed judicious economic judgment into a social philosophy.

Muscovy possessed some concept of investment, but economic investment was subordinate to religious investment in *Household Management*. Anyone who lent money for interest or advanced money to finance a trading expedition understood the concept of profit, even without a stock market generating dividends. Within the framework of *Household Management*, however, the reward for abstaining from conspicuous consumption came in the form of salvation, not luxury in retirement following deferred gratification. The Orthodox theology at the base of *Household Management* had nothing to do with Calvinist predestination or a "calling." Nevertheless, the text idealized behavior congruent with Weber's "Protestant ethic," such as making economic decisions on rational grounds and avoiding laziness, waste, and ostentation.[47]

The appearance in Muscovy during the 1550s of a book of household management, the first of its kind, was no accident. Concern with social behavior and economic management reflected ongoing, and threatening, change. The text's obsession with social control cannot be separated from church and state concern for regulating sinful or criminal behavior. No hysterical apocalyptic thoughts marred its mood of controlled discipline. The very creation of this text attests to a perceived need to defend the existing social order. As in England, social mobility produced insistence on social immobility.[48] Its obsession with increasing material assets, economic self-improvement, rational allocation of resources, indeed with *managing* a household as an economic enterprise, bespeaks a bourgeois mentality previously unattested in Muscovite literature.

The moderation of *Household Management* contrasts sharply with the "extremism" of the early seventeenth-century vita of Iuliianiia Lazarevskaia Osor'ina, a rare laywoman saint who was not a martyr, nun, princess, or holy fool.[49] Iuliianiia's vita conforms to the traditional ascetic ethos of Russian Orthodoxy. During a famine Iuliianiia gave away all her possessions to feed the hungry, going hungry herself. She gave charity far in excess of her means. Her extreme asceticism and aversion to bathing violate the sober propriety and personal cleanliness of a housewife abiding by *Household Management*. An admitted illiterate such as Iuliianiia could not have kept the written records it prescribed. In contrast to *Household Management*, Iuliianiia emphasized the spirit, not the letter, of ritual. She ran her household in a far less authoritarian style than prescribed by the text and never inflicted corporal punishment on her servants.[50] *Household Management* advocated multiplying economic assets, not depleting them to the point of bankruptcy. Iuliianiia's religious enthusiasm and philanthropic excesses seem far more traditional than the punctilious religiosity of the author of *Household Management*. Comparing *Household Management* to the vita of

Iuliiannia demonstrates the former's economic and religious atypicality, despite its sincere Orthodox faith.

Muscovite prosperity during the first half of Ivan's reign reflected economic progress and development, even if Muscovy remained a mixed natural and money economy. The economic mentality of *Household Management* resonated with the rational elements of Muscovite culture during the 1550s, such as bureaucratic administration. Of course traditional conspicuous consumption, so alien to *Household Management*, continued to dominate the court and the boyars, and an ascetic monastic culture still prevailed in the Russian Orthodox Church, despite the existence of monastic entrepreneurial activities.

Economic prosperity directly affected political reform and foreign policy. Prosperous peasants and artisans could afford to pay double their tax rate in order to have local self-government in allotting and collecting state revenue. Peasant prosperity funded the gentry cavalry and musketeers who fought Muscovy's wars and expanded its borders. Territorial expansion not only depended upon adequate financing of Muscovy's military regime, but it also facilitated economic prosperity. When Muscovy conquered the Kazan and Astrakhan khanates, it acquired control of the entire Volga River to the Caspian Sea and opened up new, very profitable, opportunities for foreign trade to the Orient, which, in turn, increased cash imports. The arrival of the English via the Arctic Ocean stimulated Muscovite trade with England and other countries. When Muscovy conquered Narva, it acquired direct access to more economical trade routes via the Baltic Sea, thus creating even more profitable opportunities for trade with northern countries.

12

Early Foreign Policy

A healthy adult tsar could and did direct Muscovite foreign policy, could and did lead and inspire Muscovite armies to defend or expand Muscovite territory. Muscovy could neither have conquered Kazan in 1552 nor undertaken the Livonian War without Ivan's participation. As in domestic policy, historians disagree on Ivan's role in Muscovite foreign policy after his coronation. Muscovy faced issues on two fronts: to the south and the southeast, the Tatars in Crimea and Kazan; to the west, Livonia. In 1553 the arrival of the English via the Arctic Ocean led to direct commercial and diplomatic relations, but in the long run it did not alter the dynamic of Muscovy's relations with the Baltic powers as much as Ivan hoped.

The conquest of Kazan and Astrakhan raised Moscow's confidence that it could accomplish its goals on the battlefield. Early victories in the Livonian War seemed to confirm that optimism. By the turn of the 1560s, however, Muscovite campaigns in Livonia had stalled and the diplomatic situation worsened. Eventually, during the *oprichnina*, Muscovy's involvement in Baltic affairs cost it dearly on the southern front, when the Crimeans burned Moscow.

THE CONQUEST OF KAZAN

Russian historiography glorified Muscovy's conquest of Kazan in 1552 more than any other event during Ivan's reign. Historians hailed the conquest of Kazan as the victory of Christianity over Islam, the Cross over the Crescent, the forest over the steppe, and European civilization over Asiatic barbarism.[1] Church spires replaced minarets. Ivan endowed the new Kazan archbishop, equal in rank to that of Novgorod, the second-highest hierarch in the Russian Orthodox Church after the metropolitan himself, with a tithe of state revenues, reviving a Kievan institution from the Church Statute of St. Vladimir.[2]

Military reforms that gave Muscovy superiority in gunpowder weapons made the conquest of Kazan possible. Muscovy caught on quickly to the "gunpowder revolution." The Muscovites started casting falconets eleven years after the Italians invented them in 1536. Muscovy was ahead of the curve in loading cannon from the chamber. Muscovy's iron industry improved significantly.[3] Although Muscovy imported some raw materials it lacked and some guns, essentially it was self-sufficient in artillery, achieving parity with, and sometimes superiority over, its enemies. After the failure of the 1549–1550 Kazan campaign, Ivan created the musketeers (*strel'tsy*), professional infantry, and Russia's first standing army to supplement its mounted archers.[4] By contrast, even under Philip II, Spain had no standing army and needed to import virtually all its weapons, especially field guns. Previously, Muscovite cities raised gunpowder infantry with matchlocks locally and temporarily, not countrywide or permanently.[5] At first the central government established six companies of five hundred musketeers. The Russian words "*prikazy*" (which also meant bureaus) and "*pribory*" (companies) later replaced the original Russian word for their units, "*stat'i*," "detachments" (literally: "grades"). A few musketeer units rode horses, but musketeers could only fire muskets on the ground, using their poleaxes as a prop. Gentry captains (*golovy*) commanded each unit. The musketeers possessed limited battlefield mobility but fought quite effectively behind a "moving wall" (*guliai gorod*) or from city walls. The Muscovite government was obviously satisfied with the performance of the musketeers; by 1577 it had doubled their number.[6]

The Muscovite military had to meet the challenge of moving men, weapons, and supplies down and along the Volga River to arrive simultaneously at Kazan. Before 1552 campaigns foundered because flooded rivers or rain destroyed supplies. Moscow solved this logistical problem by building an advance armory and supply depot at Sviiazhsk, overlooking Kazan. An attempt by the Crimeans to divert Muscovite forces from Kazan failed.[7] A mysterious Razmysl, presumably a foreigner, led Muscovy's sappers, who first blew up the city's water supply and then its walls. Nevertheless, it took a lengthy siege and a bloody storm to take the city. The Muscovites enslaved so many captured Kazan women and children that they sold them very cheaply. The Muscovites slaughtered the men.[8]

Muscovite writers advanced largely spurious legal, religious, historical, and dynastic claims to justify the conquest of Kazan: Kazan had become Ivan's patrimony (*yurt*) when it succeeded Grand Bolgar, supposedly conquered by Ivan's ancestor, Vladimir Grand Prince Andrei Bogoliubskii. Muscovite rulers had installed previous khans. Muscovy claimed Kazan by right of conquest and by its right to liberate enslaved Muscovite captives. One text even asserted that Kazan sat on native Rus' soil.[9] Different rationales appealed to different audiences: some to Muscovites, some to foreign Christians, and some to steppe inhabitants.[10]

Contemporary sources written in Muscovy gave Ivan credit for the conquest of Kazan because of his bravery, piety, and wisdom. Narratives about the conquest of Kazan borrowed from literary works about the battle of Kulikovo Field in 1380, when Dmitrii Donskoi defeated emir Mamai of the Juchid *ulus*. Although those sources showed Donskoi fighting in the front ranks, Ivan never engaged in hand-to-hand combat. The ruler had become too valuable to risk his life. The tsar's most important function in battle was praying for victory. Ivan fought for victory by praying for it. No hint of cowardice was attached to this role.[11]

Not all sources praised Ivan's actions. Whereas the Nikon Chronicle and the *Tsar's Book* wrote that Ivan ordered Kazan captives killed when the city would not surrender, as if that did not reflect badly on him, Kurbskii, who accused Ivan of cowardice at Kazan, claimed that the Tatars killed those captives because it was better for them to die at the hands of co-religionists rather than "infidels." (Sergei Eisenstein filmed Kurbskii's version.) Kurbskii ignored the Muslim belief that death at the hands of infidels guarantees martyrdom. An early seventeenth-century chronicler impugned Ivan's image by recounting the legend that upon Ivan's birth, the tsaritsa of

Kazan, Suyunbike, told a Muscovite envoy that a man had just been born in Moscow with two sets of teeth, one of which would devour Kazan, the other Muscovy, an allusion to the oprichnina.[12]

Historians have described the Muscovite campaigns as "crusades."[13] If only a pope can launch a crusade by issuing indulgences, then the campaigns against Kazan cannot qualify as crusades, although the Russian Orthodox Church actively supported the 1552 campaign by sending monks, holy water, and icons to inspire the troops. The Muscovites expelled any surviving Tatars from Kazan, which became a Christian city. Ivan patronized the establishment of monasteries and churches within and around the city and adorned them with sacred objects, including miracle-working icons.[14] The expedient use of Muslim Nogai or Kasimov Tatars in Ivan's army did not impugn the religious motive for conquering Kazan. (Founded in the middle of the fifteenth century, the Kasimov Khanate, bordering on the steppe, became a Muscovite vassal; its Tatars served in Muscovite armies against other Tatars and on the western front).[15] Earlier, when Muscovy promoted a Muslim, the Chingissid Shah-Ali, as its choice of puppet ruler over Kazan, Muscovite sources refrained from criticizing his religion. Muscovite chronicles and sermons promised eternal life to those who died in battle against Kazan, equivalent to papal indulgences. The illustrations in the *Illustrated Chronicle Compilation* portray Muscovy's war against Kazan as a holy war.[16] Historians, can, therefore, speak of crusader themes in Muscovite propaganda.

Russian Orthodox Church missions in Kazan differed from New World Catholic missions. The Muscovite state funded them, not the church, and the missionaries lived in towns, not frontier missions. Despite these efforts Muscovy failed to convert the Tatars as intended.[17] To convert such a massive Muslim population proved impractical. Political considerations dictated that attempts to convert the Muslim population of the middle Volga region be played down. It took years for Muscovy to pacify the region fully. Resistance required punitive campaigns as late as the early 1580s. Yet Muscovy could not have left its entire conquest army on site in 1552 to subdue the region without leaving the Muscovite heartland defenseless against Crimean attack.[18]

With the acquisition of Astrakhan at the mouth of the Volga River in 1556, Muscovy possessed untrammeled access to the Caspian Sea and trade with Persia, Central Asia, and even India.[19] Regional trade in honey, fish, salt, and wax, and luxury international trade in Indian spices or Iranian silk generated attractive profits. Faith did not exclude commerce as a motivation for Muscovite policy.[20]

Muscovy lacked the resources to impose its control over the Kazan region without co-opting local elites and tolerating local differences. Unlike the Spanish in Mexico or the Portuguese in India, the Muscovites in Kazan did not make up the difference between available and needed administrative cadres by using non-Muscovites in prominent local administrative positions. Wherever possible, Moscow did permit local self-government of native communities.[21]

Many historians have utilized the *Kazan History* to describe Muscovy's conquest of Kazan because some of its narrative and themes (for example, criticism of boyars) seem to date to the 1560s. None of its manuscripts date to earlier than the seventeenth century, however, and all derive from a prototype with clear anachronisms. The text's reference to Third Rome was probably written after 1589. No literary scholar has succeeded in re-creating a mid-sixteenth-century version of the *Kazan History*. Therefore, its contents should not be taken as evidence of Muscovite opinion during Ivan's reign.[22]

Whether the conquest of Kazan changed Muscovy into an empire depends upon one's definition of "empire." There are different types of empire—universal and finite, with colonies and without. Muscovites did not conceive of Kazan as a colony, but sometimes treated it as one. The Kazan Tatars living under Muscovite rule undoubtedly thought of themselves as subjects of a foreign power; whether they understood the concept of a colony is another matter. The way in which Muscovy integrated Kazan into the Muscovite state set the pattern for future Muscovite and Russian acquisition of non-Russian, non-Orthodox Christian territories, a process that continued long after Ivan's death. Tatarstan remains part of the Russian Federation, the longest-lasting accomplishment of Ivan's reign, although Kazan's Tatars did not and do not necessarily view it in this light.[23]

No matter how great their achievement in conquering Kazan, the Muscovite government and elite did not appreciate the extent to which by doing so they had already exhausted Muscovy's material and human resources. This misjudgment influenced Muscovite conduct of the Livonian War.

THE ARRIVAL OF THE ENGLISH

In August 1553 one of three English ships searching for a northern passage to China reached Muscovy instead; the other two perished. Ivan invited the survivors to Moscow and permitted the opening of direct English-Muscovite trade via the northern route. The Arctic route remained open fewer months of the year than the Baltic route, but it enabled the English to avoid the Danish Sound tolls, Livonian German markups, Baltic pirates, and prying eyes when England shipped war supplies to Muscovy, despite disclaimers that it was not doing so.[24] Ships on the Baltic did not risk the icebergs in the Arctic, but they did suffer severe storms. Land routes took longer and entailed equally high customs. The northern route had distinct advantages for the English.

The English founded the Muscovy Company, England's first joint-stock company. Ivan granted it a monopoly on Arctic trade and total customs exemption.[25] The surviving English text of that charter almost certainly contains the draft English proposal.[26] It is likely that no one in Muscovy understood the corporate nature of a joint-stock company. The Muscovites treated the company's personnel as individuals.[27]

As a result of the opening of Anglo-Muscovite relations, English diplomats, merchants, and artisans became common in Muscovy. Muscovite diplomacy escaped its Baltic and regional confines and, for the first time, reached the Atlantic Ocean. England figured prominently in Muscovite foreign policy after 1553. When the Crimeans burned Moscow in 1571, the number of Englishmen who died and the amount of English property that was destroyed attest to the extent of English commercial penetration of Muscovy.[28]

Changing international circumstances affected Muscovite-English diplomatic and commercial relations, and none more so than the Livonian War, which drastically altered the conditions of Muscovite trade with its Baltic neighbors.

THE LIVONIAN WAR

The Livonian War began with Muscovy's invasion of Livonia in 1558 and lasted for twenty-five years. Nearly all Baltic powers were eventually involved. The war drained Muscovy of manpower and resources and opened the way for the Crimeans to burn Moscow in 1571. Worst of all, Muscovy lost.[29] Referring to "the" Livonian War misstates its narrative, like referring to "the" Hundred Years' War. The Livonian War took place as a series of related wars that historians conceptualized in hindsight as "the" Livonian War. Ivan played a leading role in the diplomatic and military conduct of the war. Ivan's management of the war looms large in evaluations of his leadership skills and decision making. The Livonian War inspired the anti-Muscovite propaganda that to this day dominates Ivan's image outside Russia. It is a distortion of history, however, to view the Livonian War as a conflict between "Europe" and "Russia" or as a precursor of Peter the Great's "Great Northern War."

Historians disagree about various aspects of the Livonian War, beginning with whether Muscovy needed to fight it at all;[30] whether the annexation of Livonia should have taken precedence over invading Crimea; Muscovy's war goals; and the reasons Muscovy lost. Muscovy's occupation of Livonia sheds light on Muscovy's "imperial" policy toward non-Orthodox, non-Russian, non-steppe conquered populations.

Causes of the Livonian War

Ivan declared Livonia's failure to pay tribute for use of some Muscovite land, actually a never-enforced provision of a medieval treaty between the city of Dorpat and then-independent Pskov, as its casus belli. He claimed Dorpat by right of inheritance because of his ancestor, Grand Prince Iaroslav of Kiev, who founded it as the city of Iur'ev. Ivan rightly complained that iconoclastic Lutheran Livonians had destroyed Orthodox icons and churches in Dorpat. Metropolitan Makarii sponsored the vita of an Orthodox martyr in Livonia.[31] Ivan blamed his minority for Muscovy's earlier failure to contest Livonian treaty violations. After years of fruitless negotiations and Livonia's unfulfilled promises to pay, in 1558 Ivan sent an army into Livonia.[32] Ivan must have known all along that the fractious Livonian Knights, city-states, and episcopal lords would never actually pay any money.[33]

Historians have ascribed various goals to Ivan in initiating the Livonian War. He may have intended Muscovy's initial "invasion" merely as a raid for plunder, the idea of conquest not coming up until the inability of Livonia to resist Muscovite arms became apparent. Or Ivan may have intended the first campaign into Livonia as a means to coerce it into paying tribute because payment meant recognition of Muscovite sovereignty. Ivan had other economic motives for conquest too, such as collecting customs and booty or facilitating Muscovite trade with the Baltic by breaking the Livonian monopoly. When Muscovy tried to hire foreign artisans and technicians, the Livonian cities barred their travel to Muscovy; Ivan wanted to remove this barrier. He did not seek to increase cultural contacts between "backward," "uncivilized" Muscovy and progressive, "civilized," Renaissance "Europe." Unlike Peter the Great, Ivan did not think that Muscovy was backward or that "Europe" or "European civilization" were superior, especially in terms of the cultural issue that was most important to him, religion. Whatever Ivan's motive, his Livonian policy constituted an ambitious innovation in Muscovite foreign policy. Neither his father nor his grandfather had ever attempted to invade Livonia.[34]

Robert Kerner famously attributed Russian expansion to its "urge to the sea," a motive Eisenstein assigned to Ivan. Kerner oversimplified. Muscovy had reached the Baltic Sea when it annexed Novgorod, although it lacked a Baltic port until it acquired Narva during the Livonian War. Under Ivan, Muscovy did reach the shores of the Caspian Sea. It already bordered the White Sea and the Arctic Ocean. Muscovy avoided the Black Sea, lest the Ottomans take umbrage. Muscovy did appreciate the need to circumvent Poland-Lithuania by a northern sea route to communicate with the Holy Roman emperor, but this is hardly what Kerner had in mind. Muscovy under Ivan certainly evinced no desire to reach the Pacific Ocean, even if late in Ivan's reign it penetrated Western Siberia, the Sibir Khanate.[35] Nevertheless, Kerner correctly interpreted getting to the Baltic as the key to the Livonian War.

The Livonian cities justified their monopoly of Muscovy's Baltic trade by the need to prevent Muscovy's importation of advanced military technology that would make her a threat to all Baltic powers, an argument invoked by the Holy Roman Empire and Poland-Lithuania to persuade England to stop providing Muscovy with military supplies. England did not stop, but Muscovy imported only very small quantities of non-gunpowder weapons such as swords, hardly advanced military technology.[36] Livonian propaganda actually defended Livonian profit, not Baltic security.

The Baltic trade mattered to Ivan. While he welcomed higher customs revenue, his Livonian policy was also inspired by the desire to increase Muscovite-Baltic trade. Muscovite terms for peace with Livonia stipulated that

Livonia must permit Muscovite merchants to trade directly with non-Livonian merchants in Livonian cities, breaking the Livonian monopoly and saving Muscovite merchants the expense of Livonian middleman profits. Moscow did not need to attain naval dominance in the Baltic Sea to change the conditions of trade. Ivan also pushed reciprocity in commercial relations in treaties with Sweden and Denmark. To acquire free trade in the Baltic, Muscovy had to acquire the Livonian ports and enough Livonian territory to provide access.[37] Despite mutual recriminations between Livonia and Muscovy, lack of good faith on both sides did not slow down commerce. Muscovite merchants doing business in Livonian cities voiced the same complaints—of fraud, corruption, and debt default—voiced by foreign merchants in Muscovy.[38] Too many historians have taken the latter at face value and ignored the former.

Muscovite merchants trading with the Baltic did not oppose the Livonian War because it would interrupt their trade. On the contrary, at the Assembly of the Land in 1566 merchants supported continuing the war. Their willingness to lend Livonian emissaries the funds needed to pay the tribute before 1558 reflected their desire to make a profit, not to prevent war. Because he rightly doubted that the Livonians would pay it back, Ivan forbade the loan. The Muscovite government supported Muscovite merchants doing business in Livonia.[39]

Although Ivan criticized Elizabeth I for putting commercial matters above political ones, he still valued commerce. He told English envoy Richard Jenkinson that he knew the importance of merchants' affairs—in fact, he was Muscovy's leading merchant—but politics came first.[40] Historians have overdrawn the contrast between anti-merchant Ivan and pro-merchant Elizabeth. The Tudors did not patronize the entire English middle class. They favored a clique of London bankers at the expense of everyone else. Ivan demeaned Elizabeth I for letting "filthy trading peasants" (*torgovye muzhiki*) or "uneducated peasants" run her realm. In his letters to Swedish King Johann III, Ivan maligned the social origin of the Swedish Vasa dynasty as from "trading peasants."[41] These insults did not impair Ivan's patronage of Muscovite merchants.

The Muscovite bourgeoisie does not deserve its reputation for backwardness, nor should it be compared invidiously to the middle classes of Tudor England, Flanders, the Upper Rhine, or parts of Italy.[42] When Muscovite merchants complained that they were losing money because they could not compete with foreign merchants who were granted tax exemptions, they did so in order to deprive their competitors of those privileges or to acquire those privileges for themselves. Historians have failed to locate a bourgeoisie in Muscovy that conforms to the idealized contours of the rational, acquisitive, socially confident, and politically influential bourgeoisie of the Weber thesis, but that ideal type never existed anywhere. Capitalism does not require a dominant bourgeoisie or any bourgeoisie. Landowning aristocrats can create capitalism. Therefore, the absence of a Weberian bourgeoisie in Muscovy cannot explain the supposed absence of capitalism in Muscovy.[43]

Muscovy did have an active and acquisitive commercial bourgeoisie with some political influence. Muscovite merchants played a far from negligible role in Muscovite affairs. They probably had a hand in Ivan's refusal to let English merchants travel to and trade in Persia, where Muscovite merchants had already established commercial connections. The largest contingent of Muscovite merchants abroad went by land via Smolensk to Livonia, Lithuania, and Poland. War between Muscovy and Poland-Lithuania did not interrupt this trade. Overland trade to Poland-Lithuania, Germany, and the Habsburg lands constituted at least a fifth of sixteenth-century Muscovite exports.[44] Muscovite merchants must have traveled by sea to Copenhagen and Dordrecht because thieves robbed them there. In a 1566 letter two Muscovite trading people in Copenhagen informed their employer at home of the projected four-week business trip to Amsterdam of a third trading person. Muscovite merchants took full advantage of the new opportunities for trade with foreign merchants when Muscovy conquered Narva. Trade through Narva surged during the Muscovite occupation.[45]

English merchants felt so superior to Muscovites at free enterprise that they besought their own and the Muscovite governments to enforce their trading monopoly by the use of police force.[46] By barring Muscovite merchants from using English shipping to transport goods to England, the Muscovy Company illegally forced them to sell their goods to English merchants in Muscovy. Ivan expected reciprocal retail and wholesale commercial privileges for Muscovite merchants in England, but he acquiesced to this violation of Muscovite commercial rights, partially to let the English take the shipping risks and partially as leverage to get English military assistance in the Livonian War. He did not entirely sacrifice the interests of Muscovite merchants because he also barred English merchants in Muscovy from the retail trade, which forced them to sell their goods wholesale to Muscovite merchants, and he limited where they could reside. On the whole, then, Ivan's desire to increase merchant profit from international trade probably equaled his desire to increase state customs revenue; he did not need to choose between them. Whether Ivan sought to increase his customs revenues from the Livonian cities or to increase Muscovite commerce by breaking the Livonian trade monopoly that precluded direct Muscovite trade with other Baltic parties, the Muscovite economy's seemingly infinite demand for imported silver could have played a role not only in Ivan's thinking but also in that of the foreign policy establishment. Muscovy did not seek to annex Livonia for coinage, but the cash value of Livonia would not have escaped their attention.[47]

Crimea or Livonia

At the same time that Muscovy launched the Livonian War, it also conducted its first offensive operations against Crimea. The Crimean Chingissid khans, the Gireids, vassals of the Ottoman Empire, led raids against Muscovy, sometimes with the participation of nomad Nogai Tatars who inhabited the steppe between Crimea and Muscovy. Only rarely did Ottoman forces participate. Muscovite armies reached the Crimean peninsula in 1558–1559. The Muscovites were assisted by Don Cossacks and the forces of Prince Dmytro Vishnevetsky, who had left Lithuania to enter Ivan's service and constructed a fortress on the river Psel to interdict Crimean raids on Muscovy. In 1563, to appease Crimea and remove an irritant to the Ottomans, Ivan ordered the destruction of the Psel'sk fortress. Muscovy had difficulty provisioning so distant an outpost.[48] Muscovite campaigns against Crimea sought not to annex it but to check Crimean raiding activity just enough, without upsetting the Ottomans, to permit safely reassigning Muscovite troops from the southern to the western front. Unfortunately the Muscovites miscalculated. Muscovy so weakened its southern defenses when it redeployed troops to the Livonian front that not only did Nogai raids increase but also the Crimean Tatars broached the Oka River line in 1571 and burned Moscow almost to the ground.[49]

If no Muscovites opposed the Livonian War, no debate about the war's advisability could have taken place. We have no evidence that Aleksei Adashev, the priest Sylvester, boyars supposedly averse to fighting fellow

Christians, boyars of Lithuanian descent, or anyone at the Council of the Land in 1566 opposed the war. When Ivan complained, in his first letter to Kurbskii, that his putative enemies, Aleksei Adashev and Sylvester, sabotaged the war against Livonia, he lied.[50] Adashev, for example, held military and civilian offices in Livonia after his disgrace at the same time that his brother Danilo served in a raid on Crimea. In the 1550s Muscovy more than once unsuccessfully proposed an entirely unrealistic anti-Crimean alliance with Lithuania. Numerous conflicting interests, in particular over the territories of Kievan Rus', precluded such an alliance. Muscovy and Lithuania each sought an alliance with Crimea.[51] It is true that the Muscovite gentry failed to show up for muster in the later stages of the Livonian War in such numbers that punitive expeditions had to be sent out to round them up, and Ivan had to make up the shortfall in manpower by increasing the numbers of Tatars and non-Russian troops in his armies. But the gentry did not shirk military service out of political opposition to the Livonian War. Rather they did so from a lack of arms, horses, armor, and provisions. Gentry had no objections to participating in, and profiting from, Muscovy's early victories in Livonia.[52]

A Muscovite invasion of Crimea remained unfeasible in the second half of the sixteenth century. Over a century later, Sofiia Alexeevna, regent for her brother Tsar Ivan Alexeevich and half-brother Tsar Peter (later, the Great), found the logistical problems insurmountable. Muscovite men and horses lacked water in the arid steppe, and, after the Crimeans set the steppe grass on fire, the horses lacked fodder. Muscovy could not establish an advance post against Crimea in the steppe. The temporary weakness of the Crimean Tatars in the late 1550s, whether due to disease or lack of rain, did not create an opportunity that Ivan missed. The Ottoman Empire would have responded immediately to a Muscovite invasion of its vassal.[53] War with the sultan so terrified the Muscovites that Moscow politely returned Ottomans captured during Muscovite raids on Crimea to the Porte unharmed, with abject apologies for the inconvenience. In 1569 a joint Ottoman–Crimean Tatar attempt to retake the sultan's yurt, Astrakhan, failed disastrously, but it so successfully signaled Ottoman displeasure at Muscovite policy toward Crimea, on the Volga River and in the North Caucasus, that Ivan and the Muscovite government retreated.[54] Ivan insisted to the sultan that, despite his conquests of Kazan and Astrakhan, he did not intend to harm Muslims. Ivan declared that Muslims could practice Islam without hindrance in his lands. He had built the Terek fortress to assist his father-in-law, the Kabarda Circassian ruler Temriuk, not to harm Ottoman interests. (Ivan tactfully omitted to note that the fortress defended Temriuk against Crimean Tatars.) Muscovy could not project its power into the North Caucasus in the face of determined Crimean and Ottoman resistance.[55] Ivan reopened Astrakhan to Central Asian Muslims making the Hajj to Mecca and Medina, and he promised to destroy the fortress constructed on the Terek River. He did not actually destroy the fortress, but he did withdraw its Muscovite garrison. Ivan also apologized profusely to the sultan for the "misunderstanding."[56]

Losing the Livonian War

Ivan did not try to invade Crimea, but his attempt to conquer Livonia ultimately failed. Explanations of Muscovy's defeat run the gamut from Ivan's insanity to Muscovite military backwardness, from military logistics to diplomatic incompetence.[57]

One popular theory argues that Muscovy could not satisfy its contradictory needs for mounted archers in the south-southeast and musketeers and artillery in the northwest. To the contrary, Muscovy deployed artillery and musketeers against Kazan and light cavalry against Livonia. Cavalry remained crucial to Muscovy's neighbors as well, constituting nearly half of the Ottoman, Polish-Lithuanian, and Swedish armies for another century. Muscovy understood and successfully managed to adjust the proportions of its forces on the two fronts. In the south it put forth a cavalry army supported by infantry and artillery; in the northwest an artillery and infantry army supported by cavalry.[58]

From 1558 until 1577, time and again it looked as if Muscovy would win the Livonian War, but the lack of a Baltic fleet doomed its chances for success. In 1563 the Muscovites took the Belarusian city of Polotsk, which directly threatened Vilnius, and secured the Livonian flank. If Ivan thought that the fall of Polotsk would motivate Poland-Lithuania to concede Livonia to him, he was painfully mistaken.[59] In 1577 Ivan could still muster a formidable field army with sufficient musketeers and artillery to invade Livonia and wrack up an impressive list of captured Livonian cities.[60] Unfortunately, without a Baltic fleet Muscovy could not take the port cities of Riga and Revel (Tallinn), because despite any Muscovite siege by land, they continued to receive supplies and reinforcements from the sea.[61] Muscovy had boats and ships, but the wrong kind for Baltic warfare. The Don and Zaporozhian Cossacks used galleys to cross the Black Sea to raid Asia Minor. Muscovy possessed river transport. Muscovite merchants found their way in the Baltic and Caspian Seas on vessels that hugged the shore, but such vessels could not engage in Baltic naval warfare.[62] Ivan's attempts to build—or have built for him—his own Baltic navy failed.[63] First, he hired Danish privateers led by Carsten Rode (Karsten Rhode), but, unfortunately, the Danes soon arrested him. (Vasilii III may have tried the same method.[64]) Ivan's compelling need for English naval intervention in the Baltic on Muscovy's side drove his obsessive efforts to arrange an English dynastic marriage as the basis for an offensive-defensive military alliance. Elizabeth I resolutely avoided both such a marriage and such an alliance, lest it hurt English commercial profits from trade with Muscovy's enemies. England commanded sufficient naval power in the Baltic to protect English, Dutch, and French ships from Swedish privateers, but she did not place that naval power at Ivan's disposal.[65]

Ivan began the Livonian War at the most propitious time possible to avoid the risk either that other Baltic powers would intervene or that Muscovy's southern neighbors would take advantage of Muscovy's involvement in a war on its northern and western borders. Denmark and Sweden were at war; Lithuanian resistance to incorporation into Poland made the Poles unwilling to assist Lithuania against Muscovy; frosts and epidemics weakened Crimea and the Nogais.[66] Then Denmark and Sweden made peace, Poland and Lithuania created the Polish-Lithuanian Commonwealth in the Union of Lublin, and Crimea and the Nogais recovered.

Ivan tried to play Sweden and Poland-Lithuania off against one another to no avail. He tried to neutralize Poland-Lithuania via another marriage project. Regrettably, his pursuit of Catherine (Katarzyna Jagiellonka/Katarina Jagellonika), sister of Sigismund Augustus II of Poland and already married to Duke Johann of Finland, brother of King Erik XIV of Sweden, proved disastrous. Ivan later insisted that he thought that Johann had died, else he would never have asked for a married woman as bride. He lied. He expected Erik to have his brother assassinated to make his sister-in-law

available. With equal deceit Ivan later told Johann that he had never intended to marry Katerina but only to ransom her to her brother in return
for Livonia. Erik signed a treaty promising Catherine to Ivan, but he also
became homicidally insane. When Johann overthrew Erik, Sweden joined
Poland-Lithuania against Muscovy in Livonia. Ivan even plotted, with no
serious hope of success, to rescue Erik from Swedish prison and offer him
asylum in Muscovy.[67]

Historians have unfairly criticized Ivan for never being willing to compromise his goal of occupying all of Livonia. In 1566 Ivan did reject a
compromise. But in 1567 and 1578 Ivan proposed a partition of Livonia with
Poland-Lithuania, based upon current possession, that would have denied
him Riga and Revel. Poland-Lithuania turned down these offers because,
like Sweden, it wanted all of Livonia for itself.[68]

Some factors worked in Muscovy's favor. Its native infantry did not mu-
tiny over missing wages, as its enemies' mercenaries did. Because of its tax
base, Muscovy could mount engineering and logistical operations superior to
Poland-Lithuania.[69] Muscovite light cavalry were as good as Polish hussars.

Muscovy could *conquer* all of Livonia except for Riga and Revel, but
it lacked sufficient resources to *hold* its territorial acquisitions. Defeats in
open battle did not matter. Musketeers, crucial for garrisons in heavily
urbanized Livonia, required supplies. A small number of expensive German
and Scottish mercenaries captured in Livonia chose to enroll in Muscovite
service, such as the German horse and infantry mercenaries recruited by
Elert Kruse, a captive Livonian noble who entered Ivan's service. The largest
unit, commanded by Iurii Franzbek (Georg Franzbeck), numbered at most
several hundred men. Ivan deployed such troops against the Tatars, not
against his western enemies.[70]

Ivan never gave up. He favored truces when it suited his purpose, but
he wanted victory. He considered the "end" of the war in 1582 just a respite
until he could resume hostilities. Even during the oprichnina, fear of domestic unrest did not impede Ivan from leading Muscovite field armies
into Livonia. His presence in Livonia would not have enabled Muscovite
garrisons to defend conquered cities. Only rarely did a Muscovite garrison
surrender to Batory and petition to enter Polish service; Muscovite garrisons usually either fought to the death or, when they could no longer hold
out, surrendered and marched home. Ivan looked for scapegoats, of course,

accusing commanders of sabotage for not doing what they did not have the resources to do. Once he even sent state secretary Andrei Shchelkalov to the front to get military units moving.[71] Nothing availed.

When he became King of Poland and Grand Duke of Lithuania, Stefan Batory of Transylvania raised Polish and Lithuanian troops and recruited multinational mercenaries to recover Polish-Lithuanian territory and invade Muscovy. He retook Polotsk, but even his mercenaries and military genius did not suffice to capture Pskov (he used the same trench warfare strategy that had worked successfully for Ivan at Kazan). Neither Ivan nor anyone else in Moscow could have anticipated that a military opponent of Batory's skill would tip the balance of the Livonian War.[72]

The debate among historians over whether Muscovy should have invaded Crimea instead of Livonia misses the point. Muscovy could neither project its military force into Crimea nor retain Livonia. Invading Livonia was discretionary, but the need to defend the southern frontier against Crimean raids was not. Muscovy could not sustain a two-front war in the west and the south. It could not avoid military action in the south, but it could do so in the west. Any western military action created avoidable problems.[73] Prudence dictated that Ivan concentrate on defensive measures against Crimea, such as the enhancement of the Oka River intelligence network in the steppe implemented in the 1570s. A defensive strategy against Crimea could have taken good advantage of Muscovy's Ukrainian Cossack, Don Cossack, and Circassian surrogates.

Had it tried to conquer Crimea, Muscovy would have overreached. By trying to conquer Livonia, it did overreach. However unwise, Ivan's excessive ambition remains understandable. Ivan and the elite drew the wrong conclusion from their success at Kazan. Their euphoria blinded them to the extent to which Muscovy had already taken its best shot. They jumped to excessively optimistic conclusions about Muscovy's capacity to expand. The huge expenditure of resources needed to conquer Kazan and to hold it during years of popular resistance to Muscovite rule precluded undertaking any other prolonged, territorial expansion. Muscovy became a victim of its own success.[74]

The Livonian War was aggressive, not defensive. It was a "war for expansion" (*zakhvatnicheskaia voina*).[75] Although contemporary Tatarstan historians present the Muscovite conquest of Kazan as an example of Russian imperialism, Muscovy's conquest of Kazan originated in defensive needs. Kazan Tatars raided Muscovite territories and captured and sold Muscovite slaves.[76] Even if Muscovy needed—meaning that it would genuinely have benefited from—Baltic access, Livonia did not pose a military threat to Muscovy. Greed does not justify aggression. Muscovy did not have a choice about fighting Kazan or Crimea. It chose to fight Livonia.

The Muscovite Occupation of Livonia

Muscovy faced serious problems dealing with the Livonian territory it occupied, which was heavily urban, Protestant or Catholic in religion, ethnically German, Estonian, or Latvian, and institutionally very different from the Muscovite homeland. Initially, Ivan generously promised to respect the rights, privileges, and property of Livonian burghers and knights who swore loyalty to him and not to deport any German knights or burghers. Despite his aversion to Lutheranism, he also swore not to interfere in Livonia's religious life. Ivan kept the latter promise. Although the Muscovites constructed Russian Orthodox churches in every Livonian city they occupied, Moscow never sought to impose Orthodox Christianity upon the Livonian population. Although Muscovy always had some support among Livonian Germans, it never possessed enough local support to secure Livonian acquiescence to Muscovite sovereignty.[77] The insincere Livonian surrender masked a refusal to accept Muscovite rule. When they revolted against Muscovite rule, Ivan deported many Livonians and probably overrode his previous grants of rights to them.[78]

To maintain his army of occupation, Ivan had to transfer Muscovy's political and economic systems to Livonia.[79] Muscovite musketeers garrisoned the cities, as in conquered Polotsk. To sustain Muscovite gentry cavalry stationed in Livonia, Ivan assigned them the land of dead or fled Livonian Knights as conditional land grants.[80] Shortening supply lines, not a dearth of landed estates at home, motivated this policy. Livonian cities had the privilege of self-government under the medieval German Magdeburg Law. Historians have not traced how long it continued to function after Muscovy took over. Ivan granted the Livonians in Dorpat most, but not all, of the privileges they requested.[81] The Muscovite government did not permit residents of conquered Polotsk, like the Tatars in conquered Kazan, inside the "city" (the citadel) without permission, and even then, only if unarmed. Perhaps a similar rule applied in Livonia. Moscow extended its postal system to occupied Lithuanian and Livonian territory. Muscovite census takers periodically surveyed Livonian territorial and human resources. Ivan added "Livonia" to his title. Administratively, then, Livonia became an integral part of the Muscovite state.[82]

In order to lessen Livonian resistance to direct Muscovite rule, Ivan explored means of indirect rule. First he asked captured Master of the Livonian Order, Prince Wilhelm von Fürstenberg, to remain in office as Muscovy's vassal, but he refused. Then, with equal creativity but an equal lack of success, Ivan recruited a Danish prince, Magnus, brother of King Fredrick II, to be his vassal "King of Livonia."[83] Ivan even let Magnus remain Lutheran when he married Ivan's first cousin once removed, the daughter of Prince Vladimir Staritskii. Ivan wrote Magnus a long exposition of their mutual obligations and his plans for Magnus's kingdom. Unfortunately, Magnus failed to appreciate his dependent status. When he tried to claim Livonian cities other than those that Ivan had assigned to him, both Magnus and the occupants of those cities suffered severely. Ivan threatened to exile Magnus to Kazan.[84] Magnus eventually defected to Poland-Lithuania. These ploys had no effect on Livonian resistance to Muscovite rule.

We cannot know if Ivan would have respected the liberties he granted the Livonians had they sincerely accepted Muscovite sovereignty instead of conspiring to revolt.[85] Ivan punished a Muscovite commander whose troops violated a safe-conduct to a surrendering Lithuanian garrison. He would have done no less for his Livonian subjects. Ivan assiduously protected the activities of German merchants from Muscovite-occupied Livonia, such as when they were victimized by Baltic piracy.[86] There was absolutely no chance, however, that the Livonians would accommodate Muscovite control. Pamphlets detailing Muscovite atrocities and Ivan's barbarism flooded Livonia at the time. The usual depredations by an occupying army did not help matters. The Livonians made up in arrogance toward the "barbaric Asiatic" Muscovites what they lacked in military or political competence. The Muscovite occupation of Livonia demonstrates its willingness to accommodate religious, social, and cultural differences if and only if the subject population recognized Muscovite political domination. Ivan's rational policies toward Livonia ran aground on the Livonian hatred of Muscovy.[87]

Ivan demonstrated courage and leadership in the conquest of Livonia, and he showed creativity and flexibility in trying to find an administrative modus vivendi with its refractory residents—until things went bad. Then Ivan succumbed to blaming scapegoats for military losses and taking punitive measures against rebellious subjects. Given the situation, it can be argued that he acted no differently than any other sixteenth-century monarch would have in the same situation.

"Lion of Revel" (now Tallinn) cannon by Karsten Middledorp of Lübeck, 1559. Artillery Museum, St. Petersburg. Photo by Sergei Bogatyrev. Reproduced with permission

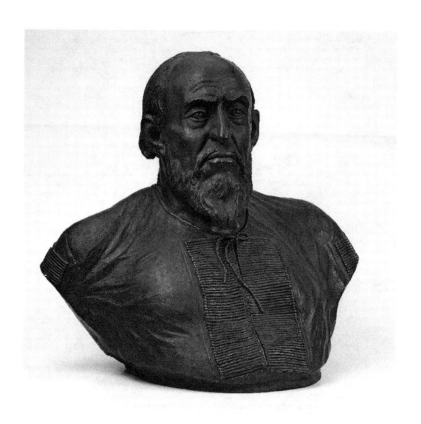

Mikhail Mikhaylovich Gerasimov's forensic facial reconstruction of Ivan IV, 1953.

"Copenhagen Portrait" of Ivan IV, seventeenth century. National Museum, Copenhagen.

↑ Ilya Repin, *Ivan the Terrible and His Son Ivan on 16 November 1581*, 1885. Oil on canvas, 78.5 in × 100 in. Tretyakov Gallery, Moscow.

➔ Viktor Mikhailovich Vasnetsov, *Tsar Ivan the Terrible*, 1897. Oil on canvas, 97.2 in. × 51.9 in. Tretyakov Gallery, Moscow.

Nikolai Cherkasov as Ivan IV in Sergie Eisenstein's *Ivan the Terrible* (*Ivan Groznyi*), 1944.

Part IV

*Ivan and Muscovy during and
after the Oprichnina*

13

The Oprichnina and Its Aftermath, 1564–1584

The *oprichnina* lasted from 1565 to 1572, seven years out of the fifty years of Ivan's reign or the thirty-seven years of Ivan's rule. Yet these seven years constitute the litmus test of any evaluation of Ivan's personality and rule. No Rus'/Russian ruler before Ivan had ever employed mass terror as a political instrument. Even if Ivan continued to pursue the same policies as during the period of reform but using different methods, the qualitative difference in those methods constitutes a drastic change. The following four chapters address the oprichnina period of Ivan's reign. This chapter lays out the basic narrative details. Chapter 14 will discuss general interpretations of the nature of the oprichnina in order to lay the groundwork for a more detailed examination of key events in Muscovite history during this period in chapter 15. That chapter will also assess the impact of the oprichnina upon Muscovy at the time and upon subsequent Russian history. Finally, chapter 16 will present a new explanation of the evolution of the oprichnina as the result of the interaction of Ivan's political ideology and developments in Muscovite society over the preceding century.

Regardless of how we explain the oprichnina, no excuse can obviate Ivan's moral responsibility for its atrocities. Ivan must have executed some innocent people. Even if all of his elite male victims had been guilty, the lower-class men and the elite and commoner women and children killed on Ivan's orders had committed no crimes, with perhaps the lone exception of Princess Evfrosiniia Staritskaia. Because some boyars and gentry committed treason by emigrating, Ivan invoked guilt by association to take reprisals against blameless boyars and gentry. He invented conspiracies and assassination plots against him. Mass terror constituted a wholly disproportionate response to whatever degree of political disaffection existed in Muscovy. It far exceeded the selective use of violence previously employed by Ivan's predecessors. Some historians minimize Ivan's "excesses" by referring to the "spirit of the times," arguing that other contemporary rulers committed equally inhuman acts, such as the repression of the Peasants' Revolt in Germany, the revolt of the Netherlands against Habsburg rule, or the St. Bartholomew's Day massacre.[1] That such rulers deserve equal moral condemnation does not exonerate Ivan. If Ivan's actions were no worse than those of other rulers, neither were they better than them. That said, moral condemnation does not terminate historical analysis of the oprichnina.

Historians must attempt to understand why and how Ivan and Muscovy degenerated to the level of violence of the oprichnina. To explain the oprichnina, historians must place Ivan's actions within the context of Muscovite society of the time. They must distinguish between Ivan's intentions and the actual consequences of his actions. Ivan might not have planned to launch mass terror when he created the oprichnina. The oprichnina evolved in response to changing circumstances. There are parallels to Ivan's abdication and to mass terror in world history, but the ideological and institutional mix of the oprichnina retains unique characteristics. For example, the symbolism of dogs' heads had no precedent or parallel anywhere at any time. The complexity of the oprichnina precludes simplistic monocausal explanations. It is not possible to separate the problem of explaining Ivan from that of explaining the oprichnina.

In December 1564 Ivan ordered his courtiers (*dvoriane*), members of the royal court (*dvor*), to assemble in full military garb, accompanied by their families.[2] Ivan left Moscow accompanied by boyars, privy personnel, state officials, courtiers, and selected gentry. He took with him the state treasury and the treasures of Moscow—coins, jewels, and plate of precious metals— as well as religious valuables, icons, and crosses. He kept his destination secret. These unusual features of his departure created no little drama.[3] Ivan usually indicated his destination in advance so that proper accommodations could be prepared for him. He first went to Kolomenskoe, his vacation lodge, where he prayed at the St. Nicholas Monastery. From there he went to the Trinity-Sergius Monastery, a frequent site of royal pilgrimages. After a delay occasioned by road problems, he turned in the opposite direction and wound up at Aleksandrovskaia Sloboda, a favorite royal retreat and hunting lodge, about one hundred kilometers northeast of Moscow.

From Aleksandrovskaia Sloboda Ivan sent two letters to Moscow. The first, to Metropolitan Afanasii and the boyars, announced that he had abdicated because he could no longer tolerate the treason of his servitors or the church's protection of those traitors. Since his father's death, the boyars, military commanders, and state officials had embezzled money from the treasury and "feedings," stolen patrimonies and conditional land estates, oppressed the Orthodox, and failed to defend the land against Crimean Tatars, Germans, and Lithuanians. Ivan also directed his anger against the archbishops, bishops, archimandrites, and abbots who had protected these miscreants. He put boyars, majordomos, the equerry, associate boyars, treasurers, secretaries, gentry, and all state officials in disgrace. Ivan declared that he would wander whither God led him. He addressed a second letter to the populace of Moscow, the lower classes, primarily artisans and merchants. In that letter, read aloud on Red Square, he announced that he felt no rancor toward them. He had not placed commoners in disgrace, and they should not fear Ivan's anger.

The population of Moscow panicked. The lower classes (*chern'*) lamented that they could not possibly survive without their shepherd. All governmental, commercial, and religious activity in the city ceased. The population petitioned the metropolitan and the boyars to persuade Ivan to return and to permit Ivan to deal with evildoers as he saw fit. In this atmosphere it is very likely that anyone Ivan named as an evildoer would not have lived long, but Ivan had not named names.[4] The boyars and clergy, accompanied by commoners, undertook to walk to Aleksandrovskaia Sloboda to implore Ivan to return to Moscow. The metropolitan remained in Moscow to maintain order.

At Aleksandrovskaia Sloboda, now an armed camp, Ivan deigned to receive the elite but not the commoners. He informed the elite delegation that he would return to the throne and lift his disgrace only upon certain nonnegotiable conditions. Ivan must have the freedom to reward and to punish whomever he chose, without interference by boyars or clergy. He would establish the oprichnina, a separate realm in which only his authority obtained, and would create a personal corps of servitors and bodyguards, *oprichniki*. Ivan wanted his own oprichnina "court" (household) of servants, artisans, boyars, associate boyars, majordomos, treasurers, state secretaries, state officials, lower household officials, and musketeers.[5] The boyars in the Royal Council and officials in the Moscow bureaus should continue to perform their duties, consulting Ivan on major issues. Ivan provided a long list of territories to be included in the oprichnina, including a street-by-street delineation in Moscow. The territory not included in the oprichnina would become the "land," later called the *zemshchina*. The "land" must provide 100,000 rubles for the oprichnina's maintenance. The elite agreed. The tsar's archive contained Ivan's decree (*ukaz*) establishing the oprichnina; eventually, it disappeared or someone destroyed it.[6] That same winter Ivan ordered the execution of four boyars and associate boyars and banished two others to a monastery. He put some courtiers and gentry in disgrace anew and confiscated all their property.

Ivan did not abandon the Kremlin entirely. At first he spent most of his time at Aleksandrovskaia Sloboda. Later he had an oprichnina court (compound) constructed in Moscow outside the Kremlin. Ivan still ran Muscovite foreign policy; diplomatic negotiations and receptions still took place in the Kremlin. He continued to pray at the Annunciation Cathedral.[7] Ivan must have lived in the Kremlin while in Moscow before the completion of the oprichnina court in 1567 and again after it burned down in 1571.[8]

In 1567 Ivan prepared to go on campaign to the west, but he turned back, reportedly after the discovery of a plot to capture him in the field, turn him over to the Lithuanians, and replace him on the throne with his cousin, Prince Vladimir Staritskii. Foreigners report either that Ivan tricked Prince Vladimir Staritskii into naming all the conspirators or that Staritskii did so on his own in the hope of saving his own neck. Ivan probably invented this plot. Staritskii's betrayal of the conspirators, however obtained, probably qualifies as a court rumor. The conspiracy resembles the one that Henry VIII invented to justify executing his Yorkist relatives, including a near seventy-year-old countess.[9] Staritskii could not have been stupid enough to believe that Ivan would spare his life in return for the lives of those accused of being his supporters.

Ivan ordered the estates of boyar Ivan Fedorov-Cheliadnin, master of horse and titular head of the "land" Royal Council, looted in retribution for his supposed role in the conspiracy. According to Albert Schlichting, a German renegade who entered Ivan's service and later defected, Ivan first dressed Fedorov in the imperial regalia. Ivan told Fedorov that he had now achieved his goal of becoming ruler and added that just as he could make Fedorov ruler, he could remove him as ruler. Ivan then drew his knife and stabbed Fedorov to death. While this narrative resembles other episodes of Ivan's playacting, it contains too many errors to be reliable. Schlichting erroneously called Fedorov a prince and recounted Fedorov's tender goodbye to his nonexistent children. Fedorov died, certainly at Ivan's orders, but it is very unlikely that the cause of death was a stab wound inflicted by Ivan himself. As far as I can tell, in no Muscovite miniature, icon, fresco, or mural does Ivan carry a knife, even when hunting. He carries a spear when he appears in the guise of St. George on coins and seals, but that is a different matter.[10] Ivan's ceremonial dress would have made carrying a knife awkward. Ironically, in a letter in Fedorov's name—whose authorship historians attribute to Fedorov, Ivan, or both—"Fedorov" insisted to Lithuanian Hetman Chodkiewicz that Ivan never executed anyone who was innocent.[11]

In 1566 Ivan selected Filipp, abbot of the Solovetskii Monastery, to become the next metropolitan of the Russian Orthodox Church. Filipp at first refused to accept the position unless Ivan abolished the oprichnina. Ivan and Filipp reached a compromise, embodied in a formal agreement. Filipp agreed not to interfere with the oprichnina, in return for which Ivan permitted him to retain the traditional right of the metropolitan to intercede for mercy on behalf of those judged guilty by the ruler. This truce did not last. Filipp openly criticized the oprichnina. Ivan had him deposed on trumped-up charges of personal misconduct and ordered him incarcerated in a Tver monastery.[12]

Repression escalated in 1569, as Ivan prepared a punitive expedition against the cities of the northwest: Tver, Klin, Novgorod, and Pskov. He forced Staritskii and some members of his family to take poison. En route to Novgorod he ordered his oprichnina henchman Maliuta Skuratov to secure Filipp's approval of his punitive expedition against Novgorod. Ivan must have been counting on Filipp's animosity toward the archbishop of Novgorod, Pimen, who had supported Filipp's removal from office, to induce Filipp to comply with his wishes. Filipp refused to endorse Ivan's campaign, so Skuratov strangled him.

Upon completion of the devastation he wrought in the northwest in 1570, Ivan staged gruesome public executions in Moscow. The sack of Novgorod and the Moscow executions constitute the height, or perhaps the depth, of the oprichnina's atrocities, the culmination of the mass terror that Ivan had unleashed upon his own subjects.

Ivan could not avoid foreign affairs during the oprichnina. In 1569 the Ottoman-Crimean campaign to conquer Astrakhan forced him to abandon his ambitious plans for increasing Muscovite influence in the North Caucasus. In that year the Grand Duchy of Lithuania, unable to resist Muscovite expansion into its territory, reluctantly agreed to the Union of Lublin with Poland that created the Polish-Lithuanian Commonwealth (Rzeczpospolita) in order to induce Poland to commit its vaster military resources to the war effort against Muscovy.[13] In 1571 the Crimean Khan Devlet Girei breeched Muscovy's depleted southern defensive line and reached Moscow, which his forces put to the torch. In 1572 Muscovite troops from both the "land" and the oprichnina defeated Devlet at the battle of Molodi.[14] Soon thereafter Ivan abolished the oprichnina in name and, by my definition, in fact.

When he abolished the oprichnina in 1572, Ivan was forty-two. The remaining twelve years of his life cannot be called anticlimactic. A depression struck Muscovy during the 1570s and 1580s. After King Sigismund II Augustus of the Polish-Lithuanian Commonwealth died, Ivan actively sought to secure its throne for himself or for his younger son, Tsarevich Fedor, as a means of securing Muscovite control of Livonia. In 1575 Ivan abdicated again, placing the converted Chinggisid Simeon Bekbulatovich on the throne "of All Rus'" and taking for himself the modest title of "Prince of Moscow."[15] Within a year Ivan removed Simeon from his throne, as consolation making him Grand Prince of Tver. Before the abolition of the oprichnina Ivan had begun a game of marital musical chairs that spun completely out of control during the remainder of his reign. Before 1569 he had married twice, to Anastasiia and Mariia Cherkasskaia, but between 1569 and 1581 he married five more times. In 1582–1583, although married to Mariia Nagaia, who had just given birth to a son, Ivan made yet another futile attempt to secure an English bride, the nadir of his increasingly dysfunctional marital life. In 1577 Ivan led a major campaign into Livonia that captured many cities, but the Muscovite army could still not take Riga or Revel. The new king of the Polish-Lithuanian Commonwealth, Stefan Batory, launched a counteroffensive that did not stop until it reached the walls of Pskov, where his unsuccessful siege demonstrated the exhaustion of both countries.[16] Ivan secured peace through the mediation of the Jesuit Antonio Possevino after he requested papal arbitration.

In 1581 Ivan supposedly accidentally killed his elder son, Tsarevich Ivan, whose death, regardless of its cause, cast a pall over his declining years.[17] The death of Tsarevich Ivan also left his younger brother, the mentally and physically deficient Tsarevich Fedor, as heir. Out of grief or in yet another byzantine plot to uncover disloyalty, Ivan offered to abdicate in favor of Fedor. After Tsarevich Ivan's death, his father made donations in memory of his victims, something he had previously not done. Memorial lists documented these donations and provide a frightening catalogue of Ivan's victims. Even Ivan's death remains shrouded in controversy. Some historians claim that Ivan died from poison. Thus, Ivan's life began in controversy, with questions about his parentage, and ended in controversy, with questions about his cause of death.

14

The Problem of the Oprichnina

The lack of consensus among historians about the *oprichnina* seems to grow every time a new monograph or article on the subject appears. Older interpretations of the oprichnina never disappear. They either survive intact or morph into new forms. This is particularly true in Russia, where the fall of the Soviet Union in 1991 freed historians from censorship. Historians in Russia, professional or amateur, have published numerous studies of the oprichnina with ever more diverse interpretations. The paucity and bias of the existing sources permit the creation of such varied theories. Historians in Russia continue to find new sources that speak to technical issues of its history, but no archival find could possibly resolve the conundrum of the oprichnina itself.

This chapter selectively surveys the major interpretations of the oprichnina that have been put forward by historians. We then turn to specific questions related to its territory, personnel, structure, and local impact. Disagreements about these issues animate disputes over its purpose, operation, and consequences.

INTERPRETATIONS OF THE OPRICHNINA

Gunnar Opeide best made the case that evaluations of the oprichnina vary because definitions of the oprichnina vary.[1] The word "oprichnina" sometimes refers to everything that happened in Muscovy between 1565 and 1572, at other times to the institution of the oprichnina, the methods of terror employed by the oprichnina, or, most vaguely, "the tsarist regime." The oprichnina has been considered everything from an episode of social engineering to a private security force run amok. Until recently the oaths, black horses, black robes, dogs' heads, brooms, and pseudo-monastic brotherhood of the *oprichniki* have been treated as extraneous sidebars, the "form" of the oprichnina rather than its "content," which concerned land or power.[2] Recent religious interpretations of the oprichnina treat these formal elements as semiotic symbols. In a culture dominated by symbolism, form *was* content.

Because of the absence of documentation other than Ivan's propaganda, historians sometimes infer Ivan's motives for creating the oprichnina from its consequences or from the identity of its victims—a very risky business. Such an approach assumes that the oprichnina turned out as Ivan intended.[3] Different historiographic schools focus on different facts and, naturally, derive different conclusions therefrom. We may group the major interpretations of the oprichnina into three categories: psychiatric, political, and religious.

The Oprichnina as Mental Illness

The insanity theory of the oprichnina renders any rational explanation of its realia superfluous. If Ivan were insane, of course the details of the oprichnina would make no sense. Undocumented assertions that Ivan derived sexual pleasure from sadistic torture and first committed rape at age eleven do not require further comment. Ivan's arbitrary choice of victims supposedly derived from his delusions and psychoses. His self-destructive policies emanated from his megalomania. Ivan's paranoia inspired his fear of threats against his life. It must be kept in mind, however, that sane politicians lie, pursue failed policies, and have exalted opinions of themselves all the time.

Assertions about Ivan's sadism rest upon dubious atrocity stories. Documentation of Ivan's role in torture suggests a more restrained conclusion. Ivan personally supervised the interrogation of Muscovites who had escaped Crimean captivity after the Tatar raid in 1571 and returned to Moscow. He posed leading questions incriminating boyars in inviting Devlet Girei to raid Moscow. Ivan decided which tortures to apply, to whom, and with what frequency, but he never applied the fire or other instruments of torture himself. Physically torturing his subjects was probably beneath his imperial dignity.[4]

Psychiatric theories overlook all Ivan's rational political decisions during the oprichnina.[5] The related biological reductionist argument that Ivan abdicated because he could not physically perform the duties of tsar lacks evidence.[6]

The Oprichnina as Politics

It would require a monograph in itself to describe adequately the numerous, sometimes mutually exclusive political theories of the oprichnina. Such theories argue that Ivan tried to overthrow institutional restraints upon his authority or to remove political opposition to his policies by actual or potential enemies. That opposition variously included boyars, the Suzdal elite, the appanages, Novgorod, the court (royal household), or the Russian Orthodox Church.

Historians have marshaled evidence that supposedly contradicts each political theory, but contradictory evidence cannot disprove the existence of a policy. A policy may be pursued inconsistently or it may produce contradictory results or collateral damage. A policy can change in response to changing circumstances. Moreover, even if a policy fails or proves to be unnecessary, it remains a policy. For example, the oprichnina impaired centralization by dividing the realm in two, but Ivan still might have thought that the oprichniki would eliminate opposition to centralization in the "land" so that centralization could resume unimpeded once the oprichnina was abolished.[7] The same inverted logic applies to the relationship of the oprichnina to the Livonian War. The oprichnina weakened the war effort by diverting financial and military resources, but Ivan may have thought that the oprichniki would quash opposition to the war and make additional land available to support gentry military service, thus contributing to eventual victory. Such mental gymnastics miss the point. Even if some Muscovites opposed centralization or the Livonian War, Ivan's response to such opposition created worse problems. Ivan did not need the oprichnina or mass terror to deal with individual opponents of his policies.[8]

The concepts of reform and counter-reform do not apply to the *oprichnina*. Describing the *oprichnina* as a reform is a distortion. The *oprichnina* did not envisage the revision of existing political institutions to improve their operation. The *oprichnina* did not continue the anti-boyar policies of the 1550s by different methods because the 1550s reforms did not attack the boyars as a class, and neither did the *oprichnina*.[9] The *oprichnina* did not repeal any of the 1550s reforms, so describing it as counter-reform misstates its purpose.

Judging the purpose of the oprichnina by its victims overlooks the fact that the selection of those victims may not reflect Ivan's decisions alone. Ivan's advisors may have manipulated him to repress their rivals. Ivan may have disgraced or executed some boyars at the behest of other boyars, although no one has ever identified who sabotaged whom. Rivalries among the oprichniki could have resulted in executions. Intrigue by Vasilii Griaznoi and Maliuta Skuratov may have led to the fall of the Basmanovs, father Aleksei and his son Fedor.[10] The Shchelkalov brothers, Andrei and Dmitrii, leading bureaucrats, denounced bureaucrat Viskovatyi because they wanted, and ultimately received, his jobs. According to Filipp's vita, clerics motivated by ambition or corruption, such as Archbishop of Novgorod Pimen, who supposedly wanted to become metropolitan, supported the removal of Metropolitan Filipp from office but not necessarily his murder. To be sure, Ivan's suspiciousness created the soil in which rivalries could grow into fatalities, so final blame would still fall on Ivan's shoulders. The oprichnina amplified opportunities for false denunciations, but such intra-elite feuding did not produce the oprichnina.

Ivan did not seek to "operationalize" his unlimited rule via the oprichnina. Ivan's childhood reading is sometimes said to have given him an exalted conception of himself as ruler, one at odds with the hypocritical behavior of boyars who deferred to him in public but mistreated him in private. This theory rests upon Ivan's fictionalized autobiography. Custom, tradition, and religion could constrain Ivan's actions somewhat, but he still had more than enough flexibility within the Muscovite political system to achieve his policies without an oprichnina.

Ivan did not expect to achieve unlimited power.[11] His actions demonstrate that he appreciated the difference between theory and practice. Ivan asserted his total authority neither to create a facade to mask his impotence nor to succor his megalomania. His claims to unlimited authority functioned as a negotiating tactic, a means to achieve more leverage with the elite, as part and parcel of an ongoing political process. The oprichnina did not lessen Ivan's dependence upon institutions any more than it did his dependence upon advisors. Rather, in some cases it doubled the number of institutions with which he had to deal: two Royal Councils, two royal households, two treasuries, the "land's" and the oprichnina's bureaus. Ivan complicated his relations with his bureaucracy by creating the oprichnina; he did not remove a layer of bureaucracy between himself and his subjects.[12]

Ivan's political ideology did not pervert his perception of reality. He adapted to circumstances. If a domestic policy failed, he changed it. When all is said and done, that was the fate of the oprichnina. Experimentation in local government never stopped. Ivan's foreign policy demonstrates his undogmatic flexibility very well. When necessary, Ivan could address "inferior" rulers, even kings of Sweden or Poland, as "brothers." He could abrogate his own insistence that Sweden conduct its foreign relations with Novgorod. He could violate Muscovite tradition by sending Muscovite envoys to Batory rather than insisting that Batory send his envoys to Moscow. He could imitate composite states by offering to recognize the institutions and privileges of Livonian cities and knights. He could compromise on religion, the most inflexible element of his belief system. Although he hated Protestants, he welcomed Protestant English merchants to Muscovy and permitted the Lutheran Magnus to marry into the royal family. Ivan did not permit the construction of a Catholic church in Moscow but he allowed private Catholic services and utilized a Jesuit to extricate Muscovy from a debilitating war. Ivan could inform Batory of the unity of the Latin and Greek faiths and allude sympathetically to the Union of Florence, by which a failing Byzantine Empire had accepted the union of the Orthodox and Catholic churches in 1438–1439 in order to secure Catholic military support against the Ottomans, although it was vehemently rejected by the Muscovite Orthodox Church at the time.[13] The existence of the flexible Ivan contradicts the image of the rigid ideologue Ivan who inflicted mass terror on Muscovy in order to achieve the impossible—absolute servility to his arbitrary will.

The Oprichnina as Religious Institution

Some historians have recently approached the oprichnina not as—or not only as—a political institution but also—or primarily—as a religious institution. They argue that hitherto neglected visual and performance elements of the oprichnina reveal its true purpose. Ivan reacted to expectations of the Apocalypse by creating the oprichnina in order to purify the Russian people of sin and help them achieve salvation.

As tsar, Ivan believed that no one but God could judge him and that he remained sacred even as he acted sinfully. His redemptive sacred violence anticipated the Last Judgment. Ivan saw himself as both a martyr and a merciless judge. Indeed, he was a martyr *because* he had to be a merciless judge.[14] Ivan expected the Apocalypse in 7070 (1562) or 7077 (1569), dates based upon the calculation that the end of the seventh millennium (the year 7000 in the Byzantine calendar) would witness the End of Days, on a date with sevens. According to Staden, Ivan or someone in his employ designed the oprichnina court in Moscow on the model of the Temple of Jerusalem, the site of the Second Coming of Christ. (Pavel Lungin re-created that building as the Temple of Solomon in his film *Tsar'*.) Excavations in 1989 are supposed to have confirmed Staden's description.[15] Ivan mortified the flesh of his "body," the Russian people. He chose modes of execution saturated with the religious symbolism of fire, water, and bridges.[16] All of his actions derived from his obligation before God to punish sinners. Ivan did not egoistically inflate his own absolute power. Rather, he piously defended God's authority.[17] Ivan modeled the oprichnina upon Catholic religious orders, either the Dominicans (the "dogs of God," hence the dogs' heads on the manes of the horses of the oprichniki), the Jesuits, or military monastic brotherhoods such as, of all people, the Livonian Knights.

Such religious theories of the oprichnina fail to provide a satisfactory explanation of the evidence. Of course Ivan expected the End of Days but not imminently. A few cliché theological terms in Kurbskii's and Ivan's letters do not constitute evidence of a serious apocalyptic mood. No text from the 1560s repeated the speculations of the 1490s that the Apocalypse might occur in 1562 (7070) or 1569 (7077) rather than 1492 (7000).[18] During the oprichnina Ivan denied his victims last rites. Sometimes he exterminated all relatives who could have arranged memorial prayers for them. Sometimes he had their bodies dismembered, which precluded their resurrection.[19] If relatives survived, they could perhaps have said private memorial prayers for the victims, but without Ivan's approval no major church or monastery would have commemorated the disgraced, until Ivan made his own donations for their commemoration. Rather than save his victim's souls for eternal life, Ivan was at least trying to doom them to Hell for eternity. In his first letter to Kurbskii Ivan wrote that anyone who disobeyed him doomed himself and all his relatives to Hell. The oprichniki were neither monks nor a chivalric order. Ivan did not lead them into northwest Muscovy under a banner of an icon of Christ, as he did his pre-oprichnina armies in the campaigns against Kazan or Livonia.[20] The mood in Muscovy during the oprichnina does not match that of 1492.[21]

Existing psychiatric, political, and religious interpretations of the oprichnina fall short of adequately explaining its purpose, meaning, and evolution.

THE CREATION OF THE OPRICHNINA

A Muscovite chronicle contains the only complete narrative of the oprichnina's creation. The narrative survives in the sixteenth-century Synodal manuscript and in a seventeenth-century copy in the "continuation" of the Aleksandro-Nevskaia Chronicle, both parts of the *Illustrated Chronicle Compilation*. Therefore, we may consider the narrative authentic, which does not, however, guarantee its reliability.[22] The two letters that Ivan sent to Moscow survive only in the chronicle's paraphrase, so we cannot verify their contents.

Ivan pretended to act spontaneously, as if he did not know what the outcome of his political maneuver would be, but his actions suggest otherwise. If he had actually abdicated, he should have left the state treasury in Moscow for his successor, and he should have sent his military servitors back to Moscow from Aleksandrovskaia Sloboda to protect that successor. A ruler who had abdicated could not place elite subjects or commoners in disgrace. Aleksandrovskaia Sloboda must have been prepared to house a far larger entourage than Ivan usually took with him when he went hunting because his servitors brought their families. The circuitous route Ivan took to arrive there could not have reflected indecision as to his destination on his part; perhaps he deliberately disguised where he was going. Ivan brought state officials with him because he expected to set up a new, separate administration.[23] His scribes immediately provided the delegation from Moscow with a detailed list of territories to be included in the oprichnina, down to names of streets in the city of Moscow. Planning to establish the oprichnina must have taken months. Ivan was clearly prepared for his manoeuver to succeed and could not have expected it to fail.

Ivan's "abdication" was political theater, a spectacle designed to make an impression on the Moscow elite and populace. Ivan neither invented nor monopolized the technique of threatening to abdicate in order to secure concessions from his subjects. In 1527 in order to acquire the authority to impose the Reformation on Sweden, King Gustav Vasa tearfully asked the Swedish Estates to let him abdicate. In 1570 King Fredrick III of Denmark had to threaten to abdicate to secure supplies for Denmark's continued participation in the Livonian War. Ivan involved the "people" in his gambit because he anticipated that they would invite him to retake his throne on whatever conditions he set.[24] His talents as a political tactician and strategist far exceeded those of anyone else in Muscovy.[25]

The narrative of the creation of the oprichnina refutes the traditional anti-boyar interpretation of its purpose and reveals the duplicity of Ivan's political rhetoric. Except for clergy, the categories of people Ivan took with him matched the categories of people he excoriated in his letter to the metropolitan and the boyars. His entourage included boyars, but Ivan's letter attacked the boyars' behavior during his minority and the reform period. Ivan could not have intended to use the oprichnina to attack the boyars exclusively because he accused a dozen other social groups of the same misdeeds. As Muscovy's premier class, the boyars figured first on the list of those Ivan criticized, but they also held pride of place among those who accompanied him, following only royalty. The list of malefactors consisted overwhelmingly of non-boyars, including significant members of the royal household, gentry, and bureaucrats. The oprichnina could not have been aimed exclusively at the court because Ivan also blamed clergy, who were not members of his royal household.[26] Ivan's letters did not criticize the appanage system, although he did not take Prince Vladimir Staritskii with him. When Ivan blamed the entire "establishment," lay and clerical, for driving him from the throne, he "overlooked" those members of the establishment who accompanied him to Aleksandrovskaia Sloboda. By blaming everyone, Ivan justified repressive actions against anyone.

The solicitous attitude toward the lower classes that Ivan expressed in his second letter to Moscow should not be construed as a sign of his democratic or populist leanings. He often expressed contempt for "boorish merchants" and "filthy peasants." It is conceivable, but improbable, that Ivan feared a popular uprising or riot in Moscow in 1564 like the one that occurred in 1547. Ivan's demagogic second letter to Moscow sought to manipulate the populace of Moscow to pressure the elite recipients of his first letter.[27]

Ivan had no meritocratic agenda in mind for the oprichnina. The oprichniki and the elite of the "land" drew from the same social base. Their social profiles did not differ. Gentry cavalry warriors presumably supplied the bulk of the mounted, armed oprichniki; no one else had horses and skill at arms. If Ivan had intended an oprichnina corps of gentry to replace the boyars, he would not have brought some boyars with him or included boyars in the oprichnina corps or deported or executed so many gentry.[28]

The narrative of the creation of the oprichnina belies assertions that Ivan had class motives in establishing the oprichnina. Ivan's disingenuous rhetoric makes extracting anything concrete from the narrative about his motives problematic. We can conclude that Ivan did and said whatever he thought necessary to get approval to establish the oprichnina, but his motives for wanting to establish the oprichnina cannot be deduced from this narrative.

IVAN AS HOLY FOOL AND MINSTREL

Some scholars unconvincingly view the theatricality of Ivan's establishment of the oprichnina in the context of other occasions on which he supposedly played the role of a holy fool or a minstrel in his prose and conduct. These scholars invoke Mikhail Bakhtin's theory of carnival.[29]

Reports do attribute theatrical actions to Ivan. He is said to have dressed the boyar Ivan Fedorov in his regalia and sat him on the throne before stabbing him to death. He reportedly enjoyed wearing the mask of a minstrel, a very disreputable profession in the eyes of the Russian Orthodox Church. He supposedly had the boyar Prince Mikhail Repnin executed for criticizing such unseemly behavior. Ivan summoned bears and bear trainers from Novgorod to Moscow to entertain at his wedding to Anna Koltovskaia. In his petition to Simeon Bekbulatovich he indulged in exaggerated self-deprecation like a holy fool, as he did in his letter to the Kirillo-Beloozero Monastery and the prologue to his testament. He dressed in rags to convey his poverty when the Crimean khan asked for a huge tribute after the burning of Moscow in 1571.[30] He referred to musical instruments used by minstrels in a letter he ghostwrote for a boyar.[31] He also enjoyed using pseudonyms, most plausibly in the letters written in the name of the boyars, much less plausibly as Parfenii the Holy Fool, author of a canon to the Archangel Michael, or as Peresvetov.[32]

This evidence can be questioned or reinterpreted. I doubt that Ivan insulted the royal regalia by dressing a boyar in them. It would have been beneath Ivan's dignity to wear a minstrel mask or dress in rags before a foreign envoy, even a Crimean Tatar. Specialists dispute Ivan's authorship of the canon to the Archangel Michael. On the other hand, Ivan's enjoyment of entertainment by minstrels, including at his wedding to Koltovskaia in 1572, despite their prohibition by the Church Council of 1551, occasions no surprise. Minstrels voiced no social criticism.[33]

Ivan's literary or theatrical poses differed in important ways from those of holy fools or minstrels. He certainly never walked around Moscow in winter naked or wearing only a loincloth or chains to cover his private parts, he never spoke in tongues, and he did not deliberately commit social gaffes to earn the opprobrium of the court. The opening sections of Ivan's letter to the Kirillo-Beloozero Monastery and his testament contain purely literary modesty motifs, not homages to holy fools.[34] The humility of Ivan's petition to Simeon Bekbulatovich was artificial, not genuine. Ivan did not play the mutually exclusive and incompatible roles of holy fool or minstrel. He did not apply the principle of carnival to his deportment.[35] Ivan's self-abasement, unlike that of a holy fool, did not uncover the moral shortcomings of the powers that be. He *was* the powers that be. According to Bakhtin, the carnival "terror" of medieval and Renaissance folk culture resembled, in modern parlance, children's stories. It was comic and farcical but not serious. It never included violence. Authority never employed it. Ivan's violent "terror," imposed by state authority, bears no resemblance to Bakhtin's theory. Carnival involves social inversion, but Ivan could not imitate his superiors because he had none. Ivan impersonated an abbot of the pseudo-monastic brotherhood at Aleksandrovskaia Sloboda, a sacrilegious but not carnivalesque act. The oprichnina did not belong to the realm of carnival.[36]

PROBLEMS IN ANALYZING THE OPRICHNINA

The different interpretations of the oprichnina rest on a foundation of disagreements about the factual details of the oprichnina's existence, the size of its territory, the number of oprichniki, and the extent of land confiscations and landowner deportations it generated. Absent the oprichnina archive or the continuation of mainline Moscow chronicle writing after 1567, such disputes remain unavoidable and irresolvable.[37]

The territory of the oprichnina changed. Ivan probably incorporated

Iaroslavl and Rostov into the oprichnina. Unquestionably, he added two of
the five regions of the former Novgorod hinterland and half of the city itself.
At its largest extent the oprichnina may have encompassed two-thirds of
Muscovy.[38] Given different regional population densities, such a territorial
measurement has less value than an estimate of what percentage of Muscovy's population lived in the oprichnina. No one has attempted to calculate
such an estimate.

The size of the oprichniki corps also changed concomitantly: as its territory increased the size of the corps presumably increased proportionally.
Ivan judged political reliability on an individual basis. He had no qualms
about adding gentry to the oprichnina after gentry at the Assembly of the
Land of 1566 protested its existence.[39] Novgorod territory added to the oprichnina, if assigned proportionally, would have increased the size of the
oprichnina corps by 50 percent. Some estimates conclude that Ivan recruited
4,500 to 5,000 oprichniki. An estimate that at its height there were 6,000
oprichniki may rest upon a misreading of a passage declaring that Ivan
summoned 6,000 gentry to Moscow. The passage might not have referred
to oprichniki.

Not all residents of the oprichnina became oprichniki. Not all servants,
artisans, or employees of Ivan's oprichnina household qualified as members
of the oprichnina corps, those armed men riding black horses with dogs'
heads and brooms. Neither did most infantry musketeers in the oprichnina.
Whether the oprichniki corps included only the pseudo-monastic brotherhood at Aleksandrovskaia Sloboda, about three hundred in number, or
also the larger troop of bodyguards, remains unresolved. So, the size of the
oprichniki corps remains an open question. Ivan began with a thousand oprichniki, who probably increased in number later by an unknown amount.
A register of members of the royal household, dated March 20, 1573, does
not provide a complete list of oprichniki, even if Ivan did not abolish the
oprichnina, but merely renamed it the "household." The list included cooks,
artisans, and even two minstrels who were employees of the oprichnina but
not oprichniki.[40]

The scattering of foreigners who belonged to the oprichnina has received disproportionate attention. The oprichniki included a few Germans
(probably not including Staden); one Circassian, the convert Prince Mikhail
Cherkasskii, Ivan's brother-in-law; and no Muslims.[41] Contemporary foreigners and some later Muscovites accused Ivan of favoring foreigners over

natives because he thought foreigners more loyal. The former attributed to Ivan the typical tyrant's fear of his own people; the latter sought to blame foreigners for Ivan's misdeeds. At some point Ivan must have noticed how many foreigners in his service (Schlichting, Staden, Taube, Kruse, and Magnus) eventually defected. No historian has ever asked whether non-Orthodox foreigners could take the oprichnik oath or belong to the oprichnina pseudo-monastic brotherhood.

Disagreement over the size of oprichnina confiscations and deportations derives from disagreement about which territories Ivan incorporated into the oprichnina. The evidence supports assertions of massive gentry relocation.[42] Of course the impact of the oprichnina varied from region to region. Some suffered more than others, depending upon location, economic profitability, and the social makeup of their population.

Historians assert that Muscovite society responded to the oprichnina with shock, social anomie, moral debasement, numbness, and disorientation. No Muscovite private memoirs or letters survive to corroborate the notion that members of the elite thought that they had to denounce someone else before they were denounced.[43] Analysis of all appearances of the terms "oprichnina" and "oprichniki" in Muscovite sources written in Muscovy between 1565 and 1572 demonstrates that Muscovites expressed two primary perceptions of the oprichnina. On the one hand, the oprichnina was a fact of life. Registers unemotionally recorded the appointment of elite military officers "from the oprichnina." Charters and cadastres recounted in a perfectly matter-of-fact tone that gentry lost estates when Ivan incorporated their districts into the oprichnina or acquired new estates to compensate them for their losses. On the other hand, numerous passages in cadastres from late in the oprichnina also detail in gruesome detail the illegal actions of oprichniki, but they do so without criticizing Ivan. Such depictions of oprichnik illegalities portray the oprichnina as a criminal enterprise, and may have served Ivan as an excuse to abolish the corps.[44]

The termination of the Moscow tradition of all-encompassing chronicle writing in 1567 vastly complicates analysis of the oprichnina. This discontinuity, not the shift from the "good" to the "bad" Ivan and not any substantive event, constitutes the most significant chronological divide during Ivan's reign, and it should drive the division of Ivan's reign into two periods.[45] No one knows why Moscow chronicle writing stopped, in part because no one knows who wrote chronicles in the first place. If government bureaus supervised the compiling of chronicles, then it seems illogical that they would stop this activity when they did not cease compiling diplomatic or office-assignment records. The end of chronicle writing did not coincide either with the establishment of the oprichnina in 1565 or the murder of Metropolitan Filipp in 1569, although either event could have been traumatic enough to induce a chronicle writer to put down his quill. The last potential apocalyptic year in the Byzantine calendar would have been 7077, which ran from September 1568 to August 1569, but if central chronicle writing ceased in anticipation of that event, regional and private chronicle writing did not.[46] During Ivan's reign the Moscow chronicle never included all the news. The issuance of the Law Code of 1550 and the Church Council of 1551 went unmentioned. Even so, the Moscow chronicle tradition provides the most comprehensive narrative account of events available. Historians cannot compensate for its discontinuance. We have a narrative of the creation of the oprichnina but not of its ongoing activities or termination. Instead historians have to rely heavily upon foreign denunciations of Ivan's tyranny or upon narrowly focused regional chronicles such as the Novgorod chronicles or upon very haphazard and unsystematic documentary sources.[47] The Moscow chronicle did not resume after the oprichnina, similarly handicapping studies of Ivan's reign from 1572 to 1584.

Historians writing about the oprichnina, especially in Russian, sometimes use anachronistic terminology. Skrynnikov structured his narrative around "cases" (*dela*) and "purges" (*chistki*), vocabulary taken from the 1930s. He also employed the Imperial Russian concept of a "state of emergency," literally an "extraordinary situation" (*chrezvychainoe polozhenie*). Two historians who criticized Srynnikov's employment of "current terminology" themselves described a man promoted because of the oprichnina as an "upwardly mobile person" (*vydvizhenets*), a term for those people promoted to higher positions vacated by victims of Stalin's purges. Another historian referred to the division of Muscovy into the oprichnina and the "land" as "dual authority" (*dvoevlastie*), the term for the relationship between the Provisional Government and the Petrograd Soviet after the Russian Revolution of February 1917.[48] Of course historians cannot avoid anachronistic vocabulary entirely; no alternative to the word "repression" presents itself, for example. Other misleading and anachronistic terms include "*zemstvo*," boyar "commissions," and gentry "corporations." Gratuitous anachronistic language modernizes and distorts sixteenth-century Muscovite history.

THE NATURE OF THE OPRICHNINA

Ivan established the oprichnina as an appanage, a private territory with its own administrative apparatus, judicial extraterritoriality, and finances, assigned to a member of the royal dynasty. It took time to staff the oprichnina infrastructure, but the oprichnina began operating immediately.[49] The royal who held the oprichnina distinguished it from any other appanage because he simultaneously ruled his appanage and the entire country.

Unique distinguishing features characterized the oprichniki. They wore distinctive garb and insignia; they rode black horses and dressed in black. (Did the two Muscovite defectors who tricked the guards of Izborsk into letting them enter the city by pretending to be oprichniki, only to betray it to the Lithuanians, "dress" the part?) The oprichniki took an oath to sever all personal ties to anyone living outside the oprichnina, including members of their own families, and to give absolute obedience to Ivan. The oath forbade social contact between oprichniki and non-oprichniki, even the exchange of "a single word."[50] The dogs' heads and brooms on the necks of oprichniki horses symbolized that the oprichniki were the dogs of the tsar and would sweep the land free of traitors.[51] Muscovite sources written in Muscovy during Ivan's reign do not mention any of these semiotic elements of the oprichnina, either because they were too obvious or too controversial to mention.[52] Muscovite sources written outside Muscovy by Muscovites during Ivan's lifetime, namely by the émigré Kurbskii, or written in Muscovy after Ivan's death and foreign sources do provide information on these semiotic aspects of the oprichnina.

The oprichniki belonged to a sacrilegious pseudo-monastic brotherhood (monks in the Russian Orthodox Church were not organized into orders as in the Roman Catholic Church) at Aleksandrovskaia Sloboda with Ivan as pseudo-abbot—"pseudo" because they did not take the cowl and did not observe monastic celibacy or poverty. Nevertheless the pseudo-monastic brotherhood very strongly suggests that the oprichnik oath imitated the ritual of becoming a monk.[53] Whether Ivan created this brotherhood immediately after he instituted the oprichnina remains unknown, but he did not do so as a burlesque or a parody for entertainment purposes.[54] The brothers observed a rigorous daily routine of church services. Oprichniki not residing in Aleksandrovskaia Sloboda probably could not participate in these pseudo-monastic activities. Even if the pseudo-monastic brotherhood had

a short life span, because Ivan spent rather little time at Aleksandrovskaia
Sloboda during the later years of the oprichnina, its very creation speaks to
Ivan's conception of the oprichnina as a society isolated from the Muscovite
population at large. In legitimate monasteries the abbot was obligated to
consult collegially with the council of (monastic) elders on all important decisions, but the oprichnina brotherhood lacked such an institution because
it did not constitute a legitimate Orthodox monastery.[55]

Unfortunately for Ivan, he could not, in practice, isolate oprichniki
from non-oprichniki to the extent mandated by their oath. The two halves
of the realm, however hostile to one another, had to interact. Oprichniki
continued to own land in the "land," and residents of the "land" continued
to own land in the oprichnina. Oprichnina and "land" boyars together
negotiated with Polish-Lithuanian envoys in 1566 and with Magnus in 1570.
The oprichnina had its own Royal Council. Whether it had its own Privy
Council remains obscure. Even if oprichnina and "land" members of either
council met jointly, Ivan probably met separately with his oprichnina boyars
at times. Anti-brigandage charters authorized anti-brigandage elders in the
oprichnina to cooperate with anti-brigandage elders outside the oprichnina
in the hot pursuit of known brigands. Some districts had both oprichnina
and "land" anti-brigandage elders.[56] Although no oprichnina service register
survives, for an oprichnik to sue a noble from the "land" over precedence
entailed that they were serving together. Ivan disappointed oprichniki
who assumed that he would always favor them in precedence lawsuits.
In all such cases known to us he obfuscated, declaring service "without
place." This resolution also awaited oprichniki who sued each other over
precedence. Sometimes a joint oprichnina/"land" court, in lieu of Ivan,
adjudicated a precedence lawsuit that crossed the oprichnina divide. Ivan
issued a blanket prohibition on precedence lawsuits when, after 1569, he
merged the oprichnina and "land" armies for service on the Oka River
with dual commands in every division.[57] Oprichniki boyars could no more
segregate themselves from their "land" counterparts than could oprichnina
anti-brigandage elders.

The oprichnina created an administrative quagmire at the local level.
The city of Moscow dealt with its division into oprichnina and "land"
streets by establishing two land bureaus (*zemskie prikazy*), one for each
jurisdiction.[58] After Ivan's sack of Novgorod, he divided that city in two
administratively, between the oprichnina "trade" side and the "land" St.

Sophia side. This partition was more coherent geographically than that of Moscow.[59] In 1571, when two military officers, one an oprichnik and the other not, arrived in Novgorod en route to Kolyvan (Revel) in Livonia, the former stayed at the household of an oprichnina boyar and the latter billeted on the "land" side of the city.[60] Oprichniki stood surety for non-oprichniki.[61] How the oprichnina functioned at the local level requires more study, but it is clear that oprichniki interacted far more with non-oprichniki than Ivan anticipated or preferred.

Conflicting interpretations of the oprichnina—psychological, political, or religious—create a confusing historiographic and historical landscape for trying to make sense of Ivan's complex and idiosyncratic institutional innovation. Of course, the oprichnina did not remain static, but the problem lies elsewhere. The lack of consensus among historians derives from different conceptions of what the oprichnina was and emphasis upon different aspects of the oprichnina. Nevertheless, one conclusion seems inescapable: without Ivan—without his personality, beliefs, and proclivities—there would have been no oprichnina. Ivan, not his advisors, designed the oprichnina. He remains solely responsible for the actions of the oprichniki and for the devastation that the mass terror of the oprichnina wrought upon Muscovite society.

15

The Oprichnina in Action

Atrocities dominate the narrative of the *oprichnina* in action: the murder at Ivan's order of former metropolitan Filipp and of Prince Vladimir Staritskii and family members; Ivan's "invasion" of his own northwestern territories; the gruesome public executions in Moscow in 1570; and the use of mass terror. The oprichnina years do contain two redeeming reforms: the creation of a new institution, the Assembly of the Land, and the establishment of a new frontier reconnaissance service, but the former did not play a prominent role in Muscovite history until after Ivan's death and the latter did not prevent the Crimean burning of Moscow in 1571. This chapter discusses Ivan's atrocities, the two reforms, and then examines his motivation for abolishing the oprichnina. Mass terror always degenerates to the point that the instruments of terror become its last victims, which is exactly what happened in Muscovy. Ivan liquidated the oprichnina by liquidating some of the *oprichniki*. We will also address various conclusions about its impact upon Muscovite history, in Ivan's time and since.

METROPOLITAN FILIPP

When, after the break-up of the Soviet Union, a fringe group of Great Russian chauvinists, Russian Orthodox Christian extremists, monarchists, and anti-Semites proposed that the Russian Orthodox Church canonize Ivan, their campaign crashed against the rock of Ivan's responsibility for the murder of Metropolitan Filipp, now a saint. The man who ordered the murder of a saint, the Patriarch of Moscow declared, could not be made a saint. Ivan's treatment of Filipp undermines his image as a devout Orthodox Christian.

In 1566 Metropolitan Afanasii resigned "for reasons of health," but he lived such a productive retirement that some historians argue that his resignation was actually a muted protest against the oprichnina. Nevertheless, a strong case can be made for the health motivation. Regardless of whether grand princes chose earlier metropolitans, during the oprichnina Ivan must have had the decisive voice on who would succeed Afanasii.[1]

Before becoming metropolitan, Filipp had been abbot of the Solovetskii Monastery.[2] As abbot he directed a major construction program that enhanced the monastery's entrepreneurial activities. His concern for profit did not intrude into his largely patrimonial and pastoral relations with peasants living on monastic lands.[3] As a condition of his selection Filipp insisted that Ivan abolish the oprichnina because it was impious to divide a land under divine protection. Ivan refused. In a compromise Filipp became metropolitan upon signing a written agreement not to interfere in the oprichnina. In return he retained the right of intercession on behalf of the disgraced. When Ivan abdicated in 1564, he had complained of church protection of traitors and criminals by its right of intercession. It is assumed that the Russian Orthodox Church had renounced that right in order to induce Ivan to return to the throne. If so, then Filipp restored the metropolitan's right to request mercy for malefactors. (Asking for mercy did not impugn the legitimacy of Ivan's judgment that such individuals were guilty. For the wrongly convicted one asks for justice, not mercy.) Why Ivan chose an opponent of the oprichnina to become metropolitan remains unfathomable. No existing explanation adequately explains this choice. Ivan was not so naive as to believe that his previous generosity toward the Solovetskii Monastery would guarantee that its abbot would become a compliant metropolitan.[4]

Filipp's vita, composed during the 1590s and partially confirmed by a German account, recounts his opposition to the oprichnina. For unknown reasons the vita, the "most negative picture" of Ivan produced in Muscovy, stopped short of directly accusing Ivan of suborning the perjured testimony that convicted Filipp of impropriety to justify his removal from office. Nor did the vita accuse Ivan of ordering Maliuta Skuratov to murder Filipp if

Filipp refused to "bless" Ivan's punitive campaign against the northwest. Skuratov would not have dared to exceed his instructions in dealing with Filipp. The vita, like the Muscovite chronicle, omitted reference to Filipp's agreement not to criticize the oprichnina, although it later inconsistently noted that Filipp violated his "oath" not to do so.[5] Different versions of the vita criticized Ivan as a "tormentor" only once or applied the term only to Skuratov.[6] The author of the vita manipulated Agapetus's mirror of princes, used to laud Ivan in the *Book of Degrees*, to criticize him for impiety.[7] Whatever the accuracy of the vita's rendition of Filipp's sermons and dialogues with Ivan, the metropolitan undoubtedly opposed the oprichnina. Filipp certainly did not acquiesce to Ivan's policies. Kurbskii's *History* and the vita declared Filipp's removal at the insistence of the laity uncanonical, but it is unclear who judged Filipp, whether clergy or boyars.[8] In any event his judges convicted Filipp and removed him from office. Ivan surely must have instigated and approved that action because he had the power to preclude it. According to the vita, Filipp's opposition to the oprichnina did not garner the support of the Holy Council. Ironically, Filipp had ordained five of its eleven bishops. The vita noted approvingly the later punishment of the bishops and abbots who had voted to remove Filipp from office and thus slandered a saint, but it does not opine that God, the church, or Ivan punished them because of their role in Filipp's removal. During the oprichnina Ivan reversed the restrictive policies on monastic immunities inaugurated in 1552, supposedly to secure monastic support against the metropolitan and the bishops.[9] Ivan incorporated some monasteries into the oprichnina. No monastery, including Filipp's, opposed the oprichnina. Filipp largely stood alone against Ivan and the oprichnina, without support from ecclesiastical institutions.

Muscovite church-state relations cannot be reduced to a single incident, even the murder of a deposed metropolitan. Ivan certainly was not the only monarch of the time who ordered the execution of clergy. Henry VIII had some abbots hung from church towers. Piety no more inhibited Ivan's treatment of individual bishops or monks than it did Philip II's. Muscovy imported the Byzantine ideal of church-state "symphony," but in Byzantine practice it was sometimes the emperor and sometimes the patriarch who had the upper hand. In sum, Ivan displayed the same combination of religious piety and high-handed interference in ecclesiastical affairs as his fellow monarchs.[10]

After Filipp, no metropolitan in Moscow openly opposed the oprichnina. Ivan omitted Filipp's name from his memorial list, adhering to Skuratov's cover story, repeated in but disputed by Filipp's vita, that Filipp had died of asphyxiation before Skuratov entered his cell. Nevertheless, Ivan cannot escape guilt for the murder of a political opponent who was a metropolitan and later became a saint.

THE STARITSKII APPANAGE

In 1569, the same year as Filipp's murder, Ivan ordered the execution of his cousin, the appanage Prince Vladimir Staritskii. Oprichniki compelled Staritskii, his wife, and one or more of his children (the evidence is confused but at least one) to take poison. They escorted Staritskii's mother, the nun Princess Evfrosiniia Staritskaia, out of her convent and apparently asphyxiated her in a cart. Ivan made memorial donations on their behalf; dead royal family remained royal family. Ivan spared at least three of Vladimir's progeny, two daughters and a son, Vasilii. Ivan betrothed the elder daughter, Evfimiia, to Magnus; when she died, Magnus married her sister, Mariia. Ivan later granted the son, Vasilii, a portion of his father's appanage. Vasilii probably died a natural death, although a late chronicle accused Ivan of murdering him too.[11] Thus ended the Staritskii collateral line.

Contradictions abounded in Ivan's relations with his cousin. At different times Vladimir served as a potential regent for Ivan's minor heir, a military commander, and acting governor of Moscow. After the dynastic crisis of 1553 Ivan demanded that Vladimir agree to denounce his mother, should she conspire against Ivan and his family. In 1558–1559 Ivan let Vladimir select which of his boyars he would send to Kashira for defense against the Crimeans. Vladimir served prominently in the 1563 Polotsk campaign. Makarii blessed him as a member of the royal family in his 1563 testament. In 1563 Ivan pardoned Vladimir after his conviction on vague treason charges of conspiring against the tsar. Yet in 1564 Vladimir accompanied Ivan to Aleksandrovskaia Sloboda. In 1565 a boyar had to take an oath that he would not switch from serving Ivan to serving Staritskii.[12] In 1566 Ivan ordered another territorial exchange, in which Vladimir lost Staritsa district to the oprichnina.[13] Shortly thereafter Ivan imposed his last territorial exchange on Staritskii, taking Vereia for Zvenigorod. In these territorial alterations Ivan sometimes permitted landowners freely to choose whether to serve himself or Vladimir. Therefore, severing Vladimir's ties to his appanage servitors did not motivate the exchanges. In 1566 another boyar had to promise not to engage in a conspiracy with Vladimir. When Ivan ordered construction of his own oprichnina court in Moscow outside the Kremlin in 1566, he permitted Vladimir to resume occupancy of his court (compound) in Moscow.[14] Interpreting these shifts in policy remains problematic. Perhaps Ivan vacillated between trusting and distrusting Staritskii; perhaps it took him from 1553 to 1569 to find the resolve to do what he always wanted to do—order Staritskii's execution.

The Staritskii clan anticipated which way the wind would eventually blow. Between 1558 and 1561 they constructed a church in Staritsa in honor of the princely martyrs Saints Boris and Gleb. Vladimir was cast in the role of innocent martyr and Ivan in the role of the "accursed" Prince Sviatopolk Vladimirovich, an early eleventh-century Kievan Rus' prince who ordered the assassination of Boris and Gleb because they blocked his way to the Kievan throne. Evfrosiniia's needlework assigned that same role to Ivan. Perhaps the construction of the Boris and Gleb Church constituted another response to the conquest of Kazan in competition with Ivan's architectural monument, St. Basil's, also completed in 1561.[15] Neither Ivan nor anyone else among the elite could have mistaken the message of this Staritskii political propaganda, despite its guise of religious patronage.

The sources do not reveal much about Vladimir's character. Perhaps he was an able military and political leader; perhaps he was Eisenstein's fool. That Ivan compelled Evfrosiniia to take the cowl, while leaving her son at large, suggests that Ivan considered Evfrosiniia the greater threat. Ivan might have assigned Vladimir high political and military roles only as a pretense, demonstrating to the public the absence of friction within the Moscow house. No one forced Ivan to designate Vladimir as regent in 1554 and 1556. It is unlikely that Vladimir plotted to poison Ivan, the crime for which he died. Ivan's death would hardly have benefitted Vladimir because Tsarevich Ivan Ivanovich would have become tsar and would not have viewed Vladimir kindly.[16]

Muscovites, contemporary and after 1584, knew that Ivan bore responsibility for Staritskii's death. Ivan acted out of purely dynastic motives: Vladimir's claim to the throne as grandson of Ivan III posed a potential threat to the succession of one of Ivan's sons. Appanages, autocracy, or "feudal" division had nothing to do with it. Yet another territorial division could have neutralized any danger posed by Staritskii's appanage. Forcing Vladimir to take the cowl would have sufficed to remove him from politics, without murdering Vladimir's mother, wife, and one or more of his children. Ivan, however, chose to employ the most extreme solution to the Staritskii problem. His choice of self-induced poison as a means of capital punishment required his victims to commit the sin of suicide, but they avoided public humiliation. For whatever reason or for no reason, Ivan refused any longer to tolerate the risk of a rival contender for the throne, even one who never came close to the degree of hostile plotting that compelled Queen Elizabeth I of England, after years of stalling, finally to order the execution of Mary Stuart.[17]

NOVGOROD

The city-state of Lord Novgorod the Great (Gospodin Velikii Novgorod) looms large in the history of medieval Rus', in part because it is mistakenly viewed as a "democratic" alternative to "autocratic" Moscow and in part because it was a major economic and cultural center. Ivan IV's grandfather, Ivan III, "the Great," conquered the city in 1478. Ivan III liquidated Novgorod's autonomous political institutions and executed or deported the Novgorodian boyars, carving up their estates to assign to immigrant Muscovite gentry as conditional land grants. The metropolitan in Moscow together with the ruler appointed the archbishop of Novgorod. Therefore, by Ivan IV's reign Novgorod's elite consisted of third-generation pro-Muscovite servitors and Moscow-appointed clerics.

Ivan's justification for his repression of Novgorod lacks credibility. During his reign Novgorod displayed no serious signs of political disaffection such as separatist or "democratic" tendencies. Few Novgorod gentry supported Prince Andrei Staritskii in 1537. Ivan's conflicts with Novgorodians in 1546 and 1552 had no lasting import.[18] He accused Novgorod of contradictory aims, of wanting to replace him on the Muscovite throne with Prince Vladimir Staritskii and of planning to switch its allegiance from Moscow to Poland-Lithuania. Oprichniki probably invented both lies. Archbishop Pimen had played a significant role in the development of the doctrine of royal authority. During Ivan's punitive campaign, he removed Pimen from office, humiliated him by making him ride backward on a donkey, and hauled him off to Moscow.[19]

The history of the city of Smolensk reveals the artificiality of Ivan's accusations against Novgorod. When Vasilii III conquered Smolensk from Poland-Lithuania in 1510, he guaranteed the elite's corporate rights and privileges. These guarantees became void when the Smolensk gentry rebelled against Muscovite rule. Moscow deported the indigenous elite to various central Muscovite provinces, and imported Muscovite gentry. Their descendants did not "go native" or dream of restoring Polish-Lithuanian rule in Smolensk. The oprichnina did not touch Smolensk. Ivan never leveled any accusations of treason against the city. The Muscovite gentry in Novgorod behaved no differently from the Muscovite gentry in Smolensk, despite Ivan's charges.[20]

Only the "Tale of the Destruction of Novgorod" (*Povest' o razgrome Novgoroda*), extant in seventeenth-century Novgorod chronicles, provides an extensive Russian narrative of the sack of Novgorod.[21] Muscovite sources described the campaign as a "sack," "plundering," or "destruction" (*plenenie, pokhod, prikhod, razgrom*). Historians commonly describe the attack as a "pogrom," a term not found in any Muscovite source depicting this event, although other contemporary sources used the word to mean a "raid" or "robbery," not in its modern sense of an anti-Semitic riot.[22] According to the "Tale," the destruction lasted six weeks, slightly longer than the St. Bartholomew's Day massacre outside Paris. The earliest version of the "Tale" did not mention oprichniki in Ivan's army, just boyars, gentry, and musketeers. Nor did the "Tale" allude to the musketeers stationed in Novgorod at the time. One late chronicle version included serving Tatars from Kazan in Ivan's forces, although no Tatars served in the oprichnina.[23] Later versions of the "Tale" interpolated the word "oprichniki" into the title of the "Tale" but never into the body of the text. Nevertheless, historians almost always write that Ivan attacked Novgorod with oprichniki.[24] Of course we may assume that Ivan would not have left Aleksandrovskaia Sloboda in 1569 without an oprichnik bodyguard. Why the author of the first version of the "Tale" did not use the word "oprichniki" remains an open question. (Coincidentally, a late chronicle describing Ivan's friendly visit to the city in 1568 did not use the word either.) The "Tale" blamed Ivan's attack on "our" sins, which permitted slanderers to inflame Ivan's anger against the city of "our" fathers. It is clear that a Novgorodian wrote the "Tale," although when it was written remains debatable.[25]

Despite its inconsistencies, historians have taken the "Tale" literally, with two notable exceptions: the eighteenth-century aristocrat Prince Mikhail Shcherbatov and the twentieth-century American Hugh Graham.[26]

According to this narrative, Ivan ordered hundreds of Novgorodians drowned in the Volkhov River daily for weeks on end in December and January, months when the river should have been frozen. If as many people had been executed as this account enumerated, the city would have been virtually uninhabited by the time Ivan left—and certainly, given the looting, uninhabitable. Yet soon thereafter Ivan stayed in Novgorod en route to Livonia, and later even temporarily moved his family and treasury there. The Novgorod mint remained in operation. Novgorod's sack did not irretrievably impoverish the city. Empty shops attest that Novgorod did decline some but not so severely as proposed and not exclusively because of the oprichnina. Extraneous factors such as the Livonian War and changes in Baltic trade, and indigenous factors such as bad harvests and epidemics, also negatively affected the city's economy.[27]

According to the memorial lists of Ivan's victims compiled after the death of Tsarevich Ivan in 1581, approximately three thousand victims died in Novgorod, about the same number of casualties as in Paris during the St. Bartholomew's Day massacre, in the same range as the "at least" two thousand Dutch executed as heretics in the Netherlands by Charles V, and less than the eight thousand fatalities in Antwerp when unpaid Spanish troops rioted.[28] All segments of the Novgorod population suffered, especially clergy and boyars of the archbishop as well as merchants, artisans, and even state secretaries.

Ivan's campaign also claimed victims outside Novgorod and Novgorodian territory. To disguise his approach, Ivan treated Novgorod as quarantined. Foreign sources claim that Ivan ordered his army to kill everyone it met on its way to Novgorod so no one could warn the city of his approach.[29] This sensational detail seems fictional. Ivan's punitive expedition also sacked several cities en route to Novgorod, including Tver and Klin, and prepared to do the same to Pskov until the holy fool Nikola intervened. Pskov still suffered, but less than Novgorod.

Some passages in the "Tale" suggest that Ivan acted from a mercenary motive, to replenish the coffers of the oprichnina. Ivan's forces looted St. Sophia Cathedral, removing its iron doors and sending them to Aleksandrovskaia Sloboda, where they still stand. Ivan's soldiers also pillaged all the Novgorod monasteries. They extorted money from clerics, merchants, and artisans.[30] One register identified Ivan's goal as plunder. Sixteenth-century Novgorod's cultural production bespeaks wealth. There is no evidence, however, that Ivan lacked money at this time. If he intended to collect as much money as possible, then burning commercial assets such as grain and killing livestock make no sense. Two historians, Igor Kurukin and Andrei Bulychev, suggest that the Bible influenced Ivan to perceive this property as "tainted" by the sins of its owners, so Ivan had to order its destruction. More likely, such senseless vandalism derived from Ivan's desire to terror- ize the inhabitants of the city. Whether Ivan's troops visited such wanton destruction upon the merchandise of Muscovite merchants in Dorpat or Narva, as claimed by a Livonian chronicle, remains uncertain.[31]

In scale the northwest expedition qualifies as Ivan's worst atrocity. Kill- ing the military servitors of the St. Sophia eparchy when he lacked sufficient personnel to fight the Livonian War was self-destructive. Even if the fan- tastic number of victims cited in the traditional accounts is adjusted, the monstrous level of the assault on Novgorod and other northwest cities seems totally mindless. The death of several thousand innocent men, women, and children remains a horrendous atrocity.

After its sack, life in Novgorod went on but not unchanged. Ivan in- corporated two of its "fifths" (*piatiny*; provinces) into the oprichnina. He added Novgorod gentry conditional landholders to the oprichnina corps, accompanied by the usual deportations and confiscations. Ivan attached the trade side of the city, across the Volkhov River from the St. Sophia side, to the oprichnina. Oprichnina state secretaries arrived to administer the new additions to Ivan's personal domain. Ivan issued a new commercial statute in the expectation that tax farmers would continue to have customs dues to collect on the trade side, and that merchants from central Muscovy and Smolensk, as well as Germany and Lithuania, would continue to visit Novgorod. Novgorod remained a regional, statewide, and international trade emporium. Oprichnina authorities did not forbid traffic across the bridge between the St. Sophia and trade sides. If merchants from the "land" St. Sophia side crossed over to the oprichnina trade side, they had to pay customs. Obviously, the ban on personal contact between members of the oprichnina and members of the "land" did not apply to Novgorod. In 1571 the government deported to Moscow 40 families from Novgorod's "land" side, along with sixty merchants from the oprichnina side, and/or, in either a new deportation or a different calculation of the same action, 5 Pskov families and 145 Novgorod families, as part of replenishing the commercial population of Moscow after it was burned by the Crimean Tatars. However much Novgorod's bifurcation disrupted its normal life, obviously the city could still support central government officials.[32]

The 1569–1570 campaign ravaged the entire northwest, although Ivan did not bother to propagate accusations against the cities that his army looted other than Novgorod. Looking for the expedition's purpose in the heritage or political disaffection of Novgorod's population is unproductive. Mass terror aims at intimidating everyone, regardless of behavior. Random terror, such as the Duke of Alva's (Alba's) "reign of terror" in the Netherlands, has a far more chilling impact than selective terror. Perhaps Ivan launched his attack neither for the excuses he articulated at the time nor for the reasons historians have ascribed to him but simply to terrorize Muscovy on a larger scale.[33] At the same time, the momentum of terror always entails an escalation from controlled, "rational" to uncontrolled, "irrational" violence, as the French Revolution attests.

THE MOSCOW EXECUTIONS OF 1570

In 1570, after his return to Moscow from his depredation of the northwest, Ivan staged public executions as horrible as anything in the sixteenth century.[34] To demonstrate his mercy, he spared 184 of the 300 potential victims who were marched onto Red Square. For comparison, in just under four years, Queen Mary Tudor of England had 284 men and women burned at the stake in her attempt to reinstate the Catholic Church, for which she acquired a reputation almost as bad as Ivan's. In a much longer reign Queen Elizabeth I of England had about 250 men and women hanged, drawn, and quartered; around 50 others died in prison.[35] Ivan's Moscow victims came from neither the boyars nor the appanages. They included some deported Novgorod ecclesiastical gentry, state officials, and their families. Leading Moscow bureaucrats were the most prominent objects of Ivan's ire. Ivan Viskovatyi, conciliar state secretary, keeper of the seal, and erstwhile head of the Ambassadorial Bureau, headed the list, which included onetime treasurer Nikita Funikov and the heads of the Bureau of Conditional Land, Main Revenue, and the Anti-Brigandage Bureau. A bureaucrat and an oprichnina boyar in Ivan's "court" managed to avoid disgrace by taking the cowl.[36] Viskovatyi, who did not belong to the oprichnina, fell out of favor with astonishing speed: he worked normally on July 12 and died on July 25, 1570. Why Ivan executed his "right-hand men," especially Viskovatyi, remains unknown. Viskovatyi's standard operating procedure of pursuing back-channel contacts with Tatar or Ottoman intelligence assets in Crimea did not constitute treason. No evidence tied Viskovatyi or any other bureaucrat to an anti-oprichnina protest, Novgorod separatism, or boyar opposition. Ivan did not blame Viskovatyi for failures in Livonian War diplomacy. Of all the members of the Muscovite elite, one would expect the greatest loyalty to Ivan from the highest non-noble bureaucrats because their careers rested entirely on royal patronage. That Viskovatyi denounced the oprichnina as he endured fatal torture cannot be confirmed.[37] Ivan did not have a monopoly on venting obviously bogus charges against someone he wanted executed. As was usual by now, sometimes Ivan ordered men executed with their families. Novgorod gentry wives and children also died in the carnage. On the other hand, Ivan sometimes spared relatives. The younger brother of an executed treasurer became keeper of the seal.[38] Ivan continued to mix mercy and brutality, compassion and vengeance, in his repression, governed by personal whim and arbitrariness.

Michel Foucault observed that public torture and execution by governmental authorities served as ritualistic political theater, a "bacchanalia of executions" intended to demonstrate the power of the sovereign. This concept applies to Spanish Inquisition autos-da-fé and the English disemboweling and quartering of traitors. Crowds everywhere always turned out to watch the new versions of bread and circuses.[39] The Moscow executions of 1570 belong to the same phenomenon.

THE ASSEMBLY OF THE LAND OF 1566

The first meeting of an Assembly of the Land in Muscovy in 1566 qualifies as a beacon of light in Muscovy during the years of the oprichnina, a new reform promulgated when Ivan was undoubtedly in control of the government.

In 1566 Ivan summoned an Assembly of the Land to discuss whether to continue the Livonan War or accept a Polish-Lithuanian peace offer to partition Livonia based upon the status quo, meaning that Muscovy would not get Riga and Revel.[40] The document produced by the assembly did not call itself an "assembly" or "council" (*sobor*). Historians infer that denotation from the later history of the institution. Like most monarchs who summoned representative institutions, Ivan did not actually want advice.[41] He expected public support for a policy decision that he had already made. The Assembly of the Land of 1566 was the first of its kind. Previous candidates for that distinction between 1549 and 1566 do not qualify as Assemblies of the Land. No other assembly met during Ivan's reign.[42] The 1566 assembly is thus doubly unique: it was the first and the only such assembly during Ivan's reign.

Muscovite sources inform us about many, but not all, aspects of the assembly. Boyars, clergy, gentry, and merchants attended. Whether any oprichniki were present remains disputed. Technically the oprichnina did not belong to the "land" whose representatives Ivan summoned.[43] "Land" and oprichnina boyars jointly conducted the negotiations with the Polish-Lithuanian delegation at the time of the assembly. Clerics at the assembly offered their "advice" (sovet), laymen only their "thoughts" (mysli). The chronicle passage on the assembly noted that Ivan "spoke" (govoril) to members of various social classes, not that he "consulted" (posovetoval) with them. The central government selected the participants. The government may have assumed that the opinion of any member of a class represented the views of that class as a whole, obviating the necessity for elections. Curiae met by class. All of them unanimously rejected the Polish-Lithuanian offer and advised continuing the war, which they promised to support with their prayers, weapons, or money. We know of no voting rules or debate procedures. Ivan summoned the 1566 assembly specifically for a consultative, not a legislative, function, to advise him, but Muscovites would not have understood that functional distinction. The assembly's resolutions reflected considerable familiarity with the military and diplomatic situation, suggesting government briefing.[44] Ivan permitted Viskovatyi, the state secretary in charge of foreign affairs, to express an individual opinion, but Ivan and the assembly deemed his proposal too clever—to accept the Polish-Lithuanian offer under conditions that permitted Muscovy to violate it.

Historians should take seriously the formal similarity and synchronicity of the Assemblies of the Land to foreign institutions such as Parliament, the Cortes, the Riksdag, the Estates-General, or the Sejm. Those representative assemblies vary so much in structure, timing, development, composition, authority, and influence that the Muscovite Assembly of the Land easily finds a place among them. In the sixteenth century some representative assemblies rose in influence, while others fell. Some became more important in subsequent centuries, but many virtually disappeared. Some defended local noble rights, but most served, and did not oppose, central monarchs. The "non-constitutional" nature of the Muscovite Assembly of the Land does not disqualify it as a comparable institution. Although Muscovy possessed royal and ecclesiastical councils for inspiration, the Muscovite assembly originated much later than its counterparts. Royal need for additional revenue drove the development of representative assemblies elsewhere, but Muscovite rulers could rely on their patrimonial possessions and customary taxation to fund the central government. They did not need a countrywide assembly to vote on new taxes. Nor did any previous foreign policy issue require such an assembly.[45] After Ivan's death, at times Assemblies of the Land elected tsars, passed laws, and ran the country, but such actions have nothing to do with Ivan's conception of the assembly.

Ivan summoned the 1566 assembly to impress the Polish-Lithuanian delegation with a parallel to the Polish and Lithuanian Sejms and to facilitate mobilizing additional domestic support for the Livonian War. If Ivan assumed that everyone would agree with him, then the question of whether he thought the opinions of the participants worthwhile becomes moot.[46]

Ivan never summoned another assembly after 1566. Perhaps he never again needed to mobilize his subjects' support for his foreign policy. Representative assemblies met rarely in England and France at the time, but what representative assemblies accomplished exceeded in importance how frequently they met.[47] Ivan probably decided not to summon another assembly because he took umbrage at an unwelcome by-product of the 1566 meeting. According to Schlichting, some attendees took advantage of the opportunity of gathering together in Moscow to petition Ivan to abolish the oprichnina. No such petition survives. Historians speculate whether metropolitan-designate Filipp, who opposed the oprichnina, colluded with this opposition. Ivan would have been astonished and infuriated. He expected loyal agreement and nothing more. He got loyal agreement on the Livonian War, but much more than he bargained for on the oprichnina. He waited until the Lithuanian delegation left town to react. He ordered the leaders of the petition drive executed and three hundred gentry imprisoned, although he later released them. Historians disagree about the severity and duration of Ivan's all-out war on the properties of the senior "land" boyar Ivan Fedorov-Cheliadnin and about its possible connection to the assembly protest. It was Fedorov-Cheliadnin's leadership of the "land" protest against the oprichnina and not, per Schlichting, his role in a conspiracy to assassinate Ivan or aspirations to sit on the tsar's throne that motivated Ivan's death sentence.[48]

The fate of the attendees at the assembly indicates either extremely widespread dissent against the oprichnina among members of the elite or indiscriminate repression by Ivan. Ivan eventually executed nine of seventeen boyars, the treasurer, the keeper of the seal, three of six conciliar state secretaries, eleven of thirty-three rank-and-file bureaucrats and state officials, and twenty-nine gentry participants in the assembly.[49] Some, perhaps most, of these deaths may have been unrelated to the assembly, but one wonders how enthusiastically Muscovites would have responded after 1566 to an invitation to another assembly.

The 1566 assembly protest and its denouement conform to the usual dynamic of political terror. Repression generates its own opposition. Evidence of opposition to the oprichnina outside the Assembly of the Land is sparse. Staden's reports that oprichniki faced violent popular wrath lack credibility. He claimed that he had rescued six oprichniki from three hundred infuriated members of the "land," and that he had "heard" that people from the "land" massacred five hundred oprichnina musketeers.[50] Distance from Moscow would have permitted greater resistance. Oprichniki depredations must have faced some resistance. If Ivan intended the oprichnina to repress a certain kind of opposition to his rule, he now faced opposition from entirely different segments of society—specifically, from the gentry on whom he supposedly depended to counter the influence of the boyars. It is not clear whom the oprichnina was originally meant to repress. However, no one has suggested that in 1565 Ivan thought that the gentry, the social base of his regime, constituted his primary enemy. Nevertheless, the oprichnina generated opposition precisely among the gentry, despite the fact that gentry predominated among the oprichniki. If Ivan created the oprichnina to deal with existing political dissent, it then made the situation worse by creating additional opposition.

THE CRIMEAN RAID OF 1571 AND THE ABOLITION OF THE OPRICHNINA

Despite the ongoing Livonian War, Moscow remained acutely conscious of the threat of Crimean slave raids on its southern and southeastern frontier. For two decades after the conquests of Kazan and Astrakhan and during the oprichnina, Ivan continued building new fortress-cities on the southern frontier. Muscovite diplomacy had tried to check Crimean raids by going over the head of the Crimean khan to the Ottoman sultan, but that tactic failed.[51]

In 1571 a series of Royal Council decrees established a new, more sophisticated system of frontier scouts and lookout posts, under the direction of Prince Vasilii Vorotynskii, to provide advance warning of impending raids. Government employees, gentry, town Cossacks, serving Tatars, and Mordva (a Finno-Ugric people living in the middle Volga region) provided the personnel, not, as before, independent Don Cossacks or men from the frontier Sever district.[52] Muscovite intelligence facilities advanced farther into the steppe. Unfortunately, the new system did not begin functioning quickly enough to prevent the Crimeans from reaching Moscow in 1571. Russian scouts sent early warnings, but efforts to anticipate Khan Devlet Girei's route failed. After 1572 the government made strenuous efforts to correct a serious shortfall in manpower and material support on the southern frontier. It established a "border command" separate from the regular mobilization of a field army along the Oka River line.[53] A stronger Muscovite intelligence network and southern defense eventually enabled greater colonization of the southern region.

Devlet Girei originally planned a normal raid. He changed his objective to reaching Moscow on the recommendation of dozens of Muscovite turncoats, identified by name in Muscovite sources, who emphasized his clear path to the defenseless city. The defectors came from Kaluga, Kashira, and Serpukhov, non-oprichnina cities that served as staging areas for defense of the Oka River crossings. Whether anti-oprichnina sentiment animated this betrayal remains an inference. Some defectors bear names that might be Tatar, but it is not clear whether ethnicity influenced their actions. A turncoat Nogai Tatar in the service of an oprichnik defected to Lithuania and then proceeded to Crimea in time to inform Devlet Girei that the situation in Muscovy favored a raid. At least one turncoat returned to Crimea with Devlet Girei and eventually petitioned Ivan for pardon. The disposition of his petition remains unknown. What happened to most of these collaborators escaped notice in the surviving sources. Some of Ivan's subjects had provided the enemy with crucial intelligence before but without such disastrous consequences.[54]

In 1571 Ivan executed his brother-in-law, Prince Mikhail Temriukovich

Cherkasskii. It is unclear why he did so. The confused chronology connecting Cherkasskii's death to the Crimean raid raises unanswerable questions. Was Cherkasskii executed because his father, the Kabarda Circassian Temriuk, joined Devlet Girei's raid, or did Temriuk join the Crimean raid because his son had been executed? Was Cherkasskii executed because a relative defected to Lithuania, or did the relative defect after Mikhail was executed? Was Cherkasskii executed because Ivan *thought* that Temriuk had aided the Crimeans, only to find out afterward that he had not? Was Cherkasskii the victim of disinformation planted by Devlet Girei?[55] Ivan had put Cherkasskii in command of the army defending Moscow from the Crimeans. One way or another his death contributed to that army's poor performance.

Ivan's flight from Moscow could not have helped, either; although the wisdom of not risking the life of the tsar remained paramount. Eventually, Ivan wound up as far away from the scene of the action as he could get, in Rostov. He returned to Moscow only after Devlet Girei got away scot-free. Ivan wept at the number of dead.[56]

Ivan made boyar Prince Ivan Mstislavskii the scapegoat. Mstislavskii admitted "inviting" Devlet Girei to attack. He signed a number of surety charters with enormous penalties should he repeat his offense. Of course Mstislavskii lied to cover for Ivan.[57] Had Ivan believed Mstislavskii's confession, he would have sentenced him to death. Instead, at the intercession of the metropolitan, probably arranged in advance, Ivan pardoned Mstislavskii.

Some historians have argued that the poor performance of oprichnina military units in 1571 and the success of joint oprichnina and "land" forces a year later at Molodi, where they soundly defeated Devlet's second major raid, convinced Ivan to abolish the oprichnina. In fact, steps to reunite the oprichnina and "land," including combining the two halves of Novgorod, the fusion of the "land" and oprichnina treasuries, joint diplomatic activities by "land" and oprichnina boyars, and cooperation of oprichnina and "land" military units, began well before Molodi. Although the oprichnina and "land" still remained separate before 1572, Ivan had already begun phasing out the oprichnina before the battle of Molodi.[58]

Diane Smith convincingly contested the notion that the oprichnina was more effective at murdering unarmed civilians than at fighting Muscovy's enemies. The oprichnina army duplicated the army of the "land" in recruitment, social composition, structure, officer assignment, promotion, precedence, and military effectiveness. Sole blame for the failure to prevent the Crimean burning of Moscow in 1571 does not belong to the oprichnina. Oprichnina forces fought well side by side with those of the "land" as early as 1565. Many oprichnina division commanders, including a few very successful generals, had prior military experience. Some held military appointments as commanders after 1572. Devlet Girei had not defeated the Muscovite armies in 1571, he had avoided them. Ivan executed both oprichnina and "land" commanders after the burning of Moscow. The better prepared, combined oprichnina and "land" army in 1572 forced Devlet Girei to fight on ground of its choice. Historians dispute whether oprichnik Prince Dmitrii Khvorostinin deserved more credit for the victory by his tactical skill than his commander-in-chief from the "land," Prince Mikhail Vorotynskii, but both fought well and deserve credit. For unknown reasons, Ivan later executed Vorotynskii. Historians have tarred all oprichniki with the same reputation as the worst oprichniki executioners, but some served purely military functions honorably.[59]

The burning of Moscow sullied Ivan's international reputation. The story became headline news on the international pamphlet circuit. A vignette repeated with variations by contemporary foreign sources and a later Muscovite chronicle had it that Ivan dressed in a peasant coarse-cloth caftan to plead poverty to the Crimean khan's emissary who was demanding tribute after the burning of Moscow. The envoy supposedly gave Ivan a rusty knife with which to commit suicide. According to the diplomatic archives, the Crimean envoy presented Ivan with a gold knife, an honorable present from a superior to an inferior, which Ivan politely returned. Ivan would not have "dressed down" in public. His typically theatrical protestations of poverty, on the other hand, reflected his usual mixture of humility and arrogance.[60] Circumstances dictated that in his letter to Devlet, Ivan write that he "petitioned" (*bit chelom,* "beat his head," kowtowed to) the Crimean khan, a monumental acknowledgment of subservience and the first time he had so humbled himself. Ivan had to perform such damage control. He was stalling for time for Muscovy's military to recover, seeming to agree to Crimean demands to abandon his conquest of Astrakhan but stipulating impossible conditions. He knew that the Crimea would never consent to the continued presence of a Muscovite official in Astrakhan, which would turn it into a Muscovite vassal state like Kasimov, or to placing it under joint Muscovite-Crimean rule. Muscovy did recover at Molodi in 1572. In 1573

Ivan delivered a long speech to a Crimean envoy regurgitating the history of Muscovite-Crimean relations. Ivan's sense of humor had not deserted him. To Devlet's complaints about Ivan's puny gifts, he responded by citing Devlet's self-proclaimed disinterest in wealth.[61]

The Muscovite defeat by the Tatars in 1571 and the Muscovite victory over the Tatars in 1572 complicate the question of Ivan's military competence. Ultimate responsibility for the burning of Moscow falls on Ivan's shoulders. As tsar, he directed Muscovy's armed forces. He depleted the southern defenses by transferring troops to the Livonian front. On the other hand, if Muscovy still had enough military talent to defeat the Crimeans at Molodi, then Ivan's execution of the Muscovite officer corps during the oprichnina had not left Muscovite forces under the command of only incompetent second- or third-rate officers.[62]

THE EVOLUTION OF THE OPRICHNINA

Ivan the Terrible was the first Rus' ruler to use mass terror as a political weapon. Ruslan Skrynnikov brilliantly encapsulated this defining characteristic of the oprichnina and of Ivan's reign in a single short phrase (two words in Russian, three in English), "reign of terror" (*tsarstvo terrora*), for the title of his most-cited monograph. Mass terror has a logic of its own. In its last phase, terror always makes victims of its own instruments. The oprichnina conformed to this logic. After the attack on Novgorod, Ivan began executing oprichniki such as Prince Andrei Viazemskii, accused of trying to warn that city of Ivan's intentions. For obvious political reasons, Ivan kept these executions less public than those of non-oprichniki. The oprichnina now went to war not only against the "land" but also against itself.[63]

Ivan applied mass terror inconsistently. He had most of his victims arrested, tortured, and executed summarily, without any trial, although he sometimes granted due process to boyars accused of treason for trying to flee the country. Trials followed proper investigations before the normal authorities. If convicted, the accused suffered punishment or enjoyed pardons. Some of the accused even survived the oprichnina and Ivan's reign. In high-profile cases Ivan abandoned all procedural restraint, such as the executions of boyar Ivan Fedorov, appanage Prince Vladimir Staritskii and his family, or bureaucrat Ivan Viskovatii. Historians do not need to rely on lurid and sensational foreign accounts or Kurbskii's *History* to document the scale of these atrocities, often involving desecration of corpses, because of the memorial lists and other documentary sources. "Explaining" this orgy of violence by Ivan's irrationality addresses neither the rationale of mass terror—atrocities create more terror—nor its social context.[64]

It is unlikely that Ivan intended to authorize the oprichniki to rob, torture, or murder anyone other than those victims chosen by him. According to Staden, Ivan instructed his courts always to judge the oprichniki innocent of all charges, although the oprichniki did not get away with unlimited lawlessness, rapine, murder, extortion, or theft. One attempt of an oprichnik to extort land from a resident of the "land" failed.[65] Such occasions were admittedly rare. The oprichniki deserved their reputation for illegality and legal immunity.[66]

The oprichnina consisted of at least three phases: its establishment, its response to the opposition generated by its creation, and its self-liquidation. Skrynnikov deserves credit for recognizing that the oprichnina lacked a single, coherent policy or unified goal. At different times the oprichnina had different objects. Skrynnikov may have exaggerated the number of phases, but all historians divide the oprichnina into phases, whether they realize it or not.[67]

Staden reported that in 1572 Ivan abolished the oprichnina and banned anyone from even saying the word. Some historians contend that the oprichnina continued to exist under another name, the royal household. Ivan did transfer some oprichnina personnel and territory to the royal household. He did not demote, let alone execute, all oprichniki. No decree abolishing the oprichnina survives; no surviving short chronicle mentions its dissolution. Kurbskii would not have mentioned the abolition of the oprichnina because that would have reflected well upon Ivan. The word "oprichnina" did disappear from general usage after 1572, although complete censorship of the word proved impossible in a manuscript culture. The taboo placed upon the word "oprichnina" might explain its absence from monastic short chronicles covering Ivan's reign from 1572 to 1584.[68]

The royal household did not continue the oprichnina under another name. The oprichnina had its own household to administer royal estates and enterprises in oprichnina territory. Oprichnina household majordomos and treasurers duplicated "land" royal household offices.[69] A 1573 document defining the "household" committed a lapse in the supposed taboo on usage of the word by indicating that one man received fifty rubles in the "land" but had no allotment in the oprichnina. This error does not mean that the oprichnina still existed as the royal household. If Ivan originally thought that he could administer the oprichnina with a skeleton staff of members of his household, reality soon disabused him of that delusion.[70] The contrast between "land" and royal household personnel in the registers after 1572 reflected the usual division between them before 1564, no more. The post-1572 royal household lacked the symbols of the oprichnina and mass terror.

THE OPRICHNINA AND THE COURSE OF MUSCOVITE HISTORY

Historians have drawn dire conclusions about the impact of the oprichnina on Muscovite history. Makovskii concluded that it aborted the growth of capitalism in Muscovy. Pavlov and Perry concluded that it terminated the development in Muscovy of an estate monarchy in which corporate estates would have acquired legal rights and privileges that would eventually have restricted the autocratic power of the ruler. Other historians have concluded that Ivan permanently turned Russia away from the path leading to democratic constitutional monarchy and onto the path leading to "Asiatic despotism."[71] In the sixteenth century "constitutional development" or "democracy" did not exist, and Muscovy's Western neighbors did not adhere to a single path of development. "Asiatic" or "Oriental despotism" does not constitute a form of government. The rulers of Muscovy's Tatar neighbors, as the Muscovites knew full well, were answerable to various vested interests among their subjects.[72] The "great man in history" paradigm has its value, but Ivan did not personally exercise enough influence to decide Russia's fate by himself. Such fatalism deprives Ivan's successors of any historical agency. Ivan abolished the oprichnina, and no later Muscovite tsar employed mass terror.

EVALUATING THE OPRICHNINA

Whether the oprichnina can be said to have succeeded depends upon what we assume to have been its goals. If Ivan was insane, then the oprichnina had no goal. If he wanted to extinguish boyar conspiracies to assassinate him, he failed because there were none. If he intended to destroy the power base of the aristocracy or the aristocracy itself and replace it with the gentry, he failed. If he sought to destroy the appanage system or nonexistent Novgorodian separatism or the autonomy of the Russian Orthodox Church, he failed. If he sought personal security, even he thought that he had failed. If he intended to establish a personal dictatorship, he failed. If he intended the oprichnina as a lasting contribution to Muscovite administration, he failed. If he sought to make the Muscovite state more centralized, he failed. As an experiment the oprichnina failed so badly that not one of Ivan's successors imitated it. He did not intend for the oprichnina to wreck the Muscovite economy, but it did.[73] He did not intend to reduce the country to chaos, but he did. He abolished the oprichnina because of its unintended consequences.

To punish traitors, or any political opponents, Ivan did not need oprichniki in black clothes riding black horses with dogs' heads on their necks and brooms. A musketeer and gentry bodyguard would have sufficed. For such bodyguards it would have been superfluous to imitate a monastic brotherhood, impose residential segregation, or require oaths not to communicate with non-bodyguards. Yet Ivan created the oprichnina with precisely those characteristics. In the next chapter I will propose a different interpretation of Ivan's goal in establishing the oprichnina, one that foregrounds precisely its unique features.

We can conclude here that, despite positive reforms such as the creation of the southern frontier intelligence service and the creation of the Assembly of the Land, the oprichnina defies any justification on political or religious grounds. Ivan deserves all the opprobrium heaped upon him for its atrocities. Gaining a better understanding of the process by which Ivan came to commit such inhuman acts cannot alter that judgment.

16

Ivan's Ideology, the Oprichnina, and Muscovite Society

A viable interpretation of the *oprichnina* should take into account two fundamental but separate factors: Ivan's intentions in creating it, and how Muscovite society responded to his actions. The evolution of the oprichnina resulted from the interaction of Ivan and society. He felt morally and intellectually (but *not* physically) overburdened by the multiple layers of Muscovite ruler-myth ideology. He could not resolve the contradiction between his personal wish to be pious and the demands of his office, which required him to act impiously, so he pretended to abdicate, knowing that he could not or would not actually renounce power. In this sense Ivan programmed the oprichnina to fail. He had staged a spectacle, not perpetrated a coup d'état. He could not seize power because he already had power.

Because Ivan did not abdicate, his personal act had political consequences. Ivan created an autonomous zone that he tried, but failed, to isolate from society. The residential and social isolation of the *oprichniki* from non-oprichniki reflected Ivan's desire to divorce himself from the rest of Muscovite society. Politically, Ivan's actions in establishing the oprichnina institution—such as deporting population—created political opposition. The spontaneous lawlessness of the oprichniki exacerbated that opposition. When fighting that opposition elevated repression from a secondary by-product of the oprichnina to its primary function, Ivan turned to mass terror. Mass terror, in turn, fed upon the long-repressed strains on Muscovite society resulting from a century of directed change in the form of social mobilization and social engineering—integration of the boyars and the creation of the gentry and the bureaucracy. This combination of terror and social malaise proved explosive. Mass terror drew its dynamism from Muscovite social disorder, and it followed its own inexorable logic to self-destruction. The elite used the oprichnina to settle intra-class feuds. Mass terror produced the massacres of the northwest campaign and the horrors of the Moscow mass executions. The antisocial behavior of the oprichniki inflicted huge harm upon Muscovite society and forced Ivan to terrorize the oprichniki. Everybody in Muscovy lost, including Ivan. The interaction between Ivan's intentions and actions, and between Muscovite society's reactions and social problems, determined the evolution of the oprichnina.

This chapter elucidates the Muscovite ruler cult that animated and confounded Ivan until he sought respite off the throne. Then it will analyze the evolution of Muscovite society, which generated the destructive energy unleashed by the oprichnina.

THE OPRICHNINA AS IDEOLOGICAL OVERLOAD

Michael Cherniavsky interpreted Ivan's actions as the product of the accumulation of ideological burdens on the Muscovite ruler. Ivan's political ideology consisted of three layers of myths, the first two of which consisted of two images in tension: Mongol khan and Byzantine basileus, saintly prince and pious tsar, and Renaissance prince.

The first layer comprised the tension between the ruler as Mongol khan, a secular image rooted in conquest, and the ruler as Byzantine basileus, a religious image rooted in Orthodox Christianity. The unresolved conflict between the two images manifested itself tragically in Ivan's "killing by day and praying by night."[1]

The tension between the ruler as saintly prince and the ruler as pious tsar comprised the second layer. The earlier image of the saintly prince of Kievan Rus' had obviated the distinction between the king's two bodies, as ruler and as person. The image of the pious tsar, obligated to preserve the purity of Muscovite Orthodox Christianity, superseded the image of the saintly prince and generated apocalyptic consequences. Ivan fused the two.

He internalized his divine function to such an extent that, in his first letter to Kurbskii, he argued that opposition to him meant opposition to God. Anyone who opposed Ivan not only forfeited his body but also his soul and the souls of his ancestors. If the tsar was a saint and Christlike, then anyone who claimed the right to share the tsar's authority committed blasphemy. Political opposition to the tsar became heresy. The ruler led the people to salvation. Anyone who interfered with the fulfillment of the state's purpose contradicted divine will.[2]

The image of Ivan as a Renaissance prince comprised the third layer. Ivan had not read Machiavelli's *The Prince*. Ivan's self-image as a Renaissance prince resulted from parallel development, not Italian influence.[3] Cherniavsky related Ivan to a cohort of contemporary or near contemporary rulers who acquired reputations as "terrible" (regardless of the accuracy of that reputation), including Kings Richard III and Henry VIII in England, King Louis XI in France, King Philip II in Spain, *condottieri* (mercenary) "Lord" Sigismondo Malatesta, Pope Alexander VI (Rodrigo de Borja), and power broker and warlord Cesare Borgia in Italy, King Christian (Kristian, Christiern) II of Denmark, and Erik XIV of Sweden.[4]

Cherniavsky, extrapolating from Ivan's first letter to Kurbskii, connected Ivan's conception of rule with his use of terror: "The tsar ruled through terror reasonably, that is, deliberately, and through terror saved men, both their souls and their bodies. . . . What was new was the emphasis on the power of fear, the conscious and deliberate use of terror as an instrument of policy and of justice itself."[5] Ivan internalized the Agapetan dichotomy of ruler as human and divine by insisting that a monarch who drew upon the worst in human nature became the best of rulers. Unfortunately, this required the ruler to act like a bad Christian, which made Ivan feel guilty. Such guilt was characteristic of the northwestern or northern Renaissance, in countries along the Baltic Sea and Atlantic Ocean, but absent in the southern Renaissance, primarily Italy. Ivan was wicked in order to be just. Cherniavsky correlated his ideas with contemporary writings by Peresvetov and the "Valaam Discourse." As in Machiavelli, a pessimistic opinion of human nature dictated the need for firm rule. However, in addition to rational terror, this theory of rule also facilitated "the irrational, the personal, humanly monstrous aspects of Ivan's nature—the savagery, the incredible, blasphemous cruelty, the vengefulness," which associated him with the prototypical sadistic ruler, Dracula. Thus, Ivan's actions made him tragic, although not quite a Hamlet. "The terrible ruler is not only terrible in his function but . . . in his person as well, for he has broken though human limitations and cannot be judged by human standards." Cherniavsky cited Jan Kott's *Shakespeare, Our Contemporary* as Shakespearian confirmation of this interpretation of Renaissance monarchy. Foreigners who described Ivan as cruel but just shared this Renaissance ambivalence about the morality of the ruler.[6]

> Ivan the Terrible as a Renaissance prince reflected a Renaissance fusion of two strands of thought and feeling: the idea of the ruler, terrible in his function as ruler, guaranteeing through cruel terror justice and order in a world of weak and evil men and of evolving strong centralized monarchies; and the idea of the awe-inspiring free personality, autonomous of old standards, above human law, and independent of divine law in a world where any means to gain immortality could be considered and utilized. But the fusion was explosive, for it combined political autonomy with an autonomous ego. It legitimized in one persona absolute political power with no limitations except his own interests, and the untrammeled human personality fulfilling itself by exceeding all human limitations. The result frequently was awe-inspiring and monstrous.[7]

The combination of multiple layers of ruler myth gave Ivan ideological flexibility. He could play saintly prince, pious tsar, imperious khan, imperial basileus, or arbitrary and playfully cruel Renaissance prince as the occasion warranted. However, the awareness of his own evil tortured Ivan.[8] The doom and gloom, defeat and disaster, of the later years of Ivan's reign reflected an "enormous ideological escalation, on the part of Ivan certainly, and in the Russian setting as a whole. The events appear to be part of a cosmic drama; everything is measured on a cosmic scale; and Muscovite Russia is a cosmic stage. The political terror is absolute, the defeats catastrophic, the *terribilita* of the tsar world-shaking, and the countryside depopulated."[9]

Recent scholarship has corrected Cherniavsky's exposition on several minor points. He exaggerated the role of Third Rome theory in state ideology in the image of the pious ruler. His dating of the *Kazan History* as a contemporary source has largely been abandoned; the later dating precludes citing it as evidence of Ivan's desire for fame and greatness. To Ivan, aspirations to greatness, fame, or glory would have constituted the sin of pride, although the problem of pride is of course much more complicated. Divine favor toward the Rus' dynasty or toward Ivan personally was supposed to produce humility in the recipient, not arrogance.

Cherniavsky gave too much credence to unreliable atrocity stories about Ivan.Cherniavsky did not explain to his readers that his conception of a Renaissance prince differed from other definitions. By describing Ivan as a Renaissance prince, he did not mean to imply that Ivan patronized Renaissance humanism or art. Recent historians focus on the personalities, ideals, and values of monarchs during the Renaissance period, all of whom shared an overarching ambition to achieve greatness.[10] Cherniavsky implied that Ivan committed excesses to express his individuality and to demonstrate his superiority to mortal law. This was Cherniavsky's greatest error concerning Ivan. Ivan expressed his individuality in his writing. He always insisted upon his subordination to divine law. His atrocities reflect the dynamic of terror, not the Renaissance impulse to achieve fame via infamy. Finally, in print Cherniavsky never integrated his three layers of the ruler myth.

Nevertheless, Cherniavsky's exposition on the whole retains its value. His analysis of the differences between the northern and southern Renaissance makes a great deal of sense. Cesare Borgia, had he lived in England, would never have agonized like Henry VIII over the refusal of Queen Catherine of Aragon to give him a divorce, like Mary Tudor over whether to order the death of Elizabeth I, or like Elizabeth I in hesitating to pronounce a death sentence on Mary Stuart. With total equanimity and no sense of guilt, Borgia would have ordered the immediate assassination of anyone who stood in his way politically, as he did when he ordered the murder of his brother-in-law, the husband of his sister Lucrezia Borgia. Moreover, other historical judgments, older and recent, corroborate Cherniavsky's approach. Gratuitous, monstrous cruelty and deliberate terrorism definitely resonate with Jakob Burckhardt's depiction of Renaissance Italian condottieri. Even the great humanist Erasmus accepted the need to tolerate rulers who violated the Gospel in their public actions.[11]

Cherniavsky presented a persuasive context in which to understand Ivan's desire to escape his ideological burden, the obligation to commit un-Christian acts in order to rule effectively, by ceasing to be a ruler. Evidence supporting this view includes Ivan's pseudo-abdications in 1564 and 1575, fantasies of asylum in England, and delusions about becoming a monk, which Cherniavsky did not explicitly invoke.[12] (Historians often interpret

these events as proof of Ivan's paranoia.) Historical and contemporary foreign rulers had set precedents for voluntary abdication to become monks:
in 889 Bulgarian Khan Boris; in 1196 Serbian ruler Stepan Nemanja; and
between 1539 and 1556 Holy Roman Emperor Charles V (Charles I of Spain),
who definitely retired to a monastery but may not have actually become a
monk. Louis of Bavaria disguised himself as a pilgrim, worked as a gardener,
and thought himself a monk, suggesting a combination of mental illness
and abdication. Ivan certainly knew about Nemanja, could have known
about Boris, and should have been aware of Charles V.[13] If Ivan had read the
Nikon Chronicle, he could have learned about Vojshelk, son of Lithuanian
Grand Duke Mindaugus, who took the cowl but left his monastery to
suppress his father's assassins and then returned to his cloister.[14] Ivan did not
take the cowl until he lay dying, and he performed only sham abdications.
His refusal to cut the Gordian knot of his ideological overload by actually
giving up power resulted in repeated phony abdication scenarios.

Cherniavsky's analysis provides an ideological explanation for the attempted isolation of the oprichniki from "normal" Muscovite society. Ivan
sought symbolic and physical autonomy from his role as ruler. In Muscovite
society, to achieve salvation apart from the temptations of daily life, one became a monk: hence the pseudo-monastic brotherhood at Aleksandrovskaia
Sloboda and the equivalent of monastic vows, not of poverty, asceticism,
or silence but, in the oath of the oprichniki, of obedience to Ivan, isolation
from families, and abstention from socializing with outsiders.

Of course, Ivan did not renounce power or his political obligations. He
retained power not only within his appanage, the oprichnina, where he
possessed autonomy, but also in Muscovy, where he remained in control of
foreign policy, warfare, and major policy decisions. He was constrained, as
before his "abdication," by custom. Ivan enjoyed no social isolation from
the "land." Although a personal desire to avoid politics inspired the creation
of the oprichnina, its establishment had tangible political consequences.
The opposition it inspired fed Ivan's violent excesses. In this sense the lack
of restraint by the oprichniki mimicked Ivan's own lack of restraint in
his behavior. Moreover, the oprichnina became the vehicle through which
several elite classes of Muscovite society—boyars, gentry, and bureaucrats—
could relieve the tensions created by a century of social change in the most
dysfunctional way imaginable, with unmitigated violence. Cherniavsky correlated the development of the seventeenth-century schism in the Russian

Orthodox Church to changes in Muscovite society,[15] but he never attempted to relate the social pathology of the oprichnina—mass terror, lawlessness, and crime—to the inability of sixteenth-century Muscovite society to tolerate degrees of social change and mobility beyond the limits of a traditional society. I use the term "traditional society" to emphasize the contrast to "modern" societies in which upward social mobility is viewed as far more legitimate, in the United States even encouraged, than in societies that see all social mobility, upward or downward, as a threat to stability, and caste societies, in which all social mobility is forbidden. Cherniavsky focused on the cultural context of Ivan's Renaissance moral contradiction, to the exclusion of its social context. We will now try to fill that lacuna.

THE OPRICHNINA AND MUSCOVITE SOCIETY

Muscovite society influenced the evolution of the oprichnina. Social change created problems in all contemporary states, lethally in France, where aristocratic assassination politics unleashed the popular mayhem of the St. Bartholomew's Day massacre.[16] Choices between central and indigenous values, processes, and priorities drove provincial Muscovite political culture. To understand its interaction with the oprichnina, it is necessary to examine Muscovite society.[17] Anti-banditry legislation, the increase in slavery, the rise of social critics such as the holy fools, and elite concern with social problems reflect social change and tension during the pre-oprichnina era.[18] Historians usually see the oprichnina as the cause of the social instability of the Time of Troubles, but social instability contributed to transforming the oprichnina into mass terror and social chaos.

Descriptions of Muscovite society during Ivan's reign lack precision. Historians refer to estates during that period, although Muscovy did not become a caste or estate society, in which everyone inherited his social place and social mobility was forbidden, until passage of the Conciliar Law Code of 1649, if then. Some Western historians resist applying the term "class" to social groups in the sixteenth century for fear of the Marxist definition of class. Because historians cannot describe social groups during Ivan's reign as "estates," they should use the term "class" with a social definition, to describe a group of people with a common social identity.[19]

Muscovite society during Ivan's reign constituted a typical traditional society, in which most people inherited their social status and some social mobility was tolerated, in contrast to Burckhardt's Renaissance Italian ideal, in which by and large birth did not matter. Social consensus and social conflict obtained in all sixteenth-century societies in unstable ratios.[20] Traditional societies can tolerate a limited amount of upward and downward social mobility. Up to and during Ivan's reign, Muscovite society experienced a degree of social mobility well beyond those limits. The excessive strains on Muscovite society manifested themselves in the excesses of the oprichnina.

This process began at the end of the fifteenth century, when Muscovy embarked on a large-scale program of social engineering.[21] The government began creating the service gentry and bureaucratic classes to supplement the boyars. Boyars were too few in number to staff all military and civilian offices and too noble to fulfill the role of paper-pushers. Such social engineering created social dislocation. Ivan's social policies exacerbated this social instability.

The Muscovite regime lacked the institutional apparatus—a large standing army, a national police force, a bureaucracy that projected central authority into the provinces—to rule by coercion alone. It had no choice but to utilize nonviolent mechanisms to create social consensus. The beliefs, rituals, and practices of the Russian Orthodox Church united the elite and lower classes in the quest for salvation. Precedence, consultation, and court ritual and ceremony fostered cohesion between the ruler and the elite.[22] The concepts of dishonor and collective responsibility applied to Muscovite society from top to bottom. The philanthropy and mercy of the tsar also applied to everyone; all his subjects could petition him to request succor. As in every contemporary state, violence or the threat of violence reinforced social integration, but these cohesive forces could not contain Muscovy's rising social tensions indefinitely.

The Components of Muscovite Society

As in all contemporary states, Muscovy's social classes formed a hierarchy. Each social class stood in a position of superiority or inferiority to every other social class. For example, all well-born nobles outranked all bureaucrats. We will examine evidence of social change among boyars, princes, gentry, bureaucrats, merchants, peasants, slaves, clergy, musketeers, women, and Cossacks. Social divisions within each of these classes remain outside this discussion.[23]

The boyars occupied the highest social rank in Muscovy, exceeded only by the ruling dynasty. "Boyar" referred both to an assigned office in the Royal Council and to an inherited social status, membership in one of the forty to sixty elite clans that supplied boyars. Historians referring to "the boyars" usually subsume associate boyars within that category. Only a boyar could hold the most prestigious governorships, generalships, and usually the highest diplomatic ranks (a conciliar state secretary in charge of the Ambassadorial Bureau such as Viskovatyi could, although less often, head a diplomatic mission). Like some other powerful aristocracies, the boyars did not need inherited office to maintain their influence. Purchases, royal grants, and conditional landholding more than offset the supposedly destructive impact of partible inheritance and the absence of primogeniture upon inherited boyar landed wealth. The boyars comprised the wealthiest class in Muscovy.[24]

The preeminent social status of the boyars as a class did not preclude instability among individual boyars, boyar clans, and boyar lineages. The lethal boyar feuds of Ivan's minority and the sometimes lethal process of boyar accommodation to the pretensions of a maturing grand prince and then tsar increased the insecurity of boyar life. Most boyars achieved their rank because of genealogical seniority in their clans,[25] although powerful boyar clans could arrange boyar status for lesser relatives or deny it to otherwise deserving heads of rival clans. A clan could lose boyar status when death in war, disease, or high infant mortality deprived it of male heirs. The disappearance of one lineage of a boyar clan might provide an opportunity for a junior lineage of that clan to acquire boyar status. Many descendants of boyar clans lost boyar status.[26] Although boyars resided at court in Moscow, they did not need the social skills of Castiglione's courtiers and did not incur the risks of court life he described. Nevertheless, the boyars still remained vulnerable.[27]

An adult ruler regulated boyar clan rivalries but added other sources of unpredictability. Favorites and royal in-laws could rise to boyar rank. Such parvenus were few in number, as few as the members of the English gentry or bourgeoisie who bought their way into the English titled nobility, but they attracted disproportionate attention from traditionalists. New aristocrats everywhere assimilated old aristocratic values and lifestyles. The disgrace or execution of a family member could destroy a boyar clan's standing, although a demoted boyar could be pardoned and sometimes the clan survived a member's disgrace. Similarly, boyar favorites could lose favor, and the ruler could discard boyar in-laws when he discarded royal wives. Members of a boyar clan could suffer different fates.[28] A new ruler usually increased the number of boyars in order to gain political support. Only a handful of disgruntled boyars resorted to the extreme measure of emigrating to Lithuania, Sweden, or Crimea. During the oprichnina Ivan did not replace most boyars, whether they died naturally or unnaturally. The Royal Council in 1572 included only eight of its fifty-two members from 1564. The size of the ("land") Royal Council shrank from sixty bo-yars and associate boyars to eighteen, approximately its number in 1533. Notwithstanding kinship customary rights, boyar membership experienced considerable, even excessive, turnover.[29]

Despite boyar clan competition, the boyars as a class possessed consid-erable social cohesion. The precedence system fostered mutual suspicion and engendered endless lawsuits, but it also united the boyars (and gentry who qualified for inclusion in the system) against those not included in the system. Neither the distinction between princely and non-princely boyars nor differences in real or legendary ethnic origin produced boyar factions.[30]

Like the English aristocracy of the time, boyars, but not the boyar class as a whole, underwent considerable strain during Ivan's reign as a result of upward and downward social mobility. Unlike French nobles, boyars did not have to deal with the Reformation, lawyers, and domination by nobles of high clerical office. Historians disagree about the vaunted antagonism between the nobilities of the sword and the robe in France.[31] While gentry, bureaucrats, and merchants in Muscovy could purchase estates, they could not as elsewhere rise in social status by emulating the boyar lifestyle. Pro-portionally, no class suffered more from the oprichnina than the boyars, but, despite complaints by Kurbskii in his *History* about social-climbing bureaucrats, boyars experienced insecurity individually, not collectively.

Class, ethnic origin, place of service, and category divided princes. Princes included descendants of the legendary founder of the Rus' dynasty, Riurik, or more accurately of St. Vladimir, the baptizer of Rus'; descendants of the Lithuanian grand duke Gedminas; and converted non-Chinggisid Tatar begs. Some princes belonged to the boyars, but the vast majority be-longed to the gentry. A non-princely boyar outranked a prince gentry-man. Precedence suits testify that princes competed against each other for status.[32] Three distinct categories of princes existed: appanage, "special princes," and "serving princes." Appanage princes, as members of the royal family, were completely separate from all other princes.

No currently proposed definition of "special princes" (*kniazhata*) is satisfactory.[33] Special princes differed from boyars, but their special status did not make them equal to boyars. Because they were not members of the royal household, special princes could not serve as master of the horse, armorer, or majordomo. The resolutions of the Assembly of the Land of 1566 did not list special princes as a separate curia, but the summary of its proceedings attributed its recommendations to "special princes, gentry and courtiers [*dvoriane*]."[34] Inadequate sources preclude adequate study of this subset of princes: no individual is ever identified as a "special prince."

Southwestern "serving princes," after they switched their loyalty to Muscovy, retained their own courts, boyars, and even musketeers. The registers grouped serving princes by clan family name in field armies. It took several generations for the descendants of serving princes to become fully integrated into the boyar elite. They then lost their serving prince status and regalian rights and sometimes their patrimonies. Whether Ivan opposed their autonomous status as such remains unclear. Legislation attempted to preserve their family landowning, but the oprichnina victimized serving princes.[35]

Princely status mattered socially. A prince always remained a prince and had to be addressed as a prince. Before the sixteenth century, some princely lines had lost their princely status, but apparently none did so during the sixteenth century.[36] Male princely status depended entirely on inheritance. Generic lists of Muscovite social groups usually listed princes immediately after members of the royal family. Prince Kurbskii recounted princely martyrs first in his *History*. Plinth inscriptions violated funerary egalitarianism by noting the deceased's princely title.[37] If boyar princes favored military careers, sons of princely gentry, unlike sons of non-princely gentry, almost never became clerks, preferring judicial or administrative service.[38]

The social problems of boyar and gentry princes derived from their class affiliations, not their princely status. Dynastic politics destroyed some appanage princes. The abolition of serving princely status turned serving princes into boyars or gentry with princely titles. The fate of special princes remains as mysterious as their identity.

The gentry (*deti boiare*) constituted the largest, fastest growing, most economically vulnerable, and most socially unstable segment of the elite. Population growth within the gentry alone probably could not have met

Ivan's need for additional military servitors. Additional gentry derived most-ly from families of clerks and bureaucrats.[39]

To serve, gentry needed land with labor. Partible inheritance did not inevitably lead to impoverishment among gentry any more than among boyars. Most gentry had only conditional land grants. The government promised serving gentry a certain amount of land and a cash allotment, but in practice it guaranteed neither. Gentry often successfully petitioned the government to assign a father's conditional estate to his son, even a minor son, but that did not make conditional estates legally inheritable.[40] A servitor deprived of his conditional estate for not appearing for service could petition for its return, but he had to provide a valid excuse for his ab-sence. Conditional landed estates endured the same economic insecurity as small patrimonial estates. The poorest gentry had no peasants and worked the land themselves. They probably could not afford to perform military service. A significant minority of gentry servitors with peasants needed supplemental government grants in money, grain, or military equipment to support their service. A servitor who ruined his estate, seeking short-term gain on the premise that he or his heir would not retain it, risked not receiv-ing another estate. Turnover in conditional landholding varied by district and period. The greatest discontinuity occurred during the oprichnina.[41]

A change in conditional landholders' rights toward peasants may reflect economic and social change. Beginning in 1541 grants of conditional land increasingly shifted from obliging peasants to pay rent according to tradi-tion (*po starine*) to peasants paying whatever rent the lord imposed (*obrok vam izobrochit*).[42] Over sixty charters contain the new language. The change spread most notably during and after the 1560s. The traditional formula continued to appear in a majority of charters, however. The change in language may represent a change in practice. The authority of the lord to set the level of peasant exploitation probably reflected a greater need for revenue among the gentry because of more frequent, lengthier, and more costly military service. The new formula did not imply an open invitation to predatory gentry treatment of the peasantry, lest the peasantry be ruined.[43] Perhaps the government altered the phrase to give gentry the flexibility to adjust existing customary dues to current economic conditions. In the last analysis what stands out most is the partial abandonment of a formula invoking tradition.

Gentry accumulated significant debts. The Law Code of 1550 forbade gentry to sell themselves into limited-contract slavery. As early as 1558 the government provided debt relief for insolvent gentry. By the later stages of the Livonian War gentry constituted the bulk of the growing number of draft dodgers (*netchiki*) who failed to show up for muster. Well-to-do gentry donated money or land to monasteries. Impoverished gentry, fighting a losing battle with epidemics, crop failures, runaway or stolen peasants, and the burden of incessant warfare, might have been attracted to the solace of the monastery, but they could not afford to purchase cells. Some gentry fled the country.[44]

On the other hand, service as anti-banditry or local government tax collectors reinforced the gentry's social identity as the leading provincial social class. Gentry remained socially selective in their marriage partners. They did not marry into peasant, merchant, or clergy families.[45]

Historians have assumed rather than demonstrated what the gentry thought about the boyars who dominated the government. The number of gentry from déclassé boyar descendants and from princes who had lost their princely title was probably too small, compared to the size of the gentry class as a whole, to have much weight in determining that opinion. Andrei Staritskii's largely unsuccessful 1537 appeal to the Novgorod gentry constitutes the only evidence of class antagonism between gentry and boyars. The social boundary between gentry and boyars was porous; demoted boyars and upwardly mobile gentry broached it, and sources describe sons from boyar families who had not yet attained boyar rank as "gentry." Nevertheless, boyars and gentry remained distinct social classes. It was unusual for the son of a boyar (literally, not a member of the gentry called in Russian a "son of a boyar" [*syn boiarskii*]) to be made a conciliar gentry-man (*dumnyi dvorianin*), keeping in mind that "*dvorianin*" means "gentry" rather than "member of the royal household/court" only in this term.[46]

Gentry suffered significant dislocations during Ivan's reign. The oprichnina involved major deportations of gentry into and out of oprichnina districts.[47] Gentry had some room to maneuver to avoid relocation or deportation but probably less than before or after the oprichnina. Gentry might lack emotional attachment to a specific estate, but they could still prefer land in a home district because of proximity to relatives who could help out in times of need. This consideration might have induced gentry to decline or exchange conditional estates. If so, then the dislocations of the oprichnina disrupted gentry lives even more. During the Livonian War, the government relocated over four hundred gentry to, and then back from, Livonia.[48] Whether from warfare or natural causes, young male gentry suffered atrocious mortality rates. Cadastres list numerous conditional estates held by widows with very young children. Dead, missing, or captured gentry constituted a quarter of the Riazan contingent that served in Livonia in 1577.[49] On the other hand, to provincial gentry the oprichnina constituted an opportunity for promotion to previously unattainable military assignments.[50] The gentry constituted a majority of the oprichniki. Given the enormous strains imposed upon the gentry by Ivan's government, granting armed gentry servitors what they took as immunity from the law became a prescription for social disaster, which, ironically and tragically, redounded badly back on the gentry class as a whole.

The class of "scribes" or "secretaries" (*d'iaki*), like the gentry, grew in numbers during Ivan's reign. The highest-ranking bureaucrats, the conciliar state secretaries (*dumnye d'iaki*), ran Moscow bureaus, but they constituted only a small percentage of the government clerks, copyists, and sub-clerks (*pod"iachie*) in Muscovy.[51] The increase in the number of secretaries from non-secretary families masks an enormous and unappreciated social transformation.

The traditional view that secretaries were sons of priests (Russian Orthodox priests had to be married and therefore had sons) is partially true, but most secretaries originated in the (non-princely) gentry.[52] Scores of secretaries belonged to gentry families. Some individuals even moved back and forth between working as scribes and serving in the cavalry. By the mid-sixteenth century sources identify some scribes as the sons of scribes, but scribe families could not satisfy the growing personnel needs of the expanding government apparatus and a society increasingly dependent upon written documentation for land transactions.[53]

Mutually beneficial ties existed between state secretaries and boyars. State secretaries lent money to boyars, served as executors of boyar testaments, and witnessed boyar donations to monasteries. However, only an extraordinary state secretary from a gentry family could rise to the rank of military commander (*voevoda*), and only as an oprichnik. His promotion did not turn out well; he lost his life and the lives of his wife and five relatives, although probably not because of his social origin.[54] With rare exceptions, the social gap between boyars and secretaries precluded intermarriage.

The social consequences of the permeable wall between the gentry and bureaucrats remain unstudied. Service as a state secretary did not convey gentry status. No state secretary became a conciliar gentry-man. Gentry did not improve their social status by becoming secretaries because gentry outranked secretaries. Gentry were included in the precedence system; even the highest ranked conciliar state secretaries were not. Gentry claimed noble birth regardless of their poverty, but status as secretaries derived from professional expertise and secretaries were not nobles regardless of their wealth. In Ivan's reign a father's service as a bureaucrat did not inhibit the careers of his gentry sons.[55] Gentry and scribes did not share a common social identity. The penalties for dishonoring gentry and scribes differed. Historians have no idea how members of the same family shared different social statuses and interacted with each other. Poverty could not induce a gentry-man to abandon his status as "well-born" to become a non-noble bureaucrat, the motive for gentry self-sale into slavery, because only the highest-ranking bureaucratic clerks became rich. How individuals who crossed the social divide between gentry and clerk viewed their changing social identities remains unknown.

All bureaucrats in the central administration depended entirely upon the goodwill of the ruler for their livelihoods. This was a source of greater instability during Ivan's adulthood, especially during the oprichnina, than during his minority. The state-building enterprise that produced the gentry also magnified the size of the class of scribes, which derived from the gentry. Scribes from the gentry experienced not only changes in profession but also a drastic change in social identity.

Merchants in Moscow played a more varied and vigorous role in the economy and society than traditional scholarship allows. Two legal categories of Muscovite merchants existed during Ivan's reign: "select merchants" (*gosty*; literally, guests) and "trading people" (*torgovye liudi*). The government chose select merchants. Because the profit justified the risk of losing royal favor or incurring popular wrath with government officials via guilt by association, merchants sought this designation, which carried tax exemption. On their own or as royal agents, select merchants dominated foreign trade.[56] Some select merchants became prominent enough to be singled out for execution during the oprichnina, especially merchants from Novgorod, as opposed to artisan casualties who became collateral damage.

Trading people dominated local trade, but not everyone engaged in trade qualified legally and/or socially as a merchant. In the countryside many peasants earned their living as traders.[57] De facto middling merchants and artisans, whether "taxable" (*tiaglye*) urban dwellers or peasants, served as collectors of customs tolls (*tamga*), tax farmers, and collectors of revenue from state-run taverns (*kabaki*).[58] Merchants made money serving as government officials, which changed their social status, or fulfilling government functions.

Scattered evidence suggests that the government tried to move all major provincial merchants to Moscow after the 1571 fire to repopulate its commercial ranks, forcibly relocating merchants from many regional cities. Merchants, like gentry, resisted relocation by retaining ties to their former domiciles.[59] Select merchants did not disappear from the countryside, however.

Muscovite merchants enjoyed a respectable social status and economic well-being. They did not hesitate to exhibit their wealth by endowing churches and making religious donations. Merchants did not feel the need to hide their wealth from Ivan, lest he confiscate it.[60] Merchants traveled by land or sea to Central, Northern, and Eastern Europe, the Middle East, and Central Asia on commercial, diplomatic, and philanthropic missions. The effects of such international experience upon merchant mentality remain unstudied. International entrepreneurial travel refutes the cliché image of the isolated, passive, conservative, and dependent Muscovite merchant. The Stroganovs achieved exceptional economic success in salt manufacture and fur trapping, but other merchants also displayed economic initiative unimpaired by Muscovy's economic, social, or political structure. Such activity bespeaks social confidence.

In the sixteenth century international commerce always involved great risks from both natural and human hazards. As the Livonian War progressed Muscovite merchants had to adjust first to trading in Narva and then to not trading in Narva. Oprichnina devastation of Novgorod and Pskov and Tatar destruction of Moscow hurt merchants. The murder of merchants and confiscation of their property during the oprichnina, along with compulsory relocation, must have had an impact. The merchants as a class survived these vicissitudes well, but individual merchants faced greater insecurity, with the exception of the Stroganovs. Declines in merchant income and the state revenue collected by merchants affected everyone dependent upon government economic resources.

Peasants constituted the overwhelming majority of the population—at least 90 percent. Peasants included not just farmers but people engaged in commerce, extractive industries, and artisan trades. Despite periodic crop failures and local famines, subsistence agriculture fed the country. One way or another, peasants paid for the dynasty, the boyars, the gentry, the bureaucrats, and the church, as well as sustaining the merchants and artisans who sold them goods or services.[61] The economy placed great pressure upon the peasantry.

The transformation of the peasants into serfs, which restricted their right of movement and increased the rights of private landowners, lay or clerical, over the peasantry, dominates scholarship on the peasantry. Serfdom did not exist during Ivan's reign, and calling Muscovite peasants at this time "serfs" misstates their legal status. The Law Code of 1550 tinkered with peasant departure fees, but otherwise it left the right to peasant movement unchanged.[62] Peasants who left the countryside to live in urban enclaves could not become free in a year and a day, as happened in medieval imperial German cities, where "urban air makes free," because they were not "unfree" to begin with. Ivan's decrees forbade the illegal "export" of peasants, coerced peasant movement, and peasant movement without due process. Monasteries, gentry, and princes, who needed more peasant labor than they had, cheated. Illegal peasant movement disproportionately hurt conditional landholders and "black" (state) peasants.[63] The mobility of peasants varied geographically, chronologically, and depending on whose land they occupied. Muscovy did not experience anything equivalent to the massive enclosure movement in England that drove peasants from the land. Some Muscovite peasants moved voluntarily, others involuntarily.[64]

Because of the collapse of the economy in the 1580s, the central government issued the Forbidden Years (*zapovednye leta*) decrees, forbidding all peasant movement, which historians have almost always interpreted as a step toward serfdom because peasants never reacquired the right to move. (During the early seventeenth-century famines peasants were temporarily allowed to move to avoid starvation.)[65] The sources that refer to the Forbidden Years during Ivan's reign all date to after 1584 and may have been projecting the practice back in time to shift responsibility from Tsar Fedor to his father. Even if Ivan did begin to issue Forbidden Years decrees, annual prohibitions on peasant movement did not constitute serfdom because peasants remained technically free to move as soon as the Forbidden Year decree for a given year expired. Events, not Ivan's intentions, altered the impact of the Forbidden Years decrees.[66]

The status of some peasants did decline during Ivan's reign. Ivan transferred "black" peasant settlements to the gentry, which deprived them of
some autonomy. "Owners of their own land" (*svoezemtsy*), who owned land
like servitors but engaged in agriculture like peasants, became state peasants
socially (without losing their land); this clearly represented downward social
mobility.[67] Peasant activity reflects continued common identity. Despite their
geographic dispersal, peasants petitioned the state collectively from villages,
or even districts, for redress of grievances. We can assume that they petitioned landlords in a similar way, although no petitions to landlords survive.
Most peasant petitions asserted a violation of custom, although we have no
petitions objecting to the shift in rents from custom to landlord discretion.

Not many peasants escaped oppression in the center and northwest by
fleeing to the newly acquired lands of the middle Volga. Peasants would
hardly move to regions in the midst of rebellions and punitive expeditions.[68]
Only the areas of the former Kazan Khanate contiguous with core Muscovite territory experienced some peasant in-migration. Nor did peasants
migrate in large numbers across the Urals to Siberia because annexation of
the Khanate of Sibir came after Ivan's death.[69]

Peasants did move geographically and socially. Increasingly, physical
movement from a poorer landed estate to a richer one resulted from pirating
(*vyvoz*; literally, "export") of peasants, as richer owners paid off peasants'
debts so that they could "voluntarily" migrate to newer settlements, or from
outright kidnapping by powerful landowners, including oprichniki. Some
peasants also ran away socially to join the Don Cossacks.[70] The ranks of
the peasantry increased with the migration to Muscovy of Tatars, some
of whom converted to Orthodox Christianity, some of whom did not.[71]
Peasants must have contributed to the increasing ranks of priests, clerks,
and musketeers, which constituted upward social mobility. Some must have
joined the rural proletariat by becoming free hired labor confusingly also
called "Cossacks" (*kazaki*). Others definitely moved down the social scale
to become slaves; "wandering people" (*guliashchie liudi*, "rural vagrants"), a
social substratum found in other countries too; or to join the always volatile
urban lumpen proletariat of day laborers, beggars, urban vagrants, and
criminals.[72] Historians cannot quantify any of this peasant social instability.

The most often cited evidence of peasant flight from the economic crisis,
the cadastres from the 1570s and early 1580s, especially in the northwest
and center, recorded up to 90 percent of all peasant households as "empty."

The cadastres listed the causes of peasant flight very specifically, including famine, disease, death, taxes, war, or the oprichnina, but often described the current whereabouts of their former occupants more vaguely as "unknown." Census takers (*pistsy*) did not visit every peasant hut to record its occupancy or vacancy. Instead, they traveled from district center to district center, querying local informants. No doubt many homesteads were empty, and some landlords did have to adjust to labor shortages. Some peasants could, no doubt, disappear without a trace, and many just died.[73]

However, it is unlikely that half to three-quarters of the peasants of any district could just vanish. We lack evidence of sufficient peasant in-migration to the middle Volga region, the Don Cossacks, or anywhere else, for that matter. After Ivan's death, most depopulated regions seemingly miraculously rediscovered much of their population, tax revenue recovered, and the state resumed aggressive spending without forced loans. It seems plausible to infer that "empty" meant "unable to pay taxes" and that some peasants had fled only locally, to nearby forests or marshes, neighboring and more prosperous estates, or the borders of their province, and returned to their homesteads a short time later. Of course, some landowners simply hid some settlements from the census takers in old-fashioned tax evasion. It remains true that we cannot account for the whereabouts of approximately half the peasants who had occupied the abandoned homesteads described in the cadastres.

Even if many peasants had not permanently departed from their homes, there is no question that during the last years of Ivan's reign the peasant economy declined drastically. Homesteads unable to pay taxes represent severe economic hardship. While some peasant flight may have been illusory, peasant impoverishment was not.[74]

Peasant instability created boyar, gentry, and bureaucratic anxiety. Peasant responses to the increasingly heavy tax burdens and the ancillary depredations of Ivan's political repression directly affected the operation of the machinery of the state. Nonviable peasant households could not afford to pay taxes or rent. Records of criminal proceedings illustrate that the state apparatus noticed peasant robbery and murder of lay landowners and monks. Rising rents to owners and taxes to the state, more frequent famines and epidemics, and greater susceptibility to foreign incursion drove peasants to despair, slavery, beggary, banditry, bankruptcy, poverty, or death. Their fate shook Muscovy's economic foundation.

Slavery expanded in Muscovy during the second half of the sixteenth century.[75] Elite slaves, either military slaves or slave estate administrators (*kliuchniki*; literally "key holders"), enjoyed higher status, but the latter gradually disappeared during Ivan's reign. Some slaves engaged in agriculture on their lords' demesnes, while others worked their own plots. Household slaves predominated, as in contemporary Spain and Italy. Slaves contributed significantly to the economy via their labor. They constituted perhaps 10 to 15 percent of the population.[76]

Slaves in Muscovy included both natives and foreigners. Prisoners of war probably comprised a minority of the slave population.[77] Muscovy permitted the resale of non-Muscovite slaves to the Nogais, who held them for ransom or resold them in Central Asian or Ottoman slave markets. Children of slave captives did not become slaves, as children of limited-contract debt slaves did. For a while the law emancipated slave captives upon the death of their owners. The government treated skilled captives differently. Between a quarter and a third of all slaves ran away, rendering their lifelong status as slaves or that of their offspring moot. Between two-thirds and three-quarters of all slaves, therefore, did pass lifelong slavery on to their progeny. Slave owners spent years trying to recover runaways.[78]

Slaves—even runaway slaves—also became free via testamentary emancipation, as widespread in Muscovy as in Seville. Such charitable acts retained slave service while the owner lived, encouraged slaves to behave and not run away, and enabled the testator to die with a clear conscience.[79] Although Orthodox Christians could be slaves, conversion of non-Christian slaves to Orthodox Christianity brought emancipation. The government restricted the right to issue slave emancipation charters to certain government officials in selected cities, but it did not inhibit emancipation of slaves.[80]

The composition of the slave class remained in a state of constant flux. As other categories of slaves grew obsolete, a new category of slavery, limited-contract debt slavery, arose and became predominant. Free people became slaves, while slaves became free. Farmer slaves gradually fused with the peasantry.[81] Elite slave administrators disappeared. Captives became slaves or left slavery by ransom. Children of slave captives grew up to be free. Slaves ran away or were returned to slavery upon recapture. Although the government benefitted from the services performed by boyar or gentry military slaves, runaway military slaves posed a greater danger than runaway civilian slaves because they knew how to use weapons. No slave revolts occurred during Ivan's reign, but elite concern about slavery as a problem of social control resulted in frequent legislative initiatives and lengthy gentry searches for runaways. Both drained elite resources. Overall, slavery contributed to social insecurity.

In Muscovy religion was the main source of social cohesion, but it served as a social unifier only through the agency of the clergy.[82] Institutional and social divisions within the Russian Orthodox Church, and between the clergy and laity, mitigated the efficacy of shared religious values, although some pious laity undoubtedly remained completely devoted to Russian Orthodox Christianity despite the human foibles of clerics. Russian Orthodox clergy consisted of the "white" parish clergy—priests who had to marry—and the "black" regular clergy—monks and nuns who lived according to monastic rules. Priests whose wives died were supposed to move to monasteries, but the social divide between priests and monks bifurcated the church. All bishops were chosen from among the monks, creating a social disconnect between the episcopal administration and the clergy it supervised. Episcopal spiritual responsibility over monasteries could lead to disputes between bishops and monasteries. To be sure, donations to monasteries by bishops and priests suggest that such divisions could be overcome through shared religious respect for the monastic state.

The parish clergy were not a closed caste during Ivan's reign. Because the population of Muscovy grew during the first half of the sixteenth century and because of territorial expansion the Russian Orthodox Church had to expand its parish structure. It therefore required the services of a greater number of priests; it would not have been enough to replace priests who died or became monks. Priestly names that included the phrase "son of a priest" (*syn popov*) demonstrate that the priestly vocation could remain in the family. Clearly, the hierarchy sympathized with priests who wanted qualified members of their families to succeed them.[83] Even if one son might replace his father as the priest in their home parish, other sons still needed jobs. We may infer that the demographic growth of existing priestly families did not suffice to fill all clerical openings in the church's growing infrastructure because many priests were not described as "sons of priests." Peasants might become priests if they had the calling or if they thought it would improve their status. At the same time some sons of priests did not continue their fathers' occupation. Anfim, the son of the priest Sylvester, became a merchant and government official. Most sons of priests who did not enter the clergy, such as the Shchelkalov brothers, became secretaries, although few rose to the political heights (and wealth) of the Shchelkalovs.[84]

The parish clergy became economically enmeshed in their congregants' lives. Proprietary churches predominated.[85] Rural churches rested on private land, "black" land, or monastic land, while townspeople established parish churches in their houses. Unless a priest owned his church, he answered to whoever did. Priests' income depended upon fees for their services. For this period little evidence exists of social tension between priests and their congregants. The Russian Orthodox Church at this time began making a concerted effort to replace "founder" authority over proprietary churches with a genuine parish structure responsible to the hierarchy, a change that may have created some lay-clerical disagreements. Economic disruption of the peasantry or urban population affected the well-being of the parish priesthood as well.

Although the Russian Orthodox Church, unlike the Catholic Church, had no monastic orders, Orthodox monasteries varied in social composition, size, and wealth. Social tensions within a given monastery could derive from clashing personalities, degree of discipline, or contradictory preferences for an individual hermit existence or communal organization. Some monasteries reproduced the outside world's social hierarchy within their walls; others did not.[86] Although its most famous sixteenth-century abbot and later metropolitan, Filipp Kolychev, came from the boyar class, state peasants dominated the Solovetskii Monastery. Only the Iosifov and Kirillo-Beloozero Monasteries served the same food to all monks. Given Muscovy's hierarchical society, the question of monastic egalitarianism resonated outside monastic walls, but advocates of lay social hierarchy could still object to social inequality within monastic walls.[87]

Monasteries served social functions that contributed to social harmony. They provided hospitals, soup kitchens, poor houses, convalescent homes for injured soldiers, and retirement homes for donors. Monasteries became refuges for laity overwhelmed by the problems of secular existence. The Church Council of 1551 expressed concern for those who chose the monastic life for secular motives.[88]

Even for men who became monks to "leave the world," economic enterprises, particularly those of large and wealthy monasteries, could impair their vocation. The worldly institutional needs of monasteries required monks to intrude into lay society and, concomitantly, required lay society to intrude into monasteries. Monks lived in monastic compounds ("courts") in cities or in distant villages to supervise entrepreneurial activities. They could be sent off on assignment to make deliveries or purchases.[89] Monasteries became major landowners. Donations of land to monasteries and purchase of land by monasteries spiked during the oprichnina, although the increase may have been exaggerated by better recordkeeping, mandated by the Church Council of 1551. Regardless, litigation over lands and privileges between monasteries and lay landowners could not be avoided and could create ill will.[90]

Like every class of Muscovite society during Ivan's reign, the clergy underwent social change. Sons of clergy left the priestly class to become clerks or merchants; sons of non-clergy entered the clergy as priests or monks. Social strains upon their congregants affected the parish priests; social strains among the inhabitants of monastic lands affected monks. Concerns over social inequality among the laity penetrated monasteries. The church strove to sustain societal cohesion in Muscovy—ideologically, by propagating the faith, and institutionally, by providing social services for people who had no other recourse—but one wonders if conflicts within its ranks or with the laity, involving criminal and sometimes violent encounters, distracted clergy from that purpose.

In 1551 Ivan created a new social entity, the musketeers. The social origin of the musketeers remains elusive. The first six companies of five hundred musketeers consisted of reorganized gunners, but where additional manpower was recruited cannot be determined. Only free men not registered as taxpayers in a rural or urban unit could volunteer. Serving in the musketeer ranks was beneath the dignity of gentry-men, although they did serve as musketeer captains.[91] During Ivan's reign there is no evidence to suggest social tensions between those gentry officers and "commoner" enlisted men. Nor is there any evidence to support the widespread assumption that urban artisans, such as blacksmiths with expertise in working with metal, comprised the recruiting base. Scattered references suggest that some musketeers came from the countryside.[92] The government exempted musketeers from taxes and domiciled them in tax-exempt enclaves. In Ivan's time, the musketeers formed an occupational group, not a caste.[93]

Collective grants to land just outside their garrison's urban location reinforced musketeer identity, but apparently some musketeers received individual conditional land grants in the countryside (if *strelok* ["shooter"] meant *strelets*, the singular of *strel'tsy*). All musketeers lived in urban areas. They mostly engaged in artisan crafts and trade to supplement their government-issued supplies and salaries. The musketeers' uniforms distinguished them from other urban dwellers. Inevitably, the musketeers acquired some urban police functions. They could fight fires or enforce the government liquor monopoly, but during Ivan's reign they did not serve as riot police.[94] The government sent musketeer garrisons to Livonia and later brought them home.

The establishment of the musketeers constituted a major social innovation. Historians have not studied what social tensions resulted from their creation or how their development changed the rural and urban social landscape. How many musketeers existed at one time during Ivan's reign cannot be determined. Register data on Ivan's 1577 campaign against Livonia suggests that between five and seven thousand could be mobilized for a single field army, perhaps double the number of musketeers created in 1550.[95] The initial recruitment of the musketeers drained thousands of able-bodied males from somewhere, and the presence of hundreds of musketeers in a suburb with tax-exempt shops and stalls would have altered cities. The musketeers changed the social environment around them, but, even more profoundly, they changed themselves. The recruits underwent a transformation from their previous occupations and social identities to a new profession and identity constructed around their units. For the time being at least, the musketeers did not create mayhem—they did not riot over missing pay, like mercenaries or Janissaries—but the consequences of the establishment of the musketeer corps for the stability of sixteenth-century Muscovite society have not been studied.[96]

The role and status of women in a society serves as a sensitive barometer of social change. Unfortunately, no consensus exists among historians regarding how social change in sixteenth-century Muscovy affected women. Some historians argue that women's status improved; others argue that it deteriorated. Because class determined a woman's social status, generalizing about women remains problematic.[97]

Royal and boyar women lived in secluded women's quarters, but it is not known when this institution arose. Some historians argue that it reflected the enhanced value of royal and boyar women in marriage politics. The homes of middle-class women did not have separate women's quarters, but women still did not socialize with men. To honor exceptional guests a host might present his wife and daughters to them in a brief courtesy ceremony.[98] Peasant, artisan, merchant, priestly, and slave women worked as hard as their menfolk and could hardly live in seclusion.

Whether the rights of elite women to own property changed in the sixteenth century remains under discussion.[99] Restrictions on bequeathing clan patrimonial land negatively affected women's property rights. The conditional landholdings of widows, with or without children, probably increased, as the state assumed a welfare responsibility for families of deceased military servitors. The right of a widow to receive a portion of her late husband's conditional land grant to support her and, if necessary, her minor children, called the "widow's portion," evolved without benefit of legislative regulation. This state welfare program remained atypical of sixteenth-century states.[100]

Non-class legislation honored and protected women. In new dishonor legislation, women of all classes enjoyed a dishonor fee double that of their husbands because an insult to a wife also insulted her husband. A 1555 decree nullified a woman's testament naming her husband executor because the wife would have dictated what her husband told her to. *Household Management* did not follow the foreign model of assigning gender-based parenting roles, such as the disciplinarian father versus the nurturing mother.[101] Whether this enhanced or minimized women's role remains an open question. We cannot draw any definitive conclusions about the effects of social change on sixteenth-century Muscovite women, other than the obvious one: whatever social changes affected men also affected women.

The Cossacks were of, but not in, Muscovite society. They began serving Moscow as steppe scouts and guides, but in the second half of the sixteenth century they graduated to direct military action in coordination with regular Muscovite forces against Crimea.[102] The Cossacks supplemented their income from hunting, fishing, and beekeeping through banditry and piracy. Cossacks proliferated on the Don, the Iaik (Ural), the Volga, and the Terek (Greben) Rivers. They frequented Astrakhan. During Ivan's reign the Cossacks remained somewhat peripheral to Muscovy, like other border irregulars such as the Uskoks of Senj and the Croatian Grenzer.[103] Only males joined the Cossack brotherhoods, so their population growth derived exclusively from in-migration.

The social impact of the Cossacks cannot be measured. Their social origin cannot be determined, but members of almost all social groups could have joined the Cossacks. The Cossacks drew people away from the heartland, although becoming a Cossack meant more than geographic relocation. It meant adopting a new identity as a freebooter—an even greater social transformation than becoming a musketeer.[104] Crossing the Muscovite border to live in the "wild steppe" or "wild field" (*dikoe pole*) meant severing all ties with Muscovite society.

Muscovite sources provide numerical data on "free" Cossacks serving in Muscovite field armies or "settled" garrison Cossacks during Ivan's reign. Nearly 3,000 Cossacks participated in the 1563 Polotsk campaign. In 1570 the Pskov garrison included 250 Cossacks. These numbers suggest the visibility of the Cossacks in Muscovite society. They could not have attracted recruits unless Muscovites of various social classes had acquired knowledge of Cossack social and political organization. By Ivan's reign, would-be Cossacks in Poland-Lithuania joined Cossack groups there.[105] Such awareness of a class-free, democratic, lower-class brotherhood might also have influenced the social views of the peasantry and artisans.

We cannot document how Cossack military service in field armies or garrisons affected Muscovites. Cossacks disdained discipline. Their contempt for Muscovy's social hierarchy would have been painfully obvious to any Muscovite who came into contact with them. Tatars and Cossacks considered each other deadly enemies.[106] The commander of a field army in which both served probably kept them as far apart as possible. During Ivan's reign the migration of Muscovites to the steppe to join the Cossacks, the establishment of settled Cossack garrisons, and interaction between regular Muscovite military forces with Cossack units might not yet have had tangible consequences. However, clearly the development of the Cossacks did contribute to social discontinuity in Muscovy by providing an alternative to Muscovy's hierarchical social order, even if this was as yet more symbolic than manifest.

THE CONSEQUENCES OF SOCIAL CHANGE

Ivan's reign witnessed enormous social change.[107] A traditional society can tolerate only so much social change, and during Ivan's reign change exceeded Muscovy's limits. The oprichnina magnified preexisting strains on Muscovite society beyond the breaking point. Ivan had a personal purpose in establishing the oprichnina, but its creation had consequences beyond what he intended. At first the effects of the oprichnina were confined to massive deportations and the formation of a new social identity for oprichniki. Executions played a secondary role. The escalation of terror to mass executions of entire families and mass repression in rural areas, cities, and regions exacerbated these social strains.[108]

The notion that Ivan was deranged cannot alone account for the scale of the mass terror during the oprichnina. To accomplish the looting of Fedorov's estates or of the northwest cities in 1569–1570, and to perform the Red Square executions in 1571, Ivan required the assistance of thousands of oprichniki, recruited not from the dregs of Muscovite society but from the Muscovite elite. Non-oprichnina members of various elite Muscovite classes, including notably boyars, bureaucrats, and upper clergy, took advantage of the situation to advance their careers by joining the orgy of denunciations accompanying these atrocities.[109] These phenomena require a society-wide explanation.

The level of violence in Ivan's Muscovy probably did not exceed that in other contemporary societies. Corporal punishment of children and adults occurred equally everywhere. In theory Muscovite custom exempted adult boyars from corporal punishment, but in Muscovy, as in England, where adult peers supposedly shared that exemption, that privilege was not respected in treason cases. State violence against political and criminal deviance exhibited no more savagery in Muscovy than among its neighbors and contemporaries. Despite Muscovy's supposedly domineering central government, Moscow could not eliminate violent crime.[110] The level of violence, sadism, barbarity, and inhumanity of the oprichnina rose precipitously, as it did in the French wars of religion,[111] the German Peasants' Revolt,[112] the English repression of Ireland, the Habsburg response to the Dutch Revolt, Renaissance Italian politics, and the Spanish repression of the revolt of Moriscos (forcibly converted Muslims) in Grenada.[113] Historians perceive a lower level of violence in these other contexts than in Muscovy because its causes—religion, class warfare, or ethnic bigotry—seem to make sense. Ivan's violence, especially the oprichnina, is categorized as gratuitous and, thus, worse.[114] Regardless of how much Ivan exceeded the customary Muscovite limits on violence, his actions did not distinguish him among contemporary or near contemporary rulers. Kings Henry VIII of England and Philip II of Spain used secret police and lethal repression just as much as Ivan, albeit in different contexts, outright rebellion at home or abroad.

The atmosphere of intrigue, envy, and insecurity at Ivan's court resembled that of the foreign courts of the native lands of foreign visitors to Muscovy.[115]

When Ivan turned to mass terror to repress opposition to the oprichnina, he unintentionally unleashed the tensions germinating in the Muscovite elite by over a century of territorial expansion, state building, and social mobilization. Elite social stress fed upon the uncertainties created by an unprecedented and intolerable level of elite and popular social mobility. Boyars became gentry; gentry became boyars, bureaucrats, or slaves; bureaucrats became gentry; merchants became bureaucrats; peasants became slaves, priests, bureaucrats, musketeers, or Cossacks. The synergistic interface of the oprichnina with the destructive consequences of Muscovite social change produced the oprichnina's massive social dysfunction, a social pathology in which the normal constraints upon antisocial behavior evaporated.

To escape the contradictions among the multiple levels of the ruler myth in Muscovy Ivan created an appanage, the oprichnina, in which he would possess total autonomy. To carry out this policy it was necessary to give the oprichniki autonomy from the law. The oprichniki came primarily from the gentry, the most vulnerable segment of the elite, armed and dangerous but lacking any mechanism to express their angst, frustration, resentment, or social animosity. Ivan's reign of terror unintentionally created just such a mechanism. If the gentry had been complacent and satisfied, they might very well have confined themselves to following Ivan's orders. Instead, and in violation of Ivan's wishes, they ran rampant on their own. Ivan's ideological dilemma and the gentry's social anxiety combined to produce mass violence, which affected the gentry class as well as the entirety of Muscovite society.

17

Muscovy, 1572–1584

During the period between the abolition of the *oprichnina* in 1572 and Ivan's death in 1584, it becomes nearly impossible to separate Ivan's actions from Muscovite history. This chapter discusses Muscovite economic and foreign policy during this period. Ivan's policies at first exacerbated the economic depression and then ameliorated it. Throughout, it was Ivan who determined the course of Muscovite diplomacy and warfare.

ECONOMIC DEPRESSION

War, crop failure, epidemics, and political conflict drove the Muscovite economy into a deep depression by the 1570s and 1580s, comparable to the economic collapse that followed the French Wars of Religion. In some regions, upwards of 97 percent of all arable land could not pay taxes. Lost taxes forced the government to demand loans from monasteries and subsidies from the Muscovy Company.[1] Poverty induced gentry to dodge military service. Nevertheless, transient causes produced a reversible depression. Some sectors of the economy recovered even during Ivan's reign, and the downturn was largely overcome for the entire economy after his death.

The poor harvest of 1567 initiated a cycle of economic problems. Because of increased taxes, peasants had no reserves to tide them over, resulting in famine. Grain prices rose precipitously. Wages rose and rents fell, developments that hurt rent-dependent gentry. From 1568 to 1571 the economy crashed. The oprichnina raised expenditures and lowered revenues.[2]

Even at its worst, however, the depression did not spell economic doom for the entire country. Ulfeldt described the burned-out remains of Novgorod and Tver after Ivan's punitive expedition, but he saw signs of prosperity when he entered central Russia. Changing policies ameliorated fiscal exactions somewhat and permitted some economic revival. If a significant minority of peasants had not actually fled, but merely taken a leave of absence when the census-takers came to town, it would have been easier for them to reconstitute the agricultural sector when the most oppressive features of the economy—wars, the oprichnina—were removed. Perhaps to compensate for lost revenue, in 1572–1573 Moscow experimented with letting conditional landholders purchase their estates, transforming them into patrimonies. Given the poor financial situation of so many gentry, the likelihood of a large revenue windfall must have been slim. A northern fishing community recovered almost completely from the oprichnina. Gentry in the Novgorod region in the 1580s relied upon a variety of management techniques to cope with the depression, including using slave labor on demesnes and turning abandoned arable land into hayfields to sell the hay or engage in animal husbandry. Almost all found a workable survival strategy.[3] Historians have underestimated the resilience of the economy. If government policy played no small role in creating the economic catastrophe, it also made a contribution to economic recovery.

Ivan's donations in memory of Tsarevich Ivan demonstrate that he still had large cash resources at his command.[4] As ever, specie came from abroad. As a result of the loss of Narva, Baltic trade shifted to the White Sea, while eastern trade with Turkey, Persia, and Central Asia continued unabated.[5] The domestic economy functioned at a sufficiently high level to sustain foreign trade and import currency in precious metals to Muscovy. Terminating the Livonian War released even more economic resources for domestic needs. The building programs initiated by Tsar Fedor Ivanovich and Tsar Boris Godunov after Ivan's death strongly suggest that the economic depression did not result from structural causes.

THE THRONE OF POLAND-LITHUANIA

Ivan's role as a candidate for the throne of the Polish-Lithuanian Common-wealth during the 1570s illustrates very well the inseparability of dynastic issues from international relations. Historians sometimes criticize Ivan's actions, but he pursued a consistent strategy to achieve his highest foreign policy objective, winning the Livonian War to secure Baltic ports.

Lithuania needed military assistance from Poland to stop the Musco-vite military juggernaut that produced Muscovite annexation of Polotsk in 1563. To secure that support Lithuania had to agree to a stronger union with Poland, the 1569 Union of Lublin. Even worse, Lithuania had to pay Poland to enter the Livonian War by transferring its Ukrainian territories to Poland. The aged Polish King Sigismund II Augustus had little interest in waging war, however. He died childless in 1572, the first and last Jagellon on the throne of the Polish-Lithuanian Commonwealth. Foreigners could campaign for the post since there were no restrictions on whom the com-monwealth, meaning the magnates and gentry, could elect to replace him. The candidates during the First Polish Interregnum, 1572–1573, included Ivan and his son Fedor.[6]

Divergent priorities, interests, and mentalities undermined Ivan's can-didacy. Some Lithuanians favored Ivan because he could defend Lithuania against the Tatars and Ottomans. Ivan's Polish supporters arrogantly in-sisted that Polish civilization would "tame" his "barbarity," but Ivan would not play Polish politics by Polish rules. He felt it beneath his dignity to campaign or to bribe electors. Ivan wanted the electors to invite him to assume the throne. He colluded with Holy Roman Emperor Ferdinand in an attempt to prevent the election of the "Ottoman" candidate, Henri of Valois (France was an ally of the Ottoman Empire). Ivan failed to persuade King Frederick II of Denmark to interdict Henri's travel across Danish soil to reach Poland. Ivan lied to Frederick that the Poles and Lithuanians had invited him to become king first.[7] Upon the death of his brother, Henri left Poland as soon as he could, preferring to rule in Paris, which initiat-ed the Second Polish Interregnum (1574–1576). Despite opposition from Ivan and Ferdinand, another "Ottoman" candidate, Stefan Batory from Transylvania (an Ottoman vassal), won the resumed election campaign.[8] It took Batory several years to suppress Ferdinand's supporters, who had elected him as rival king, and to impose his will upon the city of Danzig

(Gdansk). Only then could he begin regaining Lithuanian territory from Muscovy.

Ivan's conditions for his election as king of Poland prove that he saw his candidacy as no more than a means to an end, winning the Livonian War. He would not convert to Catholicism. The Orthodox metropolitan of Moscow had to crown him. The Polish throne would be inherited by his male heirs. Ivan sought not to rule Poland-Lithuania but to neutralize it.[9]

Some factions in Poland-Lithuania proposed the young, and therefore suitably pliable, Tsarevich Fedor as king. If they knew of his mental and emotional limitations, they said nothing. In his maliciously clever and mendacious response, Ivan declared that the Poles and Lithuanians intended to turn Fedor over to the sultan as a peace offering to secure the end of Crimean raids on Ukraine and southern Poland. Ivan terminated Fedor's candidacy.

Ivan's diplomatic dance with Ferdinand proved equally fruitless. He offered to support the candidacy of Ferdinand or his son Archduke Ernst in return for Livonia, which was in theory an imperial possession. Meanwhile Ferdinand sought to persuade Ivan to abandon his Livonian ambitions. As an alternative, Ivan proposed the partition of the commonwealth. The Habsburgs could have Poland (thus sacrificing the Ukrainian lands transferred to Poland in 1569) and Ivan would take Lithuania, which virtually guaranteed that Ivan would keep Livonia. (With Polish withdrawal from Livonia, I suspect that Ivan expected to retrieve Livonian territory occupied by Sweden). Batory's military aptitude laid all this plotting to rest, but Ivan's creativity in trying to solve the Polish-Lithuanian problem anticipated Poland's later partitions in the eighteenth century.

Although Ivan would not have turned down the Polish throne if offered on his own terms, conflict between the territorial interests of Poland and Muscovy proved insurmountable and precluded the election of any Muscovite candidate. Ivan knew what he was doing, however, and knew with whom he was dealing. He addressed an electoral letter, which urged the election of Archduke Ernst, to every influential lay or clerical noble in Poland or Lithuania by name. Ivan kept his options open.[10] He did not lose the Polish-Lithuanian election because of arrogance or ignorance. He was arrogant, but he was not ignorant. He formulated his priorities well—Livonia first, Ukraine second (even if claims to Kiev served only as leverage), Lithuania a distant third, Poland not even fourth—and stuck to them. Unfortunately for him, he could not prevent the election of a military genius as king of Poland, and he and Muscovy suffered the consequences.

THE END OF THE LIVONIAN WAR

By the late 1570s Ivan knew that he had to cut his losses in Livonia. He showed himself to be decidedly less obstinate than Philip II of Spain was on the issue of war against the Netherlands and a bit more realistic than Philip on his war with France.[11] Muscovy had exhausted its economic and military resources. The Livonian War left Muscovy as impoverished as Henry VIII's 1540s wars with France left England. As Polish and Swedish forces methodically seized Muscovite possessions in Livonia, Ivan knew that he could not extricate himself from the situation on his own. For the first time in his reign, Ivan took the initiative to make peace.[12]

The Russian Orthodox tsar took the bold diplomatic step of inviting the pope to mediate a truce between Muscovy and the Polish-Lithuanian Commonwealth. (As precedent, Grand Prince Ivan III, grandfather of Ivan IV, had let the pope play matchmaker between himself and Sophia Palaiologa.) Ivan dangled the chimera of a joint crusade against the Ottomans before the pope's eyes. Ivan knew that the pope would salivate at the prospect of inducing him to change his religious affiliation and transfer his support from the Patriarch of Constantinople to the papacy. Ivan fully intended to keep the illusion of his interest in a religious union alive while avoiding any practical commitments, a tactic he did not need to learn from Elizabeth I's treatment of Muscovite proposals for an English-Muscovite military alliance. He also knew full well that the pope would elevate his interest in church union and crusade above the interests of Catholic Poland and its very Catholic ruler, Stefan Batory, an active instrument of the Counter-Reformation. Papal hopes for, and Polish fears of, a papal-Muscovite alliance proved equally unfounded. Ivan's grasp of the politics of the situation demonstrates that he remained in complete command of his mental faculties, fully capable of outthinking his enemies. Ivan's continued tactical—not delusional—bluster against Batory demonstrated Muscovy's resolve to continue the war in order to negotiate better terms. Ivan knew that Batory needed to end the war as much as he did because Batory's siege of Pskov had stalled.[13] To be sure, for Ivan desperate times called for desperate measures.

The pope sent the Jesuit Antonio Possevino to mediate the truce.

Possevino's account and the official Muscovite diplomatic report differ. The former made Possevino look good; the latter favored Ivan. Evaluations of Possevino's role as honest broker and judgments as to whether Ivan or Batory "won" the negotiations varied then and continue to do so. Batory was not pleased by the expectation that he subordinate his plan to conquer Muscovy to papal priorities, but he had no choice. The treaty of Yam Zapol'skii cost Ivan what he should have expected it to cost him: all his gains in Livonia that Batory had seized.[14] The defenders of Pskov saved Ivan from worse terms. He managed to retain his freedom of action against Sweden, which had taken Dorpat; he mistakenly hoped to recoup some losses in Livonia at Swedish expense. In the end, though, Muscovy gained nothing from the separate Plyusa treaty with Sweden, since each side kept what territory it already held.

Although Muscovy wound up with essentially the same boundaries it started with, the Livonian War was a major event in Ivan's reign. The waste of lives and resources involved in fighting the Baltic powers to a draw cannot be minimized. The Livonian War contributed significantly to Muscovy's temporary economic collapse.[15]

Ivan's diplomatic end game in the Livonian War made the best of the bad situation that his foreign policy had created.[16] Historians accuse Ivan of being too stubborn to know when to quit while he was ahead in Livonia, but he was clearly smart enough to quit when he was behind. Contemporary states never conceded the failure of their acquisitive dreams. Truces and treaties just laid the groundwork for future wars.[17] The Polish-Lithuanian Commonwealth still wanted to recover more territory from Muscovy, as its actions during the Time of Troubles attest.

Ivan expected to live to fight another day in his pursuit of Livonia, but he exaggerated his own life expectancy. The state of the economy and the embarrassing loss of the Livonian War cast a shadow over Ivan's last years on the throne. Ivan's personal life between 1572 and 1576 did nothing to lift that shadow.

18

Ivan, 1572–1584

Compared to Ivan's image as a young, newlywed conqueror of Kazan in the late 1540s and early 1550s or a mature reformer and victorious warrior during the "long" 1550s, Ivan's life during his last years paints a depressing picture. That his behavior at least constituted an improvement over the putative homicidal maniac of the *oprichnina* provides little relief. Ivan's pessimism after the Crimean Tatars burned Moscow in 1571 was reflected in his 1572 testament. This mood passed with the Muscovite victory at Molodi in 1572, but Ivan's increasingly chaotic married and personal life, marred most of all by the death of Tsarevich Ivan in 1581, bore no silver lining. The Simeon Bekbulatovich episode of 1575–1576 still confuses historians. After Tsarevich Ivan's death, Ivan made memorial donations not only for him but also for all his victims, a somber comment on the legacy of Ivan's reign. Historians disagree about the cause of Ivan's death—a fitting close to his life, paralleling disagreement over his parentage, and framing his life in uncertainty.

IVAN'S 1572 TESTAMENT

Ivan's 1572 testament, the only one extant from his reign, reflected his mind-set just before he abolished the oprichnina. The testament begins with Ivan's extensive mea culpa detailing his seemingly endless vices. This preamble, unique among Muscovite royal testaments, strongly resembled in its self-flagellation Ivan's letter to the Kirillo-Beloozero Monastery in which he established his bona fides for correcting monastic laxity by emphasizing his humility. As usual, Ivan employed a literary cliché to excess.

Ivan named Tsarevich Ivan as his heir, while granting Tsarevich Fedor an appanage. Ivan admonished Tsarevich Fedor to obey his older brother and Tsarevich Ivan to take care of his younger brother. He instructed both not to use violence blindly to achieve their goals. He specifically authorized his sons to retain or abolish the oprichnina as they saw fit.[1] Most studies of the testament date it to after the Crimean sack of Moscow—arguing that this is the best explanation for Ivan's despondency and unenthusiastic attitude toward the oprichnina—and before the victory of Molodi restored Ivan's confidence. The content of the testament suggests a work in progress, one undergoing continuous revision. For example, it contains three different accounts of who held territories originally belonging to the princes Vorotynskii. Ivan could not have written that his sons could decide the fate of the oprichnina after Ivan himself abolished it in 1572. The testament became inoperative on the death of Tsarevich Ivan in 1581. The lack of a contemporary manuscript, therefore, occasions no surprise. The wonder is that any copy survived. To be sure, the provenance of the surviving manuscript, a copy of a copy of a copy, does not inspire tremendous confidence. It likely dates to the early nineteenth century, from an eighteenth-century prototype. Some particularly confusing passages in the testament require further study.[2]

No historian has explained the real mystery of the testament, which is why Ivan did not replace it after Tsarevich Ivan's death, especially after the birth of the second Tsarevich Dmitrii, of Uglich, to Tsaritsa Mariia Nagaia. There is no evidence to support assertions that Ivan wrote a subsequent testament after 1582 that was later deliberately destroyed.[3] After 1584 no tsar left a testament allocating his territories and personal possessions to his designated heir or other progeny. For unknown reasons, Muscovite rulers abandoned a practice initiated in the fourteenth century. Ivan's failure to modify his testament set a precedent for not composing testaments at all.

SIMEON BEKBULATOVICH

It is not clear why Ivan put the converted Chingissid Simeon Bekbulatovich on the throne in 1575 and seemingly treated him as his overlord, only to remove him a year later. Supposedly, astrologers predicted the death of the ruler, but Ivan did not believe in astrology enough to let this determine his actions. He did not permit anyone to bear arms in his presence. Bodyguards accompanied him everywhere. At diplomatic receptions foreigners had to relinquish their weapons. He did not need to worry about an assassination plot, although of course he claimed that he did.[4]

Ivan did not randomly choose a Christian Chingissid to sit on his throne (no Muslim Chingissid could do so, of course). The Chinggisid lineage enjoyed considerable prestige among the Muscovite elite, but Ivan did not give Simeon any independent authority. The registers during his year on the throne did not consistently attribute decisions to him.[5] Ivan chose to give Simeon the title of "Grand Prince of All Rus'," not "Tsar," which Simeon held as former khan of the vassal khanate of Kasimov. Ivan bluntly insisted to an English envoy that Simeon was his puppet. Ivan kept Simeon hidden from Poland-Lithuania as he had officially kept the oprichnina secret from his worst enemy.

Ivan's titles at this time remain confused. Most often he took for himself the modest title of "Prince of Moscow" (*kniaz' moskovskii*). One historian suggests that Ivan also claimed to be "Prince of Moscow and Pskov and Rostov."[6] Ivan issued immunity charters to the Trinity-Sergius Monastery for estates in the former Kazan Khanate in which he titled himself "Tsar and Grand Prince of All Rus'," but not "Tsar of Kazan." Ivan's use of "tsar" while Simeon reigned was erratic.[7] Two "Grand Princes of All Rus'" makes little sense, unless the second was the son and designated heir and coruler of the first, which did not obtain during 1575–1576.

After Ivan resumed the throne, he had to reissue now invalid documents he had issued to monasteries as "Prince of Moscow." He made no attempt to destroy the earlier documents. He also had to reissue or confirm Simeon's grants of privileges and decrees.[8] Pro forma, therefore, Simeon's acts as "Grand Prince of All Rus'" and Ivan's as "Prince of Moscow" carried the force of law.

The ambiguities of Ivan's relationship to Simeon as "Grand Prince of all Rus'" surfaced in a curious case. In 1576 Prince Ivan of Moscow needed evidence from the Moscow state archives concerning a precedence case. His secretary in Staritsa ordered state secretary Andrei Shchelkalov in Moscow to deliver the relevant documentation. Technically, Shchelkalov was Simeon's official, but, of course, he obeyed Ivan's order. He addressed Ivan by referring to himself as "your slave," not Simeon's. Simeon, Grand Prince of All Rus,' did not decide precedence cases, but Ivan, Prince of Moscow, did.[9]

After he placed Simeon on the throne of "All Rus,'" Ivan petitioned Simeon for permission to set up an appanage. Ivan utilized the abject terminology obligatory for a subject addressing his ruler.[10] Servitors could leave Simeon's domain for Ivan's but not vice versa. Ivan requested that those relocating to his domain be permitted to take with them moveable property, standing grain, and money without being robbed, an interesting commentary on the treatment of previous servitors who had changed lords. Of course Simeon acceded to Ivan's "request." As Prince of Moscow Ivan issued charters allocating conditional land grants to his new servitors. Simeon reassigned the estates of the men who had left his jurisdiction.[11] Ivan's petition epitomized his flexibility as an actor and dexterity as a writer. It is vintage Ivan, a masquerade played out in all seriousness on a par with Ivan's humility topos in his letter to the Kirillo-Beloozero Monastery and the preface to his testament.

In a second petition Ivan eschewed the use of self-deprecating diminutives for himself when informing Simeon that he and his son, "Prince" (not "Tsarevich") Ivan were preparing to depart for military service on the Oka River. He requested whatever subsidy God instructed Simeon to grant him. Only a later chronicle supplies the amount of money Ivan desired: forty thousand rubles.[12] This brief, business-like document shows that Ivan could turn his role-playing on and off at will. The subsidy does echo the hundred-thousand ruble subvention of the oprichnina that Ivan demanded and got in 1565.

When Ivan resigned the throne of Moscow in 1575, his eldest son, Tsarevich Ivan, should have succeeded him, but Ivan named someone else as his heir. Apparently, Ivan assumed that if he were alive, his sons would share his fate. In 1575, as in 1564, he abdicated with his sons. In 1575 the twenty-year-old Tsarevich Ivan was old enough to rule, let alone reign. In a letter in the name of Tsarevich Ivan to the Crimean *kalga*, the khan's heir apparent, in 1564 Tsarevich Ivan called himself Ivan's heir. Although Danish envoy Paul Juusten claimed that he dealt with both of Ivan's sons, in Muscovite documents only the elder brother, Tsarevich Ivan, not the younger brother, Tsarevich Fedor, joined his father in diplomatic receptions. Tsarevich Fedor only began attending diplomatic events after his brother's death.[13] According to a Danish diplomat and a Danzig burgher, Ivan flattered Germans and Magnus by proposing that Magnus would succeed him, disregarding Tsarevich Ivan altogether.[14] Some historians believe that Ivan's flattery of Magnus and the façade of Simeon Bekbulatovich impugned Tsarevich Ivan's status as his designated successor. Tsarevich Ivan and his entourage supposedly felt insulted by Ivan's actions, an interpretation relevant to the issue of Tsarevich Ivan's death.

Some historians explain Ivan's installation of Simeon as an excuse for him to create his own appanage, reprising the oprichnina in order to resume executions.[15] Ivan's 1575 removal of Archbishop of Novgorod and Pskov Leonid for personal and professional abuses occurred before the Bekbulatovich episode. Leonid died in prison, but according to seventeenth-century legends Ivan dressed him in a bear costume and sicced hunting dogs on him. Ivan also ordered two archimandrites and some priests executed, but why remains unknown. Later Muscovites and modern historians confused the Simeon Bekbulatovich episode with the oprichnina by making Simeon ruler of the "land" between 1565 and 1572,[16] but executions predate and postdate the oprichnina and Ivan never needed the oprichnina to carry them out. Unlike Henry VIII, Ivan's executions declined in number in his last years. Partial continuity of personnel between the oprichnina and Ivan's appanage does not prove continuity of policy. His appanage did not reproduce the mass terror of the oprichnina. Its servitors did not take an oath to renounce their families outside the appanage. They did not wear black clothes, ride black horses with dogs' heads and brooms, or constitute a pseudo-monastic brotherhood.[17]

Ivan's petition to Simeon to establish his appanage provides the key to understanding the episode. The petition both was and was not a parody. It was not a parody in that it was a legal instrument in the real world that led to physical consequences. It was a parody, however, in the sense that the puppet Simeon had no choice but to approve it. Its flawlessly subservient terminology shows Ivan assuming another of his theatrical poses, a common contemporary royal activity.[18] Ivan played a joke on himself by abdicating to Simeon, even if no one laughed. He lampooned his own pretensions as Tsar of All Rus'. Ivan was never more serious than when he was joking.[19]

IVAN'S MARRIAGES

Ivan's marital life was unexceptional until the death of Tsaritsa Mariia Cherkasskaia in 1569. His first wife, Anastasiia, died in 1560, and Ivan remarried in 1561. The history of Ivan's five later marriages strongly suggests that Ivan would never take a woman into his bed whom he did not consider his wife, despite his literary mea culpas. Russell Martin has established that Ivan had wives, not concubines. Only unproven propaganda accused Ivan of rape and sexual perversion.[20] Queen Elizabeth I of England did not go further than crediting him with an eye for beautiful women.[21]

Martin has definitively established the number and identities of Ivan's wives, while throwing the fantasies of a nineteenth-century forger into the trash bin of history.[22] As Ivan grew older, the duration of his marriages grew shorter. Ivan never imprisoned, exiled, or poisoned any of his wives. Unlike Henry VIII, Ivan never sent no-longer-desirable wives to the block. Instead, he deposited discarded wives in convents. No man could touch a woman who had shared Ivan's bed. Even in convents, Ivan's ex-wives, like the former wives and widows of Prince Iurii Vasil'evich and Tsarevich Ivan, retained their status as royal women.[23] Ivan continued to respect the institution of marriage and the status of royal women even after his marital life became chaotic.

In 1571 Ivan married his third wife, the seriously ill Marfa Sobakina, who soon died. How she passed muster at a bride show remains a mystery. In his April 29, 1572, petition to the Consecrated Council for permission to marry for an uncanonical fourth time, Ivan wrote that Anastasiia had been poisoned, a charge he had not previously made. Her death left him with two sons. For that reason he had married Mariia Cherkasskaia, but she died eleven years later. (Ivan miscounted; Cherkasskaia died eight years and one month after her marriage to Ivan.) Upon Cherkasskaia's death in 1569 he could not become a monk because he could not resign the throne, but because of his bodily needs, he also could not lead a holy life as a bachelor. Because his children had not yet achieved their majority, he had married a third time, to Marfa Sobakina, but she died a virgin. He did not suggest poisoning as the cause of death. Because his third marriage remained unconsummated, Ivan asked the council not to count it and to give him permission to marry for what he said was the third time.[24]

In Orthodox canon law, once the priest performs the sacrament of marriage, the marriage becomes valid, regardless of whether the couple consummates it, so the council did count Ivan's marriage to Sobakina as his third marriage. Ivan was over forty and had children. He had not been entitled to dispensation to remarry even for a third time. Nevertheless, the church granted Ivan's request for permission to take a fourth wife on the grounds of expediency. Implicitly, it accepted the logic of Ivan's argument that he had to remain tsar, and therefore he had to marry.

In 1572 Ivan counterintuitively suggested that he had to marry for a third time in 1569 because his sons, Tsarevich Ivan and Tsarevich Fedor, then aged fifteen and twelve, were so young that they could not live without maternal care, whereas in 1560 he told Makarii that he had not intended to remarry because his sons were six and three years old and no longer needed such care. Obviously, on both occasions Ivan manipulated the needs of his children to justify his actions.

The church imposed penances barring Ivan from communion for the rest of his life and made it clear that no one else should get any ideas about imitating his multiple marriages. (Ivan enclosed part of a gallery of the Annunciation Cathedral to create a small room from which he could hear the service without entering the church.) Ivan then married Anna Koltovskaia. The chronology of this marriage remains murky. Within a few years either she voluntarily took the veil or he repudiated her.[25] He did not even ask for permission for further marriages. Nevertheless, priests performed the marriage sacrament as part of the usual marital panoply of bride shows and banquets. The Russian Orthodox Church did not defrock the priests who performed Ivan's uncanonical weddings.

When Ivan abdicated to Simeon in 1575, Tsaritsa Anna Vasil'chikova abdicated with him, resuming her title when he resumed his. Vasil'chikova died by 1577. Ivan then married Vasilissa Radilova Melent'eva, his only previously married wife, an extraordinary violation of royal marriage etiquette. The date of her death remains uncertain. He married his seventh wife, Mariia Nagaia, in 1580. In negotiations for an English bride the Muscovite ambassador to England first insisted that Ivan's current marriage did not constitute an obstacle because Nagaia was low-born and unimportant. Ivan did not find her suitable (*ne po sebe*). When confronted by information from English merchants that she had just given birth to the second Tsarevich

Dmitrii, the ambassador lied. Religion and politics stood in the way of Ivan's marriage to Mary Hastings, a relative of Elizabeth I. Ivan's death made Mariia Nagaia his widow.[26]

Ivan did not obsessively pursue a foreign wife in order to raise the prestige of the Muscovite throne. As Orthodox tsar he had all the prestige he required. He married Cherkasskaia for reasons of foreign policy. His marriage proposals for Polish, Polish-cum-Swedish, or English brides possessed the same rationale. He wanted an English bride as leverage, to establish an offensive-defensive military alliance that would put the English fleet in the Baltic at his disposal.[27] He wanted a Polish bride, with or without a Swedish connection, to get Livonia.

Ivan's later marriages to Muscovite women lacked any political rationale, domestic or foreign.[28] Historians infer that his closest political advisors of the moment influenced Ivan's selections, but, even if true, that would at most explain whom he chose, not his desire to remarry. Ivan's later marital instability—five marriages during the last thirteen years of his life—derived from his personal deterioration. He would not give up having a wife, but he was unable to find one who would retain his favor as long as Anastasiia or even Cherkasskaia. Because his judgment in marital affairs ceased to be sound, domestic stability eluded him.

THE DEATH OF TSAREVICH IVAN

Ivan's marital mayhem seems like no more than a minor inconvenience compared to the aftermath of the tragic death of Tsarevich Ivan at Aleksandrovskaia Sloboda on November 19, 1581. Contemporary registers recorded his death without comment.[29] Ivan had earlier written from Aleksandrovskaia Sloboda to Moscow that he could not return to the capital because of his son's illness. No eyewitness account describes the circumstances of Tsarevich Ivan's death; surviving stories consist of rumors, court gossip, retrospective speculation, and fantasy. According to Possevino, Ivan found his pregnant daughter-in-law, Elena Sheremeteva, improperly attired and struck her, causing a miscarriage. Tsarevich Ivan accosted his father, complaining that Ivan had selected three wives for him, compelled him to send the first two to convents, and had now caused his third wife's miscarriage. Enraged, Ivan struck Tsarevich Ivan with the iron point of his staff, fatally wounding him.[30]

This story presents a number of logical flaws. For example, Sheremeto-va's ladies-in-waiting would not have permitted Ivan to barge in on her if she were not dressed appropriately. Ivan's jewel-tipped royal staff cannot have been the iron-tipped staff he supposedly wielded against Tsarevich Ivan.[31] Given Ivan's spinal problem, it is doubtful whether he even could have swung such a weapon. Nevertheless, accusations that Ivan accidentally murdered his son rest largely upon Possevino's narrative.[32]

Paul Bushkovich has persuasively discredited Possevino's Sheremeteva story.[33] Possevino lied about how he heard, and when he wrote down, that Ivan had struck his son while arguing about his treatment of his daughter-in-law. Possevino gave more than one account of the death of Tsarevich Ivan. Although he had ample opportunity to do so earlier, he did not tell the Sheremeteva tale until he wrote his *Moscovia* in 1586, only after he had "consulted" a number of Polish and papal "referees." To make matters worse, translations of the Latin text into German, Russian, and English take liberties that obscure its anomalies. Possevino either made his story up or acquired it from a Polish informant. Conflict between Ivan and his son, like tales of discord between Ivan and the boyars, fed the Polish desire for political unrest in Muscovy, which was seen as conducive to Polish victory in the Livonian War. Historians should no more hold Ivan responsible for the death of Tsarevich Ivan than Philip II for the death of his son Don Carlos.[34]

Ivan's relations with Tsarevich Ivan pose a number of problems. First of all, we cannot be sure why Ivan ordered Tsarevich Ivan's first two mar-riages terminated. Chronology does not support the inference that he did so because of the inability of his daughters-in-law to provide him with a grandson. Five years of marriage passed before Elena Glinskaia gave birth to Ivan. It was three years after her marriage to Ivan before Anastasiia gave birth to her first child, a daughter. Ivan compelled Tsarevich Ivan to divorce his first wife after four years of marriage, and his second after only two years. The inconsistency in duration of his first two marriages suggests a different but unknown rationale behind their termination.[35] Tsarevich Fedor married Irina Godunova in 1575, and until 1581 all her pregnancies ended in miscarriages. Ivan should have begun to feel some urgency at the lack of a grandson, yet he did not compel Tsarevich Fedor to divorce Irina, even when Tsarevich Fedor became heir apparent. As is so often the case, we do not and cannot know what motivated Ivan's actions or inactions.

Theories of long-standing rivalry between Ivan and Tsarevich Ivan lack credibility. Ivan cannot have disapproved of Sheremeteva as his son's wife, even if Ivan had just executed her father, because Ivan chose her. Once she was pregnant, any animosity would have evaporated at the prospect of a royal grandson.[36] In Muscovite sources Tsarevich Ivan remains a cipher. He never expresses an independent opinion. Foreigners and later Muscovites painted him either as a sadist, as cruel as his father, or as a humane man, his subjects' hope for a better life after his father's death. We cannot corroborate either the demonized or the idealized stereotype.[37] No source expresses Tsarevich Ivan's feelings about his father. Some historians infer animosity between father and son over Ivan's seeming selection of Magnus and Simeon Bekbulatovich as his successor. Other historians may have viewed their relationship through the distorting prism of Peter the Great's relationship to Tsarevich Aleksei.

Tsarevich Ivan shared his father's erudition, piety, and literary aptitude. Scribes prepared copies of the *Great Menology*, the *Book of Degrees*, and a "short chronicle" for Tsarevich Ivan, the latter as a history textbook.[38] Ivan, like Henry VIII, wrote hymns. Tsarevich Ivan wrote a redaction of the vita of Antonii Siiskii, as well as a laud and hymns to him.[39] Scholars cannot firmly establish whether Ivan and Tsarevich Ivan composed the music as well as the texts of these hymns. A stone slab in a church consecrated in 1564 and the accompanying tale recorded that Ivan sang in a church choir. Reliable sources attest that Ivan loved sacred music. He patronized hymnographers and a royal church choir.[40] During Ivan's reign, the church deemed assigning authorship to hymns prideful. Few manuscripts of hymns violated this rule of propriety. We know that at least one hymn later attributed to Ivan was not written by him because it is included in a manuscript written before his birth.[41] The manuscripts attributing hymns to Ivan all date to after his death. The earliest manuscript of the Svirskii vita and the hymns ascribed to Tsarevich Ivan have watermarks from Tsarevich Ivan's lifetime. To my knowledge, no expert in hagiography or hymnography has addressed the verisimilitude of such an attribution of a hymn to a living royal author.[42]

Other stories of Tsarevich Ivan's death also circulated as rumors. A Pskov chronicle written after Ivan's death recounted that Tsarevich Ivan berated his father for not dispatching troops to alleviate the siege of Pskov. Ivan's son volunteered to command such a relief expedition. Enraged at his son's presumptuousness and jealous of the popularity his son would accrue should he succeed in such a mission, Ivan "stuck [or "stabbed"] [him] with a sharp object" (*ostnem pokolol*). What sharp object this problematic text meant (a scepter? an iron-pointed staff?) cannot be determined. The chronicle did not say that Ivan killed him, however. It noted Tsarevich Ivan's death, without explanation, several lines later.[43] The self-interest of a Pskov chronicler in finding a hero who wanted to do more than the implicitly cowardly Ivan to help the beleaguered city seems self-evident. A contradictory version of this story reached the Livonian Salomon Henning, although it is impossible to know when (Henning died in 1589, the chronicle appeared in print in 1590), and wound up in his chronicle. It recounted that Ivan became so enraged when Tsarevich Dmitrii urged him to make peace that he struck and killed him. (In fact, Ivan favored making peace, and Tsarevich Dmitrii of Uglich was born after the siege ended and did not die until 1591.) Ivan Timofeev wrote that "some people" said that Ivan murdered Tsarevich Ivan, without invoking either the Sheremeteva or Pskov versions. Stories about Tsarevich Ivan's death tell us a good deal about Ivan's reputation but nothing about Tsarevich Ivan's death.[44]

IVAN'S MEMORIAL LISTS

Ivan's traumatic reaction to his elder son's death motivated memorial donations in amounts that exceeded even his own previous generosity for deceased relatives. His largesse did not constitute an admission of guilt. Ivan never admitted accidentally killing his son. Any feelings of guilt he felt about Tsarevich Ivan's death would have derived from the then common belief that the death of a son, royal or not, constituted God's punishment of the sins of the father, for which donations to ecclesiastical institutions served as atonement.[45]

Ivan's donations raise the question of the source of his abundant cash. The government's lack of money had inspired extortion from monasteries and the Muscovy Company, yet Ivan had tens of thousands of rubles at his disposal.[46] The loss of Dorpat depleted the importation of silver via the Baltic. Specie did still enter the country via the White Sea littoral and from the Ottoman Empire. Three possible explanations for Ivan's cash reserves suggest themselves: 1) Ivan had been hoarding his treasure, instead of expending it to alleviate the suffering of his subjects; 2) economic disaster had not impaired his source of specie via customs dues because the elite luxury trade continued unabated; or 3) historians have exaggerated the depression. Historians should reassess the likelihood of these scenarios.

In addition to donations to monasteries for prayers on behalf of his son, Ivan also commissioned memorial lists of all his victims to be sent to monasteries, with yet more donations for prayers for the dead. (Unlike such administrative sources as genealogies, the memorial lists included Ivan's female victims.)[47] The lists are not identical, but all contain names from what we presume was a master list, which does not survive. The victims included Muslim Tatars and Catholic and Protestant Germans, Poles, and Lithuanians. The efficacy of prayers on their behalf by Orthodox monks seems problematic, but Ivan had clearly reversed himself on the question of permitting commemoration of his victims. Although he acknowledged that God had punished him for his sins and that he needed to balance the scales, he did not repent of his deeds. Ivan remained a bundle of mutually exclusive traits—humility and arrogance, piety and blasphemy.[48]

The memorial lists constituted a kind of posthumous amnesty. The lifting of disgrace from the executed greatly improved the prospects of their descendants, if they had any, by erasing their social stigma.[49] Whether this measure resulted in the restoration of any confiscated estates or the political rehabilitation of any surviving elite relatives remains unknown. When monasteries received Ivan's requests for memorial prayers for his victims, they did not assume that the deceased were innocent.[50] Monasteries prayed for deceased sinners as much as for deceased innocents, although some monasteries may later have changed their views on the guilt or innocence of Ivan's victims.

Most of the surviving manuscripts of the memorial lists lack the last names of victims, making identification difficult. Many victims remained unnamed. The memorial lists referred to anonymous groups, whose individual names God alone knew. Even so, the lists of almost three thousand men, women, and children make somber reading. The lists excluded Metropolitan Filipp, because Ivan stuck to the cover story that Filipp died of asphyxiation.[51] Ivan did list many other clergy, including Vassian Muromtsev and Kornilii of the Pskov Caves Monastery.

Skrynnikov, continuing Stepan Veselovskii's pioneering research, made one of his greatest contributions to scholarship about Ivan's reign by sorting out the manuscripts of the memorial lists and discovering the key to deciphering them: the lists recorded names in blocks, in rough chrono-logical order. The core of the memorial lists pertained to the Novgorod campaign, for which they probably provide close to a comprehensive enu-meration of prominent victims and an accurate estimate of the total number of victims. Coincidentally, the word "oprichnina" did not appear in the memorial lists. On the basis of this yeoman analysis Skrynnikov recon-structed a model text. He identified far more victims than any previous historian.[52]

Despite the existence of the memorial lists, it is impossible to compile a comprehensive list of all of Ivan's victims. The memorial lists did not include the names of some of Ivan's most prominent victims unrelated to the Novgorod campaign.[53] For many years its coverage is quite incomplete. Historians do not agree on the reliability of the names of Ivan's victims found in other contemporary sources, such as Kurbskii's *History* and for-eigners' accounts, because their data often lack confirmation. Similarly, data in genealogies, often preserved in seventeenth-century manuscripts, resist corroboration and lack explanation. A genealogy might indicate that so-and-so died but not whether Ivan ordered his execution. It is safe to say that all relevant sources, including the memorial lists, contain errors. Nevertheless, we can establish the approximate scale of Ivan's repression. He was directly responsible for the murders of thousands of people who were killed by people acting on his orders, perhaps over ten thousand, but not many more than that. This number approximates the total victims of the St. Bartholomew's Day massacre in all of France, falls short of the number of commoner deaths during the German Peasants' Revolt, and exceeds the number of French peasants who perished in late sixteenth-century peasant revolts.[54] Foreigners then and historians since have bandied about much higher, fantastic numbers, but the evidence from Ivan's time does not sup-port them.

The number of victims for whom Ivan bears direct responsibility pales in comparison to the estimated number of deaths in Muscovy for which he bears indirect responsibility—deaths by famine, because the oprichniki destroyed all crops and he did not organize famine relief; by epidemic, because of ineffective quarantines; in unnecessary warfare; or in Tatar raids because Ivan failed to protect the southern frontier adequately.[55] When he died, Ivan had more than enough blood on his hands to earn eternal damnation.

IVAN'S DEATH

Ivan died on March 18, 1584, after a long illness. (Some scribes continued to issue charters in his name after his death.[56]) After the Second World War archaeologists disinterred his remains and subjected them to forensic analysis. Dmitrii Gerasimov prepared a reconstruction of Ivan's face and head. He discovered that Ivan suffered from a serious bone problem, osteophytes, whose chronology and consequences remain elusive. Ivan did not lose the mobility needed to ride a horse. Juusten commented that Ivan rode in a carriage in 1570, as did many rulers, ill or not, but in 1577 Ivan rode Boris Godunov's horse from Pskov to Novgorod.[57] Horsey saw him carried into his throne room on a chair, but by then Ivan was already dying, although not from his non-life-threatening spinal condition. Ivan never became a chronic invalid. No source ever noted his nonperformance of a ceremony or ritual because of physical debility or even remarked that he was in obvious physical pain while doing so. His illness cannot explain his actions. According to sixteenth-century Russian Orthodox Christianity, God punished sin with illness. Therefore, prayer, not mass murder, constituted the appropriate response to pain. We do not know how well Ivan was able to tolerate pain or medication. In any case, his body chemistry did not determine his behavior.[58] Whatever his mental or physical disabilities, Tsar Fedor Ivanovich fully participated in Muscovite ceremonies and even went on campaign. Ivan's autopsy, however, raises a greater issue than his osteophytes.

Serious scholars, including the director of the Kremlin Museum complex, infer from the chemical levels in Ivan's bones that he was poisoned. An early seventeenth-century Muscovite chronicle reported that "some people" said that he had been poisoned. Gerasimov and his consultants found a normal level of arsenic in his skeleton but a high level of mercury, which was used externally to treat problems with limbs. Someone may have murdered Ivan deliberately or he may have died from an accidental overdose of painkillers combined with copious quantities of alcohol. These medications were not prescribed by a doctor as treatment for syphilis because, according to Gerasimov's autopsy, Ivan had not contracted that disease.[59]

It is unlikely that anyone poisoned Ivan. To poison him deliberately via food would have required finessing the circumstantial obstacles to poisoning anyone in the royal household, since food was not prepared for individuals. The only plausible way he could have been poisoned was by medical treatment, since someone prepared medications exclusively for him. The validity of the chemical analysis depends upon the absence of contamination of Ivan's sarcophagus by water or chemicals over the hundreds of years after his death. Tsarevich Ivan's corpse tested positive for the same mercury and arsenic levels as Ivan's, but no one poisoned Tsarevich Ivan.[60]

There were rumors that Boris Godunov had assassinated Ivan, believing that Ivan wanted Tsarevich Fedor to divorce Irina Godunova because she had not produced an heir. A divorce would have driven Godunov from power. No evidence corroborates such accusations, which prove only that Godunov had a bad reputation.[61]

On his deathbed, aided by the priest Feodosii Viatka, Ivan finally took the cowl as the monk Iona. The legend that he died before he became a monk originated in an unreliable early seventeenth-century chronicle that misdated Ivan's death to 1591.[62] Someone contested even Ivan's final religious act.

Although Ivan never stopped trying to achieve his foreign policy goals during his last years, despite his impressive creativity, he always failed. He gained nothing from all his diplomatic efforts in the Polish-Lithuanian interregna or his attempts to secure a Polish or English bride. Ivan extricated himself from the Livonian War as best he could. Even his continuing mental dexterity did not suffice to compensate for Muscovy's failures abroad.

Even as Ivan's domestic life deteriorated, he retained the ability to direct a theatrical enterprise—the Simeon Bekbulatovich episode—that confused contemporaries and still confuses historians. The death of Tsarevich Ivan remains unexplained, and it cast a pall upon Ivan himself, no more than partially ameliorated by his memorial gifts for his victims. Tsarevich Ivan's death had a profound impact on later Muscovite history by placing on the throne a man who would not produce a male heir, ending the Daniilovich princely line. Ivan's rule began in glory and ended in agony, both for himself and his country.

Conclusion

I van the Terrible's reign, like Ivan himself, was complex, contradictory, and paradoxical. Ivan was sacrilegious, temperamental, stubborn, and cruel. He was also pious, erudite, perspicacious, witty, playful, and philanthropic. Good or bad, Ivan always remained charismatic, the focus of attention for Muscovites and foreigners alike. Ivan violated literary rules in his compositions and behavioral rules in his conduct. He adopted a variety of literary poses in his writings and a variety of political roles in his rule. More an opportunist than a chameleon, Ivan refused to be consistent as a writer or a politician.[1] No wonder historians have failed to produce a coherent portrait of him.[2] Kliuchevskii, who saw history as contingent, accidental, and paradoxical, embraced Ivan's contradictions. Like all contemporary rulers, Ivan lived a theatrical life, but he did not mistake theater for real life and his self-image never got the better of him.[3]

Ivan's conception of his relationship to God dominated his identity. He implicitly agreed with Agapetus that in his power he was like God, but he did not try to become God. If God could judge Ivan by divine law, Ivan was not God.[4] Even in his most arrogant and self-righteous moments, he could do no more than ask God to forgive his sins, which he readily admitted committing.

To compare Ivan to his "terrible" contemporaries requires confronting the theory of Russian exceptionalism, its "special path." His detractors criticize him for being much more violent than comparable contemporary rulers, but levels of atrocity defy comparison.[5] His apologists insist that, although he acted no worse than his contemporaries, he is viewed more negatively because contemporary and subsequent Europeans and Europeanized Russians hate Russia, an attitude they call Russophobia. Such apologists fail to mention that Ivan was *no better* than his contemporaries.

Ivan's contradictory qualities also characterize most of Cherniavsky's "terrible" rulers and leaders, such as Lorenzo de Medici of Italy, Louis XI of France, Henry VIII of England, and Gustav Vasa of Sweden. Of course, no two rulers were identical. People praised Lorenzo for his tenderness toward children, but no one mentioned Ivan's paternal instincts. Unlike Henry VIII, Ivan never had any of his children legally declared illegitimate. Ivan did not share Louis XI's aversion to ceremony or his refusal to bear grudges. Like Ivan, Henry VIII deprived his subjects of their lives without trial or due process. Philip II, unlike nearly all contemporary rulers, refused flattery, hearsay, or calumny, not to mention bodyguards. Very much unlike Ivan, Henry VIII, or Elizabeth I, Philip always remained perfectly in control of himself when speaking, spoke little, and never interrupted anyone else while speaking.[6]

Russian exceptionalism loses some of its luster when faced with these comparisons. Ivan had more in common with his fellow rulers than indicated by his own arrogant rhetoric about their inferiority or biased insults of him by foreign travelers. Then again, the "Europe" against which historians judge Muscovy never existed.[7] Ivan resembled his fellow rulers in some respects, despite some significant differences between their countries and Muscovy.

In some ways Ivan's life was the stuff of classical Greek tragedy: the young and successful hero, conqueror, reformer, newlywed, and father brought low by war, degradation, insanity, and political catastrophe. His fatal flaw—hubris, his belief in the ideology of unlimited rule—caused him to disregard sensible advice and put himself above human and divine law.[8] This classical dramatic analogy falls short, however. Ivan was not insane, and he did not confuse his ideology with reality. Rather, Ivan would have made a great hero in a Shakespearean drama.[9] Calling Ivan's reign a tragedy does not explain how that tragedy occurred.

If we place too much emphasis on the contrast between the high hopes of the "long" 1550s and the despair of the late 1570s and early 1580s, we risk overlooking the significance of Ivan's minority, which was a discouraging beginning to his reign. The same risk affects contrasts between the "good" Ivan of the reform period and the "bad" Ivan of the *oprichnina* because, according to Kurbskii and other sources, Ivan was already "bad" as a child.

It is equally misleading to infer "public opinion" from elite government or literary sources that tell us nothing of what the peasants thought. Folklore, not recorded until the eighteenth century, cannot compensate for the absence of contemporary written sources conveying popular opinion. Historians cannot draw any credible conclusions about what nine-tenths of the Muscovite population thought about Ivan during his lifetime.[10]

Given the sources available to us, it remains impossible to determine how much of what happened during Ivan's reign can be attributed to him and how much was due to other factors. Ivan's contribution to events need not have been consistent. Kudos for Ivan's successes—reforms, the conquest of Kazan—tends to accrue to his advisors, while blame for his failures—the Livonian War, the oprichnina—to Ivan.[11] We face challenges in documenting Ivan's involvement in either successes or failures, even the extent to which he was responsible for devising the oprichnina, seemingly an expression of his self-identity, because some historians attribute his behavior to the influence of his advisors. Surviving sources always attribute government policy to Ivan. Historians can and should hold Ivan responsible, as ruler, for all good and all bad things during his reign. Anachronistic references to Ivan's always anonymous "stage managers," "masters of ceremonies," or "handlers" merely obfuscate. Ivan picked his advisors and chose whose advice to take.

It is not productive to divide the decades of Ivan's rule, after he became an adult, into periods of "good Ivan" and "bad Ivan," a trend that began with Kurbskii in his letters to Ivan and his *History*, the Chronograph of 1617, and some foreign accounts, and was enshrined in Karamzin.[12] Ivan did not begin to rule as "all good" and then turn into "all bad." At all times he was a frustrating combination of the two. He was always flawed and contradictory—in short, human. No one should deny the plausibility of a cruel brilliant writer or a hypocritical, devout Christian. Ivan was neither inhuman nor superhuman but all too human.

Ivan not only made an impression on Muscovy but also had an impact.[13] In his own lifetime his actions altered the lives of thousands, and perhaps tens of thousands, of members of the elite and their families: where they served, how they died, what rewards or punishments they received. Thousands perished in the oprichnina as a result of his war against his own country. Hundreds of boyars, state secretaries, gentry, and clergy suffered grisly deaths at his orders. On the other hand, Ivan's reforms lasted as long as any reforms last, until the elite preferred something else. The Law Code of 1550 remained in effect until 1649. All the decisions of the Church Council of 1551 remained in force until 1666, which revised only some of them. The institutional structure of the central government created in the mid-sixteenth century lasted until Peter the Great,[14] as did the musketeers. Ivan's successors continued to hold the title of "tsar" until 1917. Kazan and Astrakhan remain part of the Russian Federation. To bestow upon Ivan only praise for the good or blame for the bad developments in Muscovy during his reign distorts both Ivan's complexity and the complexity of Muscovite history in the sixteenth century.[15]

Ivan became the first ruler of Muscovy to employ mass terror as a political instrument, something no subsequent Muscovite or Imperial Russian ruler ever imitated.[16] Although the Romanovs falsely claimed him as their direct ancestor, they saw him as a negative role model and avoided imitating his policies. Tsar Aleksei Mikhailovich may have portrayed Ivan's reign as an ideal, but he repealed some provisions of the Church Council of 1551 on religious ritual and apologized to the relics of St. Metropolitan Filipp for the injustice done to him by Ivan. Boris Godunov and the Romanovs eschewed Ivan's cavalier treatment of the boyars. Attempts to restrict royal criminality in the seventeenth century must have had Ivan in mind, as the example Muscovy's rulers should not follow. Sixteenth-century interrogatories for confession did not query the tsar about whether he had accused anyone in anger, sent an unwanted wife to a convent so he could remarry, or ordered innocent people tortured, all sins which Ivan committed, but seventeenth-century interrogatories did.[17] Russian rulers after Ivan did not repeat the oprichnina's mass terror until the twentieth century, in part because it had obviously not worked.

Historians have not adequately studied the seventeenth-century Muscovites who copied, revised, and read the manuscripts of Ivan's correspondence with Kurbskii and Kurbskii's *History* or what they thought about Ivan.[18]

Previous analyses of this correspondence fixated on autocracy, aristocracy, and bureaucracy, whereas Ivan and Kurbskii debated whether Ivan behaved like a pious ruler and whether he executed the innocent or the guilty. Narratives and chronicles of the Time of Troubles hardly idealized Ivan.[19] No one has comprehensively analyzed the many historical reminiscences, comments, notes, and minutiae about Ivan in seventeenth-century manuscripts.

We have no more definite a picture of what Ivan looked like than we have of what he did. Ivan's likeness graces the barrel of a cannon cast in Revel in 1559.[20] Historians now date the icon-style Copenhagen Portrait of Ivan to the seventeenth century or later, so the image on the cannon becomes the only surviving contemporary, realistic portrait of Ivan.[21] Other, mid-sixteenth- and seventeenth-century Muscovite and foreign portraits were highly stylized. Gerasimov's reconstruction should be compared to both the Revel cannon and the Copenhagen Portrait.[22] None of these images, however accurate, possesses the emotional force of the contradictory depictions of Ivan in Imperial Russian painting: Il'ya Repin's image of Ivan crumpled up on the floor, cradling the bloody dead body of Tsarevich Ivan, and Vasilii Vasnetsov's portrait of Ivan standing upright, in all his imperial regalia and fierceness. Regardless of physical details, even in old age Ivan remained an impressive, charismatic figure. When he died, he was over six feet tall and weighed approximately 210 pounds.[23]

Ivan's reign was politicized in his lifetime and remains so to this day, in part because the myth of Ivan the sadistic tyrant dominates the historical Ivan, a very complicated man whose personality and rule cannot be reduced to a cliché. Works of Russian culture, some of which have had a worldwide impact (none more so than Eisenstein's films), enshrine the myth. Since the nineteenth century, historians in Russia have struggled to separate the man from the myth. Until fairly recently, Western historians by and large simply elaborated the myth, and some still do. Since the death of Stalin, Russian and Western historians have produced a bounty of valuable historical scholarship. Even this scholarship, however, has not entirely overcome Ivan's traditional image. Many historians sincerely believe in the accuracy of the myth. New scholarship creates more opinions, theories, interpretations, and conclusions, and less consensus. Given the sources, this dilemma cannot be overcome. No historian can "solve" the problem of Ivan's life or his reign; the most that any historian can do is engage these problems. Writing a "definitive" study of Ivan and his reign remains impossible. This book has offered some new answers to old questions, identified some old questions that no longer contribute to the discussion, and posed some new questions. Despite the limitations of the sources, historians still have much to learn about Ivan's life, reign, and rule. Their ultimate goal should be to achieve a historical understanding of Ivan that encompasses the "five Cs": change, context, causality, complexity, and contingency.[24]

Glossary

anti-brigandage (*guba*) institutions: Elders, sworn men, and scribes authorized to conduct inquests to identify known brigands and deal with them summarily.

appanage (*udel*): Territory assigned to a member of the royal family.

"black" lands / peasants: land not owned by a private owner or institution and the peasants who lived on it.

conditional land grant (*pomest'e*): During Ivan IV's reign, land given in return for service, usually military.

county administrator (*volostel'*): Centrally appointed administrator of a county (*volost'*).

court (*dvor*): (1) The ceremonial court: those who were present when Ivan held diplomatic and domestic receptions. (2) The institutional court: the household of the ruler, which included boyars, associate boyars, gentry, clerks, artisans, and servants who staffed Ivan's private domains and supplied the domestic needs of Ivan and the royal family.

"feeding" (*kormlenie*): The practice by which centrally appointed administrators lived off the people they administered by collecting taxes, customs, and supplies from them; a prebend.

gentry (*deti boiarskie*): Nobles below the rank of boyar or associate boyar.

governor (*namestnik*): Centrally appointed administrator of a city and its district.

"land" (*zemlia*) [noun]: The "land," Muscovite society exclusive of the dynasty or the Muscovite state.

"land" (*Zemshchina*) [noun]: The territory not included in the *oprichnina* from 1565 to 1572.

"land" (*zemskaia*) [adjective]: Local government tax collection institution composed of elders; replaced "feeding" governors and country administrators.

minstrels (*skomorokhi*): Entertainers, primarily bear tamers and musicians.

nobility, nobles: The boyars and the gentry.

***oprichniki*:** Members of Ivan's special corps, attached to the *oprichnina*.

***oprichnina*:** Ivan's personal appanage from 1565 to 1572.

patrimony (*votchina*): Alodial inherited landed estate.

precedence (*mestnichestvo*): A system for assigning a noble a relative "place" in office or ceremonially. It followed a complicated calculation based upon seniority within a clan and the offices previously held by all members of a clan.

prince (*kniaz*): Descendants of the legendary founder of the Rus' dynasty, Riurik, or more accurately of St. Vladimir, the baptizer of Rus'; descendants of the Lithuanian grand duke Gedminas; and converted non-Chinggisid Tatar begs.

"righter" (*pravezh*): Daily public beating on the shins of a debtor until he paid up.

Royal Council (*duma*): Council consisting of boyars and associate boyars; later during Ivan's reign it included conciliar gentry and conciliar state secretaries.

Notes

Abbreviations Used in the Notes

AAE   *Akty, sobrannye v bibliotekakh i arkhivakh Arkheograficheskoi Ekspeditsiei Imperatorskoi Akademii Nauk*

AI   *Akty istoricheskie, sobrannye i izdannye Arkheogracheskoiu kommissieiu*

AN   Akademiia Nauk

AZR   *Akty, otnosiashchiesia k istorii Zapadnoi Rossii, sobrannye i izdannye Arkheograficheskoiu Kommissieiu*

BAN   Biblioteka Akademii Nauk

Chteniia *Chteniia v Imperatorskom Obshchestve istorii i drevnostei rossiiskikh pri Moskovskom universitete*

DDG   *Dukhovnye i dogovornye gramoty velikikh i udel'nykh kniazei XIV–XVI vv.*

DAI   *Dopolneniia k Aktam istoricheskim, sobrannyia i izdannyia Arkheograficheskoiu Kommissieiu*

DRV   *Drevniaia Rossiiskaia Vivliofika*

II   Institut istorii

IRI   Institut rossiiskoi istorii

LGU   Leningradskii gosudarstennyi universitet

MGU   Moskovskii gosudarstvennyi universitet

PDRV   *Prodolzheniia Drevnei Rossiiskoi Vivlikofiki*

PRP   *Pamiatniki russkogo prava*

PSRL   *Polnoe sobranie russkikh letopisei*

RAN   Rossiiskaia Akademiia Nauk

RIB   *Russkaia istoricheskaia biblioteka*

SGGD   *Sobranie gosudarstvennykh gramot i dogovorov, khraniashchikhsia v Gosudarstvennoi Kollegii inostrannykh del*

SRIO   *Sbornik russkogo istoricheskogo obshchestva*

TODRL   *Trudy otdela drevnerusskoi literatury*

Introduction

1. Alex McNeil, *Total Television*, 4th ed. (New York: Penguin Books, 1996), 419.

2. N. I. Kostomarov, "Lichnost' tsaria Ivana Vasil'evicha Groznago," in *Sobranie sochinenii N. I. Kostomarova*, vols. 14–16, *Istoricheskie monografii i izsledovanii* (St. Petersburg: Obshchestvo dlia posobiia nuzhdaiushchimsia literatorov i uchenym, 1905), 415–17. This is mythology, of course; a historian might distinguish between personal cruelty (Nero, Caligula) and cruelty in conquest (Attila, Chinggis).

3. Aleksandr Aleksandrovich Zimin, *Oprichnina Ivana Groznogo* (Moscow: Mysl', 1964), 3; Natal'ia Nikolaevna Mut'ia, *Ivan Groznyi: Istorizm i lichnost' pravitelia v otechestvennom iskusstve XIX-XX vv.* (St. Petersburg: Ateleia, 2010); Kevin M. F. Platt, *Terror and Greatness: Ivan and Peter as Russian Myths* (Ithaca: Cornell University Press, 2011).

4. Edward L. Keenan, "How Ivan Became 'Terrible,'" *Harvard Ukrainian Studies* 28 (2006): 521–42; Charles J. Halperin, "The Metamorphosis of Ivan IV into Ivan the Terrible," in *Miscellanea Slavica. Sbornik statei k 70-letiiu Borisa Andreevicha Uspenskogo*, ed. F. B. Uspenskii (Moscow: Indrik, 2008), 379–97.

5. A. L. Khoroshkevich, "O Viskovatom, ego vremeni i bezvremen'i," *Russia Mediaevalis* 10 (2001), 273, 293, 302.

6. John L. I. Fennell, trans., *Prince A. M. Kurbsky's History of Ivan IV* (Cambridge: Cambridge University Press 1965).

7. Aleksandr Il'ich Filiushkin, *Izobretaia pervuiu voinu Rossii i Evropy. Baltiiskie voiny vtoroi poloviny XVI v. glazami sovremennikov i potomkov* (St. Petersburg: Dmitrii Bulanin, 2013), 289–598.

8. Cornelia Soldat, *Erschreckende Geschichten in der Darstellung von Moskovitern und Osmanen in den deutschen Flugschriften des 16. und 17. Jahrhunderts / Stories of Atrocities in Sixteenth and Seventeenth Century German Pamphlets about the Russians and Turks*, Foreword by David Goldfrank (Lewiston—Queenston—Lampeter: Edwin Mellon Press, 2014).

9. Marshall T. Poe, *"A People Born to Slavery": Russia in Early Modern European Ethnography, 1476–1748* (Ithaca: Cornell University Press, 2000), 157–61, 227–37; Filiushkin, *Izobretaia pervuiu voinu Rossii*, 508–10.

10. E. Golubinskii, *Istoriia russkoi tserkvy. Period vtoroi, Moskovskii*, vol. 2, *ot nashestviia Mongolov do mitropolita Makariia vkliuchitel'no*, pts. 1–2 (Moscow: University Typography for the Imperatorskoe Obshchestvo Istorii i Drevnostei Rossiiskikh pri Moskovskom Universitete, 1900), 2: 331n3; Irina Borisovna Mikhailova, *I zdes' soshlis' vse tsarstva. . . . Ocherki po istorii gosudareva dvora v Rossiii XVI v.: povsednevnaia i prazdnichnaia kul'tura, semantika etiketa i obriadnosti* (St. Petersburg: Dmitrii Bulanin, 2010), 323–24; Edward V. Williams, *The Bells*

of Russia: History and Technology (Princeton: Princeton University Press, 1985), 41–42.

11. Andreas Kappeler, *Ivan Groznyi im Spiegel der ausländischen Druckschriften seiner Zeit. Ein Beitrag zur Geschichte des westlichen Russlandbildes* (Bern, Frankfurt am Main: Herbert Land, Peter Land, 1972), 241.

12. Richard Hellie, "Introduction," *Russian History* 14 (1987): 1–4; Robert O. Crummey, "Ivan the Terrible," in *Windows on the Russian Past: Soviet Historiography since Stalin*, ed. Samuel H. Baron and Nancy W. Heer (Columbus: American Association for the Advancement of Slavic Studies, 1977), 57–74. Whether Ivan had an impact on modern Russian history or even on contemporary Russia or whether only the perception of Ivan in modern times, not Ivan's actual deeds, does so, falls outside the scope of this monograph.

13. Nikolai Konstantinovich Mikhailovskii, *Sochineniia*, vol. 6 (St. Petersburg: "Russkoe Bogatstvo," 1897), 186–87.

14. Charles J. Halperin, "How Quickly They Forgot: Ivan IV in Muscovite Historical Memory," *Vestnik Sankt-Peterburgskogo gosudarstvennogo universiteta*, seriia 2, istoriia, 63, no. 1 (2018): 223–43.

15. Nikolai Mikhailovich Karamzin, *Istoriia gosudarstva Rossiiskago*, vols. 8–9, ed. P. N. Polevoi (St. Petersburg: Izdanie Evg. Evdokimova, 1892).

16. Ruslan G. Skrynnikov, *Ivan the Terrible*, trans. Hugh F. Graham (Gulf Breeze: Academic International Press, 1981), xvii.

17. Maureen Perrie, *The Cult of Ivan the Terrible in Stalin's Russia* (New York: Palgrave, 2001).

18. Charles J. Halperin, "Would You Believe Saint Ivan the Terrible? Reforming the Image of Tsar Ivan IV," *Symposion* 16–17 (2011–2012): 1–22; Charles J. Halperin, "Anything Goes: Post 1991 Historiography about Ivan IV in Russia," *Journal of Modern Russian History and Historiography* 10 (2017): 3–27.

19. George Backer, *The Deadly Parallel: Stalin and Ivan the Terrible* (New York: Random House, 1950).

20. Charles J. Halperin "False Identity and Multiple Identities in Russian History: The Mongol Empire and Ivan the Terrible," *Carl Beck Papers in Russian and East European Studies*, no. 2103 (Pittsburgh: University of Pittsburgh, Center for Russian and East European Studies, 2011).

21. Charles J. Halperin, "Ivan IV the Terrible, Tsar of Russia," in *Oxford Bibliographies in Renaissance and Reformation*, ed. Margaret King (New York: Oxford University Press, 2014, www.oxfordbibliographies.com).

22. Sergei Fedorovich Platonov, *Ivan the Terrible*, ed. and trans. Joseph L Wieczynski, with Richard Hellie, "In Search of Ivan the Terrible" (Gulf Breeze: Academic International Press, 1986), 1–4.

23. Stepan Borisovich Veselovskii, *Tsar' Ivan Groznyi v rabotakh pisatelei i is-*

torikov: Tri stat'i (Moscow: Assotsiatsiia issledovatelei rossiiskogo obshchestva XX veka, 1999), 10–11; Dmitrii Sergeevich Likhachev, *Poetika drevnerusskoi literatury* (Leningrad: Nauka, Leningradskoe otdelenie, 1967), 84–108.

24. Vasilii Osipovich Kliuchevskii, *Sochineniia*, vol. 2, *Kurs russkoi istorii* (Moscow: Gosudarstvennoe izdatel'stvo politicheskoi literatury, 1957), 98. Compare with, to a lesser degree, Nancy Shields Kollmann, "Muscovite Russia 1450–1598," in *Russia: A History*, ed. Gregory L. Freeze (Oxford: Oxford University Press, 2009), 31–62, especially 61.

25. Edward L. Keenan Jr., "Muscovy and Kazan: Some Introductory Remarks on the Patterns of Steppe Diplomacy," *Slavic Review* 26 (1967): 548–58.

26. Edward L. Keenan Jr., "The Trouble with Muscovy: Some Observations upon Problems of the Comparative Study of Form and Genre in Historical Writing," *Medievalia et Humanistica* 5 (1974): 109; Donald Ostrowskii, *Muscovy and the Mongols: Cross-cultural Influences on the Steppe Frontier* (Cambridge: Cambridge University Press, 1998), 105, 153n42.

27. Edward L. Keenan, *The Kurbskii-Groznyi Apocrypha: The Seventeenth-Century Origin of the "Correspondence" Attributed to Prince A. M. Kurbskii and Tsar Ivan IV* [hereafter *Apocrypha*] with an appendix by Daniel C. Waugh (Cambridge: Harvard University Press, 1971); Charles J. Halperin, "A Heretical View of Sixteenth-Century Muscovy: Edward L. Keenan, The Kurbskii-Groznyi Apocrypha," *Jahrbücher für Geschichte Osteuropas* 22 (1974): 161–86; Charles J. Halperin, "Keenan's Heresy Revisited," *Jahrbücher für Geschichte Osteuropas* 28 (1980): 481–99; Charles J. Halperin, "Edward Keenan and the Kurbskii-Groznyi Correspondence in Hindsight," *Jahrbücher für Geschichte Osteuropas* 46 (1998): 376–403; Brian J. Boeck, "Eyewitness or False Witness? Two Lives of Metropolitan Filipp of Moscow," *Jahrbücher für Geschichte Osteuropas* 55 (2007): 161–77; Charles J. Halperin, "You Dog! Ivan IV's Canine Invective," in *Rusistika Ruslana Skrynnikova. Sbornik statei pamiati professora R. G. Skrynnikova, v chest' ego 80-letiia*, ed. G. Szvák and I. O. Tiumentsev (Knigi po rusistike XXX; Budapest -Volgograd: Magyar Ruszisztikai Intézet, 2011), 92n29.

28. Sergei Bogatyrev, "Micro-Periodization and Dynasticism: Was There a Divide in the Reign of Ivan the Terrible?" *Slavic Review* 69 (2010): 398–409.

29. Pierre Gonneau, *Ivan le Terrible: Ou la métier de tyran* (Paris: Tallender, 2017).

30. Kappeler, *Ivan Groznyi*, 246.

31. Paul Bushkovitch, *A Concise History of Russia* (Cambridge: Cambridge University Press, 2012), 48.

32. Robert O. Crummey, *The Formation of Muscovy, 1304–1613* (London: Longman, 1987), 149.

Chapter 1. Muscovy in 1533

1. Charles J. Halperin, "*Stepennaia kniga* on the Reign of Ivan IV: Omissions from Degree 17," *Slavonic and East European Review* 89 (2011): 58–59.

2. Arlette Jouanna, *The Saint Bartholomew's Day Massacre: The Mysteries of a Crime of State (24 August 1572)*, trans. Joseph Bergin (Manchester: Manchester University Press, 2013), 199–211; Robert M. Kingdon, *Myths about the St. Bartholomew's Day Massacres, 1572–1576* (Cambridge: Harvard University Press, 1988), 137–82, 216; John Lynch, *Spain 1516–1598: From Nation State to World Empire* (Oxford: Blackwell, 1991), 284–87.

3. Richard Hellie, "What Happened? How Did He Get Away with It? Ivan Groznyi's Paranoia and the Problem of Institutional Restraints," *Russian History* 14 (1987): 220; Anna Leonidovna Khoroshkevich, *Rossiia v sisteme mezhdunarodnykh otnoshenii serediny XVI veka* (Moscow: Drevlekhranilishche, 2003), 72n54; *Sbornik russkogo istoricheskogo obshchestva* [hereafter *SRIO*], vol. 59 (St. Petersburg, 1887), 443, 468–69; Vladimir Borisovich Kobrin, *Ivan Groznyi* (Moscow: Moskovskii Rabochii, 1989), 34–35.

4. Erik Tiberg, *Zur Vorgeschichte des Livländischen Krieges: Die Beziehungen zwischen Moskau und Litauen 1549–1562* (Uppsala: University of Uppsala, 1984), 52.

5. I also use the word "noble" to translate *mirza*, the title of Nogai Tatar leaders.

6. M. D'iakonov, *Ocherki obshchestvennogo i gosudarstvennago stroia drevnei Rusi*, 4th ed. (St. Petersburg: Izdanie Iuridicheskago knizhnago skrada "Pravo," 1912), 426–49; Nancy Shields Kollmann, *Kinship and Politics: The Making of the Muscovite Political System, 1345–1547* (Stanford: Stanford University Press, 1987).

7. Paul Bushkovitch, *Religion and Society in Russia: The Sixteenth and Seventeenth Centuries* (New York: Oxford University Press, 1992), 34n4.

8. Hellie, "What Happened?" 199–224; Richard Hellie, "Why Did the Muscovite Elite Not Rebel?" *Russian History* 25 (1998): 155–62.

9. D'iakonov, *Ocherki obshchestvennogo i gosudarstvennago stroia*, 198–200.

10. Isabel de Madariaga, *Ivan the Terrible: First Tsar of Russia* (New Haven: Yale University Press, 2005), 77n10.

11. S. P. Mordovina and A. L. Stanislavskii, ed., *Boiarskie spiski poslednei chetverti XVI-nachala XVII i Rospis' russkogo voiska 1604 g*, pt. 1 (Moscow: Glavnoe arkhivnoe upravlenie pri Sovete Ministrov SSSR, 1979), 84–85; Mikhail Krom, *"Vdovstvuiushchee tsarstvo": Politicheskii krizis v Rossii 30–40-kh godov XVI veka* (Moscow: Novoe literaturnoe obozrenie, 2010), 139; Hartmut Rüß, "Einige Bemerkungen zur Namestnichestvo-Problem in der ersten Hälfte des 16. Jahrhunderts," *Jahrbücher für Geschichte Osteuropas* 20 (1972): 403–11; Daryl W. Palmer, *Writing Russia in the Age of Shakespeare* (Adlershot: Ashgate, 2004), 52–53.

12. Paul Bushkovitch, *Peter the Great: The Struggle for Power, 1671–1725* (Cambridge: Cambridge University Press, 2001), 28–29; Ruslan Grigor'evich Skryn-

nikov, *Tsarstvo terrora* (St. Petersburg: Nauka, Sankt-Peterburgskoe otdelenie, 1992), 175. The translation of this book, Ruslan G. Skrynnikov, *Reign of Terror*, by Paul Williams for the Bronze Horseman Literary Agency (Leiden: Brill, 2015), appeared after I had written the first draft of this book.

13. S. N. Bogatyrev, "'Smirennaia groza': k probleme interpretatsii istochnikov po istorii politicheskoi kul'tury Moskovskoi Rusi," in *Istochnikovedenie i kraevedenie v kul'ture Rossii: Sbornik k 50-letiiu sluzheniia Sigurda Ottovicha Shmidta Istoriko-arkhivnomu institutu*, ed. V. F. Kozloz et al. (Moscow: RGMU, 2000), 79–83; Helmut Neubauer, *Car und Selbstherrscher: Beiträge zur Geschichte der Autokratie in Rußland* (Wiesbaden: Otto Harrassowitz, 1964), 69.

14. Michail Krom, "Formen der Patronage in Russland des 16 und 17 Jahrhunderts: Perspektiven der vergleichenden Forschung im europäischen Kontext," *Jahrbücher für Geschichte Osteuropas* 57 (2009): 121–45.

15. Kristen B. Neuschel, *Word of Honor: Interpreting Noble Culture in Sixteenth-Century France* (Ithaca: Cornell University Press, 1989).

16. John Eric Myles, "The Muscovite Ruling Oligarchy of 1547–1564: Its Composition, Political Behavior, and Attitudes towards Reform" (PhD dissertation, Oxford University-Bodleian College, 1987), 329n1.

17. Krom, *"Vdovstvuiushchee tsarstvo,"* 237–599, 381–87, 440–509; Aleksei Konstantinovich Leont'ev, *Obrazovanie prikaznoi sistemy upravleniia v russkom gosudarstve: Iz istorii sozdaniia tsentralizovannogo gosudarstvennogo apparata v kontse XV—pervoi polovine XVI v.* (Moscow: MGU, 1961), 60–63.

18. George Vernadsky, *The Tsardom of Moscow, 1547–1682*, pt. 1 (New Haven: Yale University Press, 1969), 22–23; A. N. Nasonov, ed., *Pskovskie letopisi*, 2 vols. (Moscow-Leningrad: AN SSSR, 1941, 1955), 1:110, 2:229.

19. *From Max Weber: Essays in Sociology*, trans. H. H. Gerth and C. Wright Mills (New York: Oxford University Press, 1958), 196–244; Geoffrey Randolph Elton, *The Tudor Revolution in Government: Administrative Changes in the Reign of Henry VIII* (Cambridge: Cambridge University Press, 1953); Christopher Coleman and David Starkey, ed., *Revolution Reassessed: Revisions in the History of Tudor Government and Administration* (Oxford: Clarendon Press, 1986); Krom, *"Vdovstvuiushchee tsarstvo,"* 616–19.

20. Leont'ev, *Obrazovanie prikaznoi sistemy upravleniia*, 21–72; Peter B. Brown, "Muscovite Government Bureaus," *Russian History* 10 (1983): 269.

21. Brown, "Muscovite Government Bureaus," 294–329; Zimin, *Oprichnina Ivana Groznogo*, 380; Leont'ev, *Obrazovanie prikaznoi sistemy upravleniia*, 136–52, 73–116; Vladimir Ivanovich Buganov, *Razriadnye knigi poslednei chetverti XV-nachala XVII v.* (Moscow: AN SSSR, 1962), 110–17.

22. Leont'ev, *Obrazovanie prikaznoi sistemy upravleniia*, 43, 55–56; Pavel Nikolaevich Miliukov, "Drevneishaia Razriadnaia kniga offitsial'noi redaktsii (po

1565 g.)," *Chteniia v Imperatorskom obshchestve istorii i drevnostei rossiiskikh pri Moskovskom universitete* [hereafter *Chteniia*] 1902, bk. 1, vol. 200, sec. 1, 185, 233; A. A. Zimin, *Reformy Ivana Groznogo: Ocherki sotsial'no-ekonomicheskoi i politicheskoi istorii Rossii serediny XVI v.* (Moscow: Izdatel'stvo Sotsial'no-ekonomicheskoi literatury, 1960), 361–64; *Razriadnaia kniga 1475–1598 gg.* (Moscow: Nauka, 1966), 152, 160.

23. Nikolai Petrovich Likhachev, *Razriadnye d'iaki XVI veka. Opyt istoricheskago izsledovaniia* (St. Petersburg: Tipografiia V. S. Belashova, 1888), 1–81; Zimin, *Reformy Ivana Groznogo*, 455–56; S. O. Shmidt, *Rossiiskoe gosudarstvo v seredine XVI stoletiia: Tsarskii arkhiv i litsevye letopisi vremeni Ivan Groznogo* (Moscow: Nauka, 1984), 65–68.

24. Andrei Pavlovich Pavlov, *Gosudarev dvor i politicheskaia bor'ba pri Borise Godunove (1584–1605)* (St. Petersburg: Nauka, St.-Peterburgskoe otdelenie, 1992), 27–29; Ronald G. Asch and Adolf M. Birke, ed., *Princes, Patronage, and the Nobility: The Court at the Beginning of the Modern Age, c. 1450–1650* (Oxford: Oxford University Press, 1991).

25. *Pamiatniki russkogo prava* [hereafter *PRP*], vol. 4: *Pamiatniki prava perioda ukrepleniia russkogo tsentralizovannogo gosudarstva. XV-XVII vv.* (Moscow: Gosudarstvennoe izdatel'stvo iuridicheskoi literatury, 1956), 263–64.

26. N. A. Popov, ed, *Akty Moskovskago gosudarstva*, vol. 1, *Razriadnyi prikaz: Moskovskii stol 1571–1634* (St. Petersburg: Tipografiia Imperatorskoi AN, 1890), no. 21, 34L–35L; A. M. Sakharov, ed., *Sbornik dokumentov po istorii SSSR dlia seminarskikh i prakticheskikh zaniatii (period feodalizma)*, pt. 3, *XVI vek* (Moscow: Vysshaia shkola, 1972), no. 35, 176–77.

27. Krom, *"Vdovstvuiushchee tsarstvo,"* 364–75, 491–509; Jack Edward Kollmann Jr., "The Moscow *Stoglav* ('Hundred Chapters') Church Council of 1551" (PhD dissertation, University of Michigan, 1978), vol. 1, 153.

28. Mikhail Krom, "Religiozno-nravstvennoe osnovanie administrativnykh preobrazovanii v Rossii XVI veka," *Forschungen zur osteuropäischen Geschichte 76* (2010): 63.

29. A. L. Iurganov, "Moskovskoe gosudarstvo v zhiznennom mire sovremennikov i issledovatelei," in *Rol' gosudarstva v istoricheskom razvitii Rossii / The Role of the State in the Historical Development of Russia*, ed. Gyula Szvák (Budapest: Russica Pannonicana, 2011), 18; Boris N. Floria, "Tsentralizatsiia i modernizatsiia Russkogo gosudarstva vo vtoroi polovine XV-pervoi polovine XVI v.," in *Modernizacja struktur władzy w warunkach opóźnienia. Europa Środkowa i Wschodnia na przełomie średniowiecza i czasów nowożytnych*, ed. Marian Dygo et al. (Warsaw: DiG, 1999), 59–72.

30. A. I. Iakovlev, *Namestnich'i, gubnyia i zemskyia ustavnye gramoty Moskovskago gosudarstva* (Moscow: Istoriko-fililogicheskii fakul'tet Imperatorskogo Moskovska-

go universiteta, 1909), 1536 to 1556: no. 7, 16–19; no. 8, 19–22; no. 9, 22–25; no. 10, 25–30; no. 11, 30–32; no. 12, 32–37; no. 13, 17–19, no. 16, 45–46.

31. Horace W. Dewey, "Immunities in Old Russia," *Slavic Review* 23 (1964): 643–59; Sergei Mikhailovich Kashtanov, *Sotsial'no-politicheskaia istoriia Rossii kontsa XV—pervoi poloviny XVI v.* (Moscow: Nauka, 1967), 275–376; Mark D. Zlotnik, "Immunity Charters and the Centralization of the Muscovite State" (PhD dissertation, University of Chicago, 1976); Nikolai Evgen'evich Nosov, *Stanovlenie soslovno-predstavitel'nykh uchrezhdenii v Rossii: Izyskaniia o zemskom reforme Ivana Groznogo* (Leningrad: Nauka, Leningradskoe otdelenie, 1969), 89–239.

32. Zlotnik, "Immunity Charters," 93–100; Andrei L'vovich Iurganov, *Kategorii russkoi srednevekovoi kul'tury* (Moscow: MIROS, 1998), 117–99; *SRIO* 38 (St. Petersburg: Tipografiia V. S. Balasheva, 1883), 7; K. V. Baranov and T. B. Solov'eva, "Novye dokumenty o prebyvanii v Rossii valashskogo voevoda Bogdana Aleksandrovicha," *Russkii diplomatarii* 4 (1998): 159–65.

33. Margarita Evgen'eva Bychkova, *Sostav klassa feodalov Rossii v XVI v. Istoriko-genealogicheskoe issledovanie* (Moscow: Nauka 1986), 29–73; A. L. Iurganov, "Udel'no-votchinnaia sistema i traditsiia nasledovaniia vlasti i sobstvennosti v srednevekovoi Rossii," *Otechestvennaia istoriia*, no. 3 (1996): 93–114.

34. Kashtanov, *Sotsial'no-politicheskaia istoriia Rossii*, 11; V. Iu. Belikov and E. I. Kolycheva, "Dokumenty o zemlevladenii kniazei Vorotynskikh vo vtoroi polovine XVI-nachale XVII vv.," *Arkhiv russkoi istorii* 2 (1992), no. 2, 110–18; Sakharov, *Sbornik dokumentov*, no. 15, 150–52; Nicholas Henshall, *The Myth of Absolutism: Change and Continuity in Early Modern European Monarchy* (London: Longman, 1992), 82.

35. Peter Burke, *Languages and Communities in Early Modern Europe* (Cambridge: Cambridge University Press, 2004).

36. John Elliot, "A Europe of Composite Monarchies," *Past & Present* 137 (1992): 48–71; Harald Gustafsson, "The Conglomerate State: A Perspective on State Formation in Early Modern Europe," *Scandinavian Journal of History* 23 (1998): 189–213.

37. Richard Hellie, *Enserfment and Military Change in Muscovy* (Chicago: University of Chicago Press, 1967); David M. Goldfrank, ed., *The Monastic Rule of Iosif Volotskii*, rev. ed. (Kalamazoo: Cistercian Publications, 2000), 10 n. 71; Marshall Poe, "The Truth About Muscovy," *Kritika* 3 (2002): 473–86.

38. Edward L. Keenan, "Muscovite Political Folkways" and "Muscovite Political Folkways: Reply," *Russian Review* 45 (1986): 15–58, 199–209; Kollmann, *Kinship and Politics*; Valerie A. Kivelson, "On Words, Sources, and Historical Method: Which Truth about Muscovy?" *Kritika* 3 (2003): 487–99; Hartmut Rüß, *Herren und Diener: Die soziale und politische Mentalität des Russischen Adels. 9.-17. Jahrhundert* (Cologne: Böhlau Verlag 1994).

39. Krom, "*Vdovstvuiushchee tsarstvo,*" 18; Bogatyrev, "Localism and Integration

in Muscovy," in *Russia Takes Shape: Patterns of Integration from the Middle Ages to the Present*, ed. Sergei Bogatyrev (Saarijärvi: Gummerus Kirjapaino Oy, 2005), 102–5; Myles, "The Muscovite Ruling Oligarchy," 85–87, 88n1; Valerie Kivelson, "Muscovite 'Citizenship': Rights without Freedom," *Journal of Modern History* 74 (2002): 465–89; Russell E. Martin, *A Bride for the Tsar: Bride-Shows and Marriage Politics in Early Modern Russia* (DeKalb: Northern Illinois University Press, 2012).

40. Charles J. Halperin, "Ivan IV as Autocrat (*samoderzhets*)," *Cahiers du monde russe* 55 (2014): 197–213.

41. Richard Wortman, *Scenarios of Power: Myth and Ceremony in Russian Monarchy*, vol. 1, *From Peter the Great to the Death of Nicholas* (Princeton: Princeton University Press, 1995), 35n38; Glenn Richardson, *Renaissance Monarchy: The Reigns of Henry VIII, Francis I and Charles V* (London: Arnold, 2002), 141–44; Robert O. Crummey, "The Silence of Muscovy," *Russian Review* 46 (1987): 157–64; Richard Hellie, "Edward Keenan's Scholarly Ways," *Russian Review* 46 (1987): 177–90.

42. Charles J. Halperin, "Muscovy as a Hypertrophic State: A Critique," *Kritika* 3 (2003): 501–7; Charles J. Halperin,, "Administrative Discretion in Ivan IV's Muscovy," *Russian History* 33 (2006): 429–46; *Dopolneniia k Aktam istoricheskim, sobrannyia i izdannyia Arkheograficheskoiu Kommissieiu* [hereafter *DAI*], vol. 1 (St. Petersburg: Tipografiia II otdeleniia Sobstvennoi EIV kantseliarii, 1846), no. 62, 124–25; no. 101, 150–51; Richardson, *Renaissance Monarchy*, 109–11.

43. Marshall Poe, "What Did Russians Mean When They Called Themselves 'Slaves of the Tsar'?" *Slavic Review* 57 (1998): 585–608.

44. Sergei Bogatyrev, *The Sovereign and His Counsellors: Ritualised Consultations in Muscovite Political Culture, 1350s–1570s* (Saarijärvi: Gummerus, 2000); Niccolò Machiavelli, *The Prince and the Discourses* (New York: Random House, 1950), 87–89.

45. *Polnoe sobranie russkikh letopisei* [hereafter *PSRL*] 13 (Moscow: Nauka, 1965), 79–234; *PSRL* 29 (Moscow: Nauka, 1965), 57–356.

46. Charles J. Halperin, "Ivan IV Consults his Elite Subjects," *Vestnik Sankt-Peterburgskogo gosudarstvennogo universiteta*, seriia 2, *Istoriia*, no. 4 (2016): 69–76.

47. *Razriadnaia kniga 1475–1598 gg*, 110; *PSRL* 13, 177; *Akty, otnosiashchiesia k istorii Zapadnoi Rossii, sobrannye i izdannye Arkheograficheskoiu Kommissiei* [hereafter *AZR*], vol. 2 (St. Petersburg: Tipografiia II Otd Sobst EIV Kantseliarii, 1848), no. 178, 328–29; Mikhail Krom, "'Die Sache des Herrschers und das Landes': Das Aufkommen der öffentlichen Politik in Russland im 16. und 17. Jahrhundert," trans. Andrea Kamp, in *"Politik": Situationen eines Wortgebauchs im Europa der Neuzeit*, ed. Willibald Steinmetz (Frankfurt: Campus/Verlag, 2007), 210–16.

48. Oleg Kharkhordin, "What Is the State? The Russian Concept of *Gosudarstvo* in the European Context," *History and Theory* 40 (2001): 206–40; M. M. Krom, "Rozhdenie 'gosudarstva': iz istorii moskovskogo politicheskogo diskursa

XVI veka," in *Istoricheskie poniatiia i politicheskie idei v Rossii XVI-XX veka: Sbornik nauchnykh trudov* (St. Petersburg: Ateleia, 2006), 54–69; *SRIO* 59, 37.

49. *Pamiatniki literatury drevnei Rusi. Konets XV—pervaia polovina XVI veka* (Moscow: Khudozhestvennaia literatura, 1984), 504–19; Aleksandr Il'ich Klibanov, *Dukhovnaia kul'tura srednevekovoi Rusi* (Moscow: Aspekt Press, 1996), 207–18.

50. *Prodolzhenie drevnei Rossiiskoi vivliofiki* [hereafter *PDRV*], vol. 6 (St. Petersburg: Imperatorskaia Akademiia Nauk, 1790), no. 188, 45–55; no. 190, 58–61; no. 191, 62–66; no. 192, 67–87; no. 193, 88–99; no. 194, 100–3; no. 195, 104–28; no. 196, 129–32; no. 197, 133–55; Horace W. Dewey and Ann M. Kleimola, "Suretyship and Collective Responsibility in Pre-Petrine Russia," *Jahrbücher für Geschichte Osteuropas* 18 (1970): 337–54; Horace W. Dewey, "Political *Poruka* in Muscovite Rus,'" *Russian Review* 46 (1987): 117–33.

51. Rüß, *Herren und Diener,* 272 n. 73.

52. A. V. Antonov, "Poruchnye zapisi 1527–1571 godov," *Russkii diplomatarii* 10 (2004): nos. 3–13, 13–18; A. M. Kleimola, "Ivan the Terrible and his 'Go-fers': Aspects of State Security in the 1560s," *Russian History* 14 (1987): 283–92; A. M. Kleimola, "The Duty to Denounce in Muscovite Russia," *Slavic Review* 31 (1972): 769.

53. Horace W. Dewey and Ann M. Kleimola, trans., *Russian Private Law in the XIV–XVII Centuries* (Ann Arbor: Department of Slavic Languages and Literatures, 1973), 16, 32–33; Jaako Lehtovirta, "Ivan IV as Emperor: The Imperial Theme in the Establishment of Muscovite Tsardom" (PhD dissertation, University of Turku, 1999), 228–29; Valerie Kivelson, "Merciful Father, Impersonal State: Russian Autocracy in Comparative Perspective," *Modern Asian Studies* 31 (1997): 655.

Chapter 2. The Young Ivan's World

1. Hartmut Rüß, "Machtkampf oder 'feudale Reaktion'? Zu den innerpolitischen Auseinandersetzungen in Moskau nach dem Tode Vasilijs III," *Jahrbücher für Geschichte Osteuropas* 18 (1970): 493.

2. Sigismund von Herberstein, *Notes upon Russia*, trans. R. H. Major, Hakluyt Society Works vol. 10 (London: Hakluyt Society, 1851), 51; Georgii Leonidovich Grigor'ev, *Kogo boialsia Ivan Groznyi? K voprosu o proiskhozhdenii oprichniny* (Moscow: "Intergraf Servis," 1998); Viacheslav Valentinovich Shaposhnik, *Tserkovno-gosudarstvennye otnosheniia v Rossii v 30–80-e gody XVI veka*, 2nd exp. ed. (St. Petersburg: Gosudarstvennoe izdatel'stvo Sankt-Peterburgskogo Universiteta, 2006), 514–16.

3. Paul Bushkovitch, "Princes Cherkasskii or Circassian Murzas: The Kabardians in the Russian Boyar Elite 1560–1700," *Cahiers du monde russe* 45 (2004): 11; *PSRL* 6 (St. Petersburg: Tipografiia Eduarda Pratsa,1853): 271; *PSRL* 34 (Moscow: Nauka, 1978): 21; *PSRL* 29: 122; V. V. Shaposhnik, "Bor'ba za vlast' v Moskve posle smerti Vasiliia III i vneshniaia politika russkogo gosudarstva," *Studia Slavica et*

Balcanica Petropolitana, no. 1 (2014): 27–37; Krom, *"Vdovstvuiushchee tsarstvo,"* 31–119.

4. Hartmut Rüß, "Elena Vasil'evna Glinskaja," *Jahrbücher für Geschichte Osteuropas* 17 (1971): 481–98; Kingdon, *Myths about the St. Bartholomew's Day Massacres*, 200–211.

5. *Prince A. M. Kurbsky's History of Ivan IV*, 190–91; Krom, *"Vdovstvuiushchee tsarstvo,"* 156–57; Natalia Pushkareva with Eve Levin, *Women in Russian History: From the Tenth to the Twentieth Century* (Armonk: M. E. Sharpe, 1997), 89; Sarah Bradford, *Lucrezia Borgia: Life, Love, and Death in Renaissance Italy* (New York: Viking, 2004); G. J. Meyer, *The Borgias: The Hidden History* (New York: Bantam Books, 2013), 238–47, 258–89, 297, 303–417, 429–41; Liudmila Evgen'eva Morozova and Boris Nikolaevich Morozov, *Ivan Groznyi i ego zheny* (Moscow: Drofa-Plius, 2005), 36.

6. Sergei Belokurov, *O biblioteke moskovskikh gosudarei v XVI stoletii* (Moscow: Tipografiia G. Lissner and A. Gesheli, 1898), lxviii; G. N. Moiseeva, ed., *Kazanskaia istoriia* (Moscow-Leningrad: AN SSSR, 1954), 87–92; O. A. Iakovleva, ed., "Piskarevskii letopisets," *Materialy po istorii SSSR* II (Moscow: AN SSSR, 1955), 86; Martin, *A Bride for the Tsar*, 101–2.

7. Morozova and Morozov, *Ivan Groznyi i ego zheny*, 38, 52.

8. Dewey and Kleimola, *Russian Private Law*, no. 1, 7–8; *Akty istoricheskie, sobrannye i izdannye Arkheogracheskoiu kommissieiu* [hereafter *AI*], vol. 1 (1841–1842), no. 136, 197–99; Charles J. Halperin, "The Minority of Ivan IV," in *Rude and Barbarous Kingdom Revisited: Essays in Russian History in Honor of Robert O. Crummey*, ed. Chester Dunning et al. (Bloomington: Slavica Publishers, Inc., 2008), 41–52.

9. Krom, *"Vdovstvuiushchee tsarstvo,"* 564–69; A. S. Mel'nikova, "Mesto monet Ivana Groznogo v riadu pamiatnikov ideologii samoderzhavnoi vlasti," *Vspomogatel'nye istoricheskie distsipliny* 17 (1985): 77–92; *AZR* vol. 2, no. 175: 246–48; *SRIO* vol. 59: 10–13, 33–34; *Posol'skie knigi po sviaziam Rossii s Nogaiskoi Ordoi 1489–1549* (Makhachkala: Dagestanskoe knizhnoe izdatel'stvo, 1995), 94, 194–95; Alan MacFarlane, review of *The Family, Sex, and Marriage in England 1500–1800*, by Lawrence Stone, *History and Theory* 18 (1979): 103–26.

10. M. M. Krom, *Starodubskaia voina 1534–1537: Iz istorii russko-litovskikh otnoshenii* (Moscow: Rubezhi XXI, 2008).

11. Herberstein, *Notes Upon Russia*, 52–53; David Starkey, *Henry: Virtuous Prince* (London: Harper Press, 2008), 88; Alison Plowden, *Elizabeth I* (Sparkford: J. H. Haynes & Co., Ltd, 2004), 42, 632; Sergei Bogatyrev, "Ivan IV (1533–84)," in the *Cambridge History of Russia*, vol. 1, *From Early Rus' to 1689*, ed. Maureen Perrie (Cambridge: Cambridge University Press, 2006), 242; Tat'iana Panova and Denis Pezhemskii, "Otravili! Zhizn' i smert' Eleny Glinskoi: istoriko-antropologicheskoe rassledovanie," *Rodina*, no. 12 (2004): 26–31.

12. *AI* vol. 1, no. 140, 202–4; *PSRL* 26 (Moscow-Leningrad: AN SSSR, 1959), 316; *AZR,* vol. 2, no. 189, 341–44; no. 206, 372; no. 207, 372–73; no. 211, 375; no. 213, 377–79; no. 217, 381–82; no. 218, 382–84; no. 224, 391; no. 226, 292; *Radzivillovskie akty iz sobraniia Rossiiskoi natsional'noi biblioteki: Pervaia polovina XVI veka* (Moscow-Warsaw: Drevlekhranilishche, 2002), no. 43, 108–12.

13. Kollmann, *Kinship and Politics,* 161–80; Paul Bushkovitch, "The Selection and Deposition of the Metropolitan and Patriarch of the Orthodox Church in Russia, 1448–1619," in Être catholique—être orthodoxe—être protestant: Confessions et identités culturelles en Europe médiévale et moderne, ed. Marek Derwich and Mikhail V. Dmitriev (Wroclaw: LARHCOR, 2003), 141–44; David B. Miller, "The Politics and Ceremonial of Ioasaf Skrypitsyn's Installation as Metropolitan on February 9, 1539," *Russian Review* 70 (2011): 234–51.

14. *PSRL* 13, 123 left column, 125–26, 140–41, 149; Rüß, *Herren und Diener,* 367; S. O. Shmidt, "Iz istorii redaktirovaniia Tsarstvennoi knigi (Izvestiia ob opale boyar letom 1546 g.)," in *Rossiia na putiakh tsentralizatsii. Sbornik statei* (Moscow: Nauka, 1982), 221–39.

15. *PSRL* 29, 45; *PSRL* 34, 27; *PSRL* 22 pt. 1 (St. Petersburg: Tipografiia M. A. Aleksandrova, 1911), 525; V. V. Morozov, "Ivan Groznyi na miniiatiurakh Tsarstvennoi knigi," in *Drevnerusskoe iskusstvo. Rukopisnaia kniga. Sbornik Tretii* (Moscow: Nauka, 1983), 235.

16. Valerie Kivelson, "Political Sorcery in Sixteenth-Century Muscovy," in *Culture and Identity in Muscovy, 1539–1584,* ed. A. M. Kleimola and G. D. Lenhoff, UCLA Slavic Studies, NS, vol. 3 (Moscow: ITZ-Garant, 1997), 267–83; Isaak Urielevich Budovnits, *Monastyri na Rusi i bor'ba s nimi krest'ian v XIV-XVI vekakh (po zhitiam sviatykh)* (Moscow: Nauka, 1966), 307–10.

17. M. M. Krom, "Politicheskii krizis 30–40-kh godov XVI veka (Postanovka problemy)," *Otechestvennaia istoriia,* no. 5 (1998): 3–19.

18. Ivan Ivanovich Smirnov, *Ocherki politicheskoi istorii russkogo gosudarstva 30–50-kh godov XVI veka* (Moscow-Leningrad: AN SSSR, 1958), 19–136; Crummey, "The Silence of Muscovy," 163; Krom, "Politicheskii krizis," 61; M. M. Krom, "Byla li 'politika' v Rossii XVI v.?" *Odissei: Chelovek v istorii,* no. 1 (2005): 290.

Chapter 3. Ivan's Minority

1. Starkey, *Henry: Virtuous Prince,* 169, 266; *Pamiatniki diplomaticheskikh snoshenii drevnei Rossii s derzhavami inostrannymi* [hereafter *PDSDR*], vol. 1 (St. Petersburg: Izdatel'stvo. II otdelenie E. I. V. kantseliarii, 1851), 47–48, 65, 127–28, 160, 262, 609, 733, 856–57; Andrei Sergeevich Usachev, *Stepennaia kniga i drevnerusskaia knizhnost' vremeni mitropolita Makariia* (Moscow-St. Petersburg: Al'ians-Arkheo, 2009), 611–14.

2. John L. I. Fennell, ed., *The Correspondence of Prince A. M. Kurbsky and*

Tsar Ivan IV of Russia 1564–1579 (Cambridge: Cambridge University Press, 1963), 72–77.

3. Isolde Thyrêt, *Between God and Tsar: Religious Symbolism and the Royal Women of Muscovite Russia* (DeKalb: Northern Illinois University Press, 2001), 39–40; S. A. Belokurov, *O posol'skom prikaze* (Moscow: Imperatorskoe Obshchestvo Istorii i Drevnostei Rossiiskikh pri Moskovskom Universitete, 1906), 94; *Posol'skie knigi po sviaziam Rossii s Nogaiskoi Ordoi 1489–1549*, 199; *Akty sluzhilykh zemlevladel'tsev XV—nachala XVII veka,* vol. 4 (Moscow: Drevlekhranilishche, 2008), no. 503, 388–97; *Akty, sobrannye v bibliotekakh i arkhivakh Arkheograficheskoi Ekspeditsiei Imperatorskoi Akademii Nauk* [hereafter *AAE*], vol. 1, *1294–1598* (St. Petersburg: Tipografiia II Otdeleniia sobstvennoi EIV Kantseliarii, 1836), no. 184, 158–63.

4. Crummey, *The Formation of Muscovy*, 146; Philippe Ariès, *Centuries of Childhood: A Social History of Family Life*, trans. Robert Baldick (New York: Alfred A. Knopf, 1962), 15–133; Adrian Wilson, "The Infancy of the History of Childhood: An Appraisal of Philippe Ariès," *History and Theory* 19 (1980): 132–53.

5. *PSRL* 29, 45; Plowden, *Elizabeth I*, 5–178; Bushkovitch, *Peter the Great*, 125–89.

6. *Prince A. M. Kurbsky's History of Ivan IV*, 10–11.

7. E. A. Solov'ev, "Ioann Groznyi," in *Ioann Groznyi. Khmel'nitskii. Potemkim. Suvorov. Skobelev* (St. Petersburg: LIO Redaktor, 1998), 38.

8. *Razriadnaia kniga 1475–1598 gg.*, 109; Krom, *"Vdovstvuiushchee tsarstvo,"* 301–26; I. B. Mikhailova, *Sluzhilye liudi severo-vostochnoi Rusi v XIV-pervoi polovine XVI veka: Ocherki sotsial'noi istorii* (St. Petersburg: SPbGU, 2003), 461.

9. Ivan Ivanovich Polosin, *Sotsial'no-politicheskaia istoriia Rossii XVI—nachala XVII v. sbornik statei* (Moscow: AN SSSR, 1963), 64–123; Nancy Shields Kollmann, "Pilgrimage, Procession and Symbolic Space in Sixteenth-Century Russian Politics," in *Medieval Russian Culture*, ed. Michael S. Flier and Daniel Rowland, vol. 2, California Slavic Studies 29 (Berkeley: University of California Press, 1994), 108; Lucy Wooding, *Henry VIII* (London: Routledge, Francis & Taylor Group, 2009), 61; Neil Samman, "The Progresses of Henry VIII, 1509–1529," in *The Reign of Henry VIII: Politics, Policy and Piety*, ed. Diarmand MacCulloch (New York: St. Martin's Press, 1995), 59–73.

10. Stephen Greenblatt, *Renaissance Self-Fashioning: From More to Shakespeare* (Chicago: University of Chicago Press, 1980), 15, 121, 136–37, 139; Richardson, *Renaissance Monarchy*, 14, 35, 170; Mark Hansen, *The Royal Facts of Life: Biology and Politics in Sixteenth-Century Europe* (Metuchen: Scarecrow Press, 1980), 15–24, 30–35.

11. M. N. Tikhomirov, "Zapiski o regenstve Eleny Glinskoi i boiarskom pravlenii 1533–1547," *Istoricheskie zapiski* 46 (1954), 286; *PSRL* 34, 27; *PSRL* 29, 47–49; Krom, *"Vdovstvuiushchee tsarstvo,"* 316–322.

12. *PSRL* 13, 448; *Pskovskie letopisi*, 1: 116, 2: 230–322; *PSRL* 4, pt. 1, vypusk tretii (Leningrad: AN SSSR, 1929), 618; Krom, *"Vdovstvuiushchee tsarstvo,"* 323–25.

13. Krom, *"Vdovstvuiushchee tsarstvo,"* 316–22.

14. A. A. Zimin, *Krupnaia feodal'naia votchina i sotsial'no-politicheskaia bor'ba v Rossii (konets XV-XVI vv.)* (Moscow: Nauka, 1977), 310.

15. David Goldfrank, "The Deep Origins of *Tsar'-Muchitel'*: A Nagging Problem of Muscovite Political Theory," *Russian History* 32 (2005): 341–54.

16. D. P. Golokhvastov and archimandrite Leonid, "Blagoveshchenskii ierei Sil'vestr i ego pisaniia. Issledovaniia," *Chteniia*, bk. 1, vol. 88 (1874): 68–87; *Sochineniia prepodobnago Maksima Greka*, 3 vols. (Kazan: Kazan Theological Academy, 1859), 1:23–39; 2:52–88, 157–84, 185–212, 251–60, 319–39, 338–46, 3:237–38; V. F. Rzhiga, "Opyty po istorii russkoi publitsistiki XVI veka: Maksim Grek kak publitsist," *Trudy otdela drevnerusskoi literatury* [hereafter *TODRL*] 1 (1934), 62–72, 117–19.

17. *Sochineniia prepodobnago Maksima Greka*, 2: 296–319, 346–57, 376–79.

18. Hansen, *The Royal Facts of Life*, 71–79, 120–25.

Chapter 4. Ivan's Coronation and First Marriage

1. *Akty sotsial'no-ekonomicheskoi istorii severa Rossii kontsa XV-XVI v. Akty Solovetskogo monastyria 1479–1571 gg.* (Leningrad: Nauka, 1988) no. 133, 84–85; *Akty sotsial'no-ekonomicheskoi istorii severa Rossii kontsa XV-XVI v. Akty Solovetskogo monastyria 1572–1584 gg.* (Moscow: Nauka, 1990), no. 854, 206.

2. *SRIO* 59, 264–629, 571–72; *SRIO* 71 (St. Petersburg, 1892), 578.

3. *PSRL* 22, 526; *PSRL* 34, 28; Skrynnikov, *Ivan the Terrible*, 16–17; Henry Kamen, *Philip II of Spain* (New Haven: Yale University Press, 1997), 13; E. Golubinskii, *Istoriia russkoi tserkvy*, 1: 767.

4. *DAI* vol. 1, no. 39, 41–57; Elpidifor V. Barsov, "Drevne-russkie pamiatniki sviashchennago venchaniia tsarei na tsarsto s sviazi s grecheskimi ikh originalami: S istoricheskim ocherkom chinov tsarskago venchaniia v sviazi s razvitiiem idei tsaria na Rusi," *Chteniia* bk. 1, sec. 1, vol. 124 (1883): 42–66, 67–90; David B. Miller, "The Coronation of Ivan IV in 1547," *Jahrbücher für Geschichte Osteuropas* 15 (1967): 559–74; Olga Novikova, "Le couronnement d'Ivan IV: La conception de l'empire à l'Est de l'Europe," trans. Élisabeth Teiro and André Berelowitch, *Cahiers du monde russe* 46 (2005): 220.

5. V. I. Savva, *Moskovskie tsari i vizantiiskie vasilevsy: K voprosu o vliianiia Vizantiia na obrazovanie idei tsarskoi vlasti moskovskikh gosudarei* (Kharkov: M. Zil'berber i synov'ia, 1901), 146–51; Boris Andreevich Uspenskii, *Tsar' i imperator: Pomazanie na tsarstvo i semantika monarshikh titulov* (Moscow: Iazyki russkoi kul'tury, 2000), 158 n. 7.

6. Jukka Korpela, *Prince Saint and Apostle: Prince Vladimir Sviatoslavič of Kiev,*

His Posthumous Life, and the Religious Legitimization of the Russian Great Power (Wiesbaden: Harrassowitz Verlag, 2001), 193 n. 1096.

7. Michael Cherniavsky, "Khan or Basileus: An Aspect of Russian Mediaeval Political Theory," *Journal of the History of Ideas* 20 (1959): 459–76; Savva, *Moskovskie tsari*, 145–61.

8. Peter Nitsche, *Grossfürst und Thronfolger. Die Nachfolgepolitik der Moskauer Herrscher biz zum Ende des Rjurikidenhauses* (Cologne: Böhlau Verlag, 1972), 261–66; B. A. Uspenskii, *Tsar' i patriarkh: Kharizma vlasti v Rossii (Vizantiiskaia model' i ee russkoe pereosmyslenie)* (Moscow: Shkola 'Iazyki russkoi kul'tury,' 1998), 13–113; A. F. Filiushkin, *Tituly russkikh gosudarei* (Moscow-St. Petersburg: Al'ians-Arkheo, 2006), 87; Sergei Bogatyrev, "Ivan the Terrible Discovers the West: The Cultural Transformation of Autocracy during the Early Northern Wars," *Russian History* 34 (2007): 161–70.

9. Savva, *Moskovskie tsari*, 146–51.

10. Vladimir Val'denberg, *Drevnerusskiia ucheniia o predelakh tsarskoi vlasti: Ocherki russkoi politicheskoi literatury ot Vladimira Sviatogo do kontsa XVII veka* (Petrograd: A. Benke, 1916), 273–356; Lynch, *Spain 1516–1598*, 370–71; Lehtovirta, *Ivan IV as Emperor*, 138–54.

11. Mariia Pliukhanova, *Siuzhety i simvoly Moskovskogo tsarstva* (St. Petersburg: Akropol',' 1995), 177; M. D'iakonov, *Vlast' Moskovskikh gosudarei. Ocheri iz istorii politicheskikh idei Drevnei Rusi do kontsa XVI veka* (St Petersburg: Tipografiia I. N. Skorokhodova, 1889), 91–132.

12. Anthony Pagden, *Lords of All the World: Ideologies of Empire in Spain, Britain, and France c. 1500–1800* (New Haven: Yale University Press, 1995), 11–28; Paul Bushkovitch, "The Formation of National Consciousness in Early Modern Russia," *Harvard Ukrainian Studies* 10 (1986): 356–63; Daniel B. Rowland, "Moscow—The Third Rome or the New Israel?" *Russian Review* 55 (1996): 591–614.

13. Michael S. Flier, "Transporting Jerusalem: The Epiphany Ritual in Early St. Petersburg," in *Rites of Place: Public Commemoration in Russia and Eastern Europe*, ed. Julie Buckler and Emily D. Johnson (Evanston: Northwestern University Press, 2013), 25.

14. Andrei Vasil'evich Karavashkin, *Russkaia srednevekovaia publitsistika: Ivan Peresvetov, Ivan Groznyi, Andrei Kurbskii* (Moscow: Prometei, 2000), 152–56.

15. Michael Cherniavsky, "Russia," in *National Consciousness, History and Political Culture in Early Modern Europe*, ed. Orest Ranum (Baltimore: Johns Hopkins University Press, 1975), 126; Michael Khodarkovsky, "'Third Rome' or a Tributary State: A View of Moscow from the Steppe," *Forschungen zur osteuropäischen Geschichte* 63 (2004): 363–74.

16. Sergei Mikhailovich Solov'ev, *Istoriia Rossii s drevneishikh vremen*, bk. 3 (vols. 5–6) (Moscow: Izdatel'stvo Sotsial'no-ekonomicheskoi literatury, 1963), 596.

17. Ron Sela, *Ritual and Authority in Central Asia: The Khan's Inauguration Ceremony* (Bloomington: Indiana University Research Institute for Inner Asian Studies, 2003); Charles J. Halperin, "Ivan IV and Chinggis Khan," *Jahrbücher für Geschichte Osteuropas* 51 (2003): 487–96.

18. *SRIO* 59, 437.

19. *SRIO* 59, 287, 309–10, 345, 373, 437; Charles J. Halperin, "The Russian Land and the Russian Tsar: The Emergence of Muscovite Ideology, 1380–1408," *Forschungen zur osteuropäischen Geschichte* 23 (1976), 69–78.

20. Mikhailova, *I zdes' soshlis' vse tsarstva*, 79–144.

21. Nancy Shields Kollmann, "The Cap of Monomakh," in *Picturing Russia: Explorations in Visual Culture*, ed. Valerie A. Kivelson and Joan Neuberger (New Haven: Yale University Press, 2008), 38–41.

22. Günther Stökl, *Testament und Siegel Ivan IV* (Opladen: Westdeutscher Verlag, 1973), 24–29; Frank Kämpfer, "*Dikanikion-posox:* Some Considerations on the Royal Staff in Muscovy," trans. Aveen Henry, *Forschungen zur osteuropäischen Geschichte* 24 (1978): 9–19; Mikhailova, *I zdes' soshlis' vse tsarstva*, 56, 120–42.

23. Giovanni Maniscalco Basile, "Power and Words of Power: Political, Juridical and Religious Vocabulary in some Ideological Documents in 16th-century Russia," *Forschungen zur osteuropäischen Geschichte* 50 (1994): 76–77; M. E. Bychkova, *Moskovskie samoderzhtsy: Istoriia vozvedeniia na prestol, Obriady i regalii* (Moscow: IRI RAN, 1995), 49–51; N. S. Demkova, "Gramoty Ivana Groznogo shvedskim koroliam Eriku XIV i Iogannu III (Po rukopisiam Shvedskogo gosudarstvennogo arkhiva)," *TODRL* 50 (1997), 496–99; N. N. Pokrovskii and G. D. Lenhoff, ed., *Stepennaia kniga tsarskogo rodosloviia po drevneishim spiskam: Teksty i kommentarii*, vol. 2, *Stepeni XI-XVII, Prilozheniia: Ukazateli* (Moscow: Iazyki slavianskikh kul'tur, 2008), 325, 346; Sergei Bogatyrev, "Bronze Tsars: Ivan the Terrible and Fedor Ivanovich in the Décor of Early Modern Guns," *Slavonic and East European Review* 88 (2010): 68–69.

24. *PSRL* 13, 76 right column; Bychkova, *Moskovskie samoderzhtsy*, 32; A. L. Khoroshkevich, *Simvoly russkoi gosudarstvennosti* (Moscow: MGU, 1993), 70–72; Aleksei Konstantinovich Levykin, *Voinskie tseremonii i regalii russkikh tsarei* (Moscow: Gosudarstvennyi istoriko-kul'turnyi muzei-zapovednik "Moskovskaia Kreml'," 1997).

25. Ch. Dzh. De-Mekelis, "Neizdannye istochniki na grecheskom iazyke ob Ivane IV," in *Rimsko-Konstantinopol'skoe nasledie na Rusi: Ideia vlasti i politicheskaia praktika* (Moscow: RAN, 1995), 231–35; S. M. Kashtanov, ed., *Rossiia i grecheskii mir v XVI veke*, vol. 1 (Moscow: Nauka, 2004), no. 89, 211–14; no. 93, 222–23; no. 128, 265–68, 317, 331; no. 129, 268–69, 272–73, 331; no. 130, 273–75, 314; no. 135, 281–84; B. L. Fonkich, "Gramota Konstantinopol'skogo patriarkha Ioasafa II i sobora vostochnoi tserkvy, utverdaiushchaia tsarskii titul Ivana IV" in S. M. Kashtanov, ed., *Rossiia i grecheskii mir v XVI veke*, vol. 1, 381–88.

26. Khoroshkevich, *Rossiia v sisteme*, 282–88; Filiushkin, *Tituly russkikh gosudarei*, 117–23; Sergei Bogatyrev, "Reinventing the Russian Monarchy in the 1550s: Ivan the Terrible, the Dynasty, and the Church," *Slavonic and East European Review* 85 (2007): 282–92.

27. Khoroshkevich, *Rossiia v sisteme*, 63–64; Savva, *Moskovskie tsari*, 400; V. V. Trepavlov, "Rossiia i kochevye stepy: Problemy vostochnykh vzaimstvovanii v rossiiskoi gosudarstvennosti," *Vostok* 1994: 2, 49–62.

28. *Drevniaia Rossiiskaia Vivliofika* [hereafter *DRV*], pt. 14 (Moscow: Nikolai Novikov, 1790, 2nd ed.), no. 17, 227–33; *DAI* vol. 1, no. 40, 53–55; Daniel H. Kaiser, "Symbol and Ritual in the Marriages of Ivan IV," *Russian History* 14 (1987): 247–62.

29. *PSRL* 34, 28; Tikhomirov, "Zapiski o regenstve Eleny Glinskoi i boiarskom pravlenii," 286–87; Bogatyrev, "Ivan IV (1533–84)," 245; Gleb Vladimidirovich Abramovich, *Kniaz'ia Shuiskie i Rossiiskii tron* (Leningrad: LGU, 1991), 81; Martin, *A Bride for the Tsar*, 114.

30. Martin, *A Bride for the Tsar*, 61–67; V. D. Nazarov, "Svadebnye dela XVI veka," *Voprosy istorii*, no. 10 (1976): 110–23.

31. Bogatyrev, "Ivan IV (1533–84)," 246–47.

32. Janet Martin, *Medieval Russia 980–1584*, 2nd ed. (Cambridge: Cambridge University Press, 2007), 373.

33. Lehtovirta, *Ivan IV as Emperor*, 320–55, 361.

Chapter 5. Life at Ivan's Court

1. David B. Miller, "Creating Legitimacy: Ritual, Ideology and Power in Sixteenth-Century Russia," *Russian History* 21 (1994): 289–315.

2. Bushkovitch, *Peter the Great*, 14–20.

3. Keenan, *Apocrypha*, 53–58; Eve Levin, "Muscovy and Its Mythologies: Pre-Petrine History in the Past Decade," *Kritika* 12 (2011): 780.

4. Daniel H. Kaiser, "Naming Cultures in Early Modern Russia," *Harvard Ukrainian Studies* 19 (1995): 271–91.

5. A. G. Mel'nik, "Praktika posviashchennikh khramov vo imia patronal'nykh velikokniazheskikh i tsarskikh sviatykh v XVI veke," in *Tsar' i tsarstvo v russkom obshchestvennom soznanii* (Moscow: IRI RAN, 1999), 38–48; Ludwig Steindorff, *Memoria in Rußland: Untersuchungen zu den Formen Christlicher Totensorge* (Stuttgart: Franz Steiner Verlag, 1994); Jennifer B. Spock, "Community Building and Social Identity: Donations to the Solovki Monastery 1460–1645," *Jahrbücher für Geschichte Osteuropas* 55 (2007): 534–65.

6. Ludwig Steindorff (Liudvig Shtaindorf), "Vklady tsaria Ivana Groznogo v Iosifo-Volokolamskii monastyr'," *Drevniaia Rus': Voprosy medievistiki* 28, no. 2 (2002): 90–100.

7. S. B. Veselovskii, *Issledovaniia po istorii klassa sluzhilykh zemlevladel'tsev* (Moscow: Nauka 1969), 94, 222; Zimin, *Krupnaia feodal'naia votchina*, 122–53; M. N. Tikhomirov, "Zapisi XIV-XVII vekov na rukopisiakh Chudova monastyria," *Arkheograficheskii ezhegodnik za 1958* (1960), no. 39, 20; no. 44, 21; no. 57, 22; no. 58, 23; no. 60, 23.

8. *Akty feodal'nogo zemlevladeniia i khoziaistva*, vol. 2 (Moscow: AN SSSR, 1956), no. 332, 349–51; no. 433, 488–89; Ann M. Kleimola, "'In Accordance with the Canons of the Holy Apostles': Muscovite Dowries and Women's Property Rights," *Russian Review* 51 (1992): 206, 209.

9. Lloyd E. Berry and Robert O. Crummey, ed., *Rude and Barbarous Kingdom: Russia in the Accounts of Sixteenth-Century English Voyages* (Madison: University of Wisconsin Press, 1968), 26, 55; Hugh F. Graham, trans., *The Moscovia of Antonio Possevino, S. J.* (Pittsburgh: University of Pittsburgh Press, 1977), 27, 47.

10. "Opis' domashnemu imushchestvu tsaria Ivana Vasil'evicha, po spiskam i knigam 90 i 91 godov," *Vremennik obshchestva istorii drevnostei rossiiskikh* 7 (1850), sec. 5, 1–46; Leonid Abramovich Iuzefovich, "*Kak v posol'skikh obychaiakh vedetsia . . .*" *Russkii posol'skii obychai kontsa XVI—nachala XVII v.* (Moscow: Mezhdunarodnye otnosheniia, 1988), 173–76.

11. Gail Lenhoff, "The Cult of Saint Nikita the Stylite in Pereslavl' and Among the Muscovite Elite," in Derwich and Dmitriev, *Fonctions sociales et politiques*, 344–45.

12. *SRIO* 71, 743–44.

13. Daniel Rowland, "Biblical Military Imagery in the Political Culture of Early Modern Russia. The Blessed Host of the Heavenly Tsar," in Flier and Rowland, *Medieval Russian Culture*, vol. 2, 197.

14. Valerii Perkhavko, "Po prozvishchu Vyrodok: Zhizn' i smert' pervogo voennogo inzhenera," *Rodina*, no. 12 (2004): 82–85.

15. Charles J. Halperin, "The Culture of Ivan IV's Court: The Religious Beliefs of Bureaucrats," in *The New Muscovite Cultural History: A Collection in Honor of Daniel B. Rowland*, ed. Valerie Kivelson et al. (Bloomington: Slavica Publishers, Inc., 2009), 93–105; *SRIO* 71, 2–4; *Akty sluzhilykh zemlevladel'tsev XV—nachala XVII veka*, vol. 3 (Moscow: Drevlekhranilishche, 2002), no. 86, 72–77; O. E. Kosheleva, "Dukhovnaia Timofeia Busurmenova vtoroi chetverty XVI veka," *Russkii diplomatarii* 7 (2001): 256.

16. Charles J. Halperin, "The 'Russian' and 'Slavonic' Languages in Sixteenth-Century Muscovy," *Slavonic and East European Review* 85 (2007): 1–24; Tat'iana Pavlovna Rogozhnikova, *Zhitiia "Makar'evskogo tsikla": Zhanr—Stil'—Iazyk* (St. Petersburg: SPbGU, 2003), 56–62, 82; Iurii Vladimirovich Ankhimiuk, *Chastnye Razriadnye knigi s zapisiami za poslednuiu chetvert' XV—nachalo XVII vekov* (Moscow: Drevlekhranilishche, 2005), 107–9, 133–46.

17. Eve Levin, "*Dvoeverie* and Popular Religion," in *Seeking God: The Recovery of Religious Identity in Orthodox Russia, Ukraine, and Georgia*, ed. Stephen K. Batalden (DeKalb: Northern Illinois University Press, 1993), 40n1.

18. L. A. Dmitriev, ed., *Povest' o zhitii Mikhaila Klopskogo* (Moscow-Leningrad: AN SSSR, 1958), 73–86, 141–67.

19. Paul Bushkovitch, "The Moscow Kremlin and its History," in *Britannia and Muscovy: English Silver at the Court of the Tsars*, ed. Olga Dmitrieva and Natalya Abramova. (New Haven: Yale Univerity Press, 2006), 245; Rüß, *Herren und Diener*, 450–71; Michael S. Flier, "Political ideas and rituals," in Perrie, *Cambridge History of* Russia, vol. 1, 387–408.

20. Daniel H. Kaiser, "Death and Dying in Early Modern Russia," Kennan Institute for Advanced Russian Studies Occasional Paper No. 228 (Washington, DC, 1988); Daniel H. Kaiser, "Quotidian Orthodoxy: Domestic Life in Early Modern Russia," in *Orthodox Russia: Belief and Practice under the Tsars*, ed. Valerie A. Kivelson and Robert H. Greene (University Park: Pennsylvania State University Press, 2003), 179–92; Daniel H. Kaiser, "The Seasonality of Family Life in Early Modern Russia," *Forschungen zur osteuropäischen Geschichte* 46 (1992): 21–50.

21. Mikhail Krom, "Religiozno-nravstvennoe osnovanie," 49–64; *AAE* vol. 1, no. 260, 286–87; no. 283, 328–89; no. 297, 560–61; no. 302, 368; no. 306, 371; no. 311, 375.

22. Sergei Bogatyrev, "Battle for Divine Wisdom: The Rhetoric of Ivan IV's Campaign against Polotsk," in *The Military and Society in Russia 1450–1917*, ed. Eric Lohr and Marshall Poe (Leiden: Brill, 2002), 325–63; K. V. Petrov, ed., *Kniga polotskogo pokhoda 1563 (Issledovanie i tekst)* (St. Petersburg: Russkaia natsional'naia biblioteka, 2004), 6–30.

23. Charles J. Halperin, "Russia Between East and West: Diplomatic Reports During the Reign of Ivan IV," in *Saluting Aaron Gurevich: Essays in History, Literature and Other Subjects*, ed. Yelena Mazour-Matusevich and Alexandra S. Korros (Leiden: Koninklijke Brill NV, 2010), 81–103; K. Iu. Erusalimskii, "Istoriia na posol'skoi sluzhbe: diplomatiia i pamiat' v Rossii XVI veka," in *Istoriia i pamiat'. Istoricheskaia kul'tura do nachala novogo vremeni*, ed. Lorina P. Repina (Moscow: Krug,' 2006), 664–731.

24. *AAE* vol. 1, no. 154, 266; *PRP* 4: 539, 563; *Zakonodatel'nye akty russkogo gosudarstva vtoroi poloviny XVI—prevoi poloviny XVII veka*, vol. 1, *Tektsy*, vol. 2, *Kommentarii* (Leningrad: Nauka, Leningradskoe otdelenie, 1986–1987), 1: 33, 52; 2: 56.

25. A. M. Kleimola, "Formulae and Formalism in Muscovite Judgment Charters," *Canadian-American Slavic Studies* 6 (1972): 355–73; *PRP* 4: 537–39, 563.

26. Valerie A. Tumins, *Tsar Ivan IV's Reply to Jan Rokyta* (The Hague: Mouton, 1971); Nikoletta Marchalis, *Liutor "izhe liut": Prenie o vere tsaria Ivana Groznogo s pastorom Rokytoi* (Moscow: Iazyki slavianskoi kul'tury, 2009).

27. John L. I. Fennell, "Ivan IV as a Writer," *Russian History* 14 (1987): 145–54; Marchalis, *Liutor "izhe liut,"* 98–146.

28. *The Moscovia of Antonio Possevino, S. J.*, 173; *PDSDR* vol. 10 (St. Petersburg 1851: Izdanie. II otdelenie EIV kantseliarii, 1851), 301–8, 312; Iakov Solomonovich Lur'e in D. S. Likhachev and Ia. S. Lur'e, ed., *Poslaniia Ivana Groznogo* (Moscow-Leningrad: AN SSSR, 1951), 518; Ostrowski, *Muscovy and the Mongols*, 211; Marchalis, *Liutor "izhe liut,"* 26–27.

29. Charles J. Halperin, "Ivan IV and Kiev," *Harvard Ukrainian Studies* 28 (2006): 461–69; Edward L. Keenan, "On Certain Mythical Beliefs and Russian Behaviors," in *The Legacy of History in Russia and the New States of Eurasia*, ed. Frederick Starr (Armonk: M. E. Sharpe, 1994), 21–24.

30. "Akty Kopengagenskago arkhiva, otnosiashchiesia k russkoi istorii," pt. 1, "1326–1569," *Chteniia* (1915) kniga 4, vol. 255, no. 54, 102–3; no. 60, 116–20; Mikhalon Litvin, *O nravakh tatar, litovtsev i moskvitian*, trans. V. I. Matuzova (Moscow: MGU, 1994), 102.

31. *Poslaniia Ivana Groznogo*, 174; Charles J. Halperin and Ann M. Kleimola, "Visual Evidence of the Cult of St. Vladimir," *Die Welt Der Slaven* 51 (2006): 266–68.

32. *PDRV* vol. 10 (St. Petersburg: Imporatorskaia AN, 1795), 317–19; Michael Khodarkovsky, *Russia's Steppe Frontier: The Making of a Colonial Empire, 1500–1800* (Bloomington: Indiana University Press, 2002), 114, 191, 222; Bulat Rakhimzyanov, "Muslim Iurts of Muscovy: Religious Tolerance of the Steppe in the XV-XVI Centuries," *Forschungen zur osteuropäischen Geschichte* 72 (2010): 181–200.

33. Immanuel Wallerstein, *The Modern World-System: Capitalist Agriculture and the Origins of the European World-Economy of the Sixteenth Century* (New York: Academic Press, 1974), 207.

34. Gary M. Hamburg, "Religious Toleration in Russian Thought, 1520–1825," *Kritika* 13 (2012): 521–25; Kaya Sahin, *Empire and Power in the Reign of Suleyman: Narrating the Sixteenth-Century Ottoman World* (Cambridge: Cambridge University Press, 2013), 136.

35. J. H. Hexter, *Reappraisals in History* (London: Longmans, Green & Co., 1961), 41–43.

36. J. Huizinga, *The Waning of the Middle Ages: A Study of the Forms of Life, Thought, and Art in France and the Netherlands in the XIVth and XVth Centuries*, trans. F. Hopman (New York: St Martin's Press, 1967), 149.

37. Charles J. Halperin, "Three 'Hands' and Literacy in Muscovy During the Reign of Ivan IV: 'I Affix My Hand,' 'By My Own Hand,' and 'My Man's Hand,'" *Canadian-American Slavic Studies* 51 (2017): 29–63.

38. Nancy Shields Kollmann, *Crime and Punishment in Early Modern Russia* (Cambridge: Cambridge University Press, 2012), 27, 49; Daniel E. Collins, *Reanimated Voices: Speech Reporting in a Historical-Pragmatic Perspective* (Amsterdam:

John Benmajins, 2001), 179; Rüß, *Herren und Diener*, 217–27; A. I. Sobolevskii, *Obrazovannost' Moskovskoi Rusi XV-XVII vekov.* Rech chitannaia na godichnom akte Imperatorskago S.-Peterburgskago universiteta, 8 fevralia 1892 (St. Petersburg: Am. M. Vol'f, 1892), 1–13; A. I. Iatsimirskii, "Obrazovannost' v Moskovskoi Rusi," in *Russkaia istoriia v ocherkakh i stat'iakh*, vol. 3, ed. M. V. Dovnar-Zapol'skii (Kiev: N. Ia. Okhloblin, 1909), 513–15.

39. Edward L. Keenan, "Ivan the Terrible and Book Culture: Fact, Fancy and Fog; Remarks on Early Muscovite Printing," *Solanus* 18 (2004): 32–35.

40. Neuschel, *Word of Honor*, 108–9; Anthony Goodman, *The New Monarchy: England, 1471–1534* (Oxford: Basil Blackwell Ltd, 1988), 39, 43.

41. *Zakonodatel'nye akty*, 1, no. 35, 53–54; 2, 56; Ann M. Kleimola, *Justice in Medieval Russia: Muscovite Judgment Charters (pravye gramoty) of the Fifteenth and Sixteenth Centuries* (Philadelphia: Transactions of the American Philosophical Society, vol. 65, pt. 6, October, 1975), 19n75; *PRP* 4: 248–49; Dewey, *Muscovite Judicial Texts 1488–1556*, 62.

42. David B. Miller, *Saint Sergius of Radonezh, His Trinity Monastery, and the Formation of the Russian Identity* (DeKalb: Northern Illinois University Press 2010), 239; Ludwig Steindorff, "Commemoration and Administrative Techniques in Muscovite Monasteries," *Russian History* 22 (1995): 433–54.

43. Halperin, "Three 'Hands' and Literacy in Muscovy," 29–63.

44. Valentin Viktorovich Morozov, *Litsevoi svod v kontekste otechestvennogo letopisaniia XVI veka* (Moscow: Indrik, 2005), 202, miniature no. 31; *The Moscovia of Antonio Possevino, S. J.*, 16, 50; F. I. Maslov, "Maslovskii arkhiv: Vypusk 1, 1569–1631," *Chteniia* 257, bk. 2, sec. 1, no. 4 (1916): 14.

45. *PDRV* vol. 7 (St. Petersburg: Imperatorskaia AN, 1791), 233, 274, 306; *PDRV* vol. 8 (St. Petersburg: Imperatorskaia AN, 1793), 168, 171, 249, 261; *PDRV* vol. 9 (St. Petersburg: Imperatorskaia AN, 1793), 149, 157, 272, 273; *PDRV* vol. 10, 16.

46. *Poslaniia Ivana Groznogo*, 566–69; Petr Alekseevich Sadikov, *Ocherki po istorii oprichniny* (Moscow-Leningrad: AN SSSR, 1950), 532–39; Bogatyrev, "Localism and Integration," 94.

47. *Dokumenty Livonskoi voiny (podlinnoe deloproizvodstvo prikazov i voevod) 1571–1580 gg*, 205–36; *Razriadnaia kniga 1475–1598 gg*, 96.

48. R. A. Houston, *Literacy in Early Modern Europe: Culture and Education, 1500–1800* (London: Longman, 1988), 3, 120–29.

49. Halperin, "Three 'Hands' and Literacy in Muscovy," 30–36.

50. *Istoriia Moskvy*, vol. 1, *Period Feodalizma XII-XVII vv.* (Moscow: AN SSSR, 1952), 206, 244; Gary Marker, "Literacy and Literacy Texts in Muscovy: A Reconsideration," *Slavic Review* 49 (1990): 78; Skrynnikov, *Tsarstvo terrora*, 439; Lawrence Stone, *The Crisis of the Aristocracy 1558–1641*, abridged ed. (Oxford: Oxford University Press, 1967), 305.

51. *Akty feodal'nogo zemlevladeniia*, vol. 2, no. 352, 390–94; no. 250, 253–54; no. 373, 416–18; *PRP* 4: 56–60; Nikolai Kalachov, ed, *Akty, otnosiashchiesia do iuridicheskago byta drevnei Rusi* (St. Petersburg: Arkheograficheskaia kommissiia, 1857), vol. 1, no. 52 V, 192–214; *Savvin Storozhevskii monastyr' v dokumentakh XVI veka (iz sobranii TsGADA)* (Moscow: Arkhiv russkoi istorii, 1992), no. 23, 30–31; *Russkaia istoricheskaia biblioteka* [hereafter *RIB*] 2 (St. Petersburg: Arkheografichesaia kommissiia, 1876), no. 186, 771–93; Houston, *Literacy in Early Modern Europe*, 126.

52. Kalachov, *Akty, otnosiashchesia do iuridicheskago byta drevnei Rusi*, vol. 1, no. 63, XIX, 453–55; N. P. Popov, "Sobranie rukopisei Moskovskogo Simonova monastyria (1-oi fototipiei)," *Chteniia* (1910) kn. 2, v. 233, otd 2, no. 21, 9.5.

53. *Akty feodal'nogo zemlevladeniia*, vol. 2, no. 140, 137–38; no. 141, 138–39; no. 142, 139–40; no. 143, 140–41; no. 146, 142; no. 152, 146–47.

54. Halperin, "Three 'Hands' and Literacy in Muscovy," 36–56; *Akty feodal'nogo zemlevladeniia i khoziaistva XIV-XVI vekov*, vol. 1 (Moscow: AN SSSR, 1951), no. 56, 67.

55. Halperin, "Three 'Hands' and Literacy in Muscovy," 57–62; *Akty feodal'nogo zemlevladeniia*, vol. 2, no. 165, 157–58; no. 219, 222; no. 259, 263–64; no. 374, 418–49.

Chapter 6. The Dynastic Crisis of 1553

1. *PSRL* 13, 230–31.

2. *PSRL* 13, 522–26; Nikolay Andreyev, "Interpolations in the Sixteenth-Century Muscovite Chronicles," *Slavonic and East European Review* 35 (1956): 95–115; Hartmut Rüss, "Adel und Nachfolgerfrage im Jahre 1553: Betrachtung zur Glaubwürdigkeit einer umstrittenen Quelle," in *Essays in Honor of A. A. Zimin*, ed. Daniel Clarke Waugh (Columbus: Slavica Publishers, 1985), 345–78; A. I. Filiushkin, *Istoriia odnoi mistifikatsii: Ivan Groznyi i "Izbrannaia Rada"* (Moscow: Voronezh Gosudarstvennyi Universitet, 1998), 77–100.

3. Crummey, *The Formation of Muscovy*, 155; Filiushkin, *Istoriia odnoi mistifikatsii*, 79.

4. PSRL 13, 75–77; Smirnov, *Ocherki politicheskoi istorii*, 36.

5. *Poslaniia Ivana Groznogo*, 179, 638; Carolyn Johnston Pouncy, "The *Domostroi* as a Source for Muscovite History" (PhD dissertation, Stanford University, 1985), 219.

6. *PSRL* 13, 232; *PSRL* 34, 229; O. A. Derzhavina, ed., *Vremmenik Ivana Timofeeva* (Moscow-Leningrad: AN SSSR, 1951), 20.

7. *Prince A. M. Kurbskii's History of Ivan IV*, 74–81, 90–91.

8. R. G. Skrynnikov, *Nachalo oprichniny* (Leningrad: LGU, 1966), 99n2; Ivan Zabelin, *Domashnyi byt russkago naroda v XVI i XVII st.*, vol. 1, *Domashnyi byt russkikh tsarei v XVI i XVII st.*, pt. 1, 4th ed. (Moscow: Iazyki russkoi kul'tury, 2000), 181–82.

9. Andrei Pavlov and Maureen Perrie, *Ivan the Terrible* (London: Pearson, Longman, 2003), 85; *PSRL* 13, 237–38; *PSRL* 29, 226–27; Shaposhnik, *Ivan Groznyi: Pervyi Russkii Tsar'* (St. Petersburg: Vita Nova, 2006), 192; Bogatyrev, "Reinventing the Russian Monarchy," 277–78.

10. Ieronym Gralia, "Varshavskii avtograf Ivana Viskovatogo," in *Paleobureaucratica: Sbornik statei k 90-letiiu N. F. Demidovoi* (Moscow: Drevlekhranilishche, 2012), 97–124; Daniil Natanovich Al'shits, *Nachalo samoderzhaviia v Rossii: Gosudarstvo Ivana Groznogo* (Leningrad: Nauka, Leningradskoe otdelenie, 1988), 207–27.

11. Filiushkin, *Istoriia odnoi mistifikatsii*, 77–100; Khoroshkevich, *Rossiia v sisteme*, 123–30.

12. Charles J. Halperin, "What Is an 'Official' Muscovite Source from the Reign of Ivan IV?" in *The Book of Royal Degrees and the Genesis of Russian Historical Consciousness / "Stepennaia kniga tsarskogo rodosloviia" i genezis russkogo istoricheskogo soznaniia*, ed. Gail Lenhoff and Ann Kleimola, UCLA Slavic Studies, NS vol. 7 (Bloomington: Slavica Publishers, 2011), 81–93.

13. *The Correspondence of Prince A. M. Kurbsky and Tsar Ivan IV*, 210–13; A. I. Filiushkin, *Andrei Mikhailovich Kurbskii: Prosopograficheskoe issledovanie i germenevticheskii kommentarii k poslaniiami Andreia Kurbskogo Ivanu Groznomu* (St. Petersburg: SPbGU, 2007), 29; Nitsche, *Grossfürst und Thronfolger*, 293–94; Edward L. Keenan, "The Privy Domain of Ivan Vasil'evich," in Dunning et al., *Rude & Barbarous Kingdom Revisited*, 82n37; Charles J. Halperin, "Ivan the Terrible's Younger Brother: Prince Iurii Vasil'evich (1533–63)," *Court Historian* 22, no. 1 (2017): 1–16.

14. Charles J. Halperin, "Metropolitan Makarii and Muscovite Court Politics during the Reign of Ivan IV," *Russian Review* 73 (2014): 458.

15. Smirnov, *Ocherki politicheskoi istorii*, 231–57.

16. Solov'ev, *Istoriia Rossii*, bk. 3, vols. 5–6, 534; Filiushkin, *Istoriia odnoi mistifikatsii*, 309–25; Carolyn Johnston Pouncy, "The Blessed Sil'vestr' and the Politics of Invention in Muscovy, 1550–1700," *Harvard Ukrainian Studies* 19 (1995): 548–72.

17. Mel'nikova, "Mesto monet Ivana Groznogo," 131–32.

18. *PDRV* vol. 6, no. 183, 34–39; *Sobranie gosudarstvennykh gramot i dogovorov, khraniashchikhsia v Gosudarstvennoi Kollegii inostrannykh del* [hereafter *SGGD*] (Moscow: Tipografiia N. S. Vsevolozhskago, 1813), vol. 1, nos. 167–169, 460–68; Ann Kleimola, "Ivan IV and the Staritskie: Post-Modern Narratives from a Pre-Modern State," in Lenhoff and Kleimola, *The Book of Royal Degrees*, 231–47.

19. Bogatyrev, "Ivan IV (1533–84)," 250, 251; Martin, *A Bride for the Tsar*, 12.

20. Ann Kleimola, "'I will not listen to my mother': Vladimir Staritskii's Oaths of 1554," in *Rusistika Ruslana Skrynnikova: Sbornik statei pamiati professora R. G. Skrynnikova, v chest' ego 80-letiia*, ed. Gyula Svák and Igor O. Tiumentsev (Budapest-Volgograd: Rossica Pannonica, 2011), 76–88.

21. A. M. Kleimola, "*Kto kogo:* Patterns of Duma Recruitment, 1547–1564," *Forschungen zur osteuropäischen Geschichte* 38 (1986), 208; Filiushkin, *Istoriia odnoi mistifikatsii,* 77–100.

Chapter 7. The Prehistory of the Oprichnina

1. Charles J. Halperin, "Royal Recreation: Ivan the Terrible Goes Hunting," *Journal of Early Modern History* 14 (2010): 293–316; Horace W. Dewey and Kira B. Stevens, "Muscovites at Play: Recreation in Pre-Petrine Russia," *Canadian-American Slavic Studies* 13 (1979): 193–94, 199; *Istoriia Moskvy,* vol. 1, 133.

2. Veselovskii, *Tsar' Ivan Groznyi v rabotakh pisatelei i istorikov,* 30; Martin, *A Bride for the Tsar,* 122; *PSRL* 13, 327–30; *PSRL* 29, 287–89; Thyrêt, *Between God and Tsar,* 53–57.

3. Berry and Crummey, *Rude and Barbarous Kingdom,* 264–65; V. I. Buganov and N. M. Rogozhin, "Kratkii Moskovskii letopisets nachala XVII v. iz g. Galle (FRG)," *Arkhiv russkoi istorii* 8 (2007): 563–64; N. N. Pokrovskii and A. V. Sirenov, ed., *Latukhinskaia Stepennaia kniga 1676 g.* (Moscow: Iazyiki slavianskoi kul'tury, 2012), 537–38; Andrei Popov, ed., *Izbornik slavianskikh i russkikh sochinenii i statei vnesennykh v Khronografy russkoi redaktsii* (Moscow: Tipografiia A. I. Mamontova, 1869), 183; Thyrêt, *Between God and Tsar,* 57–64.

4. *PSRL* 13, 328–89; *Razriadnaia kniga 1550–1636* (Moscow: II AN SSSR 1975), 103–4; Rüß, *Herren und Diener,* 78.

5. Halperin, "*Stepennaia kniga,*" 67–68.

6. *PSRL* 13, 329; *SRIO* 71, no. 1, 1–10; Martin, *A Bride for the Tsar,* 122, 131; Shaposhnik, *Ivan Groznyi: Pervyi Russkii Tsar,* 235.

7. Morozova and Morozov, *Ivan Groznyi i ego zheny,* 114–59; Wooding, *Henry VIII,* 190–201.

8. Bushkovitch, "Princes Cherkasskii or Circassian Murzas," 9–29; Murat Yasar, "The North Caucasus in the Second Half of the Sixteenth Century: Imperial Entanglements and Shifting Loyalties" (PhD dissertation, University of Toronto, 2011), 233–36.

9. *PSRL* 13, 333; O. V. Gladkova, "'Vozliubikh bo razum ee i blagochestie': Obraz ideal'noi liubvi v drevnerusskoi literatury," and P. V. Snesarevskii, "Predstavleniia o liubvi v pamiatnikakh pis'mennosti Rusi XIV-XV vv.," in *"A se grekhi zlye, smertnye." Liubov', erotika, i seksual'naia etika v doindustrial'noi Rossii (X-pervaia polovina XIX v.), Tektsy. Issledovaniia,* ed. N. L. Pushkareva, vol. 1 (Moscow: Nauchno-izdatel'skii tsentr "Ladimir," 1999), 492–500, 516–50; *DRV* vol. 13 (Moscow: Nikolai Novikov, 1790), no. 5, 36; no. 6, 46.

10. Prince Mikhail Shcherbatov, *Istoriia rossiiskaia ot drevneishikh vremen,* vol. 5, pt. 2 (St. Petersburg: Tipografiia M. M. Stasiulevicha, 1903), 189–90, 312; Morozova and Morozov, *Ivan Groznyi i ego zheny,* 145.

11. *PSRL* 13, 372.

12. Halperin, "Metropolitan Makarii," 447–64; Henry Rudolph Huttenbach, "The *Zemsky Sobor* in Ivan IV's Reign" (PhD dissertation, University of Washington, 1961), 141.

13. *PSRL* 13, 339–40; *PSRL* 29, 297.

14. *PSRL* 13, 344; *PSRL* 29, 301; Boris Floria, *Ivan Groznyi* (Moscow: Molodaia gvardiia, 1999), 145.

15. *PSRL* 13, 368, 370, 372; *PSRL* 29, 303; Ann M. Kleimola, "The Road to Beloozero: Ivan IV's Reconciliation with the 'Devil in a Skirt,'" *Russian History* 42 (2015): 64–81.

16. Filiushkin, *Andrei Kurbskii*, 85–86; Skrynnikov, *Tsarstvo terrora*, 116.

17. *Prince A. M. Kurbsky's History of Ivan IV*, 82–83; V. O. Kliuchevskii, *Boiarskaia Duma Drevnei Rusi*, 3rd ed. (Moscow: Sinodal'naia Tipografiia, 1902), 285–86; Victor Leontowitsch, *Dis Rechtsumwälzung under Iwan dem Schrecklichen und die Ideologie der Russischen Selbstherrschaft* (Stuttgart: F. F. Koehler Verlag, c. 1947), 91n1.

18. *The Moscovia of Antonio Possevino, S. J.*, 49.

19. *Pskovskie letopisi*, 2: 245; A. I. Filiushkin, "Mifologiia i realii bitvy pod Nevelem," *Studia Slavica et Balcanica Petropolitana*, no. 1 (2012), 197–202; *PSRL* 13, 383.

20. *SRIO* 71, 321, 454, 467, 468, 513, 517, 523–24, 531, 532, 537, 538–40, 540–2, 546–49, 777–78, 795–96, 806; S. O. Shmidt, ed., *"Vypiska iz posol'skikh knig" o snosheniiakh Rossiiskogo gosudarstva s Pol'sko-Litovskim za 1487–1572* (Moscow-Warsaw: Arkheograficheskii tsentr, 1997). 254; *Poslaniia Ivana Groznogo*, 272.

21. *Posol'skaia kniga po sviazam Rossii s Pol'shei (1575–1576 gg.)*, 26–27; Filiushkin, *Izobretaia pervuiu voinu Rossii*, 733; M. Koialovich, *Dnevnik pokhoda Stefana Batoriia na Rossiiu (osada Pskova) i diplomaticheskaia perepiska togo vremeni, otnosiashchaiasia glavnym obrazom k zakliucheniiu Zapol'skogo mira* (St. Petersburg, 1867), 584–85 (I am grateful to Paul Bushkovitch for this citation).

22. *SRIO* 71, 540–42; Inge Auerbach, *Andrej Michajlovič Kurbskij: Leben in osteuropäischen Adelsgesellschaften des 16. Jahrhunderts* (Munich: Otto Sagner, 1985), 120–21; Konstantin Iur'evich Erusalimskii, *Sborniki Kurbskogo*, vol. 1, *Issledovanie knizhnoi kul'ture* (Moscow: Znak, 2009), 75n322; Filiushkin, *Andrei Mikhailovich Kurbskii*, 85, 414; *Razriadnaia kniga 1475–1605*, vol. 2, pt. 1 (Moscow: II AN SSSR, 1981), 165.

23. *SRIO* 59, 122–23; D. K. Uo, "Neizvestnyi pamiatnik drevnerusskoi literatury: 'Gramota gosudaria tsaria i velikogo knigia Ivana Vasil'evicha vsea Rusii k Stepanu, koroliu pol'skomu,'" *Arkheograficheskii ezhegodnik za 1971 goda* (1972): 359–61.

24. V. I. Malyshev, ed., *Povest' o prikhozhdenii Stefana Batoriia na grad Pskov* (Moscow-Leningrad: AN SSSR, 1952), 41.

25. S. B. Veselovskii, *Issledovaniia po istorii oprichniny* (Moscow: AN SSSR, 1963), 290–91; Filiushkin, *Istoriia odnoi mistifikatsii*, 213–47; Jouanna, *The Saint Bartholomew's Day Massacre*, 157–78; Kingdon, *Myths about the St. Bartholomew's Day Massacres*, 91–92, 96, 100–101, 108–10, 129.

26. "Poslanie tsaria Ivana Vasil'evicha k Aleksandriiskomu patriarkhu Ioakim s kuptsom Vasil'em Pozniakovym i Khozhdenie kuptsa Pozniakova v Ierusalim i po inym sviatym mestam 1558 goda" *Chteniia* t. 128, 1884 bk. 1, I–XII, 4; *SRIO* 59, 338, 341–42; A. V. Vinogradov, "Krymskoe posol'skie knigi kak istochnik po istorii russko-krymskikh otnoshenii 60–70-kh XVI veka," in *Vneshniaia politika Rossii. Istochniki i istoriografiia* (Moscow: II AN SSSR, 1991), 11.

27. *SRIO* 71, 331, 597, 461, 591, 593, 597, 638, 651; *Poslaniia Ivana Groznogo*, 266, 270–71; Mikhailovskii, *Sochineniia*, vol. 6, 190–91; Iuzefovich, "*Kak v posl'skikh obychaiakh vedetsia*," 92.

28. *Kabardino-russkie otnosheniia v XVI-XVIII vv.*, vol. 1 (Moscow: Izdatel'stvo AN SSSR, 1957), no. 20, 33–34; V. B. Kobrin, "Sostav oprichnogo dvora Ivana Groznogo," *Arkheograficheskii ezehgodnik za 1959* (1960): 86–87; "Priezd v Moskvu poslannika Geliasha Pelgrimovskago s izvestiem o posylke sudei dlia razmena plennykh," *Starina i novizna* 4 (1901): 408–30.

29. *The Correspondence of Prince A. M. Kurbsky and Tsar Ivan IV*, 2–11, 180–85, 198–247; Bjarne Nørretranders, *The Shaping of Czardom under Ivan IV Groznyj* (Copenhagen: Munksgaard, 1964), 65–86.

30. *Prince A. M. Kurbsky's History of Ivan IV*, 152–59; Veselovskii, *Issledovaniia po istorii oprichniny*, 96–108; Valerie Kivelson and Jonathan Shaheen, "Prosaic Witchcraft and Semiotic Totalitarianism: Muscovite Magic Reconsidered," *Slavic Review* 70 (2011): 23–44.

31. I. N. Lebedeva claims to have found a sample of Kurbskii's handwriting in Cyrillic in a manuscript's marginalia (I. N. Lebedeva, ed., *Povest' o Varlaame i Ioasafe: Pamiatnik drevnerusskoi perevodnoi literatury XI-XII vv.* [Leningrad: Nauka, Leningradskoe otdelenie, 1985], 106), but I have seen no commentary on her discovery and I am not in a position to evaluate it.

32. *The Correspondence of Prince A. M. Kurbsky and Tsar Ivan IV*, 2–11; I. U. Budovnits, *Russkaia publitsistika XVI veka* (Moscow-Leningrad, Izdatelstvo AN SSSR, 1947), 280–303.

33. Goldfrank, "The Deep Origins of *Tsar'-Muchitel'*," 341–54; Andrei Karavashkin, "Vlast' muchitelia. Konventsional'nye modeli tirannii v russkoi istorii," *Rossiia XXI 2006*, no. 4, 63–64.

34. Wooding, *Henry VIII*, 1–2, 221–22.

35. Inge Auerbach, "Die politischen Vorstellungen des Fürsten Andrej Kurbskij," *Jahrbücher für Geschichte Osteuropas* 17 (1969): 170–86; Auerbach, "Identity in Exile: Andrei Mikhailovich Kurbskii and National Consciousness in the Sixteenth

Century," in Kleimola and Lenhoff, *Culture and Identity*, 11–25; Filiushkin, *Andrei Mikhailovich Kurbskii*, 161–578; Karavashkin, *Russkaia srednevekovaia publitsistika*, 299–400, 402–3.

36. *The Correspondence of Prince A. M. Kurbsky and Tsar Ivan IV*, 244–45.

37. Val'denberg, *Drevnerusskiia ucheniia*, 309–21.

38. Nikolay Andreyev, "Kurbsky's Letters to Vas'yan Muromtsev," *Slavonic and East European Review* 33 (1955): 414–36.

39. *Prince A. M. Kurbsky's History of Ivan IV*, 86–87, 96–97; Shmidt, *Stanovlenie rossiiskogo samoderzhavstva*, 189; *RIB* 31 (St. Petersburg: Imperatorskaia Arkheograficheskaia komissiia, 1914), 489–92.

40. *The Correspondence of Prince A. M. Kurbsky and Tsar Ivan IV*, ix, 8–9, 208–9; Leontowitsch, *Dis Rechtsumwälzung under Iwan dem Schrecklichen*, 51–64.

41. Oswald P. Backus, "A. M. Kurbsky in the Polish-Lithuanian State (1564–1583)," *Acta Baltico-Slavica* 6 (1969): 29–50.

42. Mykhailo Hrushevsky, *History of Ukraine-Rus'*, vol. 6, *Economic, Cultural and National Life in the Fourteenth to Sixteenth Centuries*, trans. Leonid Heretz, ed. Myron M. Kapral and Frank E. Sysyn with Uliana M. Pasicznyk (Edmonton-Toronto: Canadian Institute of Ukrainian Studies Press, 2012), 342–44, 353, 356–57, 363–64, 366; Ferdinand Liewehr, *Kurbskijs "Novyj Margarit." Untersucht und in Auswahl editert* (Prague: Taussig and Taussig, 1928).

43. *The Correspondence of Prince A. M. Kurbsky and Tsar Ivan IV*, 184–85; *Prince A. M. Kurbsky's History of Ivan IV*, 176–77, 226–27, 228–29, 234–35, 238–39, 288–89, 294–95; Karavashkin, *Russkaia srednevekovaia publitsistika*, 316–17, 327–34; Filiushkin, *Andrei Mikhailovich Kurbskii*, 37–50, 225, 548–50.

44. Karavashkin, "Vlast' muchitelia," 91–99; Erich Donnert, *Die Livländische Ordensritterschaft und Rußland. Der Livländische Krieg und die baltische Frage in der europäischen Politik 1558–1583* (Berlin: Rütten and Loenig, 1963), 235–36.

45. *Prince A. M. Kurbsky's History of Ivan IV*, 126–31, 152–53.

46. Ia. S. Lur'e and Iu. D. Rykov, ed., *Perepiska Ivana Groznogo s Andreim Kurbskim* (Leningrad: Nauka, Leningradskoe otdelenie, 1979); Jaako Lehtovirta, "Terrible Ideas—Some Sources of the *Groza* of Ivan IV," *Faravid: Acta Societas Historicae Finlandiae Septentrionalis* 17 (1995): 121.

47. *The Correspondence of Prince A. M. Kurbsky and Tsar Ivan IV*, 12–179, 186–97; *Poslaniia Ivana Groznogo*, 9–138, 208–11; Val'denberg, *Drevnerusskiia ucheniia*, 355–56.

48. *The Correspondence of Prince A. M. Kurbsky and Tsar Ivan IV* annotated every such lapse.

49. *The Correspondence of Prince A. M. Kurbsky and Tsar Ivan IV*, 124–25, 142–43; *Poslaniia Ivana Groznogo*, 263–64, 68–69; A. V. Karavashkin, "Avtor,

tekst, chitatel': Problema tvorcheskoi individual'nosti v russkoi publitsistike XVI v. (poslaniia Ivana Groznogo)," in *Actio Nova (sbornik nauchnykh statei)*, ed. A. I. Filiushkin (Moscow: Globus, 2000), 157–210.

50. Belokurov, *O biblioteke moskovskikh gosudarei;* Daniel Clarke Waugh, "The Unsolved Problem of Tsar Ivan's Library," *Russian History* 14 (1987): 395–408; A. A. Amosov, "'Antichnaia' biblioteka Ivana Groznogo: K voprosu o dostovernosti sokhranivshikhsia izvestii ob inoiazychnom fonde biblioteki moskovskikh gosudarei," in *Knizhnoe delo v Rossii v XVI-XIX vekakh: Sbornik nauchnik trudov* (Leningrad: BAN AN SSSR, 1980), 6–31; Sergei Bogatyrev, "The Ostroh Bible from the National Library of Finland," *Slavonic and East European Review* 92 (2014): 707, 712–13.

51. Nikolai Vasil'evich Vodovozov, *Istoriia drevnei russkoi literatury* (Moscow: Gosudarstvennoe uchebno-pedagogicheskoe izdatel'stvo Ministerstva Prosveshcheniia RSFSR, 1962), 255; V. V. Kalugin, "Tsar' Ivan Groznyi: stili khudozhestvennogo myshleniia," in *Kul'tura srednevekovoi Moskvy XIV-XVII vv.* (Moscow: Nauka, 1995), 193.

52. *Poslaniia Ivana Groznogo*, 272–73.

53. Sigurd Ottovich Shmidt, *Rossiia Ivana Groznogo* (Moscow: Nauka, 1999), 61.

54. *The Correspondence of Prince A. M. Kurbsky and Tsar Ivan IV*, 66–67, 106–7, 190–91; Vasilii Vasil'evich Kalugin, *Andrei Kurbskii i Ivan Groznyi (Teoreticheskie vzgliady i literaturnaia tekhnika drevnerusskogo pisatelia)* (Moscow: Iazyki russkoi kul'tury,1998), 236; Ia. S. Lur'e, ed., *Povest' o Drakule* (Moscow-Leningrad: Nauka, 1964), 119; *Poslaniia Ivana Groznogo*, 252, 270; *SRIO* 71, 102–15, 230, 465, 775; Filiushkin, *Izobretaia pervuiu voinu Rossii*, 491.

55. Michael Cherniavsky, "Ivan the Terrible as a Renaissance Prince," *Slavic Review* 27 (1968): 195–211; Lehtovirta, "Terrible Ideas," 119–28.

56. *Poslaniia Ivana Groznogo*, 241–77, 417–45, 574–75, 668–76; Charles J. Halperin, "False Identity and Multiple Identities," 56–61; Starkey, *Henry: Virtuous Prince*, 13; Greenblatt, *Renaissance Self-Fashioning*, 29, 129–30; Plowden, *Elizabeth I*, 177, 680, 692; Shmidt, *Rossiia Ivana Groznogo*, 203–12; Kalugin, "Tsar' Ivan Groznyi: stili khudozhestvennogo myshleniia," 193.

57. *The Correspondence of Prince A. M. Kurbsky and Tsar Ivan IV*, 180–81; Likhachev, 202–13, and Lur'e, 214–49, in *Perepiska Ivana Groznogo s Andreim Kurbskim.*

58. Kliuchevskii, *Sochineniia*, vol. 2, *Kurs russkoi istorii*, 164–70.

59. Filiushkin, *Istoriia odnoi mistifikatsii*, 215–17; Khoroshkevich, *Rossiia v sisteme*, 78–79.

60. *Poslaniia Ivana Groznogo*, 213–38, 390–414, 573–74, 656–68; Filiushkin, *Izobretaia pervuiu voinu Rossii*, 178–91, 752, 754, 761, 771; Andrew Pettegree, *Europe*

in the Sixteenth Century (Oxford: Blackwell Publishers, 2002), 22; Huizinga, *The Waning of the Middle Ages*, 84–86.

61. Iuzefovich, *"Kak v posl'skikh obychaiakh vedetsia,"* 18–20; *SRIO* 59, 535; Uo, "Neizvestnyi pamiatnik drevnerusskoi literatury," 359–61; Plowden, *Elizabeth I*, 620; M. E. Bychkova, *Russkoe gosudarstvo i velikoe kniazhestvo Litovskoe s kontsa XV v. do 1569 g. Opyt sravnitel'no-istoricheskogo izucheniia politicheskogo stroia* (Moscow: IRI RAN, 1996), 121–25.

62. Iuzefovich, *"Kak v posl'skikh obychaiakh vedetsia,"* 22, 24, 26, 27; Walther Kirchner, "A Milestone in European History: The Danish-Russian Treaty of 1562," *Slavonic and East European Review* 23 (1944): 39–48; *SRIO* 59, 38.

63. *Poslaniia Ivana Groznogo*, 193–94, 370–71, 565–69, 639–42; 197–204, 374–81, 569–71, 644–49; 212, 389, 573, 655; Charles J. Halperin, "You Dog! Ivan IV's Canine Invective," in Szvák and Tiumentsev, *Rusistika Ruslana Skrynnikova*, 89–108.

64. *RIB* 15 (St. Petersburg: Arkheograficheskaia kommissiia, 1894), no. 134, 305–8.

65. Gonneau, *Ivan le Terrible*, 297–310.

66. *The Correspondence of Prince A. M. Kurbsky and Tsar Ivan IV*, 46–47, 72–73, 78–79, 80–81, 82–83, 128–29; Oswald P. Backus, "Treason as a Concept and Defections from Moscow to Lithuania in the Sixteenth Century," *Forschungen zur osteuropäischen Geschichte* 15 (1970): 119–44; Al'shits, *Nachalo samoderzhaviia v Rossii*, 95–96, 100; Lur'e in *Poslaniia Ivana Groznogo*, 474, 475; *SRIO* 129 (St. Petersburg: Tipografiia V. S. Balasheva, 1910), 39, 92.

67. Daniil Al', *Ivan Groznyi: Izvestnyi i neizvestnyi. Ot legend k faktam* (St. Petersburg: Neva, 2005), 119.

68. *SRIO* 71, 766–91; Eve Levin, "Innocent and Demon-Possessed in Early Modern Russia," in *Culture and Identity in Eastern Christian History: Papers from the First Biennial Conference of the Association for the Study of Eastern Christian History and Culture (ASEC), Inc.*, ed. Russell E. Martin and Jennifer Spock, with the assistance of M. A. Johnson (Eastern Christian Studies, vol. 1, Ohio Slavic Papers, vol. 9, Columbus: Department of Slavic and East European Languages and Literatures, Ohio State University, 2009), 123–61.

69. Skrynnikov, *Tsarstvo terrora*, 195.

70. Halperin, "Administrative Discretion," 429–46; *AAE* vol. 1, nos. 262–263, 289–97; Igor Vladimirovich Kurukin and Andrei Alekseevich Bulychev, *Povsednevnaia zhizn' oprichnikov Ivana Groznogo* (Moscow: Molodaia gvardiia, 2010), 134.

71. Donald Ostrowski, "Muscovite Adaption of Mongol/Tatar Political Institutions: A Reply to Halperin's Objections," *Kritika* 1 (2000): 275.

72. *The Moscovia of Antonio Possevino, S. J.*, 124.

73. *SRIO* 59, 299–300; *SRIO* 71, 288–96, 675–93; *SRIO* 38, 108–11.

74. Bushkovitch, *A Concise History*, 50.

Chapter 8. Domestic Political Reform

1. Robert O. Crummey, "Reform under Ivan IV: Gradualism and Terror," in *Reform in Russia and the USSR: Past and Prospects*, ed. Robert O. Crummey (Urbana: University of Illinois Press, 1989), 12–27; Mikhail M. Krom, "Les réformes russes du XVIe siècle: un myth historiographique?," trans. Olga Medvedkova, *Annales Histoires, sciences sociales* (2009): 561–78.

2. Krom, "Religiozno-nravstvennoe osnovanie," 49–64; J. D. Alsop, "The Structure of Early Tudor Finance, c. 1509–1538," in Coleman and Starkey, *Revolution Reassessed*, 150.

3. L. I. Ivina, ed., *Akty feodal'nogo zemlevladeniia i khoziaistva: Akty moskovksogo Simonova monastyria (1506–1613)* (Leningrad: Nauka, Leningradskoe otdelenie, 1983), no. 64, 75–76; Iakovlev, *Namestnich'i, gubnyia i zemskyia ustavnye gramoty*, nos. 1–8, 52–78; Horace W. Dewey, ed., *Muscovite Judicial Texts, 1488–1556* (Ann Arbor: Department of Slavic Languages and Literatures, 1966), 33–43; N. E. Nosov, *Ocherki po istorii mestnogo upravleniia russkogo gosudarstva pervoi poloviny XVI veka* (Moscow-Leningrad: AN SSSR, 1957), 201–339; Horace W. Dewey, "Muscovite *Guba* Charters and the Concept of Brigandage (*Razboj*)," *Papers of the Michigan Academy of Sciences, Arts and Letters* 51 (1966): 277–88; Tat'iana Il'inichna Pashkova, *Mestnoe upravlenie v russkom gosudarstve pervoi poloviny XVI veka: Namestniki i volosteli* (Moscow: Drevlekhranilishche, 2000), 110–19; Sergei Bogatyrev, "Localism and Integration," 59–127; Vladimir Valentinovich Bovykin, *Mestnoe upravlenie v Russkom gosudarstve XVI v.* (St. Petersburg: Dmitrii Bulanin, 2012), 178–209, 301–18, 324–42.

4. *PRP* 4: 290, 356–60; Dewey, *Muscovite Judicial Texts*, 36–40; Zimin, *Reformy Ivana Groznogo*, 255–58, 265, 312, 330.

5. Kliuchevskii, *Kurs russkoi istorii*, vol. 2, 343–46; M. M. Krom, "Status Boiarskoi dumy v pervoi polovine XVI v. (K istorii vozniknoveniia formuly "boiarskii prigovor")," in *Feodal'naia Rossiia. Novye issledovaniia*, vol. 2, *Sbornik nauchnykh statei*, ed. M. V. Sverdlov (St. Petersburg: "Tret'ia Rossiia," 1998), 49.

6. M. M. Krom, "Tvorcheskoe nasledie N. E. Nosova i problema izucheniia gubnoi reformy XVI v.," in *Gosudarstvo i obshchestvo v Rossii XV-nachala XX veka. Sbornik statei pamiati Nikolaia Evgen'evicha Nosova* (St. Petersburg: Nauka, 2007), 45–57; V. V. Vel'iaminov-Zernov, *Issledovanie o Kasimovskikh tsariakh i tsarevichakh*, pt. 1 (St. Petersburg: Tipografiia Imperatorskoi Adademii Nauk, 1863), 474–80; Carol B. Stevens, "Banditry and Provincial Order in Sixteenth-Century Russia," in Kleimola and Lenhoff, *Culture and Identity*, 594–99.

7. Michael J. Braddick, *State Formation in Early Modern England, c. 1550–1700* (Cambridge: Cambridge University Press, 2000), 30–31.

8. *PRP* 4: 363–70.

9. *Akty sluzhilykh zemlevladel'tsev*, vol. 4, no. 141, 103–4; *AAE* vol. 1, nos. 174–76.

10. Oswald P. Backus, "Muscovite Legal Thought, the Law of Theft, and the Problem of Centralization, 1497–1589," in *Essays in Russian History: A Collection Dedicated to George Vernadsky*, ed. Alan D. Ferguson and Alfred Levin (Hamden: Archon Books, 1964), 48–50.

11. Fernand Braudel, *The Mediterranean and the Mediterranean World in the Age of Philip II*, vol. 2, trans. Silan Reynolds (New York: Harper & Row, 1972), 743–54; Steve Hindle, *The State and Social Change in Early Modern England, c. 1550–1640* (New York: St. Martin's Press, 2000), 116–45.

12. *Pistsovyia knigi Moskovskago Gosudarstva*, pt. 1, *Pistsovyia knigi XVI veka*, sec. 2, *Mestnosti gubernii Iaroslavskoi, Tverskoi, Vitebskoi, Smolenskoi, Kaluzhskoi, Orlovskoi, Tul'skoi* (St. Petersburg: Imperatorskoe russkoe geograficheskoe obshchestvo, 1877), 193.

13. Kivelson, "On Words, Sources, and Historical Method," 492.

14. D'iakonov, *Ocherki obshchestvennogo i gosudarstvennago stroia*, 449–89; Lev Vladimirovich Cherepnin, *Zemskie sobory russkogo gosudarstva v XVI–XVII vv.* (Moscow: Nauka, 1978), 68–78; Shmidt, *Stanovlenie rossiiskogo samoderzhavstva*, 133–96; Ostrowskii, *Muscovy and the Mongols*, 185–86.

15. *PSRL* 22, 528–29; N. E. Nosov, "Sobor 'primireniia' 1549 goda i voprosy mestnogo upravleniia (na pereput'e k zemskim reformam)," in *Vnutrennaia politika tsarizma (seredina XVI-nachalo XX v.)* (Leningrad: Nauka, Leningradskoe otdelenie, 1975), 39n46.

16. *SGGD* vol. 2 (Moscow: Tipografiia N. S. Vsevolzhskago, 1819), no. 37, 45–46; V. N. Avtokratov, "'Rech' Ivana Groznogo' kak politicheskii pamflet kontsa XVII veka," *TODRL* 11 (1955): 255–79; S. F. Platonov, *Stat'i po russkoi istorii (1883–1912)*, 2nd ed. (St. Petersburg: Tipografiia M. A. Aleksandrova, 1912), 201–5.

17. Ellerd Hulbert, "Sixteenth-century Russian Assemblies of the Land: Their Composition, Organization and Competence" (PhD dissertation, University of Chicago, 1970), 94–96; Huttenbach, "The *Zemsky Sobor* in Ivan IV's Reign," 70–84.

18. A. P. Pavlov, "Samoderzhavie i zemskie sobory russkogo gosudarstva XVI-XVII vekov," in *Mesto Rossii v Evrope: Materialy mezhdunarodnoi konferentsii / The Place of Russia in Europe: Materials of International Conference*, ed. Gyula Szvák (Budapest: Magyar Ruszisztikai Intézet, 1999), 113–21.

19. Diula Svak, *Russkaia paradigma. Russofobskie zametki rusofila* (St. Petersburg: Ateleia, 2010), 94.

20. Golokhvastov and Archimandrite Leonid, "Blagoveshchenskii ierei Sil'vestr," 12; *Prince A. M. Kurbsky's History of Ivan IV*, 16–17, 20–21, 183n2, 230–31, 242–43; Smirnov, *Ocherki politicheskoi istorii*, 139–474.

21. Anthony N. Grobovsky, *The "Chosen Council" of Ivan IV: A Reinterpretation* (Brooklyn: Theo. Graus' Sons, Inc, 1969); Filiushkin, *Istoriia odnoi mistifikatsii*, 281–329; Inge Auerbach, "Gedanken zur Entstehung von A. M. Kurbskijs *Istori-*

ja o velikom knjaze Moskovskom," *Canadian-American Slavic Studies* 13 (1979): 166–71.

22. *SRIO* 59, 468–69, 473; *SRIO* 71, 124, 147–49; Kollmann, *Kinship and Politics,* 147n6; Bogatyrev, *The Sovereign and His Counsellors,* 144–85.

23. *Sochineniia prepodobnago Maksima Greka,* 2: 60–79, 379–86, 415–20; Filiushkin, *Istoriia odnoi mistifikatsii,* 242–43; Iakovleva, "Piskarevskii letopisets," 56.

24. *PRP* 4: 233–61; Dewey, ed., *Muscovite Judicial Texts, 1488–1556,* 47–74; Horace W. Dewey, "The 1550 *Sudebnik* as an Instrument of Reform," in *Government in Reformation Europe, 1520–1560,* ed. Henry J. Cohen (London: Macmillan, 1970), 284–309.

25. V. M. Paneiakh, pt. I, "Rus' v XV–XVII vv. Stanovlenie i evoliutsiia vlasti russkikh tsarei," in *Vlast' i reformy. Ot samoderzhavnoi k sovetskoi Rossii* (St. Petersburg: Dmitrii Bulanin, 1996), 61.

26. Scott Seregny, "The *Nedel'shchik:* Law and Order in Muscovite Russia," *Canadian-American Slavic Studies* 9 (1975): 168–78; Braddick, *State Formation in Early Modern England,* 196–202, 234–40; J. Russell Major, *From Renaissance Monarchy to Absolute Monarchy: French Kings, Nobles, and Estates* (Baltimore: Johns Hopkins University Press, 1994), 131, 138; Kamen, *Philip II of Spain,* 214; Gabrielle Scheidegger, "Zu streng oder zu milde? Die altrussische Justiz in den Augen abendländischer Beobachter," in *Ot Drevnei Rusi k Rossii novogo vremeni. Sbornik statei. K 70-letiiu Anny Leonidovny Khoroshkevich* (Moscow: Nauka, 2003), 490–501.

27. Horace W. Dewey, "The Decline of the Muscovite *namestnik,*" *Oxford Slavonic Papers* 12 (1965): 21–39; S. O. Shmidt, "Prodolzhenie khronografa redaktsii 1512 goda," *Istoricheskii arkhiv* 7 (1951): 296; N. P. Likhachev, *Sbornik aktov sobrannykh v arkhivakh i bibliotekakh.* Vypusk I–II (St. Petersburg: Tipografiia V. S. Balasheva, 1895), no. 12, 220–36.

28. Horace W. Dewey, "Defamation and False Accusation (*Iabednichestvo*) in Old Muscovite Society," *Études slaves et est européenes* 11 (1966–1967): 109–20; Dewey, "Morality and the Law in Muscovite Russia," in *Russian Law: Historical and Political Perspectives,* ed. William E. Butler (Leyden: A W Sijthoff, 1977), 56–57, 58, 64; Mariia Vladimirovna Korogodina, *Ispoved' v Rossii v XIV–XIX vekakh: Issledovanie i teksty* (St. Petersburg: Dmitrii Bulanin, 2006), 172–81.

29. Kleimola, *Justice in Medieval Russia;* Horace W. Dewey, "Judges and Evidence in Muscovite Law," *Slavonic and East European Review* 36 (1957): 189–94.

30. George G. Weickhardt, "Muscovite Judicial Duels as Legal Fiction," *Kritika* 7 (2006): 714–32; *Akty sluzhilykh zemlevladel'tsev XV-nachala XVII veka: Sbornik dokumentov,* vol. 1 (Moscow: Arkheograficheskii tsentr, 1997), no. 122, 96–97.

31. Kollmann, *Crime and Punishment,* 136, 158, 169, 215; Kleimola, *Justice in Medieval Russia,* 60; George D. Weickhardt, "Due Process and Equal Justice in the Muscovite Codes," *Russian Review* 51 (1992): 466, 468–70, 480.

32. *PRP* 4: 592–95; Evgeniia Ivanovna Kolycheva, *Agrarnyi stroi Rossii XVI veka* (Moscow: Nauka, 1987), 23–25; Smirnov, *Ocherki politicheskoi istorii*, 454–74.

33. Sergei Vasil'evich Rozhdestvenskii, *Sluzhiloe zemlevladenie v Moskovskom gosudarstve XVI veka* (St. Petersburg: V. Demakov, 1897), 90–100, 108–10; *RIB* 32 (Petrograd: Arkheograficheskaia kommissiia, 1915), no. 199, 288–89; J. H. M. Salmon, *Society in Crisis: France in the Sixteenth Century* (London: Ernest Benn Limited, 1975), 33.

34. George G. Weickhardt, "The Pre-Petrine Law of Property," *Slavic Review* 52 (1993): 36; V. B. Kobrin, *Vlast' i sobstvennost v srednevekovoi Rossii (XV–XVI vv.)* (Moscow: Mysl, 1985), 198; Oswald P. Backus III, "Mortgages, Alienations, and Redemptions: The Rights in Land of the Nobility in Sixteenth-Century Lithuanian and Muscovite Law and Practice Compared," *Forschungen zur osteuropäischen Geschichte* 18 (1973): 139–67.

35. S. B. Veselovskii, *Feodal'noe zemlevladenie v severo-vostochnoi Rusi*, vol. 1 (Moscow-Leningrad: AN SSSR, 1947), 33; Marina Sergeevna Cherkasova, *Zemlevladenie Troitse-Sergieva monastyria v XV–XVI vv.* (Moscow: Arkheograficheskii tsentr, 1996), 166–68.

36. *PRP* 4: 260, 339–40; Dewey, *Muscovite Judicial Texts*, 93; Sakharov, *Sbornik dokumentov*, no. 189, 162–63; Kleimola, *Justice in Medieval Russia*, 10.

37. Filiushkin, *Istoriia odnoi mistifikatsii*, 269–71; Skrynnikov, *Ivan the Terrible*, 22.

38. *PRP* 4: 238–39; Dewey, *Muscovite Judicial Texts*, 52–53; Horace W. Dewey, "Old Muscovite Concepts of Injured Honor (*Bezchestie*)," *Slavic Review* 27 (1968): 594–603; Nancy Shields Kollmann, *By Honor Bound: State and Society in Early Modern Russia* (Ithaca: Cornell University Press, 1999).

39. Richard Hellie, *Slavery in Russia, 1450–1725* (Chicago: University of Chicago Press, 1982), 152–53.

40. Marianna Muravyeva, "*Vergünza, Vergogne, Schande, Skar* and *Sram:* Litigating for Shame and Dishonor in Early Modern Europe," in *Shame, Blame, and Culpability: Crime and Violence in the Modern State*, ed. Marianna Muravyeva, Davis Nash, and Judith Rowbotham (London: Routledge, 2012), 24.

41. Viktor Moiseevich Paneiakh, *Kabal'noe kholopstvo na Rusi v XVI veke* (Leningrad: Nauka, Leningradskoe otdelenie, 1967); E. I. Kolycheva, "Polnye i dokladnye gramoty XV-XVI vekov," *Arkheograficheskii ezhegodnik za 1961* (1962): 53–56.

42. Donald Ostrowski, "Early *Pomest'e* Grants as a Historical Source," *Oxford Slavonic Papers* 32 (2000): 36–63; Vincent E. Hammond, *State Service in Sixteenth Century Novgorod: The First Century of the Pomestie System* (Lanham: University Press of America, 2009); Janet Martin, "*Netstvo* and the Conditionality of *Pomest'e* Land Tenure," in *Dubitando: Studies in History and Culture in Honor of Donald*

Ostrowski, ed. Brian J. Boeck et al. (Bloomington: Slavica Publishers, Inc., 2012), 461–73.

43. Hellie, *Slavery in Russia*, 467–74, 476–77; N. V. Smirnov, "Boevye kholopy v sostave pomestnoi konnitsy v pervoi polovine XVI-pervoi polovine XVII v.," in *Issledovaniia po istorii srednevekovoi Rusi. K 80-letiiu Iuriia Georgievicha Alekseeva* (Moscow-St. Petersburg: Al'ians-Arkheo, 2006), 369–82.

44. Boris Kagarlitsky, *Empire of the Periphery: Russia and the World System*, trans. Renfrey Clarke (London: Pluto Press, 2008), 75, 118; Wallerstein, *The Modern World-System*, 91.

45. *Zakonodatel'nye akty*, 1: 11–12; no. 10, 36–7; no. 18, 43; no. 22, 44–5; no. 23, 45; no. 24, 45–46; *PRP* 4: 501, 514, 515, 515–56, 517.

46. Horace W. Dewey, "Historical Drama in Muscovite Justice: The Case of the Extorted Deed," *Canadian Slavonic Papers* 2 (1957): 38–46; *DAI* vol. 1, 18, 82; no. 56, 120; V. G. Geiman, ed., *Materialy po istorii Karelii XII–XVI v.v.* (Petrozavodsk: Gosudarstvennoe izdatel'stvo Karelo-Finskoi SSR, 1941), no. 86, 190–93; *PRP* 4: 89, 92, 93, 94, 117–20; Dewey and Kleimola, *Russian Private Law*, no. 56, 176.

47. Charles J. Halperin, "Sixteenth-Century Foreign Travel Accounts to Muscovy: A Methodological Excursus," *Sixteenth-Century Journal* 6 (1975): 99–100.

48. Iakovlev, *Namestnich'i, gubnyia i zemskyia ustavnye gramoty*, no. 1, 101–2; no. 2, 103–13; no. 3, 113–16; no. 4, 116–20; no. 5, 120–23; no. 6, 123–29; no. 7, 130–33; no. 8, 134–37; no. 9, 137–42; Dewey, *Muscovite Judicial Texts*, 77–83; Nosov, *Stanovlenie soslovno-predstavitel'nykh uchrezhdenii*; Bovykin, *Mestnoe upravlenie*, 209–301, 319–77; Vladimir Anatol'evich Arakcheev, *Vlast' i "zemlia": pravitel'stvennaia politika v otnoshenii tiaglykh soslovii v Rossii vtoroi poloviny XVI-nachala XVII veka* (Moscow: Drevlekhranilishche, 2014), 179–281, 383–97, 412.

49. S. O. Shmidt, "Neizvestnye dokumenty XVI v.," *Istoricheskii sbornik*, no. 4, (1961): 153–54; Pavlov and Perrie, *Ivan the Terrible*, 76, 77, 200, 209, 214.

50. Brian Davies, "The Politics of Give and Take: *Kormlenie* as Service Remuneration and Generalized Exchange, 1488–1726," in Kleimola and Lenhoff, *Culture and Identity*, 39–67; V. A. Arakcheev, "Zemskaia reforma XVI veka: Obshcherossiiskie tendentsii i regional'nye osobennosti," *Otechestvennaia istoriia*, no. 4 (2006): 3–11.

51. *PSRL* 13, 228, 311–12; B. N. Floria, "O nekotorykh istochnikakh po istorii mestnogo upravleniia v Rossii XVI veka," *Arkheograficheskii ezhegodnik za 1962* (1963): 92–97; B. N. Floria, "Kormlennye gramoty XV-XVI vv. kak istoricheskii istochnik," *Arkheograficheskii ezhegodnik za 1970* (1971): 109–26; *Akty sluzhilykh zemlevladel'tsev*, vol. 4, no. 20, 18.

52. *RIB* 32, no. 241, 497–98; A. V. Antonov, "'Boiarskaia kniga' 1556/57 goda," *Russkii diplomatarii* 10 (2004): 82–118; Brian Davies, "The Town Governors under

Ivan IV," *Russian History* 14 (1987): 92–93; Marshall Poe, "Elite Service Registry in Muscovy, 1500–1700," *Russian History* 21 (1994): 269–73.

53. A. A. Zimin, "Novye dokumenty po istorii mestnogo upravleniia v Rossii pervoi poloviny XVI v.," *Arkheograficheskii ezhegodnik za 1965*, no. 2 (1966): 345–46; no. 3, 346–47; no. 4, 347; no. 6, 348; no. 7, 349; no. 10, 350–51; Nosov, *Ocherki po istorii mestnogo upravleniia*, 13–197; A. V. Antonov, "Ryl'skaia ustavnaia namest-nich'ia gramota 1549 goda," *Russkii diplomatarii* 3 (1998): 65–70.

54. Davies, "The Town Governors under Ivan IV," 77–143.

55. Horace W. Dewey, "Charters of Local Government under Tsar Ivan IV," *Jahrbücher für Geschichte Osteuropas* 14 (1966): 16; Davies, "The Politics of Give and Take," 47–48.

56. Matthew P. Romaniello and Charles Lipp, "The Spaces of Nobility," in *Contested Spaces of Nobility in Early Modern Europe*, ed. Matthew P. Romaniello and Charles Lipp (Farnham, Surrey, UK: Ashgate Publishing Group, 2011), 1–10; B. N. Floria, "Tsentr i provintsii v sisteme upravleniia Rossii (XVI–XVII vv.)," in *Gosudarstvo i obshchestvo*, 189–94; Ostrowskii, *Muscovy and the Mongols*, 199.

57. A. A. Zimin, ed., *Tysiachnaia kniga 1550 g. i Dvorovaia Tetrad' 50-kh godov XVI v.* (Moscow-Leningrad: II AN SSSR, 1950), 53–103; *Zakonodatel'nye akty*, 1: no. 4, 30–31; 2: 14–16.

58. Zimin, *Reformy Ivana Groznogo*, 366–75; Hulbert, "Sixteenth-century Russian Assemblies of the Land," 9–46.

59. Pavlov, *Gosudarev dvor*, 86–104; Aleksandr L. Korzinin, "Tysiachnaia kniga 1550 g. i Dvorovaia tetrad' 50-kh gg kak istoricheskie istochniki po izucheniiu Gosudareva dvora v Rossii serediny XVI v.," *Canadian-American Slavic Studies* 47 (2013): 409–12.

60. Veselovskii, *Issledovaniia po istorii oprichniny*, 77–83.

61. Horace W. Dewey, "Old Russia's Struggle with Usury," *Oxford Slavonic Papers* 18 (1985): 31–47; Lynch, *Spain, 1516–1598*, 156.

62. *PRP* 4: 360, 486–87, 542–48; *Zakonodatel'nye akty*, 1: no. 7, 35; 2: 23–24.

63. *Zakonodatel'nye akty*, 1: no. 1, 29; 2: 9; Kobrin, *Vlast' i sobstvennost*, 68–86; *Savvin Storozhevskii monastyr'*, no. 27, 51–52.

64. V. D. Nazarov, "O strukture 'gosudareva dvora' v seredine XVI v.," in *Obshchestvo i gosudarstvo feodal'noi Rossii. Sbornik statei, posviashchennyi 70-letiiu L'va Vladimirovicha Cherepnina* (Moscow: Nauka, 1975), 40–54; Pavlov, *Gosudarev dvor*, 86–104; Korzinin, "Tysiachnaia kniga 1550 g. i Dvorovaia tetrad'," 412–19.

65. Buganov, *Razriadnye knigi*, 166–78; Poe, "Elite Service Registry in Musco-vy," 267; M. E. Bychkova, *Rodoslovnye knigi XVI-XVII vv. kak istoricheskii istochnik* (Moscow: Nauka 1975), 19–105.

66. Kollmann, *By Honor Bound*, 132–67; Nancy Shields Kollmann, "Ritual and Social Drama at the Muscovite Court," *Slavic Review* 45 (1986): 486–502;

Iurii Moiseevich Eskin, *Ocherki istorii mestnichestva v Rossii XVI–XVII vv.* (Moscow: Kvadriga, 2009); Nosov, *Stanovlenie soslovno-predstavitel'nykh uchrezhdenii*, 386–420.

67. Eskin, *Ocherki istorii mestnichestva*, 378–404.

68. A. M. Kleimola, "Up through Servitude: The Changing Conditions of the Muscovite Elite in the Sixteenth and Seventeenth Centuries," *Russian History* 6 (1979): 215; A. M. Kleimola, "Status, Place and Politics: The Rise of Mestnichestvo during the Boiarskoe Pravlenie," *Forschungen zur osteuropäischen Geschichte* 27 (1980): 195–214.

69. Shmidt, *Stanovlenie rossiiskogo samoderzhavstva*, 263–311; *PSRL* 13, 445; Skrynnikov, *Tsarstvo terrora*, 133; Vladimir Pavlovich Zagorovskii, *Istoriia vkhozhdeniia tsentral'nogo chernozem'ia v sostav rossiiskogo gosudarstva v XVI veke* (Voronezh: Voronezhskii gosudarstenyi universitet, 1991), 184.

70. *PSRL* 13, 267; *Zakonodatel'nye akty*, 1: 2, 29–30; 2: 9–12; *Razriadnaia kniga 1475–1605*, vol. 1, pt. 3 (Moscow: II AN SSSR, 1978), 420.

71. *PSRL* 13, 267; *Razriadnaia kniga 1475–1598 gg.*, 125; Eskin, *Ocherki istorii mestnichestva*, 157–66; A. L. Korzinin, "Poriadok ierarkhii polkovykh voevod v Livonskuiu voinu," in *Baltiiskii vopros v kontse XV–XVI vv. Sbornik nauchnykh statei*, ed. A. I. Filiushkin (Moscow: Kvadriga, 2010), 153–60.

72. A. I. Iushkov, compiler, "Akty XIII-XVII vv. predstavlennye v Razriadnyi prikaz predstaviteliami sluzhilykh familii posle otmeny mestnichestva," *Chteniia* (1898), vol. 185, bk. 2, pt. 1, 1257–1613, no. 193, 175–76; Alexander Filjushkin, *Ivan the Terrible: A Military History* (London: Frontline Books, 2008), 39–43; Levykin, *Voinskie tseremonii i regalii russkikh tsarei*, 16–17.

73. Eskin, *Ocherki istorii mestnichestva*, 191–280; Ieronim Gralia, *Ivan Mikhailovich Viskovatyi: Kar'era gosudarstvennogo deiatelia v Rossii XVI v.* (Moscow: Radiks, 1994), 29; Eskin, *Ocherki istorii mestnichestva*, 281–438.

74. Rüß, *Herren und Diener*, 390–408; Dianne Louise Smith, "The Muscovite Officer Corps, 1465–1598" (PhD dissertation, University of California, Davis, 1989), 268–335.

75. *Razriadnaia kniga 1475–1605 gg*, vol. 3, pt. 1 (Moscow: II AN SSSR, 1984), 144–45, 162–63; *Razriadnaia kniga 1559–1605 gg.* (Moscow: II AN SSSR, 1974), 147–48; *Razriadnaia kniga 1550–1636*, 70–71; *Razriadnaia kniga 1475–1605 gg*, vol. 2, pt. 2 (Moscow: II AN SSSR, 1982), 9; Kollmann, *By Honor Bound*, 162–64.

76. Halperin, "A Heretical View of Sixteenth-Century Muscovy," 172; Halperin, "Sixteenth-Century Foreign Travel Accounts," 103.

77. Iu. M. Eskin, *Mestnichestvo v Rossii XVI-XVII vv. Khronologicheskii reestr* (Moscow: Arkheograficheskii tsentr, 1994).

78. Eskin, *Ocherki istorii mestnichestva*, 138–90, 189; *Razriadnaia kniga 1475–1605*, vol. 2, pt. 2, 343–44.

79. *Razriadnaia kniga 1475–1605 gg*, vol. 3, pt. 1, 110.

80. Hartmut Rüß, *Adel und Adelsoppositionen in Moskauer Staat* (Wiesbaden: Franz Steiner Verlag, 1975), 7n31.

81. Braddick, *State Formation in Early Modern England*, 182; John McGurk, *The Elizabethan Conquest of Ireland: The 1590s Crisis* (Manchester: Manchester University Press, 1997), 29; Michael Roberts, *The Early Vasas: A History of Sweden, 1523–1611* (Cambridge: Cambridge University Press, 1968), 192–93, 222–23; Hexter, *Reappraisals in History*, 45–70; Stone, *The Crisis of the Aristocracy*, 6, 191.

82. Brian L. Davies, *Warfare, State and Society on the Black Sea Steppe, 1500–1700* (London: Routledge, 2007), 43; Leontowitsch, *Dis Rechtsumwälzung under Iwan dem Schrecklichen*, 97–121.

83. *PSRL* 13, 267–68; *PSRL* 29, 245–46.

84. *Pistsovye materialy Tverskogo uezda XVI veka* (Moscow: Drevlekhranilishche, 2005); *Pistsovyia knigi Moskovskago Gosudarstva*, pt. 1, sec. 2, *Materialy dlia istorii Zvenigorodskogo kraia: Vypusk pervyi* (Moscow: Arkheograficheskii tsentr, 1992); M. M. Krom, "Chastnaia sluzhba v Rossii XVI veka," in *Russkoe srednevekov'e: Sbornik statei v chest' Professora Iuriia Georgievicha Alekseeva* (Moscow: Drevlekhranilishche, 2012), 422–33.

85. Janet Martin, "Peculiarities of the Pomest'e System: A Comparison of Novgorod and Tver' in the Mid-Sixteenth Century," in *Moskovskaia Rus': spetsifika razvitiia / Muscovy: Peculiarities of its Development*, ed. Gyula Szvák (Budapest: Magyar Ruszisztikai Intézet, 2003), 76–87.

86. Smirnov, *Ocherki politicheskoi istorii*, 423–40; A. V. Antonov, "K rodosloviiu Polevykh XVI veka," *Russkii dipomatarii* 6 (2000), 174–75; Antonov, "'Boiarskaia kniga' 1556/57 goda," *Russkii diplomatarii* 10 (2004): 80–118.

87. Rüß, *Herren und Diener*, 289, 294–98.

88. E. I. Kolycheva, "Ogosudarstvlenie zemel v Rossii vo vtoroi polovine XVI veka," in *Sistema gosudarstvennogo feodalizma v Rossii. Sbornik statei*, vol. 1 (Moscow: IRI RAN, 1993), 93–114.

Chapter 9. Church Reform and Heresy

1. Bushkovitch, *Religion and Society*, 80–87.

2. Kollmann, "The Moscow *Stoglav*," vol. 1, 114; Shaposhnik, *Tserkovno-gosudarstvennye otnosheniia*, 113–256; *Stoglav* (St. Petersburg: Izdanie D. E. Kozhanchikov, 1863); Elena Borisovna Emchenko, *Stoglav: Issledovanie i tekst* (Moscow: Indrik, 2000), 233–416.

3. N. K. Molchanova, "Zhalovannaia gramota Nikol'skomu Mozhaiskomu soboru 1536 goda," *Russkii diplomatarii* 4 (1998): 127–28; Emchenko, *Stoglav*, 8–9, 334.

4. Emchenko, *Stoglav*, 242–50; *PRP* 4: 576–80; *Stoglav*, 14–57, 25–35; *Poslaniia Ivana Groznogo*, 162–92.

5. Kollmann, "The Moscow *Stoglav*," 1: 5–67; 2: 614–20; Emchenko, *Stoglav*, 153–228.

6. Petr Sergeevich Stefanovich, *Prikhod i prikhodskoe dukhovenstvo v Rossii v XVI–XVII vekakh* (Moscow: Indrik, 2002), 212–17, 222.

7. Emchenko, *Stoglav*, 285–87; Jack E. Kollmann Jr., "The *Stoglav Council* and Parish Priests," *Russian History* 7 (1980): 68, 69.

8. Stella Rock, *Popular Religion in Russia: "Double Belief" and the Making of an Academic Myth* (London: Routledge, 2007).

9. Eve Levin, "*Dvoeverie* and Popular Religion," in *Seeking God: The Recovery of Religious Identity in Orthodox Russia, Ukraine, and Georgia*, ed. Stephen K. Batalden (DeKalb: Northern Illinois University Press, 1993), 31–52; Russell Zguta, *Russian Minstrels: A History of the* Skomorokhi (Philadelphia: University of Pennsylvania Press, 1978); Hindle, *The State and Social Change*, 176–203; Mikhailova, *I szdes' soshlis' vse tsarstva*, 403–96, 606–10.

10. Kollmann, "The Moscow *Stoglav*," 2: 481–87; Emchenko, *Stoglav*, 358–59; S. V. Strel'nikov, "Rostovskie gramoty XV–XVI vekov," *Russkii diplomatarii* 9, no. 2 (2003): 40–44; S. M. Kashtanov, "Deiatel'nost' pravoslavnykh monastyrei v Srednem Povol'zhe v epokhu Ivana Groznogo (1551–1556 gg.)," *Forschungen zur osteuropäischen Geschichte* 63 (2004): 293–309.

11. George G. Weickhardt, "The Canon Law of Rus' and Muscovy, 1100–1551," *Russian History* 28 (2001): 411–46.

12. Bushkovitch, *Religion and Society*, 10–31.

13. Arkhimandrit Makarii (Veretennikov), *Sviataia Rus': Agiografiia. Istoriia. Ierarkhiia* (Moscow: Indrik, 2005), 19, 20.

14. Donald Ostrowski, "Church Polemics and Monastic Land Acquisition in Sixteenth-Century Muscovy," *Slavonic and East European Review* 64 (1986): 355–79; George Ostrowski, "The *Letter Concerning Enmities* as a Polemical Source for Monastic Relations of the Mid-Sixteenth Century," *Russian History* 39 (2012): 77–105.

15. V. F. Rzhiga, "Opyty po istorii russkoi publitsistiki," 30.

16. Bushkovitch, *Religion and Society*, 15–16; Kollmann, "The Moscow *Stoglav*," 2:411n54.

17. *The Correspondence of Prince A. M. Kurbsky and Tsar Ivan IV*, 236–37; *Prince A. M. Kurbsky's History of Ivan IV*, 6–7, 73–77, 80–81, 244–45; *AI* vol. 1, no. 216, 410–11.

18. David Goldfrank, "Recentering Nil Sorskii: The Evidence from the Sources," *Russian Review* 66 (2007): 367, 375; Andrei Ivanovich Pliguzov, *Polemika v russkoi tserkvi pervoi treti XVI stoletiia* (Moscow: Indrik, 2002), 253–77, 289–92.

19. Bushkovitch, *Religion and Society*, 27–28; David Miller, "The Velikie Minei Chetii and the Stepennaia kniga of Metropolitan Makarii," *Forschungen zur osteuropäischen Gesichte* 26 (1979): 286.

20. *Sochineniia prepodobnago Maksima Greka*, vol. 2, 355–67; Jack V. Haney, *From Italy to Muscovy. The Life and Works of Maxim the Greek* (Munich: Wilhem Fink Verlag, 1973), 86; Rzhiga, "Opyty po istorii russkoi publitsistiki," 86–95.

21. *Sochineniia prepodobnago Maksima Greka*, vol. 3, 154–56, 156–64; Haney, *From Italy to Muscovy*, 90–91.

22. David Goldfrank, "Theocratic Imperatives, the Transcendent, the Worldly, and Political Justice in Russia's Early Inquisitions," in *Religious and Secular Forces in Late Tsarist Russia: Essays in Honor of Donald W. Treadgold*, ed. Charles E. Timberlake (Seattle: University of Washington Press, 1992), 40–41.

23. P. P. Sokolov, "Podlozhnyi iarlyk khana Uzbeka mitropolitu Petru," *Rossiiskii istoricheskii zhurnal*, no. 5 (1918): 70–85; S. N. Kisterev, "Delo Agrafiny Volynskoi i 'otvet' mitropolita Makariia Ivanu IV," *Arkheograficheskii ezhegodnik za 1998* (1999): 71–77; Arkhimandrit Makarii (Veretennikov), *Iz istorii russkoi ierarkhii XVI veka* (Moscow: Izdatel'stvo Moskovskogo podvor'ia Sviato-Troitskoi Sergievskoi Lavry, 2006), 71n145; Pagden, *Lords of All the World*, 32.

24. *Akty feodal'nogo zemlevladeniia*, vol. 2, no. 227, 229; *PRP* 4: 107, 127–30; Kollmann, "The Moscow *Stoglav*," 2: 427.

25. S. I. Smetanina, "K voprosu o pravitel'stvennoi politike v otnoshenii tserkovnogo zemlevladeniia v gody oprichniny," *Istoriia SSSR*, no. 3 (1978): 155–64; Ann M. Kleimola, "Holding on in the 'Stamped-Over District'—the Survival of a Political Elite: Riazan' Landowners in the Sixteenth Century," *Russian History* 19 (1992): 134; A. V. Antonov, "Iz istorii nagodchiny v Riazanskoi zemle," *Russkii diplomatarii* 4 (1998): 156.

26. M. B. McGeehan, "The Problem of Secularization in Sixteenth-Century Muscovy," in *The Council of 1503: Source Studies and Questions of Ecclesiastical Landowning in Sixteenth-Century Muscovy, A Collection of Seminar Papers*, ed. Edward L. Keenan and Donald G. Ostrowski (Cambridge: Kritika, 1977), 164–88.

27. Kollmann, "The Moscow *Stoglav*," 2: 426–36; *AAE* vol. 1, no. 227, 218–19; Emchenko, *Stoglav*, 413–16; *PRP* 4: 523–24, 524–25; P. A. Sadikov, "Iz istorii oprichniny XVI v.," *Istoricheskii arkhiv* 3, no. 78 (1940): 243–44.

28. Miller, *Saint Sergius of Radonezh*, 88–95; *AAE* vol. 1, no. 246, 268–69; S. S. Ermolaev et al., ed., *Vkladnaia kniga Serpukhovskogo Vysotskogo monastyria* (Moscow: Arkheograficheskii tsentr, 1993), appendices, no. 2, 89–90; *PRP* 4: 529–32; Rozhdestvenskii, *Sluzhiloe zemlevladenie*, 120–369.

29. *PDRV* vol. 7, 132–45; *AAE* vol. 1, no. 308, 372–73; *PRP* 4: 525–26, 558–60; Shaposhnik, *Tserkovno-gosudarstvennye otnosheniia*, 390–93.

30. Veselovskii, *Feodal'noe zemlevladenie*, vol. 1, 231–43; A. V. Antonov, "Iaroslavskie monastyri i tserkvy v dokumentakh XVI-nachala XVII veka," *Russkii diplomatarii* 5, no. 27 (1999): 52–53.

31. George G. Weickhardt, "Muscovite Law on Monasteries," *Russian History*

39 (2012): 13–41; Charles J. Halperin, "Ecclesiastical Immunities in Practice during the Reign of Ivan IV," *Russian History* 14 (2013): 153–65.

32. *PRP* 4: 242, 287–89; Dewey, *Muscovite Judicial Texts*, 56; *Stoglav* 213, 221, 302–3; Pavel Smirnov, *Posadskie liudi i ikh klassovaia bor'ba do serediny XVII veka*, vol. 1 (Moscow-Leningrad: AN SSSR, 1947), 104–59.

33. S. N. Kisterev, "Akty moskovskogo Chudova monastyria 1507–1606," *Russkii diplomatarii* 9, no. 38 (2003): 113–16; Geiman, *Materialy po istorii Karelii XII–XVI*, no. 209, 272–74; no. 211, 275–76; S. M. Kashtanov, *Finansy srednevekovoi Rusi* (Moscow: Nauka, 1988); *Puteshestviia russkikh poslov XVI–XVII. Stateinye spiski* (Moscow-Leningrad, 1954), 144.

34. B. N. Floria, "Penitential Formulas in the Relationship of Church and State in Russia in the Sixteenth and Seventeenth Centuries," *Russian Studies in History* 39 (2001–2002): 75–77; Korogodina, *Ispoved' v Rossii*, 95–101, 301–10, 509–20.

35. David Goldfrank, "Pre-Enlightenment Utopianism in Russian History," *Russian History* 11 (1984): 130–31.

36. *Stoglav*, 217; G. N. Enin, "Kormlenie tserkovnogo apparata upravleniia v XVI–XVII vv. i sistema kormlenii," in *Russkaia religioznost': problemy izucheniia* (St. Petersburg: "Zhurnal-Neva," 2000), 121–28.

37. Charles J. Halperin, "The Administrative Culture of the Russian Orthodox Church during the Reign of Ivan IV," in Martin and Spock, *Culture and Identity*, 63–81.

38. A. I. Klibanov, *Reformatsionnye dvizheniia v Rossii v XIV-pervoi polovine XVI vv.* (Moscow: AN SSSR, 1960), 93–94; J. R. Howlett, "Reformation or Reformatio? The Case of Muscovite Russia," *Polata k"nigopis'naia* 16 (1987): 141–52.

39. Bushkovitch, *Religion and Society*, 26–27; Henry Kamen, *Inquisition and Society in Spain in the Sixteenth and Seventeenth Centuries* (Bloomington: Indiana University Press, 1985), 71–80, 91–95.

40. *PSRL* 13, 232–33; Klibanov, *Reformatsionnye dvizheniia v Rossii*, 253; A. A. Zimin, "Osnovnye problemy reformatsionno-gumanisticheskogo dvizheniia v Rossii XIV-XVI vv.," in *Istoriia, fol'klor, iskusstvo slavianskikh stran. Doklady sovetskoi delegatsii. V Mezhdunarodnyi s"ezd slavistov (Sofiia, sentiabr 1963)* (Moscow: AN SSSR, 1963), 97–98.

41. O. Bodianskii, ed., "Moskovskie sobory na eretikov XVI veka v tsarstvovanie Ioana Vasil'evicha Groznago" *Chteniia* 16, no. 3 (1847): 1–23; Bodianskii, ed., "Rozysk ili spisok o bogokhulnykh strokakh i o sumnenii sviatykh chestnykh ikon, d'iaka Ivana Mikhailova syna Viskovatago v lete 7062," *Chteniia* 24, bk. 2, sec. 3 (1858): i–viii, 1–42; *AAE* vol. 1, no. 238, 241–49; Nikolai Andreyev, "O 'dele d'iaka Viskovatago,'" *Seminarium Kondakovianum* 5 (1932): 191–242; David B. Miller, "The Viskovatyi Affair of 1553–54: Official Art, the Emergence of Autocracy, and

the Disintegration of Medieval Russian Culture," *Russian History* 8 (1981): 293–332; Khoroshkevich, "O Viskovatom," 278–79, 290–94.

42. Gralia, *Ivan Mikhailovich Viskovatyi*, 416–35.

43. E. B. Emchenko and I. V. Kurukin, "K izucheniiu publikatsii 'dela Viskovatogo' i formirovaniia ego sostava," *Arkheograficheskii ezhegodnik za 1983* (1985): 68–75; *PSRL* 13, 232–33.

44. A. A. Zimin, *I. S. Peresvetov i ego sovremenniki: Ocherki po istorii russkoi obshchestvenno-politicheskoi mysli serediny XVI veka* (Moscow: AN SSSR, 1958), 168–82; Klibanov, *Reformatsionnoe dvizhenie*, 265–66.

45. Bogatyrev, "Reinventing the Russian Monarchy," 281n43; Gralia, *Ivan Mikhailovich Viskovatyi*, 122–46.

46. L. E. Morozova, *Sochineniia Zinoviia Otenskogo* (Moscow: II AN SSSR, 1990), 103–4; Arkhimandrit Makarii (Veretennikov), *Zhizn' i trudy sviatitelia Makariia mitropolita Moskovskogo i vsea Rusi* (Moscow: Izdatel'skii sovet Russkoi Pravoslavnoi Tserkvy, 2002), 90; Kollmann, "The Moscow *Stoglav*," 1: 91.

47. Golokhvastov and Archimandrite Leonid, "Blagoveshchenskii ierei Sil'vestr," 2: 88–100; Igor' Vladimirovich Kurukin, *Zhizn' i trudy Sil'vestra, nastavnika tsaria Ivana Groznogo* (Moscow: Kvadriga, 2015), 44–50.

48. Zimin, *I. S. Peresvetov*, 153–68.

49. *AAE* vol. 1, no. 239, 249–56; *RIB* 4 (St. Petersburg: Arkheograficheskaia kommissiia, 1878), 1202–1448; *Prince A. M. Kurbsky's History of Ivan IV*, 266–73; Keetje Rozemund, "Ivan Fedorov and Starets Artemyi," *Slavonic and East European Review* 63 (1985): 417–21; Auerbach, "Identity in Exile," 21n48.

50. Andrei Petrovich Bogdanov, *Pero i krest: Russkie pisateli pod tserkovnym sudom* (Moscow: Izdatel'stvo politicheskoi literatury, 1990), 13–62; David B. Miller, "The Orthodox Church," in Perrie, *The Cambridge History of Russia*, vol. 1, 335–36.

51. *Prince A. M. Kurbsky's History of Ivan IV*, 252–85; Muriel Heppell, "Feodorit, a Russian non-Possessor, priest and martyr," *Sobornost* 5 (1983): 22–34; Jukka Korpela, "Fedorit (Theodorit) Kol'skii: Missionary and Princely Agent," *Forschungen zur osteuropäischen Geschichte* 72 (2010): 201–26; *Pistsovyia knigi Moskovskago Gosudarstva*, vol. 1, pt. 2, 1522.

52. *RIB* 4, 1432–34; Donald Ostrowski, "The *Debate with* Iosif (*Prenie s* Iosifom) as a Fictive Disputation," in Ostrowski, Valeria Nolan, and Jennifer Spock, ed., *Iosif Volotskii and Eastern Christianity: Essays across Seventeen Centuries* (Washington, DC: New Academic Publishers, 2017), 199–204; Haney, *From Italy to Muscovy*, 89; Anna Yu. Seregina and Mikhail V. Dmitriev, "Two Views of Religious Toleration in the 16th C: Robert Persons and Starets Artemyi," in Derwich and Dmitriev, *Être catholique—être orthodoxe—être protestant*, 104.

53. Morozova, *Sochineniia Zinoviia Otenskogo*, 94–97, 141–49.

54. Zimin, *I. S. Peresvetov*, 182–214; Klibanov, *Reformatsionnye dvizheniia v*

Rossii, 266–301; V. I. Koretskii, "Vnov' naidennoe protivoereticheskoe proizvedenie Zinoviia Otenskogo," *TODRL* 21 (1965): 166–82.

55. R. P. Dmitrieva, *Povest' o spore zhizny i smerti* (Moscow-Leningrad: Nauka, 1964).

56. Inok Zinovii, *Istiny pokazanie k voprosivshim o novom uchenii* (Kazan: Izdatel'stvo Kazanskogo universiteta, 1863); Andrei Popov, ed., "Poslanie mnogoslovnoe. Sochenenie inoka Zinoviia po rukopisi XVI veka," *Chteniia* 112, bk. 2 (1880): i–xix, 1–305.

57. Nancy Yanoshak, "A Fontological Analysis of the Major Works Attributed to Zinovii Otenskii" (PhD dissertation, Georgetown University, 1981); Nancy Yanoshak, "The Author of *Poslanie Mnogoslovnoe:* A Fontological Inquiry," *Slavic Review* 50 (1991): 621–36; Morozova, *Sochineniia Zinoviia Otenskogo*, 150–200.

58. Yanoshak, "A Fontological Analysis," 405–21.

59. Inok Zinovii, *Istiny pokazanie*, 23–31, 48, 126.

60. Zinovii, *Istiny pokazanie*, 890–913, 921–27; Rzhiga, "Opyty po istorii russkoi publitsistiki," 8; Rudolph M. Mainka, CMF, *Zinovij von Osten'. Ein Russischer Polemiker und Theologe der Mitte des 16. Jahrhunderts* (Rome: Pontifical Institute of Oriental Studies, 1961), 18–27; Yanoshak, "A Fontological Analysis," 382–87, 393–95; Morozova, *Sochineniia Zinoviia Otenskogo*, 53–62, 72–74, 85–89.

61. Goldfrank, "Theocratic Imperatives," 45, 46 n. 82.

62. Lynch, *Spain, 1516–1598*, 342–49.

63. *Stoglav*, 136–37, 139–40.

64. Ia. S. Lur'e, "Sud'ba belletristiki v XVI v.," in *Istoki russkoi belletristiki: Vozniknovenie zhanrov siuzhetnogo povestvovaniia v drevnerusskoi literatury* (Leningrad: Nauka, Leningradskoe otdelenie, 1970), 387–99, 418–23.

65. V. I. Koretskii, "Novye poslaniia Zinoviia Otenskogo," *TODRL* 25 (1970): 119–34; David Goldfrank, "Essential Glue: Muscovy's Republic of Sacred Letters, Mid-XIV to Mid-XVI c.," *Forschungen zur osteuropäischen Geschichte* 76 (2010): 335–59.

66. Sergei A. Ivanov, *Holy Fools in Byzantium and Beyond*, trans. Simon Franklin (Oxford: Oxford Univeristy Press, 2006), 280.

67. *Razriadnaia kniga 1475–1605*, vol. 2, pt. 1, 5; A. A. Zimin, "K izucheniiu istochnikov Stepennoi knigi," *TODRL* 13 (1957): 225–30; A. A. Zimin, "Povesti XVI veka v sbornike Rogozhskogo sobraniia," *Zapiski Otdela rukopisei GBL* 20 (Moscow, 1958): 186–204; Natalie Challis and Horace W. Dewey, "Basil the Blessed, Holy Fool of Moscow," *Russian History* 14 (1987): 47–59.

68. I. I. Kuznetsov, *Sviatye blazhennye Vasilii i Ioann, Khrista radi moskovskie chiudotvortsy* (Moscow: Zapiski Moskovskogo arkheologicheskago instituta, vol. 8, 1910), 1–121, 177–308, 330–65.

69. Mikhailova, *I zdes' soshlis' vse tsarstva*, 397–400; A. M. Panchenko, "Laughter as Spectacle," trans. Priscilla Hunt, in *Holy Foolishness in Russia*, ed. Priscilla Hunt and Svitlana Kobets (Bloomington: Slavica Publishers, Inc, 2011), 140–42; Ivanov, *Holy Fools*, 291–99.

Chapter 10. Intellectual and Cultural History

1. Al'shits, *Nachalo samoderzhaviia v Rossii*, 62; Backus, "Muscovite Legal Thought," 33–68; Goldfrank, "Pre-Enlightenment Utopianism," 131–47.

2. Ihor Ševčenko, "A Neglected Byzantine Source of Muscovite Political Ideology," *Harvard Slavic Studies* 2 (1954): 141–79; Daniel Rowland, "Did Muscovite Literary Ideology Place Limits on the Power of the Tsar (1540s–1660s)?" *Russian Review* 49 (1990): 125–55.

3. William F. Ryan, "The Old Russian Version of the Pseudo-Aristotelian *Secretum Secretorum*," *Slavonic and East European Review* 56 (1978): 242–60.

4. William F. Ryan, "The *Secreta Secretorum* and the Muscovite Autocracy," in *Pseudo-Aristotle, the* Secret of Secrets*: Sources and Influences*, ed. William F. Ryan and Charles B. Schmitt (London: Warburg Institute Surveys, IX, 1982), 119.

5. Ryan, "The Old Russian Version," 250.

6. Lur'e, *Povest' o Drakule*, 117–22, 140–85.

7. *Sochineniia I. Peresvetova* (Moscow-Leningrad: AN SSSR,1956), 162–65, 359, 170–84, 331–59; S. O. Shmidt, ed., *Opis' tsarskogo arkhiva XVI veka i arkhiva Posol'skogo prikaza 1614 goda* (Moscow: Izdatel'stvo vostochnoi literatury, 1960), 31; Daniel C. Matuszewski, "Peresvetov: the Ottoman Example and the Muscovite State" (PhD dissertation, University of Washington, 1972), 110–27, 150–51, 177, 206–11; Daniil Al', *Pisatel' Ivan Perevsetov i Tsar' Ivan Groznyi. U istokov izvechnoi diskussi—kak obustroit' Rossiiu* (St. Petersburg: Sankt-Peterburgskii gosudarstvenni universitet kul'tury i iskusstva, 2000), 11–92.

8. *Sochineniia I. Peresvetova*, 123–284; Zimin, *I. S. Peresvetov*, 217–480; Karavashkin, *Russkaia srednevekovaia publististika*, 27–126.

9. Goodman, *The New Monarchy*, 68–76; Greenblatt, *Renaissance Self-Fashioning*, 121; Karavashkin, "Vlast' muchitelia," 86–88; *Kazanskaia istoriia*, 113; *Prince A. M. Kurbsky's History of Ivan IV*, 127–33; *Sochineniia I. Peresvetova*, 151–62.

10. *Sochineniia I. Peresvetova*, 181, 147–51, 160; Werner Philipp, *Ivan Peresvetov und seine Schriften zur Erneuerung des Moskauer Reiches* (Berlin: Ost-Europa-Verlag, 1935), 27n204, 48–83; Iurganov, *Kategorii russkoi srednevekovoi kul'tury*, 33–107; Neubauer, *Car und Selbstherrscher*, 42.

11. George Vernadsky, "On Some Parallel Trends in Russian and Turkish History," *Transactions of the Connecticut Academy of Arts and Sciences* 36 (1945): 25–36; Ilber Ortayli, "Suleyman and Ivan: Two Autocrats of Eastern Europe," in *Suleyman the Second and His Time*, ed. Halil Inalcik and Cemal Kafardar (Istanbul: Isis

Press, 1993), 203–10; S. A. Nefedov, "Reformy Ivan III i Ivana IV: Osmanskoe vliianie," *Voprosy istorii*, no. 11 (2002): 30–53.

12. Veselovskii, *Feodal'noe zemlevladenie*, vol. 1, 282; Jaroslaw Pelenski, "State and Society in Muscovite Russia and the Mongol-Turkic System in the Sixteenth Century," in *The Mutual Effects of the Islamic and Judeo-Christian Worlds: The East European Pattern*, ed. Abraham Ascher et al. (New York: Brooklyn College Press, 1979), 93–109; Donald Ostrowskii, "The Military Land Grant Along the Muslim-Christian Frontier," *Russian History* 19 (1992): 327–59.

13. Brian L. Davies, "The Development of Russian Military Power 1453–1815," in *European Warfare, 1453–1815*, ed. Jeremy Black (London: St Martin's Press, 1999), 156–60, 178; Gábor Ágoston, "Military Transformation in the Ottoman Empire and Russia, 1500–1800," *Kritika* 12 (2011): 281–319; Godfrey Goodwin, *The Janissaries* (London: Saqi Essentials, 2006).

14. Zimin, *I. S. Peresvetov*, 109–42; A. I. Klibanov, "Sbornik sochinenii Ermolaia-Erazma," *TODRL* 16 (1960): 188–98; Klibanov, *Narodnaia sotsial'naia utopiia v Rossii period feodalizma* (Moscow: Nauka, 1977), 35–54.

15. R. P. Dmitrieva, ed., *Povest' o Petre i Fevronii* (Leningrad: Nauka, Leningradskoe otdelenie, 1979), 209–23; Riccardo Picchio, "The Hagiographic Framing of the Old Russian Tale on Prince Petr of Murom and the Wise Maid Fevronija," in *Language and Literary Theory: In Honor of Ladislav Matejka*, ed. B. A. Stolz et al. (Ann Arbor: Department of Slavic Languages and Literatures, University of Michigan, 1984), 489–90; Pliukhanova, *Siuzhety i simvoly*, 203–32.

16. Natalia L. Pushkareva, "The Ideal Image of a Spouse and Its Evolution in Medieval Rus' and Early Modern Russia from the Twelfth until the Seventeenth Centuries," in *Das Inviduum und die Seinen. Individualität in der okzidentalen und in der russischen Kultur in Mittelalter und früher Neuzeit*, ed. Yuri L. Bessmertny and Otto Gerhard Oxle (Göttingen: Vandenhoeck & Ruprecht, 2001), 97–98.

17. Andrei Karavashkin, *Literaturnyi obychai Drevnei Rusi* (Moscow: ROSSPEN, 2011), 417, 474n1, 482–83; Pushkareva, *Women in Russian History*, 100; *Poslaniia Ivana Groznogo*, 162–92; Zimin, *Krupnaia feodal'naia votchina*, 120.

18. Dmitriev and Likhachev, *Pamiatniki literatury drevnei Rusi: Konets XV–pervaia polovina XVI veka*, 652–63.

19. Maureen Perrie, "The Muscovite Monarchy in the Sixteenth Century: 'National,' 'Popular' or 'Democratic'?" *Cahiers du monde russe* 46 (2005): 238.

20. Galina Nikolaevna Moiseeva, *Valaamskaia beseda—pamiatnik russkoi publitsistiki serediny XVI veka* (Moscow-Leningrad: AN SSSR, 1958); N. A. Okhotina-Lind, *Skazanie o Valaamskom monastyre* (St. Petersburg: "Glagol" 1996), 69–77.

21. This is a difficult phrase to translate. The second anonymous reader of this book suggested the second possibility.

22. Val'denberg, *Drevnerusskiia ucheniia*, 299–309; Huttenbach, "The *Zemsky Sobor* in Ivan IV's Reign," 60–61, 243; Moiseeva, *Valaamskaia beseda*, 76.

23. *Prince A. M. Kurbsky's History of Ivan IV*, 202–3.

24. *Kazanskaia istoriia*, 72; *PSRL* 19 (St. Petersburg: Tipografiia I. N. Skorokhodova, 1903), 42; Berry and Crummey, *Rude and Barbarous Kingdom*, 293.

25. Jacob Burckhardt, *The Civilization of the Renaissance in Italy: An Essay* (London: Phaidon Press Ltd, 1951), 286; Moiseeva, *Valaamskaia beseda*, 163.

26. Miller, "The Velikie Minei Chetii and the Stepennaia kniga," 268–313; Marija Pljuchanova, "Rhetoric and Russian Thought of the Sixteenth and Seventeenth Century," *Europa Orientalis* 5 (1986): 333–43.

27. Alexander Dvorkin, *Ivan the Terrible as a Religious Type: A Study of the Background, Genesis and Development of the Theocratic Idea of the First Russian Tsar and his Attempts to Establish "Free Autocracy" in Russia* (Erlangen: Lehrstuhl für Geschichte und Theologie, 1992), 41; D'iakonov, *Vlast' Moskovskikh gosudarei*, 67–68.

28. *PSRL* 29, 330–31; *PSRL* 13, 378–80; Donald Ostrowski, "Ironies of the *Tale of the White Cowl*," *Palaeoslavica* 10 (2002): 1–28; Miroslav Labunka, *The Legend of the Novgorodian White Cowl (The Study of Its "Prologue" and "Epilogue")* (Munich: Ukrainian Free University, 1998); Uspenskii, *Tsar' i patriarkh*, 429–39.

29. Usachev, *Stepennaia kniga*, 456–59; Gail Lenhoff, "The Cult of Metropolitan Iona and the Conceptualization of Ecclesiastical Authority in Muscovy," in *Speculum Slaviae Orientalis. Muscovy, Ruthenia and Lithuania in the Late Middle Ages / Moskoviia, Iugo-Zapadnaia Rus' i Litva v period pozdnego Srednevekov'ia*, ed. Vyacheslav V. Ivanov and Julia Verkholantsev (UCLA Slavic Studies, New Series, vol. IV; Moscow: Novoe izdatel'stvo, 2005), 122–43.

30. Gail Lenhoff (G. Lenkhoff), "Uchrezhdenie Kazanskoi eparkhii i proekt sozdaniia Stepennoi knigi," *Drevniaia Rus': Voprosy medievistiki* 4, no. 50 (2012): 95–107.

31. Miller, "The Velikie Minei Chetii and the Stepennaia kniga," 314–61; Aleksei Vladimirovich Sirenov, *Stepennaia kniga. Istoriia teksta* (Moscow: Iazyki slavianskikh kul'tur, 2007).

32. Gail Lenhoff, "The Economics of a Medieval Literary Project: Direct and Indirect Costs of Producing the *Stepennaia kniga*," *Russian History* 34 (2007): 219–37; Gail Lenhoff, "The 'Stepennaja kniga' and the Idea of the Book in Medieval Russia," in *Germano-Slavistische Beiträge. Festschrift für Peter Rehder zum 65. Geburtstag*, ed. Miloš Okuka and Ulrich Schweier (Munich: Verlag Otto Sagner, 2004), 449–58.

33. A. S. Usachev, "Metody raboty drevnerusskogo knizhnika i problema avtorstva Stepennoi knigi (chast' 1)," *Dialog so vremenem: Al'manakh intellektual'noi istorii* 25 (2008): 186; Sergei Bogatyrev, "*The Book of Degrees of the Royal Genealogy:*

The Stabilization of the Text and the Argument from Silence," in Lenhoff and Kleimola, *The Book of Royal Degrees*, 51–38; Edward L. Keenan, "The *Stepennaia kniga* and the Godunovian Renaissance," in Lenhoff and Kleimola, *The Book of Royal Degrees*, 69–79; Halperin, "*Stepennaia kniga*," 56–75.

34. Lenhoff, 143–44; and Pokrovskii, 94, 96, in *Stepennaia kniga tsarskogo rodosloviia*, vol. 1.

35. Wolf-Heinrich Schmidt, "The Serbian *Danilov sbornik* and the *Stepennaia kniga*: Toward a Comparative Analysis of their Genres and Functions," in Lenhoff and Kleimola, *The Book of Royal Degrees*, 125–39; N. N. Pokrovskii, "Istoricheskie postulaty Stepennoi knigi tsarskogo rodosloviia," in *Istoricheskie istochniki i literaturnye pamiatniki XVI-XX vv.: Razvitie traditsii* (Novosibirsk: RAN, Sankt-Peterburgskoe otdelenie, 2004), 12; Usachev, *Stepennaia kniga*, 666–84.

36. Olga Il'ichna Podobedova, *Miniatiuri russkikh istoricheskikh rukopisei. K istorii russkogo litsevogo letopisaniia* (Moscow: Nauka, 1965); Morozov, "Ivan Groznyi na miniiatiurakh," 232–40; Aleksandr Aleksandrovich Amosov, *Litsevoi letopisnyi svod: Kompleksnoe kodikologicheskoe issledovanie* (Moscow: Editorial URSS, 1998). I have not consulted *Litsevoi letopisnyi svod: Russkaia letopisnaia istoriia*, 24 vols. (Moscow: AKTEON, 2009–10).

37. A. V. Sirenov, *Stepennaia kniga i russkaia istoricheskaia mysl' XVI–XVIII vv.* (Moscow-St. Petersburg: Al'ians-Arkheo, 2010), 121–66; Gail Lenhoff, "Le *Livre des degrés*, ou l'écriture hagiographique de l'histoire (1555–1563)," in *Écrire et réécrire l'histoire russe d'Ivan le Terrible à Vasilij Ključevskij (1547–1917)*, ed. Pierre Gonneau and Ecatherina Rai (Paris: Institut d'Études slaves, 2013), 30–31.

38. M. N. Tikhomirov et al., *U istokov russkogo knigopechataniia: K trekhsot-semidesiatipiatiletiiu so dnia smerti Ivana Fedorova 1583–1958* (Moscow: AN SSSR, 1958); Evgenii L'vovich Nemirovskii, *Voznikovnovenie knigopechataniia v Moskve: Ivan Fedorov* (Moscow: Kniga, 1964).

39. Edward L. Keenan, "Paper for the Tsar: A Letter of Ivan IV of 1570," *Oxford Slavonic Papers* 4 (1971): 21–9; Natal'ia Savel'eva, "'Paper for Tsar Ivan Groznyi in the Archive (*Drevlekhranilishche*) of Pushkinskii Dom (St. Petersburg)," *Solanus* 17 (2003): 5–17.

40. Nemirovskii, *Voznikovnovenie knigopechataniia*, 263–69; Tikhomirov in *U istokov russkogo knigopechataniia*, 35–40; Anatolii Sergeevich Dëmin, *Pisatel' i obshchestvo v Rossii XVI–XVII vekov (Obshchestvennye nastroenniia)* (Moscow: Nauka 1965), 8–35.

41. M. V. Kukushkina, *Kniga v Rossii v XVI veke* (St. Petersburg: "Peterburgskoe Vostokovedenie," 1999), 164, 169, 178; Nancy Shields Kollmann, "Response to Wirtschafter. On Advising Princes in Early Modern Russia: Literacy and Performance," in Lenhoff and Kleimola, *The Book of Royal Degrees*, 345.

42. Henshall, *The Myth of Absolutism*, 114–15; Plowden, *Elizabeth I*, 518; Kap-

peler, *Ivan Groznyi*, 102; Keenan, "Ivan the Terrible and Book Culture," 29; Sergei Bogatyrev, "The Patronage of Early Printing in Moscow," *Canadian-American Slavic Studies* 51, nos. 2–3 (2017): 249–88.

43. Nadezhda Aleksandrovna Soboleva, "O datirovke bol'shoi gosudarstvennoi pechati Ivana IV," in *Rossiia na putiakh tsentralizatsii*, 179–86; Mel'nikova, "Mesto monet Ivana Groznogo," 121–33; Gustave Alef, "The Adoption of the Muscovite Two-Headed Eagle: A Discordant View," *Speculum* 41 (1966): 1–21.

44. Stökl, *Testament und Siegel Ivan IV*, 41–69; John H. Lind, "Ivan IV's Great State Seal and His Use of Some Heraldic Symbols during the Livonian War," *Jahrbücher für Geschichte Osteuropas* 3 (1985): 481–94; Isolde Thyrêt, "The *Katepetasma* of 1555 and the Image of the Orthodox Ruler in the Early Reign of Ivan IV," in Kivelson et al., *The New Muscovite Cultural History*, 43–62.

45. Rüß, *Herren und Diener*, 454–55; Michael S. Flier, "The Iconology of Royal Ritual in Sixteenth-Century Muscovy," in *Byzantine Studies: Essays on the Slavic World and the Eleventh Century*, ed. Speros Vryonis Jr. (New Rochelle: Aristide D. Caratzas, Publisher, 1992), 53–76; Burckhardt, *The Civilization of the Renaissance*, 245.

46. Richard Hakluyt, *The Principal Navigations Voyages Traffiques & Discoveries of the English Nation*, vol. 2 (Glasgow: James MacLehose and Sons, 1903), 434–35, 439–40; Michael S. Flier, "Breaking the Code: The Image of the Tsar in the Muscovite Palm Sunday Ritual," in Flier and Rowland, *Medieval Russian Culture*, vol. 2, 213–42; Uspenskii, *Tsar' i patriarkh*, 440–61; Miller, "The Politics and Ceremonial," 244–51.

47. Hakluyt, *The Principal Navigations*, vol. 2, 432–33; Paul Bushkovitch, "The Epiphany Ceremony of the Russian Court in the Sixteenth and Seventeenth Centuries," *Russian Review* 49 (1990): 1–17.

48. Giorgio G. DiMauro, "The Church and the Cult of Imperial Humility: Icons and Enactment of the Muscovite Furnace Ritual," *Harvard Ukrainian Studies* 29 (2006): 415–28.

49. M. V. Dmitriev, "Predstavleniia o vlasti i ideal 'bezvlastiia' v ucheniiakh vostochnoslavianskikh religioznykh reformatorov XVI veka," in *Rimsko-Konstantinopol'skoe nasledie*, 260.

50. O. I. Podobedova, *Moskovskaia shkola zhivopisi pre Ivane IV. Raboty v moskovskom Kremle 40-kh—70-kh godov XVI v.* (Moscow: Nauka, 1972), 59–68, 193–207 (K. Lopialo Appendix); Daniel Rowland, "Two Cultures, One Throne Room. Secular Courtiers and Orthodox Culture in the Golden Hall of the Moscow Kremlin," in Kivelson and Greene, *Orthodox Russia*, 33–57; Michael S. Flier, "Golden Hall Iconography and the Makarian Initiative," in Valerie Kivelson et al., *The New Muscovite Cultural History*, 63–75.

51. Irina Mikhailovna Sokolova, *Monomakhov tron. Tsarskoe mesto Uspenskogo*

sobora Moskovskogo Kremlia. K 450-letiiu pamiatnika (Moscow: Indrik, 2001); Michael S. Flier, "The Monomakh Throne: Ivan the Terrible and the Architectonics of Destiny," in *Architectures of Russian Identity: 1500 to the Present*, ed. James Cracraft and Daniel Rowland (Ithaca: Cornell University Press, 2003), 21–33, 216–18.

52. Isaiah Gruber, "Russia, Jews and Hebrews: The Makings of Ambivalence," *Australian Journal of Jewish Studies* 25 (2011): 119–52.

53. *Stepennaia kniga tsarskogo rodosloviia*, vol. 2, 388; *PSRL* l3, 137; A. A. Zimin, ed., *Gosudarstvennyi arkhiv Rossii XVI stoletiia: Opyt rekonstruktsii* (Moscow: II AN SSSR, 1978), vol. 2, 428–29; E. Shmurlo, ed., "Izvestiia Dzhiovanni Tedal'di o Rossii vremeni Ioanna Groznago," *Zhurnal Ministerstvo Narodnogo Prosveshcheniia* 275, no. 5 (1891): 129–30; Usachev, *Stepennaia kniga i*, 336–68.

54. Shmidt, *"Vypiska iz posol'skikh knig,"* 185; Alexander Pereswetoff-Morath, *A Grin without a Cat*, vol. 2, *Jews and Christians in Medieval Russia: Assessing the Sources* (Lund: Department of Central and Eastern European Studies, Lund University, 2002), 26–29, 122–23.

55. Kamen, *Inquisition and Society in Spain;* William Monter, *Frontiers of Heresy: The Spanish Inquisition from the Basque Lands to Sicily* (Cambridge: Cambridge University Press, 1990).

56. Rowland, "Biblical Military Imagery in the Political Culture of Early Modern Russia," 182–213; A. V. Sirenov, *Stepennaia kniga i russkaia istoricheskaia mysl' XVI–XVIII vv.* (Moscow-St. Petersburg: Al'ians-Arkheo, 2010), 39–47; Sergei Bogatyrev, "The Heavenly Host and the Sword of Truth: Apocalyptic Imagery in Ivan IV's Muscovy," in Kivelson et al., *The New Muscovite Cultural History*, 77–90.

57. *Vera i vlast': Epokha Ivana Groznogo* (Moscow: Gosudarstvennyi Istoriko-kul'turnyi muzei-zapovednik "Moskovskii Kreml'," 2007), no. 66, 160; Bogatyrev, "Battle for Divine Wisdom," 325–63.

58. A. V. Sirenov, "Stepennaia kniga v kontekste kul'turnykh sviazei Rossii serediny XVI v.," in Lenhoff and Kleimola, *The Book of Royal Degrees*, 115–17.

59. Cherniavsky, "Russia," 127; Frank Kämpfer, "Über die theologische und architecktonische Konzeption der Vasilij-Blažennyj-Kathedrale in Moskau," *Jahrbücher für Geschichte Osteuropas* 24 (1976): 481–98; Michael S. Flier, "Filling in the Blanks: The Church of the Intercession and the Architectonics of Medieval Muscovite Ritual," *Harvard Ukrainian Studies* 19 (1995): 120–37.

60. Levin, "Muscovy and Its Mythologies," 781.

Chapter 11. The Economy and Economic Management

1. Liudmila Ivanovna Ivina, *Vnutrennee osvoenie zemel Rossii XVI v. Istoriko-geograficheskoe issledovanie po materialam monastyrei* (Leningrad: Nauka, Leningradskoe otdelenie, 1985).

2. Daniil Pavlovich Makovskii, *Razvitie tovarno-denezhnykh otnoshenii v*

sel'skom khoziaistve russkogo gosudarstva v XVI veke (Smolensk: Smolenskii gosu-darstvennyi pedagogicheskii institut imeni Karla Marksa, 1963).

3. S. V. Bakhrushin, ed., *Lavochnye knigi Novgoroda Velikogo 1583 goda* (Moscow: RANION, 1930), 4; V. A. Kuchkin, "Zhalovannaia gramota 1538 g. na dve slobodki v Kolomne," *Arkheograficheskii ezhegodnik za 1959* (1960), 342–43; V. A. Kuchkin, "Materialy dlia istorii russkogo goroda XVI v. (Vypis' iz pistsovykh knig g. Muroma 1566 g. i muromskaia sotnia 1573/74)," *Arkheograficheskii ezhegodnik za 1967* (1969): 299.

4. L. S. Prokof'eva, "'Khlebnyi biudzhet' krest'ianskogo khoziaistva Belozersk-ogo kraia v seredine XVI v.," in *Krest'ianstvo i klassovaia bor'ba v feodal'noi Rossii*, 98–113; *PRP* 4: 256; Dewey, *Muscovite Judicial Texts*, 69.

5. Vladimir Ivanovich Ivanov, *Bukhgalterskii uchet v Rossii XVI–XVII vv. Is-toriko-istochnikovedcheskoe issledovanie monastyrskikh prikhodo-raskhodnykh knig* (St. Petersburg: Dmitrii Bulanin, 2005), 106; Wallerstein, *The Modern World-System*, 301–24.

6. Nosov, *Stanovlenie soslovno-predstavitel'nykh uchrezhdenii*, 289; Spock, "Community Building and Social Identity," 553; Zlotnik, "Immunity Charters," 299; *The Monastic Rule of Iosif Volotsky*, rev. ed., ed., trans, and introduced by David Goldfrank (Kalamazoo: Cistercian Publications, 2000), 105.

7. Kalachov, *Akty, otnosiashchesia do iuridicheskago byta drevnei Rusi*, vol. 2, no. 147 XXII, 361–62; Weickhardt, "The Pre-Petrine Law of Property," 663–79; Weick-hardt, "Was There Private Property in Muscovite Russia?" *Slavic Review* 53 (1994): 531–38; Weickhardt, "Registering Land Titles in Muscovy," in Dunning et al., *Rude & Barbarous Kingdom Revisited*, 441–57; Weickhardt, "The Commercial Law of Old Russia," *Russian History* 25 (1998): 361–85; Weickhardt, "The Law and the Role of Contracts in the Muscovite Tsardom," *Russian History* 36 (2009): 530–43.

8. Jennifer B. Spock, "Giving Voice to the Voiceless: Expressions of Non-Elite Identity and Perspectives in Pre-Petrine Russia," in *Religion and Identity in Russia and the Soviet Union: A Festschrift for Paul Bushkovitch*, ed. Nikolaos Chrissides et al. (Bloomington: Slavica Publishers, Inc, 2011), 29–36.

9. *Materialy po istorii krest'ian v Rossii XI–XVII vv. (Sbornik dokumentov)* (Leningrad: Izdatel'stvo Leningradskogo Ordena Lenina Gosudarstvennogo Universiteta imeni A. A. Zhdanova, 1958), no. 56, 65; *RIB* 32, nos. 201, 270, 271, 275, 282, 293, 298, 299.

10. Wallerstein, *The Modern World-System*, 112, 88.

11. Braudel, *The Mediterranean and the Mediterranean World*, vol. 1, 527; Barba-ra B. Diefendorf, *Beneath the Cross: Catholics and Huguenots in Sixteenth-Century Paris* (Oxford: Oxford University Press, 1991), 17–18; Judith Hook, *Lorenzo de' Medici: An Historical Biography* (London: Hamish Hamilton, 1964), 32–33; Ruth Pike, *Aristocrats and Traders: Sevillian Society in the Sixteenth Century* (Ithaca:

Cornell University Press, 1972), 22–53, 99–129; Richard Hellie, "Foundations of Russian Capitalism: D. P. Makovskii, *Razvitie tovarno-denezhnykh otnoshenii v sel'skom khoziaistve russkogo gosudarstva v XVI veke*," *Slavic Review* 26 (1967): 148–54.

12. Stone, *The Crisis of the Aristocracy*, 200–6.

13. A. G. Man'kov, *Tseny i ikh dvizhenie v russkom gosudarstve XVI veka* (Moscow-Leningrad: AN SSSR, 1951), 25–30.

14. Andrei Aleksandrovich Vvedenskii, *Dom Stroganovykh v XVI–XVII vekakh* (Moscow: Izdatel'stvo sotsial'no-ekonomicheskoi literatury, 1962), 29, 34; Richard Hakluyt, *The Principal Navigations Voyages Traffiques and Discoveries of the English Nation*, vol. 3 (Glasgow: James MacLehose and Sons, 1903), 113; *DAI* vol. 1, no. 118, 172; G. Man'kov, ed., *Votchinnye khoziaistvennye knigi XVI v. Prikhodnye i raskhodnye knigi Iosifo-Volokolamskogo monastyria 70–80-kh gg.*, vol. 2 (Moscow-Leningrad: II AN SSSR, Leningradskoe otdelenie, 1980), 219.

15. Mikhail Nikolaevich Pokrovskii, *Izbrannye proizvedeniia*, bk. 1, *Russkaia istoriia s drevneishikh vremen (toma I i II)* (Moscow: Mysl, 1966), 255–73.

16. Braudel, *The Mediterranean and the Mediterranean World*, vol. 1, 445; Stone, *The Crisis of the Aristocracy*, 233–48, 241.

17. Peter Turchyn and Sergey A. Nefedov, *Secular Cycles* (Princeton: Princeton University Press, 2009), 248.

18. Aleksandr Gvan'ini, *Opisanie Moskovii*, trans. G. G. Kozlova (Moscow: Greko-Latinskii kabinet Iu. A. Shichalina, 1997), 21; Aleksandr Ivanovich Tsepkov, ed., *Reinol'd Geidenshtein. Zapiski o Moskovskoi voine (1578–1582). Al'bert Shlichting. Novoe izvestie o Rossii vremeni Ivana Groznogo. Genrikh Shtaden. O Moskve Ivana Groznogo* (Riazan: Aleksandriia, 2005), 90, 126.

19. Artur Attman, *The Russian and Polish Markets in International Trade, 1500–1650*, trans. Eva and Allan Green (Göteborg: Institute of Economic History of Gothenburg University, 1973), 103–15, 270; I. G. Spasskii, "Gold Coins and Coin-Like Gold in the Muscovite State, and the First Gold Pieces of Ivan III," trans. H. Bartlett Wells, *Numismatic Chronicle*, 7th ser., 19 (1979): 165–84.

20. Mariia Vasil'evna Fekhner, *Torgovlia Russkogo Gosudarstva so stranami Vostoka v XVI veke*, 2nd ed. (Moscow: Gosudarstvennoe izdatel'stvo kul'turno-prosvetitel'noi literatury, 1956), 113; Marian Malowist, "Poland, Russia and Western Trade in the Fifteenth and Sixteenth Centuries," *Past & Present* 13 (1958): 3; Attman, *The Russian and Polish Markets*, 181.

21. Jerome Blum, "Prices in Russia in the Sixteenth Century," *Journal of Economic History* 16 (1956): 182–99; Kagarlitsky, *Empire of the Periphery*, 79–98.

22. Boris Dmitrievich Grekov, *Krest'iane na Rusi s drevneishikh vremen do XVII veka* (Moscow-Leningrad: AN SSSR, 1946), 584–85; N. P. Popov, "Sobranie rukopisei Moskovskogo Simonova monastyria (1-oi fototipiei)," no. 20, 104;

Akty moskovksogo Simonova monastyria, no. 124, 135–37; *DAI* vol. 1, no. 52, XVII, 100–101, XX, 102–4; *AI* vol. 1, no. 146, 210–11; Sergei Shumakov, *Sotnitsy (1537–1597 gg.) Gramoty i Zapisi (1561–1696)* (Moscow: Imperatorskoe Obshchestvo istorii i drevnostei rossiiskikh pri Moskovskom universitete, 1902), no. 38, 224–25.

23. Valerie A. Kivelson, "The Effects of Partible Inheritance: Gentry Families and the State in Muscovy," *Russian Review* 53 (1994): 197–212.

24. Rüß, *Herren und Diener*, 106–221.

25. Likhachev, *Sbornik aktov*, XIII, 39–49; Iurii Georgievich Alekseev, *Agrarnaia i sotsial'naia istoriia severo-vostochnoi Rusi XV–XVI vv. Pereiaslavskii uezd* (Moscow-Leningrad: Nauka, 1966), 65; Sergei Shumakov, *Sotnitsy, gramoty i zapisi 5* (Moscow: Imperatorskoe Obshchesto Istorii i Drevnostei Rossiiskikh pri Moskovskom Universitete, 1910), no. 5, 31–32; *Pistsovye materialy Tverskogo uezda XVI veka*, 145–310.

26. Rüß, *Herren und Diener*, 121–46; Jerome Blum, *Lord and Peasant in Russia from the Ninth to the Nineteenth Century* (New York: Atheneum, 1965), 192; Hellie, "The Law," 365, 384; *Akty feodal'nogo zemlevladeniia i khoziaistva*, vol. 2, no. 150, no. 166, no. 177, no. 187, no. 188, no. 197; *Materialy po istorii Tatarskoi ASSR*, 14–33; Krom, "Vdovstvuiushchee tsarstvo," 137n62; *PRP* 4: 107, 127–30.

27. Russell E. Martin, "Gifts for the Dead: Death, Kinship and Commemoration in Muscovy (The Case of the Mstislavskii Princes)," *Russian History* 26 (1999): 171–202; Daniel H. Kaiser, "Testamentary Charity in Early Modern Russia: Trends and Motivations," *Journal of Modern History* 76 (2004): 1–28; Charles J. Halperin, "Lay Cash Donations to the Trinity Sergius Monastery During the Reign of Ivan IV," *Slavonic and East European Review* 95, no. 2 (2017): 271–292; Charles J. Halperin, "Lay Cash Land Purchases During the Reign of Ivan IV," *Jahrbücher für Geschichte Osteuropas* 65, no. 2 (2017): 177–99.

28. Cherkasova, *Zemlevladenie Troitse-Sergieva monastyria*, 119, 124.

29. Rozhdestvenskii, *Sluzhiloe zemlevladenie*, 119–20.

30. Ludwig Steindorff, "Donations and Commemoration in the Muscovite Realm—a Medieval or Early Modern Phenomenon?" *Forschungen zur osteuropäischen Geschichte* 76 (2010): 496–97.

31. S. B. Veselovskii, *Selo i derevnia v severo-vostochnoi Rusi XIV–XVI vv. Istoriko-sotsiologicheskoe issledovanie o tipakh vnegorodskikh poselenii* (Moscow-Leningrad: OGIS, 1936), 101.

32. Makovskii, *Razvitie tovarno-denezhnykh otnoshenii*, 146; Kagarlitsky, *Empire of the Periphery*, 84; A. V. Mashtafarov, "Dukhovnaia gramota Ivana Iur'evicha Podzhogina 1541 g." *Russkii diplomatarii* 1 (1997): 25–37; Daniel H. Kaiser, "'Forgive Us Our Debts': Debts and Debtors in Early Modern Russia," *Forschungen zur osteuropäischen Geschichte* 50 (1994): 155–83.

33. S. N. Kisterev, "Vladimirskii Rozhdestvenskii monastyr v dokumentakh

XVI–nachala XVII veka," *Russkii diplomatarii* 6, no. 15 (2000): 108–9; *Akty moskovksogo Simonova monastyria*, no. 198, 243–44.

34. Khoroshkevich, *Rossiia v sisteme*, 257–58.

35. Carolyn Johnston Pouncy, "The Origins of the *Domostroi:* A Study in Manuscript History," *Russian Review* 46 (1987): 357–73; V. V. Kolesov, ed., *Domostroi* (Moscow: Sovetskaia Rossiia, 1990), 5–24; Viacheslav Valer'evich Khorikhin, *Ruskopisnye teksty Domostroia XVI–XVIII vv. Istoriia izdaniia i izucheniia* (Sergiev Posad: Sergievo-Posadskii gumanitarnyi institut, 2002), 29–31, 144–63, 178–79; Liudmila Pavlovna Naidenova, *Mir russkogo cheloveka XVI–XVII vv. (Po Domostroiu i pamiatnikam prava)* (Moscow: Izdatel'stvo Sretenskogo monastyria, 2003), 24–35.

36. A. L. Khoroshkevich, "Povsednevnyi byt moskvichei v seredine XVI v. (po materialem Stoglava)," in *Chelovek XVI stoletiia* (Moscow: Institut vseobshchei istorii RAN, 2000), 210–11.

37. Nancy Shields Kollmann, "Beginning a Civilizing Process: Handbooks of Morals and Behavior in Early Modern Russia," in *Everyday Life in Russian History: Quotidian Studies in Honor of Daniel Kaiser*, ed. Gary Marker et al. (Bloomington: Slavica Publishers, Inc, 2010), 329–35.

38. L. P. Naidenova, "Ideal pravednoi zhizni u russkogo gorozhanina XVI v (po materialem Domostroia)," in *Mirovospriiatie i samosoznanie russkogo obshchestva (XI–XX vv.). Sbornik statei* (Moscow: IRI RAN, 1994), 51–58; L. P. Naidenova, "'Our Own' [People] and Outsiders in *Domostroi*," *Russian Studies in History* 38, no. 4 (2000): 76–89.

39. Carolyn Johnston Pouncy, ed., *The Domostroi: Rules for Russian Households in the Time of Ivan the Terrible* (Ithaca: Cornell University Press, 1994), 37–45; Burckhardt, *The Civilization of the Renaissance*, 244–45.

40. Kollmann, *By Honor Bound*, 21–22; Naidenova, *Mir russkogo cheloveka*. 66; Pouncy, "The Origins of the *Domostroi*," 366; Bushkovitch, *Religion and Society*, 47.

41. A. A. Zimin, "Osnovnye problemy," 111; Sergei M. Soloviev, *History of Russia*, vol. 12, *Russian Society under Ivan the Terrible*, ed. T. Allan Smith (Gulf Breeze: Academic International Press, 1996), xxii; Naidenova, *Mir russkogo cheloveka XVI–XVII vv.*, 111–36; Pouncy, "The *Domostroi* as a Source for Muscovite History," 147, 267–68, 283–84; Pouncy, ed., *The Domostroi*, 50 n. 87; V. V. Kolesov, "*Domostroi* as a Work of Russian Culture," *Russian Studies in History* 40, no. 1 (2001): 28n38.

42. Jennifer B. Spock, "Administering a Right Life: Secular and Spiritual Guidance at Solovki in the Sixteenth and Seventeenth Centuries," *Russian History* 39 (2012): 148–72; Grekov, *Krest'iane na Rusi*, 769.

43. Kolesov, "*Domostroi* as a Work of Russian Culture," 32, 66; Pouncy, "The *Domostroi* as a Source for Muscovite History," 113–14; Pouncy, *The Domostroi*, 50; Burckhardt, *The Civilization of the Renaissance*, 226–27; Burke, *Languages and Communities*, 142; Korogodina, *Ispoved' v Rossii*, 347–48; Dmitrii Likhachev in

Biblioteka literatury drevnei Rusi, vol. 10, *XVI vek* (St. Petersburg: Nauka, 2000), 13–15.

44. Pouncy's translation obscures the shared use of the word "strength" (*sila*).

45. Pouncy, *The Domostroi*, 70, 75, 79, 84, 86, 92, 123, 123–24, 179, 181, 184, 190.

46. Kollmann, "The Moscow *Stoglav*," vol. 2, 538; Korogodina, *Ispoved' v Rossii*, 202; R. E. F. Smith, *Peasant Farming in Muscovy* (Cambridge: Cambridge University Press, 1977), 30, 109, 120, 229.

47. Max Weber, *The Protestant Ethic and the Spirit of Capitalism*, trans. Talcott Parsons (Los Angeles: Roxbury Publishing Company, 1998); Richard Henry Tawney, *Religion and the Rise of Capitalism* (New Brunswick: Transaction Publishers, 1998); Robert W. Green, ed., *Protestantism, Capitalism and Social Science: The Weber Thesis Controversy*, 2nd ed. (Lexington: D. C. Heath & Co., 1973).

48. Max J. Okenfuss, *The Discovery of Childhood in Russia: The Evidence of the Slavic Primer* (Newtonville: Oriental Research Partners, 1980), 5–6; Max J. Okenfuss, "From School Class to Social Caste: The Divisiveness of Early-Modern Russian Education," *Jahrbücher für Geschichte Osteuropas* 33 (1983): 323n9; Naidenova, *Mir russkogo cheloveka*, 32; Stone, *The Crisis of the Aristocracy*, 22.

49. T. R. Rudi, ed., *Zhitie Iiulianii Lararevskoi (Povest' ob Ul'ianii Osor'inoi)* (St. Petersburg: Nauka, 1996); T. A. Greenan, "Iulianiya Lazarevskaya," *Oxford Slavonic Papers* 15 (1982): 28–45; Suzanne Janosik McNally, "From Public Person to Private Prisoner: The Changing Place of Women in Medieval Russia" (PhD dissertation, University of New York at Binghamton, 1976), 133–34.

50. L. R. Lewitter, "Women, Sainthood and Marriage in Muscovy," *Journal of Russian Studies* 37 (1979): 3–11; H. W. Dewey and A. M. Kleimola, "Muted Eulogy: Women Who Inspired Men in Medieval Rus'," *Russian History* 10 (1983): 195–200.

Chapter 12. Early Foreign Policy

1. Solov'ev, *Istoriia Rossii*, bk. 3, vol. 6, 474–77; Shafiga Daulet, "Rise and Fall of the Khanate of Kazan (1438–1552): Internal and External Factors that Led to its Conquest by Ivan the Terrible" (PhD dissertation, New York University, 1984), 8, 271–72.

2. *AAE* vol. 1, no. 241: 257–61; *PSRL* 13: 249–50.

3. Marshall Poe, "The Consequences of the Military Revolution in Muscovy—a Comparative Perspective," *Comparative Studies in Society and History* 38 (1996): 607–9; Michael C. Paul, "The Military Revolution in Russia, 1550–1682," *Journal of Military History* 68 (2004): 9–45.

4. *PSRL* 22, 532; Smith, "The Muscovite Officer Corps, 1465–1598," 104–22; Filjushkin, *Ivan the Terrible: A Military History*, 19, 20.

5. Kamen, *Philip II of Spain*, 109–10, 264; Brian Davies, "The Foundation of

Muscovite Military Power, 1453–1613," in *The Military History of Tsarist Russia*, ed. Frederick W. Kagan and Robin Higham (New York: Palgrave, 2002), 25.

6. Smith, "The Muscovite Officer Corps, 1465–1598," 109; Donald Ostrowski, "The Replacement of the Compound Bow by Firearms in the Muscovite Cavalry," *Kritika* 11 (2010): 513–34; Carol B. Stevens, *Russia's Wars of Emergence, 1460–1730* (Harlow: Pearson, Longman, 2002), 72–75; Charles J. Halperin, "Ivan IV's Professional Infantry, The Musketeers (*strel'tsy*): A Note on Numbers," *Journal of Slavic Military Studies* 30, no. 1 (2017): 96–116.

7. Frank Kämpfer, "Die Eroberung von Kazan 1552 als Gegenstand der zeitgenössischen russischen Historiographie," *Forschungen zur osteuropäischen Geschichte* 14 (1969): 58–60.

8. *Latukhinskaia Stepennaia kniga 1676 g.*, 515; *PSRL* 13: 209, 218–19; *Stepennaia kniga tsarskogo rodosloviia*, vol. 3, 412; A. A. Zimin, "Uchastnik vziatiia Kazani v 1552 g. litvin Razmysl Petrov," in *Voprosy voennoi istorii Rossii XVIII i pervaia polovina XIX vekov* (Moscow: Nauka, 1969), 273–78.

9. *PSRL* 13, 170; Jaroslaw Pelenski, *Russia and Kazan: Conquest and Imperial Ideology (1438–1560s)* (The Hague-Paris: Mouton, 1974).

10. Keenan, Jr., "Muscovy and Kazan," 548–58; Ihor Ševčenko, "Muscovy's Conquest of Kazan: Two Views Reconciled," *Slavic Review* 26 (1967): 541–47.

11. Kämpfer, "Die Eroberung von Kazan," 7–161; Levykin, *Voinskie tseremonii i regalii russkikh tsarei*, 37.

12. *PSRL* 13, 209, 505; *Prince A. M. Kurbsky's History of Ivan*, 48–49, 60–61; Iakovleva, "Piskarevskii letopisets," 86.

13. *Materialy po istorii Tatarskoi ASSR*, xvi-xvii; Pelenski, *Russia and Kazan*, 203, 212–13; Miller, "The Velikie Minei Chetii and the Stepennaia kniga," 294, 301, 312; Crummey, *The Formation of Muscovy*, 153.

14. Paul Bushkovitch, "Orthodoxy and Islam in Russia 988–1725," *Forschungen zur osteuropäischen Geschichte* 76 (2010): 137–39; Michael P. Romaniello, "Controlling the Frontier: Monasteries and Infrastructure in the Volga Region, 1552–1682," *Central Asian Survey* 19 (2000): 429–43.

15. Aleksandr Filiushkin, "Religioznyi faktor v russkoi vneshnei politike XVI veka: Ksenofobiia, tolerantnost' ili pragmatizm?" *Forschungen zur osteuropäischen Geschichte* 76 (2010): 145–79; Saliam Khatipovich Alishev, *Kazan' i Moskva: Mezhgosudarstvennye otnosheniia v XV–XVI vv.* (Kazan: Tatarskoe knizhnoe izdatel'svo, 1995) 90, 104–6; Daulet, "Rise and Fall of the Khanate of Kazan (1438–1552)," 242, 277, 297.

16. Janet Martin, "The Mongol Elite in Muscovy, Rhetoric and Reality: The Portrayal of Tsar Shah Ali in *the Book of Degrees of the Royal Genealogy*," in Lenhoff and Kleimola, *The Book of Royal Degrees*, 217–29; Sabine Merten, "Die Kunst und die Krieg: Kampfbilder under Kriegsverständnis im 'Licevoij Letopisnij Svod'"

(Moskau, 2. Hälfte des 16. Jahrhunderts)," *Jahrbücher für Geschichte Osteuropas* 50 (2002): 481–518.

17. Michael Khodarkovsky, "The Conversion of Non-Christians in Early Modern Russia," in *Of Religion and Empire: Missions, Conversions and Tolerance in Tsarist Russia*, ed. Robert P. Geraci and Michael Khodarkovsky (Ithaca: Cornell University Press, 2001), 115–43; Matthew P. Romaniello, "Mission Delayed: The Russian Orthodox Church after the Conquest of Kazan,'" *Church History* 76 (2007): 511–40.

18. Matthew Romaniello, *Elusive Empire: Kazan and the Creation of Russia, 1552–1671* (Madison: University of Wisconsin Press, 2012), 40–41.

19. I. V. Zaitsev, *Astrakhanskoe khanstvo* (Moscow: Izdatel'skaia firma "Vostochnaia literatura" RAN, 2004), 147–77.

20. Stephen Frederic Dale, *Indian Merchants and Eurasian Trade, 1600–1750* (Cambridge: Cambridge University Press, 1994), 84–87; Matthew Romaniello, "The Profit Motive: Regional Economic Development in Muscovy after the Conquest of Kazan,'" *Journal of European Economic History* 33 (2004): 663–85.

21. Matthew Paul Romaniello, "Absolutism and Empire: Governance along the Early Modern Frontier" (PhD dissertation, Ohio State University, 2003), 53n25.

22. Edward L. Keenan Jr., "Coming to Grips with the *Kazanskaya istoriya*," *Annals of the Ukrainian Academy of Sciences in the United States* 31–32 (1967): 143–83; Liubov' Andreevna Dubrovina, *Istoriia o Kazanskom tsarstve (Kazanskii letopisets): Spiski i klassifikatsiia tekstov* (Kiev: Naukova Dumka, 1989).

23. Khatip Minnegulov, "Literature of the Ulus of Jochi and the Post-Golden Horde Tatar Khanates," in *The Golden Horde in World History. A Multi-Authored Monograph*, ed. Rafael Khakimov and Marie Favereau (Doumenjou) (Kazan': Sh. Marjani Institute of History, Academy of Sciences of the Republic of Tatarstan, 2017), 520–21

24. T. S. Willan, *The Early History of the Russia Company, 1553–1603* (Manchester: Manchester University Press, 1956).

25. Artur Attman, *The Struggle for Baltic Markets: Powers in Conflict, 1558–1618* (Göteborg: Kungl. Vetenskaps-och Vitterhets-Samhället, 1974), 40.

26. Hakluyt, *The Principal Navigations*, vol. 2, 297–303; J. Hamel, *England and Russia, comprising the voyages of John Tradescant the Elder, Sir Hugh Willoughby, Richard Chancellor, Nelson and others*, trans. John Studdy Leigh (New York: Da Capo Press, 1968), 139–41; Samuel H. Baron, "Osip Nepea and the Opening of Anglo-Russian Commercial Relations," *Oxford Slavonic Papers* 11 (1978): 50n35.

27. Maria Salomon Arel, "Anatomy of Discord: Sources of Friction in Muscovite Commerce in the Seventeenth Century" (paper presented at the American Association for the Advancement of Slavic Studies Convention, Denver, November 10, 2000).

28. Kagarlitsky, *Empire of the Periphery*, 81.

29. Aleksandr Filiushkin, "Diskursy Livonskoi voiny," *Ab Imperio*, no. 4 (2001): 43–80; Aleksandr Filiushkin, "Livonskaia voina ili Baltiiskie voiny? K voprosu o periodizatsii Livonskoi voiny," in Filjushkin, *Baltiiskii vopros*, 80–94; Frost, *The Northern Wars*, 23–43, 74–101.

30. Gralia, *Ivan Mikhailovich Viskovatyi*, 117, 262, 311; A. I. Filiushkin, "The Livonian War in the Context of the 16th Century East European Wars," *Studia Slavica et Balcanica Petropolitana*, no. 1 (2014): 47–64.

31. William Urban, "The Origin of the Livonian War, 1558," *Lituanus* 29, no. 3 (1983): 11–25; Filiushkin, "Diskursy Livonskoi voiny," 43–80; A. I. Rogov, "'Povest' ob Isidore Iur'evskom' kak istoricheskii istochnik i pamiatnik russkoi publitsistiki perioda Livonskoi voiny," in *Slaviano-germanskie kul'turnye sviazi i otnosheniia*, ed. V. D. Koroliuk et al. (Moscow: Nauka, 1969), 313–327.

32. *RIB* 16 (St. Petersburg: Arkheograficheskaia kommissiia, tovarishchestvo "Pechatnaia S. P. Iakovleva," 1897), no. 16, 41–52; no. 34, 125; Anti Selart, "Orthodox Churches in Medieval Livonia," in *The Clash of Cultures on the Medieval Baltic Frontier*, ed. Alan V. Murray et al. (Farnham, Surrey: Ashgate Publishing Ltd, 2009), 273–90; "Akty Kopengagenskago arkhiva," pt. 1, "1326–1569," 1–320.

33. V. D. Koroliuk, *Livonskaia voina. Iz istorii vneshnei politiki Russkogo tsentralizovannogo gosudarstva vo vtoroi polovine XVI v.* (Moscow: AN SSSR, 1954), 37.

34. Kirchner, *The Rise of the Baltic Question*, 34, 38, 47, 70, 86–122, 124; Erik Tiberg, *Moscow, Livonia and the Hanseatic League, 1487–1550* (Stockholm: Department for Baltic Studies at Stockholm University, 1995); Filiushkin, *Tituly russkikh gosudarei*, 124–51.

35. Robert J. Kerner, *The Urge to the Sea: The Course of Russian History; The Role of Rivers, Portages, Ostrogs, Monasteries and Furs* (Berkeley: University of California Press, 1942).

36. Thomas Esper, "A Sixteenth-Century anti-Russian Arms Embargo," *Jahrbücher für Geschichte Osteuropas* 15 (1967): 180–96; Thomas Esper, "Military Self-Sufficiency and Weapons Technology in Muscovite Russia," *Slavic Review* 28 (1969): 185–208.

37. *SRIO* 129, no. 3, 49–55; Samuel H. Baron, "The Muscovy Company, the Muscovite Merchants, and the Problem of Reciprocity in Russian Foreign Trade," *Forschungen zur osteuropäischen Geschichte* 27 (1979): 143–44.

38. A. Chumikov, trans., "Akty Revel'skago gorodskogo arkhiva 1450–1610," *Chteniia* (1898), bk. 4, vol. 187, otd. IV, 1–21; *RIB* 15, no. 36, 59–72; no. 20, 35–38; no. 50–54, 89–98; no. 59, 103–6; no. 60–62, 105–10; no. 57, 104–7; no. 33–34, 55–60; no. 55, 99–102; no. 63, 111–12; no. 35, 59–62.

39. A. V. Vinogradov, "Vneshniaia politika Ivana IV Groznogo," in *Istoriia*

vneshnei polikiti Rossii. Konets XV–XVII vek (Ot sverzheniia ordynskogo iga do Severnoi voiny) (Moscow: Mezhdunarodnye otnosheniia, 1999), 143.

40. *Poslaniia Ivana Groznogo*, 139–43, 329–33, 612–16; Hakluyt, *The Principal Navigations*, vol. 3, 174; A. I. Filiushkin, "Diskursy Narvskogo vziatiia," in *Gosudarstvo i obshchestvo*, 159–72.

41. Hexter, *Reappraisals in History*, 99–111; *Poslaniia Ivana Groznogo*, 144–47, 148–61.

42. Hexter, *Reappraisals in History*, 71–116; Lawrence Stone and Jeanne C. Fawtier Stone, *An Open Elite? England 1540–1880* (Oxford: Clarendon Press, 1984), 286–89; Walther Kirchner, "Entrepreneurial Activity in Russian-Western Trade Relations during the Sixteenth Century: Research Notes," *Explorations in Entrepreneurial History* 8 (1956): 245–52.

43. Samuel H. Baron, "The Weber Thesis and the Failure of Capitalist Development in 'Early Modern' Russia," *Jahrbücher für Geschichte Ostueropas* 18 (1970): 321–336; Wallerstein, *The Modern World-System*, 289.

44. Samuel H. Baron, "Ivan the Terrible, Giles Fletcher, and the Muscovite Merchantry: A Reconsideration," *Slavonic and East European Review* 56 (1978): 563–85; Jarmo T. Kotilaine, *Russia's Foreign Trade and Economic Expansion in the Seventeenth Century* (Leiden: Brill, 2005), 376.

45. *RIB* 15, no. 77, 139–42; Walter Kirchner, "The Role of Narva in the Sixteenth Century: A Contribution to the Study of Russo-European Relations," in Kirchner, *Commercial Relations between Russia and Europe*, 59–77; Attman, *The Russian and Polish Markets*, 73–84, 125–38.

46. Matthew P. Romaniello, "Through the Filter of Tobacco: The Limits of Global Trade in the Early Modern Period," *Comparative Studies in Society and History* 49 (2007): 914–15.

47. Baron, "Osip Nepea," 52–60; Attman, *The Russian and Polish Markets*, 193.

48. Mykhailo Hrushevsky, *History of Ukraine-Rus'*, vol. 7, *The Cossack Age to 1625*, trans. Bohdan Struminsky, ed. Serhii Plokhy and Frank E. Sysyn with Uliana M. Pasicznyk (Edmonton-Toronto: Canadian Institute of Ukrainian Studies Press, 1999), 88–98.

49. *Posol'skaia kniga po sviaziam Rossii s Nogaiskoi Ordoi (1576 g.)*, ed. V. V. Trepavlov (Moscow: IRI, 2003); Elena Viktorovna Kusainova, *Russko-nogaiskie otnosheniia i kazachestvo v kontse XV-XVII veke* (Volgograd: Volgogradskii Gosudarstvennyi Universitet, 2005), 86–116; Aleksei Vladimirovich Vinogradov, *Russko-Krymskie otnosheniia 50-e—vtoraia polovina 70-kh godov XVI veka*, 2 vols. (Moscow: IRI RAN, 2007), 1: 112–21.

50. *The Correspondence of Prince A. M. Kurbsky and Tsar Ivan IV*, 118–21; Norbert Angermann, *Studien zur Livlandpolitik Ivan Groznyjs* (Marburg/Lahn: J. G. Herder-Institut, 1972), 71–105.

51. B. N. Floria, "Proekt antituretskoi koalitsii serediny XVI v.," in *Rossiia, Pol'sha i Prichernomor'e v XV–XVIII vv.*, ed. B. A. Rybakov (Moscow: Nauka, 1979), 71–86; Khoroshkevich, *Rossiia v sisteme*, 191–92; "Akty Kopengagenskago arkhiva," pt. 1, "1326–1569," no. 49, 90–92.

52. Janet Martin, "Tatars in the Muscovite Army During the Livonian War," in Lohr and Poe, *The Military and Society*, 365–87; *Razriadnaia kniga 1475–1605 gg.*, vol. 3, pt. 1, 83; *RIB*, vol.17, Appendix, no. 4, 845–53.

53. Kostomarov, "Lichnost' tsaria Ivana," 401–2; Vernadsky, *The Tsardom of Moscow, 1547–1682*, pt. 1, 91–95; Alan W. Fisher, "Muscovy and the Black Sea Slave Trade," *Canadian-American Slavic Studies* 6 (1972): 575–94.

54. Halil Inalcik, "The Origin of the Ottoman-Russian Rivalry and the Don-Volga Canal (1569)," *Annales de l'Université d'Ankara* 1 (1947): 47–110; P. A. Sadikov, "Pokhod tatar i turok na Astrakhan' v 1569 g.," *Istoricheskie zapiski* 22 (1947): 132–66; Alan W. Fisher, "Muscovite-Ottoman Relations in the Sixteenth and Seventeenth Centuries," *Humaniora Islamica* 1 (1973): 207–17.

55. *Kabardino-russkie otnosheniia v XVI–XVIII vv.*, vol. 1, *XVI–XVII vv.*, no. 10, 19–21; Yasar, "The North Caucasus," 242; Chantal Lemercier-Quelquejay, "Co-optation of the Elites of Kabarda and Daghestan in the Sixteenth Century," in *The North Caucasus Barrier: The Russian Advance towards the Muslim World*, ed. Marie Bennigsen Broxup (London: Hurst and Co., 1992), 23–30.

56. *DRV* vol. 12, 30–36; Yasar, "The North Caucasus," 151–56, 159–60.

57. Filiushkin, *Izobretaia pervuiu voinu Rossii*, 701.

58. Smith, "The Muscovite Officer Corps, 1465–1598," 420; Smith, "Muscovite Logistics, 1462–1598," *Slavonic and East European Review* 71 (1993): 65.

59. D. N. Aleksandrov and D. M. Volodikhin, *Bor'ba za Polotsk mezhdu Litvoi i Rus'iu v XII–XVI vekakh* (Moscow: Izdatel'skoe predpriiatie 'Avanta+,' 1994); *Poslaniia Ivana Groznogo* (Lur'e), 502.

60. Smith, "The Muscovite Officer Corps, 1465–1598," 28–33; Smith, "Muscovite Logistics, 1462–1598," 38; *Studia Slavica et Balcanica Petropolitana* (2009): 1–2 (5–6); Brian Davies, "The Polotsk Campaign of Ivan IV and Stefan Bathory: The Development of Military Art During the Livonian War," in Filiushkin, *Baltiiskii vopros*, 106–20.

61. Filjushkin, *Ivan the Terrible: A Military History*, 265.

62. Smith, "Muscovite Logistics, 1462–1598," 57–59.

63. Fekhner, *Torgovlia Russkogo Gosudarstva*, 112; Samuel H. Baron, "Shipbuilding and Seafaring in Sixteenth-Century Russia," in Waugh, *Essays in Honor of A. A. Zimin*, 102–29.

64. "Akty Kopengagenskago arkhiva, otnosiashchiesia k russkoi istorii," pt. 2, "1570–1576," *Chteniia* (1916) bk. 2, vol. 257, no. 168, 170, 171, 174, 176, 180, 183, 184, 185, 186, 187, 190, 191, 192, 193, 195, 196, 197, 198, 199, 202, 219; *RIB* 16, no. 188, 937–51.

65. Henry R. Huttenbach, "The Correspondence between Queen Elizabeth I and Tsar Ivan IV: An Examination of Its Role in the Documentation of Anglo-Muscovite History," *Forschungen zur osteuropäischen Geschichte* 24 (1978): 101–30; Hakluyt, *The Principal Navigations*, vol. 3, 167–69; Attman, *The Struggle for Baltic Markets*, 103–6.

66. Koroliuk, *Livonskaia voina*, 25–27.

67. *SRIO* 129, 127–240; *Poslaniia Ivana Groznogo*, 146, 149–50, 159, 624–25; *Puteshestviia russkikh poslov*, 16–18, 50n3, 251–58; Demkova, "Gramoty Ivana Groznogo," 494–98; *PDRV* vol. 3, 108–40; Roberts, *The Early Vasas*, 199–241.

68. *DAI* vol. 1, 123, 178–80; Tiberg, *Zur Vorgeschichte des Livländischen Krieges* 150–52, 165, 193–202, 211–12.

69. Davies, "The Development of Russian Military Power," 159–60; Smith, "Muscovite Logistics, 1462–1598," 35–65.

70. *Razriadnaia kniga 1475–1598 gg.*, 247, 249; *The Chronicle of Balthasar Russow and a Forthright Rebuttal by Elert Kruse and Errors and Mistakes of Balthsar Russow by Henrich Tisenhausen*, trans. Jerry C. Smith with the collaboration of Juergen Eichhoff and William L. Urban (Madison: Baltic Studies Center, 1988), 260–63; Stevens, *Russia's Wars of Emergence*, 69; *Razriadnaia kniga 1475–1605 gg.*, vol. 3, pt. 1, 81.

71. Koroliuk, *Livonskaia voina*, 56; *Razriadnaia kniga 1475–1605 gg*, vol. 3, pt. 1, 36.

72. Smith, "The Muscovite Officer Corps, 1465–1598," 262; *The Moscovia of Antonio Possevino, S. J.*, xii; Dariusz Kupisz, "The Polish-Lithuanian Army in the Reign of King Stefan Bathory (1576–1586)," in *Warfare in Eastern Europe, 1500–1800*, ed. Brian Davies (Leiden: Brill, 2012), 63–92.

73. Davies, "The Foundation of Muscovite Military Power," 27.

74. *AAE* vol. 1, no. 205, 184–95; Samokvasov, ed., *Arkhivnyi material*, otdel 2: 42–43; V. V. Penskoi, "Kakuiu voinu proigral Ivan Groznyi? (Byla li Livonskaia voina glavnoi voinoi Ivana Vasil'evicha?)," *Studia Slavica et Balcanica Petropolitana*, no. 1 (2014): 38–46.

75. Alexander Yanov, *The Origins of Autocracy: Ivan the Terrible in Russian History*, trans. Stephen Dunn (Berkeley: University of California Press, 1981), 107; Filiushkin, *Andrei Kurbskii*, 101.

76. Filjushkin, *Ivan the Terrible: A Military History*, 94; Keenan, "Muscovy and Kazan," 553.

77. Edward Thaden, "Ivan IV in Baltic German Historiography," *Russian History* 14 (1987): 382–84.

78. "Akty Kopengagenskago arkhiva," pt. 1, "1326–1569," no. 23, 40–41; *RIB* 15, no. 70, 121–24; *SRIO* 71, 322.

79. V. I. Buganov, "Materialy TsGADA kak istochnik po istorii upravleniia

Pribaltikoi v gody Livonskoi voiny," *Arkheograficheskii ezhegodnik za 1968* (1970): 349–53; *Dokumenty Livonskoi voiny*, 56–93, 94–121, 122–96.

80. Petrov, *Kniga polotskogo pokhoda 1563*, 70–76, 80, 85; G. A. Novitskii, "Novye dannye o russkom feodal'nom zemlevladenii v Pribaltike v period Livonskoi voiny (1558–1582)," *Voprosy istorii*, no. 4 (1956): 134–38; B. N. Floria, "K istorii russkogo pomestnogo zemlevladeniia v Livonii," *Russkii diplomatarii* 5 (1999): 114–17; *Ivan Groznyi—zavoevatel' Polotska (novye dokumenty po istorii Livonskoi voiny)* (St. Petersburg: Dmitrii Bulanin, 2014).

81. Davies, "The Town Governors under Ivan IV," 131–38; Angermann, *Studien zur Livlandpolitik Ivan Groznyjs*, 60; A. I. Filiushkin, "Politicheskaia praktika moskovskikh vlastei v Livonii v pervye gody Livonskoi voiny (novye dokumenty)," *Studia Slavica et Balcanica Petropolitana*, no. 1 (2008): 78–83.

82. Andreas Kappeler, "Die Moskauer 'Nationalitäten Politik' unter Ivan IV," *Russian History* 14 (1987): 276; *Dokumenty Livonskoi voiny*, no. 1, 56–57; *Pistsovyia knigi Moskovskago Gosudarstva*, vol. 1, pt. 2, 421–55, 462–540, 540–49; Angermann, *Studien zur Livlandpolitik Ivan Groznyjs*, 25–70, 107–12.

83. John P Maarbjerg, "Diplomatic Relations between Denmark and Russia during the Livonian Wars 1558–1581," *Scandinavian Journal of History* 16 (1991): 167–88; Aleksandr Filiushkin, "Proekt 'Russkaia Livoniia,'" *Quaestio Rossica*, no. 2 (2012): 94–111.

84. *Razriadnaia kniga 1550–1636*, 209; *Razriadnaia kniga 1475–1605* (Moscow: AN SSSR, 1982), vol. 2, pt. 2, 331, 333; vol. 2, pt. 3, 532–33; Russell E. Martin, "Ritual and Religion in the Foreign Marriages of Three Muscovite Princesses," *Russian History* 35 (2008): 366–71, 379; "Akty Kopengagenskago arkhiva," pt. 1, "1326–1569," no. 160, 284–88; *SGGD* vol. 2, no. 48, 67–68.

85. Kirchner, *The Rise of the Baltic Question*, 33 n. 31, 104, 116.

86. *RIB* 15, no. 78–82, 141–60; no. 84, 161–64; no. 85, 163–66; no. 93, 191–92; no. 86–88, 167–78; no. 90–92, 181–90.

87. V. V. Vel'iaminov-Zernov, *Issledovanie o Kasimovskikh tsariakh i tsarevichakh*, pt. 2, *Trudy Vostochnago Otdeleniia Imperatorskago Arkheologicheskago Obshchestva*, vol. 10 (St. Petersburg, 1864), 75–76; Dmitrii Mikhailovich Volodikhin, *Voevody Ivana Groznogo* (Moscow: Veche, 2009), 46.

Chapter 13. The Oprichnina and Its Aftermath, 1564–1584

1. Crummey, "Ivan the Terrible," 60; Skrynnikov, *Tsarstvo terrora*, 5; Kollmann, *By Honor Bound*, 182–83.

2. *PSRL* 29, 341–45; *PSRL* 13, 391–96; Mikhailova, *Sluzhilye liudi*, 103–141, 335, 449.

3. Pokrovskii, *Izbrannye proizvedeniia*, bk. 1, 305.

4. Aleksandr Nikolaevich Bokhanov, *Tsar' Ioann IV Groznyi* (Moscow: Veche, 2008), 179.

5. Stanislavskii, *Trudy po istorii gosudareva dvora*, 38, 124–27.

6. *AI* vol.1, no. 179, 340–41; Sakharov, *Sbornik dokumentov*, no. 33, 60–62; *AAE* vol. 1, no. 288, 349; *Opis' tsarskogo arkhiva XVI veka*, 37; *Novgorodskie letopisi*, vol. 1 (Riazan: Aleksandriia, 2002), 105, 107.

7. Skrynnikov, *Tsarstvo terrora*, 303; Savva, *O posol'skom prikaz v XVI v.*, 85; *SRIO* 71, no. 15, 328–36; no. 16, 336–431.

8. In colloquium at Columbia University during the fall 1967, Cherniavsky said that Ivan never returned to the Kremlin after December 1564.

9. Wooding, *Henry VIII*, 232–33; Nitsche, *Grossfürst und Thronfolger*, 312–13.

10. Hugh F. Graham, ed., "A Brief Account of the Character and Brutal Rule of Vasil'evich, Tyrant of Muscovy (Albert Schlichting on Ivan Groznyi)," *Canadian-American Slavic Studies* 9 (1975): 222–25, 234, 247, 254, 258, 264, 272; Skrynnikov, *Tsarstvo terrora*, 302–41; Pavlov and Perrie, *Ivan the Terrible*, 138–39.

11. Ivan Zabelin, *Domashnyi byt russkago naroda v XVI i XVII st.*, vol. 1, *Domashnyi byt russkikh tsarei v XVI i XVII st.*, pt. 2, 4th ed. (Moscow: Iazyki russkoi kul'tury, 2000), 369; *Poslaniia Ivana Groznogo*, 276.

12. Paul Bushkovitch, "The Life of Metropolitan Filipp: Tsar and Metropolitan in the Late Sixteenth Century," in Flier and Rowland, *Medieval Russian Culture*, vol. 2, 29–46; V. A. Kolobkov, *Mitropolit Filipp i stanovlenie moskovskogo samoderzhaviia: Oprichnina Ivana Groznogo* (St. Petersburg: Ateleiia, 2004); Irina Aleksandrovna Lobakova, *Zhitie mitropolita Filippa: Issledovanie i tektsy* (St. Petersburg: Dmitrii Bulanin, 2006).

13. Robert I. Frost, *The Cambridge History of Poland-Lithania*, vol. 1, *The Making of the Polish-Lithuanian Union, 1385–1569* (Oxford: Oxford University Press, 2015).

14. *PSRL* 34, 224.

15. On variants of this title, see Charles J. Halperin, "*Rus'* versus *Ros* in Ivan IV's Muscovy," *Slavia* 86, no. 4 (2017): 367–75.

16. D. Kupish, "Russko-livonskoe pogranich'e v strategicheskikh planakh Stefana Batoriia v 1578–82," *Studia Slavica et Balcanica Petropolitana*, no. 1 (2014): 65–76.

17. E. N. Klitina et al., ed., *Vkladnaia kniga Troitse-Sergieva Monastyria* (Moscow: Nauka, 1987), 28R–29L.

Chapter 14. The Problem of the Oprichnina

1. Gunnar Opeide, "Making Sense of *Opričnina*," *Poliarnyi vestnik: Reports from Tromsø University Department of Russian*, no. 3 (2000): 64.

2. Al'shits, *Nachalo samoderzhaviia v Rossii*, 122, 228–31; Kleimola, "Ivan the Terrible and his 'Go-fers,'" 283.

3. Opeide, "Making Sense of *Opričnina*," 65.

4. "Dopros tsarem Ioannom Groznym russkikh plennikov veshedskhikh iz

Kryma," ed. S. K. Bogoiavlenskii, *Chteniia* t. 241 (1912), kn. 2, otd. 3, 26–33; Sergei Konstantinovich Bogoiavlenskii, *Moskovskii prikaznyi apparat i deloproizvodstvo XVI–XVII vekov* (Moscow: Iazyki slavianskoi kul'tury, 2006), 499–504, 553; Kollmann, *Crime and Punishment*, 306.

5. Halperin, "Ivan IV's Insanity," 207–18.

6. Keenan, "The Privy Domain of Ivan Vasil'evich," 73–88; Edward L. Keenan, "The Tsar's Two Bodies," ed. Russell Martin, *Canadian-American Slavic Studies* 51, no.1 (2017): 3–28.

7. S. N. Bogatyrev, "Administratsii Tiudorov i Riurikovichei. Sravnitel'nyi analiz," in *Zerkalo istorii: Dvadtsat' let kruzhku istorii drevnosti i srednevekov'ia. Sbornik statei* (Moscow: Rossiiskii gosudarstvennyi gumanitaryi universitet. Istoriko-arkhivnyi institut, 1992), 81–82; Kurukin and Bulychev, *Povsednevnaia zhizn'*, 240.

8. Mikhail Bentsianov, "'Kak by sluzhbu nam ustroiti': voenno-organizatsionnoe preobrazovanie seprediny XVI v.," *Quaestio Rossica*, no. 2 (2014): 80–93; Kliuchevskii, *Boiarskia duma*, 341.

9. Zimin, *Oprichnina Ivana Groznogo*, 119; Mikhailova, *I zdes' soshlis' vse tsarstva*, 308, 383n244; Dmitrii Volodikhin, *Oprichnina i "psy gosudarevy"* (Moscow: Veche, 2010), 1–95, 276–77.

10. Kollmann, *By Honor Bound*, 153; Skrynnikov, *Tsarstvo terrora*, 331, 377; *Akty Rossiiskogo gosudarstva. Arkhivy moskovskikh monastyrei i soborov XV-nachalo XVII vv.* (Moscow: Ladomir, 1998), no. 106, 242–43, 480–82.

11. Kliuchevskii, *Sochineniia*, vol. 2, 187–99; Marc Szeftel, "The Title of the Muscovite Monarch up to the End of the Seventeenth Century," *Canadian-American Slavic Studies* 13 (1979): 67, 68n28; Rüß, *Herren und Diener*, 472–74; Nørretranders, *The Shaping of Czardom*, 130–73.

12. Kashtanov, *Ocherki russkoi diplomatiki*, 170; Sadikov, *Ocherki po istorii oprichniny*, 73, 80–91; Pavlov and Perrie, *Ivan the Terrible*, 117–18; *DAI* vol. 1, no. 118, 172; Opeide, "Making Sense of *Opričnina*," 80–100.

13. D'iakonov, *Vlast' Moskovskikh gosudarei*, 133–64; Tsepkov, *Reinol'd Geidenshtein*, 162–63; Bonner and Zguta, "The Sixteenth-Century 'Account of Muscovy' Attributed to Don Felippo Prenestain," 402; *Poslaniia Ivana Groznogo*, 229.

14. Priscilla Hunt, "Ivan IV's Personal Mythology of Kingship," *Slavic Review* 52 (1993): 769–809; Karavashkin, *Russkaia srednevekovaia publitistika*, 127–298.

15. Iurganov, *Kategorii russkoi srednevekovoi kul'tury*, 306–404; Mikhailova, *I zdes' soshlis' vse tsarstva*, 308–19; Henrich von Staden, *The Land and Government of Muscovy: A Sixteenth-Century Account*, trans. Thomas Esper (Stanford: Stanford University Press, 1967), 48–52.

16. A. A. Bulychev, *Mezhdu sviatymi i demonami: Zametki o posmertnoi sud'be opal'nykh tsaria Ivana Groznogo* (Moscow: 'Znak, 2005), 88n366, 116–17, 128n573, 367–68.

17. Shaposhnik, *Ivan Groznyi: Pervyi Russkii Tsar'*, 371–91.

18. R. G. Skrynnikov, *Vasilii III. Ivan Groznyi* (Moscow: Izdatel'stvo ACT MOSKVA, 2008), 483–84; Charles J. Halperin, "Cultural Categories, Councils and Consultations in Muscovy," *Kritika* 3 (2002): 662–63.

19. Bulychev, *Mezhdu sviatymi i demonami*, 130–31, 146n647.

20. Dvorkin, *Ivan the Terrible as a Religious Type*, 97–107; V. A. Sharov, "Oprichnina Ivana Groznogo: Chto eto takoe? (Lektsiia, prochitannaia v Garvardskom universitete v 1989 g.)," *Arkheograficheskii ezhegodnik za 2003* (2004): 116–30.

21. Michael S. Flier, "Til the End of Time: The Apocalypse in Russian Historical Experience before 1500," in Kivelson and Greene, *Orthodox Russia*, 127–58.

22. Mikhail Grigor'evich Roginskii, trans., "Poslanie Ioganna Taube i Elerta Kruze," *Russkii istoricheskii zhurnal* 8 (1922): 31–36; Vadim Ivanovich Koretskii, *Istoriia russkogo letopisaniia vtoroi poloviny XVI-nachala XVII v.* (Moscow: Nauka, 1986), 24–28.

23. Al', *Ivan Groznyi: Izvestnyi i neizvestnyi*, 156–58.

24. Kivelson, "Muscovite 'Citizenship,'" 474.

25. Bokhanov, *Tsar' Ioann IV Groznyi*, 179; Skrynnikov, *Tsarstvo terrora*, 210.

26. Veselovskii, *Issledovaniia po istorii oprichniny*, 24–28.

27. Maureen Perrie, "The Popular Image of Ivan the Terrible," *Slavonic and East European Review* 56 (1978): 275–86; Perrie, "The Muscovite Monarchy," 233–41.

28. Graham, "*A Brief Account*," 219; A. P. Pavlov, "Sud'by samoderzhaviia i zemstva v Rossii XVI veka (oprichnina Ivana Groznogo)," in *Istoriia Rossii. Narod i vlast'. Iz lektsii, prochitannykh v rossiiskikh universitetakh* (St. Petersburg: Lan, 1997), 209.

29. Dmitrii Likhachev, *Velikoe nasledie: Klassicheskie proizvedeniia literatury drevnei Rusi* (Moscow: Sovremennik, 1975), 270, 277; Mikhail Bakhtin, *Rabelais and His World*, trans. Helene Iswolsky (Cambridge: MIT Press, 1968).

30. Leonid Iuzefovich, *Put' posla. Russkii posol'skii obychai, Obikhod, Etiket, Tseremonial konets XV-pervaia polovina XVII v.* (St. Petersburg: Izdatel'stvo Ivana Limbakha, 2007), 295–310.

31. *Prince A. M. Kurbsky's History of Ivan IV*, 180–81; *PSRL* 30 (Moscow: Nauka, 1965), 189; *Poslaniia Ivana Groznogo*, 162–92, 202; A. M. Panchenko, "'Dudino plemia' v poslanii Ivana Groznogo kniaziu Polubenskomu," in *Kul'turnoe nasledie Drevnei Rusi: Istoki Stanovlenie Traditsii* (Moscow: Nauka, 1976), 151–54.

32. D. S. Likhachev, "Kanon i molitva Angelu Groznomu voevode Parfeniia Urodivogo (Ivana Groznogo)," in *Rukopisnoe nasledie drevnei Rusi*, 10–27; Natal'ia Ganina, "Kanon Angelu Groznomu voevode: Problemy interpretatsii," in Sergei Fomin, *Groznyi Tsar' Ioann Vasil'evich* (Moscow: Forum, 2009), 133–48; Marchalis, *Liutor "izhe liut,"* 164–78.

33. Russell Zguta, "The Skomoroxi as Agents of Social Protest: Some Recent

Interpretations," in *Folklorica: Festschrift for Felix J. Oinas*, ed. Egle Victoria Zygas and Peter Voorheis (Bloomington: Research Institute for Inner Asian Studies, 1982), 341–48; Jack V. Haney, *An Introduction to the Russian Folktale*, vol. 1 (Armonk: M. E. Sharpe, 1999), 89.

34. Ivanov, *Holy Fools*, 285–310.

35. Svitlana Kobets, "Lice on the Iron Cap: Holy Foolishness in Perspective," in Hunt and Kobets, *Holy Foolishness in Russia*, 31–32.

36. Bakhtin, *Rabelais and His World*, 39, 90, 270; Caryl Emerson, "Tragedy, Comedy, Carnival, and History on Stage," in *The Uncensored Boris Godunov: The Case for Pushkin's Original Comedy, with Annotated Text and Translation*, ed. Chester Dunning et al. (Madison: University of Wisconsin Press, 2006), 157–86.

37. Crummey, *The Formation of Muscovy*, 162.

38. Sadikov, "Iz istorii oprichniny XVI v.," 132–33; Zimin, *Oprichnina Ivana Groznogo*, 307–41; Iu. V. Ankhimiuk, "Zapisi letopisnogo kharaktera v rukopisnom sborniki Kirillo-Belozerskogo sobraniia—novyi istochnik po istorii Oprichniny," *Arkhiv russkoi istorii* 2 (1992): 121–29.

39. Pavlov, "Sud'by samoderzhaviia i zemstva," 210; Kurukin and Bulychev, *Povsednevnaia zhizn'*, 56–57.

40. "Poslanie Ioganna Taube i Elerta Kruze," 35; V. B. Kobrin, "Istochniki dlia izucheniia chislennosti i istorii formirovaniia oprichnogo dvora," *Arkheograficheskii ezhegodnik za 1962* (1963): 121–25; Zimin, *Oprichnina Ivana Groznogo*, 314–59; Kurukin and Bulychev, *Povsednevnaia zhizn'*, 143–97; Zguta, *Russian Minstrels*, 54–55.

41. Staden, *The Land and Government of Muscovy*, 103; Crummey, *The Formation of Muscovy*, 163; Zimin, *Oprichnina Ivana Groznogo*, 356–57; *Vremennik Ivana Timofeeva*, 11–18.

42. A. L. Shapiro et al., *Agrarnaia istoriia severo-zapada Rossii XVI veka: Novgorodskie piatiny* (Leningrad: "Nauka," Leningradskoe otdelenie, 1974), 121–44; Pavlov, "Sud'by samoderzhaviia i zemstva," 212–14; V. N. Kozliakov, "Novyi dokument ob oprichnykh pereseleniiakh," *Arkhiv russkoi istorii* 7 (2002): 97–211.

43. Crummey, "Reform under Ivan IV," 22; V. I. Ivanov, *Monastyri i monastyrskie krest'iane Pomor'ia v XVI–XVII vekakh: mekhanizm stanovleniia krepostnogo prava* (St. Petersburg: Izdatel'stvo Olega Abyshko, 2007), 170–71; Kleimola, "The Duty to Denounce," 759–79.

44. Charles J. Halperin. "Contemporary Russian Perceptions of Ivan IV's Oprichnina," *Kritika* 18 (2017): 95–124.

45. Kobrin, *Ivan Groznyi*, 107; Erusalimskii, "Istoriia na posol'skoi sluzhbe," 721.

46. A. I. Filiushkin, "Izobrazhenie Livonskoi voiny v russkom letopisanii XVI–XVII vv.," in *Issledovaniia po istorii srednevekovoi Rusi*, 350n8.

47. Crummey, *The Formation of Muscovy*, 162; Kolobkov, *Mitropolit Filipp*, 152–61.

48. Skrynnikov, *Tsarstvo terrora*, 207; Kurukin and Bulychev, *Povsednevnaia zhizn'*, 16, 128; Kolobkov, *Mitropolit Filipp*, 160.

49. Kolobkov, *Mitropolit Filipp*, 136, 141–42, 160–61.

50. Valerie A. Kivelson, "How Bad Was Ivan the Terrible? The Oprichnik Oath and Satanic Spells in Foreigners' Accounts," in *Seeing Muscovy Anew: Politics—Institutions—Culture, In Honor of Nancy Shields Kollmann*, ed. Valerie A. Kivelson et al. (Bloomington: Slavica Publishers, Inc., 2017), 67–84.

51. "Poslanie Ioganna Taube i Elerta Kruze," 35, 38–40; *Prince A. M. Kurbsky's History of Ivan IV*, 248–49; Staden, *The Land and Government of Muscovy*, 30; Charles J. Halperin, "Did Ivan IV's *Oprichniki* Carry Dogs' Heads on Their Horses?" *Canadian-American Slavic Studies* 46 (2012): 40–67; Bulychev, *Mezhdu sviatymi i demonami*, 140–47.

52. Paul Bushovitch kindly offered the plausible suggestion of these elements being too obvious.

53. Valerie A. Kivelson, *Desperate Magic: The Moral Economy in Seventeenth-Century Russia* (Ithaca: Cornell University Press, 2013), 252n57.

54. Graham, "*A Brief Account*," 232; Gvan'ini, *Opisanie Moskovii*, 99; Pavlov and Perrie, *Ivan the Terrible*, 116; Cherniavsky, "Russia," 133.

55. Zimin, *Krupnaia feodal'naia votchina*, 112–22, 153–64; E. V. Krushel'nitskaia, "Zaveshchanie-ustav Gerasima Boldinskogo," *TODRL* 48 (1983): 267–70; Tom E. Dykstra, *Russian Monastic Culture: "Josephism" and the Iosifo-Volokolamsk Monastery, 1479–1607* (Munich: Otto Sagner Verlag, 2006), 195–227.

56. Kurukin and Bulychev, *Povsednevnaia zhizn'*, 59–60, 73–75, 79; Veselovskii, *Issledovaniia po istorii oprichniny*, 41; Bogatyrev, *The Sovereign and His Counsellors*, 162; Zimin, *Oprichnina*, 209; Kolobkov, *Mitropolit Filipp*, 234n209.

57. Smith, "The Muscovite Officer Corps, 1465–1598," 323–24; Iu. M. Eskin, "Oprichnina i mestnichestvo," in *Anfologion: Vlast', obshchestvo, kul'tura v slavianskom mire v Srednye veka. K 70-letiiu Boris Nikovalevicha Flori* (Moscow: Indrik, 2008), 349–56; V. B. Kobrin, "Iz istorii mestnichestva XVI veka," *Istoricheskii arkhiv*, no. 1 (1960): 214–19; Dewey and Kleimola, *Russian Private Law*, no. 57, 179–82.

58. Nørretranders, *The Shaping of Czardom*, 149; Skrynnikov, *Nachalo oprichniny*, 269n1.

59. Aleksandr Petrovich Pronshtein, *Velikii Novgorod v XVI veke: Ocherk sotsial'no-ekonomicheskoi i politicheskoi istorii russkogo goroda* (Kharkov: Khar'kovskii gosudarstvennyi universiteta imeni A. M. Gor'kogo, 1957), 208–26; appendix 3, 265–68; Davies, "The Town Governors under Ivan IV," 122–28.

60. *PSRL* 30, 196.

61. Veselovskii, *Issledovaniia po istorii oprichniny*, 124.

Chapter 15. The Oprichnina in Action

1. Sergei Bogatyrev, "The Resignation of Metropolitan Afanasii in 1566," *Canadian-American Slavic Studies* 49 (2015): 174–92; Bushkovitch, "The Selection and Deposition," 123, 144, 146.

2. George P. Fedotov, *St. Filipp Metropolitan of Moscow—Encounter with Ivan the Terrible*, trans. Richard Haugh and Nicholas Lupinin (Belmont: Nordland Publishing Company, 1978); Dmitrii Volodikhin, *Mitropolit Filipp* (Moscow: Molodaia gvardiia, 2009).

3. *AAE* vol. 1, no. 258, 283–85; no. 268, 303–4; *Materialy po istorii Karelii XII–XVI vv.*, no. 87, 193–95; *Akty Solovetskogo monastyria 1479–1571 gg.*, no. 251, 163–65.

4. *PDRV* vol. 7, no. 209, 43–46; *SGGD* vol. 1, no. 193, 557–58; Spock, "Community Building and Social Identity," 554.

5. "Poslanie Ioganna Taube i Elerta Kruze," 42–44, 48; *PSRL* 13, 403; Bushkovitch, "The Life of Metropolitan Filipp," 29–46; Lobakova, *Zhitie mitropolita Filippa*, 85, 129, 131.

6. Lobakova, *Zhitie mitropolita Filippa*, 188, 223.

7. Ševčenko, "A Neglected Byzantine Source,"141–79; N. N. Pokrovskii, "'Stepennaia kniga tsarskogo rodosloviia' i ee novoe izdanie," in Lenhoff and Kleimola, *The Book of Royal Degrees*, 6–8.

8. *Prince A. M. Kurbsky's History of Ivan IV*, 236–37, 234–35; Bushkovitch, "The Life of Metropolitan Filipp," 40 n. 22.

9. Zlotnik, "Immunity Charters," 303–49.

10. Halperin, "Metropolitan Makarii," 447–64; Wooding, *Henry VIII*, 204, 210–11; Kamen, *Philip II of Spain*, 234; Kollmann, "The Moscow *Stoglav*," 415.

11. Iakovleva, "Piskarevskii letopisets," 76, 78; Horace W. Dewey and Ann M. Kleimola, "From the Kinship Group to Every Man His Brother's Keeper: Collective Responsibility in Pre-Petrine Russia," *Jahrbücher für Geschichte Osteuropas* 30 (1987): 330; Ludwig Steindorff, "Mehr als eine Frage der Ehre. Zum Stiferverhalten Zar Ivans des Schrecklichen," *Jahrbücher für Geschichte Osteuropas* 51 (2003): 354.

12. Bogatyrev, "Reinventing the Russian Monarchy," 279–82, 292; *Razriadnaia kniga 1475–1598 gg*, 179; S. B. Veselovskii, "Poslednye udely v severo-vostochnoi Rusi," *Istoricheskie zapiski* 22 (1947): 107; *SGGD* vol. 1, no. 182, 503–6.

13. *PSRL* 13, 400; *PDRV* vol. 6, no. 203, 232–43; no. 204, 244–75; *Dukhovnye i dogovornye gramoty velikikh i udel'nykh kniazei XIV–XVI vv.* [hereafter *DDG*] (Moscow-Leningrad: Izdatel'stvo AN SSSR, 1950), no. 102, 420–22.

14. *DDG*, no. 103, 422–26; *DRV* vol. 13, no. VI, 46–57; *SGGD* vol. 1, no. 189, 533–37; *PSRL* 13, 401.

15. A. L. Iurganov, "Otrazhenie politicheskoi bor'by v pamiatnike arkhitektury (Borisoglebskii sobor v Staritse)," in *Genezis i razvitie feodalizma v Rossii. Problemy ideologii i kul'tury. Mezvuzovskii sbornik pod redaktsiei prof. I. Ia. Froianova. K 80-letiiu prof. V.V. Mavrodina* (Leningrad: LGU, 1987), 176–85; Kleimola, "Ivan IV and the Staritskie," 235.

16. Aleksandr Shitkov, *Opal'nyi rod kniazei Staritskikh* (Staritsa: Tverskoe oblastnoe knizhno-zhurnal'noe izdatel'stvo, 2001), 92, 116.

17. *PSRL* 3 (St. Petersburg: Tipografiia Eduarda Pratsa, 1841), 253; *Novgorodskie letopisi*, vol. 2 (Riazan: Aleksandriia, 2002), 336–37; *RIB* 13, 286–87; *Vremmenik Ivana Timofeeva*, 23–24; Shitkov, *Opal'nyi rod kniazei Staritskikh*, 120–21; David Hipshon, *Richard III* (London: Routledge, 2011), 136–42; Veselovskii, "Poslednye udely v severo-vostochnoi Rusi," 101–31; Plowden, *Elizabeth I*, 364–65.

18. Robert O. Crummey, "New Wine in Old Bottles: Ivan IV and Novgorod," *Russian History* 14 (1987): 61–76.

19. Bogatyrev, "Ivan the Terrible Discovers the West," 171–83; D. S. Likhachev and Aleksandr Mikhailovich Panchenko, *"Smekhovyi mir" drevnei Rusi* (Leningrad: Nauka, Leningradskoe otdelenie, 1976), 21.

20. M. M. Krom, "Mestnoe samosoznanie i tsentralizovannoe gosudarstvo: Smolensk v XVI veke," *Forschungen zur osteuropäischen Geschichte* 63 (2004): 128–36. The comparison of Smolensk and Novgorod is mine.

21. *Novgorodskie letopisi*, vol. 2, 337–45, 393–404, 468–69; *PSRL* 30, 158; Staden, *The Land and Government of Muscovy*, 25–58; *Izbornik (Sbornik proizvedenii literatury drevnei Rusi)* (Moscow: Khudozhestvennaia literatura, 1969), 477–83; S. A. Morozov, "Obzor spiskov redaktsii Povesti o plenenii Velikogo Novgoroda Ivanom Groznym," *Arkheograficheskii ezhegodnik za 1977* (1978): 268–74.

22. *Pskovskie letopisi*, 1: 115; *Skazanie Avraamiia Palitsyna*, 116; *PSRL* 13, 383, 386; *PSRL* 29, 335; *Dokumenty Livonskoi voiny*, no. 1, 25; no. 3, 42.

23. Kingdon, *Myths about the St. Bartholomew's Day Massacres*, 41; *PSRL* 28, 163; *Latukhinskaia Stepennaia kniga 1676 g.*, 547–50; Bakhrushin, *Lavochnye knigi Novgoroda-Velikogo*, 56, 75, 99–100, 103, 121, 143, 167; Iakovleva, "Piskarevskii letopisets," 83.

24. Except Evgenii Markovich El'ianov, *Ivan Groznyi—sozidatel' ili razrushitel'? Issledovanie problemy sub"evtivnosti interpretatsii v istorii* (Moscow: Editorial URSS, 2004), 90.

25. Kamen, *Philip II of Spain*, 229; *PSRL* 30, 157; Hugh F. Graham, "How Do We Know What We Know about Ivan the Terrible (A Paradigm)?" *Russian History* 14 (1987): 179–98.

26. Shcherbatov, *Istoriia rossiiskaia*, vol. 5, pt. 2, 286–96; Graham, "How Do We Know."

27. Mel'nikova, "Sistemizatsiia monet Ivana IV i Fedora Ivanovicha (1533–98),"

113–16; Skrynnikov, *Tragediia Novgoroda*, 143–47; Pronshtein, *Velikii Novgorod v XVI veke*, 5, 95, 194–95.

28. Diefendorf, *Beneath the Cross*, 3; Jouanna, *The Saint Bartholomew's Day Massacre*, 3; Kingdon, *Myths about the St. Bartholomew's Day Massacres*, 35; Salmon, *Society in Crisis*, 186–87; Geoffrey Parker, *The Dutch Revolt* (London: Penguin Books Ltd, 1977), 37, 178.

29. Petr Petrei di Erlezunda, "Istoriia o velikom kniazhestve Moskovskom, proiskhozhdenii velikikh russkikh kniazei, nedavnykh smutakh, proizvedennykh tam tremia Lzhedimitriiami i o Moskovskikh zakonakh, nravakh, pravlenii, vere i obriadakh," trans. A. Shemiakin, *Chteniia*, vol. 56 (1866): 138; A. Kappeler and R. G. Skrynnikov, "Zabytii istorichnik o Rossii epokhi Ivana Groznogo," *Otechestvenanaia istoriia*, no. 1, (1999): 135.

30. Vladimir Anatol'evich Arakcheev, *Pskovskii krai v XV–XVII vekakh. Obshchestvo i gosudarstvo* (St. Petersburg: Russko-Baltiiskii informatsionnyi tsentr BLITs, 2003), 145–49; Genrikh Nikolaevich Bocharev and Vsevolod Petrovich Vygolov, *Aleksandrovskaia sloboda* (Moscow: Iskusstvo, 1970), 5, 17–18.

31. *Razriadnaia kniga 1475–1605*, vol. 2, pt. 2, 265; Kurukin and Bulychev, *Povsednevnaia zhizn*,' 328–38; Kirchner, "The Role of Narva," 72, 76; *The Chronicle of Balthasar Russow*, 126.

32. *SGGD* vol. 2, no. 43, 53–62; *PSRL* 30, 158–61, 189, 205.

33. Braudel, *The Mediterranean and the Mediterranean World*, vol. 2, 1055; Jouanna, *The Saint Bartholomew's Day Massacre*, 51; Lynch, *Spain, 1516–1598*, 400, 405; Roberts, *The Early Vasas, 1523–1611*, 17–19; Cherniavsky, "Ivan the Terrible as a Renaissance Prince"; Myles, "The Muscovite Ruling Oligarchy," 183.

34. Graham, "*A Brief Account*," 259–65; Iakovleva, "Piskarevskii letopisets," 78–79; *Opis' arkhiva Posol'skogo prikaza 1626 goda*, pt. 1 (Moscow: Glavnoe arkhivnoe upravlenie pri SM SSSR, 1977), 257–58.

35. Eamon Duffy, *Fires of Faith: Catholic England under Mary Tudor* (New Haven: Yale University Press, 2009), ix, 7; Plowden, *Elizabeth I*, 351.

36. Daniel H. Kaiser, "Miasoed Konstantin Semenovich Vislyi: Oprichnina Victim . . . and Beloozero *zemliak*," in Svák and Tiumentsev, *Rusistika Ruslana Skrynnikova*, 109–17; Iu. D. Rykov, "Vklady gosudareva d'iaka P. M. Mitrofanova v russkie monastyry v epokhu tsaria Ivana Groznogo," in *Russkoe srednevekov'e*, 484–85.

37. Andreyev, "Interpolations in the Sixteenth-Century Muscovite Chronicles," 105; Esper in Staden, *The Land and Government of Muscovy*, xxii; Nikolai Mikhailovich Rogozhin, *U gosudarevykh del byt' ukazano . . .* (Moscow: Izdatel'stvo RAGS, 2002), 85–66.

38. Plowden, *Elizabeth I*, 324–25; Hans-Walter Camphausen, *Die Bojarenduma under Ivan IV: Studien zur altmoskauer Herrschaftsordnung* (Frankfurt am Main: Verlag Peter Lang, 1985), 279.

39. Michel Foucault, *Discipline and Punish: The Birth of the Prison*, trans. Alan Sheridan (New York: Pantheon Books, 1978), 42–57; Greenblatt, *Renaissance Self-Fashioning*, 201; Kamen, *Inquisition and Society in Spain*, 189–90; quote from Kobrin, *Ivan Groznyi*, 97.

40. *PDRV* vol. 7, no. 208, 1–42; Huttenbach, "The *Zemsky Sobor* in Ivan IV's Reign," 169–210; Hulbert, "Sixteenth-century Russian Assemblies of the Land," 119–60; Cherepnin, *Zemskie sobory russkogo gosudarstva*, 106–14; A. V. Antonov, "Prigovornaia gramota 1566 goda," *Russkii diplomatarii* 10 (2004): 171–82.

41. Michael A. R. Graves, *The Parliaments of Early Modern Europe* (Harlow, England: Longman, 2001), 219–20.

42. Huttenbach, "The *Zemsky Sobor* in Ivan IV's Reign," 87–109, 100–5, 211–60; Hulbert, "Sixteenth-century Russian Assemblies of the Land," 96–118, 161–79; Cherepnin, *Zemskie sobory russkogo gosudarstva*, 88–89, 115–25; Ellerd Hulbert, "The *Zemskii sobor* of 1575: A Mistake in Translation," *Slavic Review* 25 (1966): 320–22.

43. Hulbert, "Sixteenth-century Russian Assemblies of the Land," 146–57; Cherepnin, *Zemskie sobory russkogo gosudarstva*, 109; Camphausen, *Die Bojaren-duma under Ivan IV*, 136; Pavlov and Perrie, *Ivan the Terrible*, 132.

44. Pavlov and Perrie, *Ivan the Terrible*, 131; Cherepnin, *Zemskie sobory russkogo gosudarstva*, 108; *PSRL* 13, 402; Kliuchevskii, *Sochineniia*, vol. 2, 377–91, vol. 8 (Moscow: Gosudarstvennoe izdatel'stvo politicheskoi literatury, 1959), 5–112; Hulbert, "Sixteenth-century Russian Assemblies of the Land," 7.

45. Pelenski, "State and Society in Muscovite Russia," 93–109; Donald Ostrowski, "The Assembly of the Land (*Zemskii sobor*) as a Representative Institution," in *Modernizing Muscovy: Reform and Social Change in Seventeenth-Century Russia*, ed. Jarmo Kotilaine and Marshall Poe (London: Routledge, Curzon, 2004), 117–41.

46. Huttenbach, "The *Zemsky Sobor* in Ivan IV's Reign," 234–42; Hulbert, "Sixteenth-century Russian Assemblies of the Land," 274–86; Angermann, *Studien zur Livlandpolitik Ivan Groznyjs*, 78.

47. Goodman, *The New Monarchy. England, 1471–1534*, 49; Henshall, *The Myth of Absolutism*, 82; Graves, *The Parliaments of Early Modern Europe*, 38.

48. Graham, "A Brief Account," 248–49; V. B. Kobrin, "Iz istorii zemel'noi politiki v gody Oprichniny," *Istoricheskii arkhiv*, no. 3 (1958): 152–54.

49. Zimin, *Oprichnina Ivana Groznogo*, 208–10.

50. Staden, *The Land and Government of Muscovy*, 120–21.

51. Zagorovskii, *Istoriia vkhozhdeniia tsentral'nogo chernozem'ia*, 93–153; Mikhail Iur'evich Zenchenko, *Iuzhnoe rossiiskoe porubezh'e v kontse XVI-nachale XVII v. (opyt gosudarstvennogo stroitel'stva)* (Moscow: "Pamiatniki istoricheskoi mysli," 2008), 33–40; Vinogradov, *Russko-Krymskie otnosheniia*, 2: 164–65.

52. *Akty Moskovskago gosudarstva*, vol. 1, *Razriadnyi prikaz. Moskovskii stol 1571–1634*, no. 1–29, 1 (left column)–52 (right column); Zagorovskii, *Istoriia vkhozhdeniia tsentral'nogo chernozem'ia*, 154–87.

53. Stevens, *Russia's Wars of Emergence*, 72; Zagorovskii, *Istoriia vkhozhdeniia tsentral'nogo chernozem'ia*, 163; Zenchenko, *Iuzhnoe rossiiskoe porubezh'e*, 41–64, 80.

54. Filiushkin, *Andrei Mikhailovich Kurbskii*, 387–88, 390; Zagorovskii, *Istoriia vkhozhdeniia tsentral'nogo chernozem'ia*, 160–69; *Posol'skaia kniga po sviaziam Rossii s Nogaiskoi Ordoi (1576 g.)*, 28n 61; *Razriadnaia kniga 1550–1636*, 56–57.

55. Veselovskii, *Issledovaniia po istorii oprichniny*, 62; D. N. Al'shits, "Razriadnaia kniga moskovskikh gosudarei XVI v. (Ofitsial'nyi tekst)," *Problemy istochnikovedeniia* 6 (1958): 150; Kobrin, "Sostav oprichnogo dvora Ivana Groznogo," 86–87; Vernadsky, *The Tsardom of Moscow, 1547–1682*, pt. 1, 131.

56. *PSRL* 13, 301; *Razriadnaia kniga 1559–1605 gg*, 71; *Razriadnaia kniga 1475–1605*, vol. 2, pt. 2, 282.

57. Dewey, "Political *Poruka* in Muscovite Rus'," 179–81.

58. Zagorovskii, *Istoriia vkhozhdeniia tsentral'nogo chernozem'ia*, 165–75; Skrynnikov, *Tsarstvo terrora*, 451, 453–64, 477.

59. Smith, "The Muscovite Officer Corps, 1465–1598," 336–418, appendix XXV, 602–10; appendix XXVI, 611–13; Al', *Ivan Groznyi: Izvestnyi i neizvestnyi*, 179–94;Volodikhin, *Oprichnina i "psy gosudarevy*," 96–285.

60. Iakovleva, "Piskarevskii letopisets," 80; Berry and Crummey, *Rude and Barbarous Kingdom*, 192, 273; Iuzefovich, "Kak v posol'skikh obychaiakh vedetsia," 184–95; Vinogradov, *Russko-Krymskie otnosheniia*, 2: 196–200.

61. Vinogradov, *Russko-Krymskie otnosheniia*, 2: 204, 206, 213, 234; Andrei Lyzlov, *Skifskaia istoriia* (Moscow: "Nauka," 1990), 147, 368.

62. Volodikhin, *Ivan Groznyi. Bich Bozhii*, 37–129.

63. Kobrin, *Ivan Groznyi*, 57–59, 163; Nørretranders, *The Shaping of Czardom*, 169; Pavlov, "Sud'by samoderzhaviia i zemstva," 221.

64. Kollmann, *Crime and Punishment*, 311–21.

65. V. I. Koretskii, "Razvitie feodal'noi zemel'noi sobstvennosti v Rossii XVI veka," in *Sotsial'no-ekonomicheskie problemy Rossiiskoi derevni v feodal'nuiu i kapitalisticheskuiu epokhi. Materialy XVII sessii simpoziuma po izucheniiu problem agrarnoi istorii, Rostov-na-Donu, 1978* (Rostov: Rostovskii universitet, 1980), 46; Kurukin and Bulychev, *Povsednevnaia zhizn'*, 79.

66. V. B. Kobrin, "Ivan Groznyi: Izbrannaia rada ili oprichnina?" in *Istoriia otechestva: liudi, idei, resheniia. Ocherki istorii Rossii IX-nachala XX v* (Moscow: Izdatel'stvo politicheskoi literatury, 1991), 136; Bovykin, *Mestnoe upravlenie*, 370–73.

67. Skrynnikov, *Tsarstvo terrora*, 525; Charles J. Halperin, "Ruslan Skrynnikov on Ivan IV," in Boeck et al., *Dubitando*, 196–97.

68. Staden, *The Land and Government of Muscovy*, 52; Al', *Ivan Groznyi: Iz-*

vestnyi i neizvestnyi, 169–70, 205–26; A. V. Antonov, "Kostromskie monastyri v dokumentakh XVI–nachala XVII veka," *Russkii diplomatarii* 7, no. 33 (2007): 100–101; V. I. Koretskii, "Solovetskii letopisets kontsa XVI v.," *Letopisi i khroniki 1980 g.* (1981): 229–43.

69. Sadikov, "Iz istorii oprichniny XVI v.," no. 35, 234; Zimin, *Oprichnina*, 225–35; P. A. Kolesova, "Ustiuzhna Zheleznopol'skaia po materialam opisanii 1567 i 1597 gg.," in *Goroda feodal'noi Rossii. Sbornik statei pamiati N. V. Ustiugova* (Moscow: Nauka, 1966), 150.

70. D. N. Al'shits, "Novyi dokument o liudiakh i prikazakh oprichnogo dvora Ivana Groznogo posle 1572 goda," *Istoricheskii arkhiv* 4 (1949): 6, 51; Kolobkov, *Mitropolit Filipp*, 40n207, 143–44; Kurukin and Bulychev, *Povsednevnaia zhizn'*, 137–42.

71. Yanov, *The Origins of Autocracy;* Kobrin, *Ivan Groznyi*; Pavlov and Perrie, *Ivan the Terrible*; Al', *Ivan Groznyi: Izvestnyi i neizvestnyi*, 99–102.

72. Henshall, *The Myth of Absolutism*, 89; Ostrowski, *Muscovy and the Mongols*, 85–107; Charles J. Halperin, "The Muscovite Attitude toward the Outside World during the Reign of Ivan IV: *Stepennaia kniga*," in *Aktual'nye problemy istorii i kul'tury tatarskogo naroda. Materialy k uchebnym v chest' iubileiia akademika AN RT M. A. Usmanova*, ed. Marat Gatin (Kazan: MOiN RT, 2010), 188–201; Filiushkin, *Izobretaia pervuiu voinu Rossii*, 117, 699–717.

73. Robert O. Crummey, "The Fate of Boyar Clans, 1565–1613," *Forschungen zur osteuropäischen Geschichte* 38 (1986): 241–56; Veselovskii, *Selo i derevnia*, 130–48.

Chapter 16. Ivan's Ideology, the Oprichnina, and Muscovite Society

1. Cherniavsky, "Khan or Basileus," 459–76, quotation 476.

2. Cherniavsky, *Tsar and People*, 5–71; Cherniavsky, "Russia to 1700," in *Perspectives on the European Past: Conversations with Historians*, ed. Norman F. Cantor (New York: Macmillan, 1971), 293.

3. Cherniavsky, "Ivan the Terrible as a Renaissance Prince," 195–211; Machiavelli, *The Prince and the Discourses*.

4. Hipshon, *Richard III;* David Starkey, *Henry: Virtuous Prince;* Wooding, *Henry VIII;* Paul Murray Kendall, *Louis XI: ". . . the universal spider . . ."* (New York: W. W. Norton, 1971); Kamen, *Philip II of Spain*; Joseph Jay Deiss, *Captains of Fortune: Profiles of Six Italian Condottieri* (New York: Thomas Y. Crowell, 1967), 197–241; Meyer, *The Borgias*, 81–407; Roberts, *The Early Vasas, 1523–1611*, 17–19.

5. Cherniavsky, "Ivan the Terrible as a Renaissance Prince," 200.

6. Cherniavsky, "Ivan the Terrible as a Renaissance Prince," 208, 209; Jan Kott, *Shakespeare, Our Contemporary*, trans. Boleslaw Taborski (Garden City: Anchor Books, 1966).

7. Cherniavsky, "Ivan the Terrible as a Renaissance Prince," 211.

8. Cherniavsky, "Russia," 123; Cherniavsky, "Russia to 1700," 294.

9. Cherniavsky, "Russia," 130.

10. Kamen, *Philip II of Spain*, 21–49, 178–210; Major, *From Renaissance Monarchy to Absolute Monarchy*, xviii–xxi; Richardson, *Renaissance Monarchy*.

11. Burckhardt, *The Civilization of the Renaissance*, 4–32, 69–73, 75, 278–79; Hipshon, *Richard III*, 211; Richardson, *Renaissance Monarchy*, 24–27.

12. *Pskovskie letopisi*, 2: 262; Lehtovirta, *Ivan IV as Emperor*, 154–93.

13. Marusha A. Smilyanich, "Testative d'Explication de la Personalité d'Ivan le Terrible," *Revue des Études Slaves* 48 (1969): 122; *Poslaniia Ivana Groznogo*, 174.

14. David Goldfrank, "The Lithuanian Prince-Monk Vojšelk: A Study of Competing Legends," *Harvard Ukrainian Studies* 11, nos. 1–2 (1987): 44–76. Anonymous reader 2 called my attention to this article.

15. Michael Cherniavsky, "The Old Believers and the New Religion," *Slavic Review* 25 (1966): 1–39.

16. Hindle, *The State and Social Change*; Stone, *The Crisis of the Aristocracy*; Diefendorf, *Beneath the Cross*; Kingdon, *Myths about the St. Bartholomew's Day Massacres*; Salmon, *Society in Crisis*, 247–73.

17. Nørretranders, *The Shaping of Czardom*; Hindle, *The State and Social Change*, 235.

18. Budovnits, *Russkaia publitsistika*, 133–66; Ivanov, *Literaturnoe nasledie*, no. 216, 147–48; no. 219, 149; no. 221, 150–51.

19. D'iakonov, *Ocherki obshchestvennogo i gosudarstvennago stroia*, 191–489; V. O. Kliuchevskii, *Istoriia soslovii v Rossii*, 3rd ed. (Petrograd, 1918; Hattiesburg: Academic Interntional Press, 1969), 1–38, 96–199.

20. Burckhardt, *The Civilization of the Renaissance*, 80–103, 217–23; Hindle, *The State and Social Change*, 114–15.

21. Charles J. Halperin, "Master and Man in Muscovy," in A. E. Presniakov, *The Muscovite Tsardom*, trans. R. Price (Gulf Breeze: Academic International Press, 1978), vii–xxi.

22. Kollmann, *By Honor Bound*, 169–209; Kollmann, "Muscovite Russia, 1450–1598," 55–60; Nikolai Pavlovich Pavlov-Sil'vanskii, *Gosudarevy sluzhilye liudi: Liudi kabal'nye i dokladnye*, 2nd ed. (St. Petersburg: Tipografiia M. M. Stasiulevicha, 1909), 64–82.

23. Charles J. Halperin, "Hierarchy of Hierarchies: Muscovite Society during the Reign of Ivan IV," *Russian History* 44 (2017): 570–84.

24. Iuzefovich, *"Kak v posl'skikh obychaiakh vedetsia,"* 30; Rüß, *Herren und Diener*, 121–46, 165n55.

25. Camphausen, *Die Bojarenduma under Ivan IV*, 29–30; Kollmann, *Kinship and Politics*.

26. Kollmann, *Kinship and Politics*, 59; Eskin, *Ocherki istorii mestnichestva*, 123–37.

27. Baldesar Castiglione, *The Book of the Courtier*, trans. Charles S. Singleton (Garden City: Anchor Books, 1959); Rüß, *Herren und Diener*, 386–89; Norbert Elias, *The Civilizing Process*, vol. 1, *The History of Manners (Sociogenetic and Psychogenetic Investigations)*, trans. Edmund Jephcott (New York: Urizen Books, 1978); Norbert Elias, *Power and Civility: The Civilizing Process*, vol. 2, trans. Edmund Jephcott (New York: Pantheon Books, 1982).

28. Stone, *The Crisis of the Aristocracy*, 15–36; Stone and Stone, *An Open Elite? England, 1540–1880*; S. P. Mordovina and A. L. Stanislavskii, "Sostav osobogo dvora Ivana IV v period 'velikogo kniazheniia' Simeona Bekbulatovicha," *Arkheograficheskii ezhegodnik za 1976* (1977): 167, 178–79, 189.

29. Kleimola, "*Kto kogo*," .214; Kleimola, "Status, Place and Politics," 200n36, 209n104; Kollmann, *Kinship and Politics*, 199–241.

30. Kleimola, "Patterns of Duma Recruitment, 1505–1550," 232–58; Kleimola, "Genealogy and Identity Among the Riazan' Elite," in Kleimola and Lenhoff, *Culture and Identity*, 284–302; Rüß, *Herren und Diener*, 55, 419–20; V. V. Shaposhnik, "K voprosu o sobytiiakh avgusta 1534 g.," in *Russkoe srednevekov'e*, 351–74; Bychkova, *Rodoslovnye knigi.*, 135–44.

31. Stone, *The Crisis of the Aristocracy*; Wallerstein, *The Modern World-System*, 237–45; Salmon, *Society in Crisis*, 92–113, 222, 226; Major, *From Renaissance Monarchy to Absolute Monarchy*, xix, xxi, 103–6.

32. Rüß, *Herren und Diener*, 55–56; Solov'ev, *Istoriia Rossii*, bk. 4, vol. 7, 9; Smith, "The Muscovite Officer Corps, 1465–1598," 592–93.

33. M. N. Tikhomirov, *Rossiia v XVI stoletii* (Moscow: AN SSSR, 1962), 53; Polosin, *Sotsial'no-politicheskaia istoriia Rossii*, 59; Pavlov, "Sud'by samoderzhaviia i zemstvo," 214.

34. Shcherbatov, *Istoriia rossiiskaia*, vol. 5, pt. 1, 283n*; Zimin, *Reformy Ivana Groznogo*, 173–75; Solov'ev, *Istoriia Rossii*, bk. 4, vol. 7, 9–10.

35. K. V. Baranov, "Zapisnaia kniga Polotskogo pokhoda 1562/63 goda," *Russkii diplomatarii* 10 (2004): 120; *AAE* vol. 1, no. 227, 218–19; B. N. Floria, "O rodovom zemlevladeniia kniazei Trubetskikh vo vtoroi polovine XVI-nachale XVII veka," *Arkhiv russkoi istorii* 7 (2002): 102–6.

36. Veselovskii, *Issledovaniia po istorii klassa sluzhilykh zemlevladel'tsev*, 69, 331–32, 361, 368, 374–76, 418, 450.

37. *RIB* 15, no. 102, 207–12; Veselovskii, *Issledovaniia po istorii klassa sluzhilykh zemlevladel'tsev*, 69, 332, 359–61, 361–62, 368, 374, 418–19; L. A. Beliaev, *Russkoe srednevekovoe nadgrobie. Belokammenye plity Moskvy i Severo-Vostochnoi Rusi XIII-XVII vv.*, (Moscow: Modus-Grafiti, 1996), 252–56, 265.

38. Ieronym Gralia, "D'iaki i pisari: apparat upravleniia v Moskovskom gosu-

darstve i Velikom Knizhestve Litovskom (XVI-nachalo XVIII veka)," in *Ot drevnei Rusi*, 152–53; Volodikhin, *Voevody Ivana Groznogo*, 197–227.

39. Pavlov-Sil'vanskii, *Gosudarevy sluzhilye liudi*, 82–127; Hellie, *Enserfment and Military Change*, 21–47; Mikhailova, *Sluzhilye liudi*, 103–141, 214–31; Aleksandr Ivanovich Tsepkov, *Riazianskie zemlevladel'tsy XIV–XVI vekov* (Riazan: Fond 700-letiiu Riazani, Tovarishchestvo "Zemlia Riazanskaia," 1995), 109–11.

40. Kivelson, "The Effects of Partible Inheritance," 197–212; Hammond, *State Service*, 38–39, 23, 48, 194–95; Janet Martin, "The Heritability of Pomest'e Estates in 16th-Century Muscovy: An Analysis of the Experience of Four Families," in Marker et al., *Everyday Life in Russian History*, 231–46; Janet Martin, "From Fathers to Sons? Property and Inheritance Rights of *Pomeshchiki* in 16th-century Muscovy," in Szvák and Tiumentsev, *Rusistika Ruslana Skrynnikova*, 68–75.

41. *DAI* vol. 1, no. 52, VII, 92–93; Janet Martin, "Economic Effectiveness of the Muscovite *Pomest'e* System: An Examination of Estate Incomes and Military Expenses in the Mid-16th Century," in Davies, *Warfare in Eastern Europe*, 19–34; A. Ia. Degtiarev, "O mobilizatsii pomestnykh zemel' v XVI v.," in *Iz istorii feodal'noi Rossii. Stat'i i ocherki k 70-letiiu so dnia rozhdeniia prof. V. V. Mavrodina* (Leningrad: LGU, 1978), 85–91; Hammond, *State Service*, 132–55, 156–89.

42. *PRP* 4: 86–87 (Cherepnin); Polosin, *Sotsial'no-politicheskaia istoriia Rossii*, 45–52; A. L. Shapiro et al., *Agrarnaia istoriia severo-zapada Rossii XVI veka: Novgorodskie piatiny*, 288–89.

43. *Akty sluzhilykh zemlevladel'tsev*, vol. 4, no. 17, 15; Zimin, *Oprichnina Ivana Groznogo*, 413–15; V. I. Koretskii, *Zakreposhchenie krest'ian i klassovaia bor'ba v Rossii v vtoroi polovine XVI v.* (Moscow: Nauka, 1970), 23.

44. *AI* vol. 1, no. 154, 258–60; *Akty sluzhilykh zemlevladel'tsev*, vol. 4, no. 136, 100–101; no. 432, 321–22; no. 469, 344–45; Samokvasov, *Arkhivnyi material*, otdel 2, no. 6, 119–21.

45. Bogatyrev, "Localism and Integration," 85–101; Hellie, *Slavery in Russia*, 656.

46. Mikhailova, *Sluzhilye liudi*, 102–41; *PSRL* 8 (St. Petersburg: Tipografiia Eduarda Pratsa, 1859), 292–95; *PSRL* 13, 95 (right column); Nitsche, *Grossfürst und Thronfolger*, 250; Volodikhin, *Voevody Ivana Groznogo*, 262.

47. Kobrin, *Vlast' i sobstvennost'*, 144–49; *Dokumenty Livonskoi voiny*, no. 60, 163–68; *Akty sluzhilykh zemlevladel'tsev*, vol. 4, no. 54, 41; no. 173, 133.

48. Janet Martin, "Two *Pomeshchiki* From the Novgorod Lands: Their Fates and Fortunes during the Livonian War," *Russian History* 34 (2007): 239–53; V. A. Arakcheev, "Utrachennyi ukaz 1582 g. ob ispomeshchenii 'detei boiarskikh nemetskikh gorodov' i ego realizatsiia," in *Feodal'naia Rossiia: Novye issledovaniia*, ed. M. B. Sverdlov (St. Petersburg: Tret'ia Rossiia, 1993), 38–42; Alexander Filjushkin, "The

Livonian War and the Mentality of the Russian Nobles," *Canadian-American Slavic Studies* 47 (2013): 420–35.

49. *Novgorodskiia pistsovyia knigi*, vol. 6: *Knigi Bezhetskoi piatiny. I. 1501 g. II. 1545 g. III. 1551 g. IV. 1564 g.*, ed. S. K. Bogoiavlenskii (St. Petersburg: Arkheografich-eskaia kommissiia, 1910), 1551: 563–834; *Pistsovyia knigi Moskovskago Gosudarstva*, pt. 1, sec. 2, 1299–1595, especially 1441–1504; S. I. Kotkov, *Pamiatniki russkoi pis'mennosti XV–XVI vv. Riazanskii krai* (Moscow: Nauka, 1978), no. 44, 66, 72.

50. Volodikhin, *Oprichnina i "psi gosudarevy."*

51. Likhachev, *Razriadnye d'iaki XVI veka*, 132; N. Rozhkov, *Russkaia istoriia v sravnitel'no-istoricheskom osveshchenii (Osnovy sotsial'noi dinamiki)* (Petrograd-Moscow: Kniga, 1919–1925), vol. 4, pt. 1, 70; *Akty Rossiiskogo gosudarstva*, no. 5, 22–23.

52. A. V. Mashtafarov, "Muromskie monastyri i tserkvy v dokumentakh XVI–nachala XVII veka," *Russkie diplomartii* 6, no. 15 (2000): 64–65; *RIB* 25, no. 24, 27, 30, 51, 52, 53, 55; Likhachev, *Razriadnye d'iaki XVI veka*, 137–66, 548; Vladimir Borisovich Pavlov-Sil'vanskii, *Pistsovye knigi Rossii XVI v. Problemy istochnikove-deniia i rekonstruktsii tekstov* (Moscow: Nauka, 1991), 215–16, 222–23; Gralia, *Ivan Mikhailovich Viskovatyi*, 20–29; Alekseev, *U kormila rossiiskogo gosudarstva*, 203, 226, 236, 241, 246, 252–53, 257.

53. *Prince A. M. Kurbsky's History of Ivan IV*, 96–97; *Akty feodal'nogo zem-levladeniia*, vol. 2, no. 230, 232; S. B. Veselovskii, *D'iaki i pod'iachie XV–XVII vv.* (Moscow: Nauka, 1975), 39, 42, 47, 75, 91, 93, 93–96, 161–62, 238–40, 274, 334–45, 345–46, 408, 481, 497, 499–500, 521, 546, 559–60, 579; Halperin, "The Culture of Ivan IV's Court," 93–105.

54. Krom, *"Vdovstvuiushchee tsarstvo,"* 504–9; Veselovskii, *Issledovaniia po istorii oprichniny*, 209.

55. Kleimola, "Status, Place and Politics," 204n56; Shmidt, *U istokov rossiiskogo absoliutizma*, 319; Gralia, *Ivan Mikhailovich Viskovatyi*, 31; Likhachev, *Razriadnye d'iaki XVI veka*, 548–50.

56. N. B. Golikova, "Obrazovanie soslovnoi korporatsii gostei i ee sostav v XVI veke," *Arkhiv russkoi istorii* 6 (1995): 7–48; *Akty sluzhilykh zemlevladel'tsev XV–nachala XVII veka*, vol. 2 (Moscow: "Pamiatniki istoricheskoi mysli," 1998), no. 495, 424–25; Nosov, *Stanovlenie soslovno-predstavitel'nykh uchrezhdenii*, 186–87.

57. Pronshtein, *Velikii Novgorod v XVI veke*, 109–55; Baron, "Osip Nepea," 46–48; K. N. Serbina, *Ocherki iz sotsial'no-ekonomicheskoi istorii russkogo goroda. Tikhvinskii posad v XVI–XVIII vv.* (Moscow-Leningrad: AN SSSR, 1951), 7–19.

58. Paul Bushkovitch, "Taxation, Tax Farming, and Merchants in Sixteenth-Century Russia," *Slavic Review* 37 (1978): 381–98; K. B. Baranov, ed., *Velikii Novgorod vo vtoroi polovine XVI v. Sbornik dokumentov* (St. Petersburg: Dmitrii Bulanin, 2001), 38–40.

59. Samuel H. Baron, "The *Gosti* Revisited," in Baron, *Explorations in Muscovite History* (Hampshire: Variorum, 1991), 2: 4–7; Martin, *Medieval Russia, 980–1584*, 432, 434, 435–49.

60. Esper, "Russia and the Baltic, 1494–1558," 467; Makovskii, *Razvitie tovarno-denezhnykh otnoshenii*, 461–62, 471; V. A. Varentsov and G. M. Kovalenko, *V sostave Moskovskogo gosudarstva: Ocherki istorii Velikogo Novgoroda kontsa XV–nachala XVIII v.* (St. Petersburg: Russko-Baltiiskii informatsionnyi tsentr izdatel'stvo BLITs, 1999), 133.

61. Smith, *Peasant Farming in Muscovy;* Vladimir A. Arakcheev, "Krest'iane v sotsial'noi strukture srednevekovoi Rusi (XIV–pervaia polovina XVI v.)," *Cahiers du monde russe* 46 (2005): 113–14; Blum, *Lord and Peasant*, 220–25.

62. *PRP* 4: 258; Dewey, *Muscovite Judicial Texts*, 71; Jack M. Culpepper, "The Legislative Origins of Peasant Bondage in Muscovy," *Forschungen zur osteuropäischen Geschichte* 14 (1969): 166–68; Robert E. F. Smith, *The Enserfment of the Russian Peasantry* (Cambridge: Cambridge University Press, 1968), no. 42, 94–66.

63. *RIB*, vol. 2, no. 36, 40–41; Sakharov, *Sbornik dokumentov*, no. 29, 173–74; no. 39, 70–71; no. 40, 71; *PRP* 4: 111–12, 139–42; Smirnov, *Posadskie liudi*, vol. I, 122–44.

64. G. A. Pobedimova, "K voprosu o stabil'nosti sel'skogo naseleniia votchiny v XVI v. (Na primere Iosifo-Volokolamskogo monastyria)," in *Voprosy ekonomiki i klassovykh otnoshenii v russkom gosudarstve XII–XVII vekov* (Moscow-Leningrad: AN SSSR, 1960), 172–90.

65. Culpepper, "The Legislative Origins," 169–82; Koretskii, *Zakreposhchenie krest'ian*, 87, 118, 124–27, 148, 156.

66. S. M. Kashtanov, "K izucheniiu oprichniny Ivana Groznogo," *Istoriia SSSR*, no. 2 (1963): 96–117.

67. Alekseev, *Agrarnaia i sotsial'naia istoriia*, 168–85; Veselovskii, *Feodal'noe zemlevladenie*, vol. I, 203–16; A. L. Shapiro et al., *Agrarnaia istoriia severo-zapada Rossii XVI veka. Sever. Pskov. Obshchie itogi razvitiia Severo-Zapada* (Leningrad: Nauka, Leningradskoe otdelenie, 1978), 14.

68. Trepavlov, *Istoriia nogaiskoi ordy*, 599–647; Khodarkovsky, *Russia's Steppe Frontier*, 121–23; *Posol'skaia kniga po sviaziam Rossii s Nogaiskoi Ordoi (1576 g.)*, 54n126; Grekov, *Krest'iane na Rusi*, 806.

69. *DAI* vol. I, no. 128, 184–85; Basil Dmytryshin et al., ed., *To Siberia and Russian America: Three Centuries of Russian Eastward Expansion*, vol. I, *Russia's Conquest of Siberia, 1558–1700* (Portland: Western Imprints, Press of the Oregon Historical Society, 1985), 3–26; *PSRL* 36 (Moscow: Nauka, 1987), 32–34, 38, 45–60, 73, 92, 109–12, 118–23, 129–35, 139, 183–84, 239–45, 308, 380–81; R. G. Skrynnikov, "The Early Period of Russia's Annexation of Siberia," trans. Jean Hellie, *Soviet Studies in History* 24 (1985): 113–36.

70. Blum, *Lord and Peasant*, 251; Richard Hellie, ed., *Readings for Introduction to Russian Civilization: Muscovite Society* (Chicago: Syllabus Division, The College, University of Chicago, October 1967), 108–9.

71. Janet Martin, "The Novokshcheny of Novgorod: Assimilation in the 16th Century," *Central Asian Studies* 9 (1990): 13–38.

72. *Akty otnosiashchiesia do grazhdanskoi raspravy drevnei Rossii*, vol. 1 (Kiev: Tipografiia I. and A. Davidenko, 1860), no. 70, no. 78; *Akty Solovetskogo monastyria 1479–1571 gg.*, no. 139, 253, 255, 273; *Akty Solovetskogo monastyria 1572–1584 gg.*, no. 645, 746, 883; Braddick, *State Formation in Early Modern England*, 150–52; Hindle, *The State and Social Change*, 51–52.

73. *Pistsovye knigi Novgorodskoi zemli*, vol. 1, *Novgorodskie pistsovye knigi 1490-kh gg. i otpisnye i obrochnye knigi prigorodnykh pozhen Novogorodskogo dvortsa 1530-kh gg.* (Moscow: Drevlekhranilishche, Arkheograficheskii tsentr 1999); *Pistsovye knigi Novgorodskoi zemli*, vol. 2, *Pistsovye knigi Obonezhskoi piatiny XVI v.* (Moscow: Drevlekhranilishche, Arkheograficheskii tsentr 1999).

74. Smith, *Peasant Farming in Muscovy*, 127–28, 168–71, 174, 206; *Novgorodskiia pistsovyia knigi*, vol. 6, *Knigi Bezhetskoi piatiny. I. 1501 g. II. 1545 g. III. 1551 g. IV. 1564 g.*, 816, 827; Hammond, *State Service*, 17, 19, 229; Kolycheva, *Agrarnyi stroi Rossii XVI veka*, 28; A. L. Shapiro et al., *Agrarnaia istoriia severo-zapada Rossii XVI veka. Novgorodskie piatiny*, 6.

75. Kolycheva, *Kholopstvo i krepostnichestcho*; Paneiakh, *Kabal'noe kolopstvo*; Hellie, "Muscovite Slavery in Comparative Perspective," *Russian History* 6 (1979): 133–209; *PRP* 4: 79.

76. Braudel, *The Mediterranean and the Mediterranean World*, vol. 2, 754–55; Hellie, *Readings*, 241–42; Braudel, *Slavery in Russsia*, 625, 688.

77. *PSRL* 13, 265; *RIB* 17, no. 54, 18; no. 61, 20; no. 109, 37; no. 138, 47–48; no. 139, 48; no. 191, 69; no. 500, 182–83; no. 531, 198–99; Kolycheva, *Kholopstvo i krepostnichestcho*, 33–53.

78. *PDRV* vol. 10, 192; *Posol'skaia kniga po sviaziam Rossii s Nogaiskoi Ordoi (1576 g.)*, 14n7, 20, 26–38, 53, 54, 55; Hellie, *Slavery in Russia*, 336; Dewey and Kleimola, *Russian Private Law*, no. 54, 142–47; A. V. Antonov, "Novye istochniki po istorii polnogo kholopstva pervoi poloviny XVI veka," *Russkii diplomatarii* 4, no. 2 (1998): 124–25.

79. Pike, *Aristocrats and Traders*, 182; Kolycheva, *Kholopstvo i krepostnichest-cho*, 143–73; Daniel H. Kaiser, "Testamentary Charity in Early Modern Russia," 10n20, 10–13; *Akty feodal'nogo zemlevladeniia*, vol. 2, no. 127, 119–20; no. 157, 150–51; no. 173, 164–66; no. 176, 169–72; no. 183, 184–86; Hellie, *Slavery in Russia*, 515–16.

80. Hellie, *Slavery in Russia*, 350; Kolycheva, *Kholopstvo i krepostnichestcho*, 189–201.

81. Hellie, *Slavery in Russia*, 29–71, 679–720; Koretskii, *Zakreposhchenie krest'ian*, 19, 21, 24, 25; Kolycheva, *Kholopstvo i krepostnichestcho*, 97–142.

82. Diefendorf, *Beneath the Cross*; Steindorff, *Memoria in Rußland*, 248–51; Ludwig Steindorff, "Memorial Practice as a Means of Integrating the Muscovite State," *Jahrbücher für Geschichte Osteuropas* 55 (2007): 517–33.

83. *RIB* 32, no. 133, 240–41; no. 132, 239–40; *Akty feodal'nogo zemlevladeniia*, vol. 2, no. 154, 148–49.

84. *AAE* vol. 1, no. 229, 220–22; Kollmann, *Kinship and Politics*, 58; Kollmann, "The Moscow *Stoglav*," 340; Tom Dykstra, "*Zapisnaia kniga* (Donation Records) of Volokolamsk Monastery, for 1550–1607," *Russian History* 39 (2012): 116, 122; S. N. Bogatyrev, "The Clan of the Diaks Shchelkalov," *Istoricheskaia genealogiia / Historical Genealogy* 5 (1995): 60–70.

85. Stefanovich, *Prikhod i prikhodskoe dukhovenstvo*.

86. Dykstra, *Russian Monastic Culture*, 119–93; David Miller, "Trinity's Brotherhood: The Origins of Social and Administrative Structures at the Trinity-Sergius Monastery," *Russian History* 34 (2007): 255–62; David Miller, *Saint Sergius of Radonezhy*, 153–57, 160.

87. Goldfrank, *The Monastic Rule of Iosif Volotskii*, 89; *Poslaniia Ivana Groznogo*, 162–92; *Akty Rossiiskogo gosudarstva.*, no. 126, 300; Spock, "Giving Voice to the Voiceless," 29–36.

88. *Stoglav*, 44; Elena Romanenko, *Povsednevnaia zhizn' russkogo srednevekovogo monastyria* (Moscow: Molodaia Gvardiia, 2002).

89. M. N. Tikhomirov, *Rossiiskoe gosudarstvo XV–XVII vekov* (Moscow: Nauka, 1973), 141; Ludwig Steindorff, "Monastic Culture as a Means of Social Disciplining in Muscovite Russia—a Common European Feature," in Szvák, *Mesto Rossii v Evrope*, 112.

90. S. B. Veselovskii, "Monastyrskoe zemlevladenie v Moskovskoi Rusi vo vtoroi polovine XVI v.," *Istoricheskie zapiski* 10 (1941): 95–116; Ivanov, *Bukhgalterskii uchet*.

91. Stevens, *Russia's Wars of Emergence*, 72–75; Crummey, *The Formation of Muscovy*, 125; Stone, *A Military History of Russia*, 10.

92. Poe, "The Consequences of the Military Revolution," 612; *Materialy po istorii Karelii XII–XVI vv.*, no. 223, 283–84; Shapiro et al., *Agrarnaia istoriia severo-zapada Rossii XVI veka: Novgorodskie piatiny*, 173; Karamzin, *Istoriia gosudarstva Rossiiskago*, vol. 8, 167; Smith, "The Muscovite Officer Corps, 1465–1598," 115.

93. Paul, "The Military Revolution in Russia," 21.

94. *Pistsovye materialy Tverskogo uezda XVI veka*, 234–35, 299–300; K. V. Baranov, "Novyi istochnik po istorii Moskvy XVI veka," *Russkii diplomatarii* 6 (2000): 188; *Akty sluzhilykh zemlevladel'tsev*, vol. 4, no. 177, 136.

95. Halperin, "Ivan IV's Professional Infantry," 96–116.

96. Iu. V. Ankhimiuk, "Polotskii pokhod 1563 goda v chastnykh razriadnykh knigakh," *Russkii diplomatarii* 10 (2004): 163, 164, 165, 167; Ankhimiuk, "Rospisi Kazanskogo zimnego pokhoda v Razriadnoi knige OR RNB. Q.IV.53," in *Gosudarstvo i obshchestvo*, 183–85; *Materialy po istorii Tatarskoi ASSR*, xix, 55, 29, 179–81.

97. McNally, "From Public Person to Private Prisoner"; Joanna Hubbs, *Mother Russia: The Feminine Myth in Russian Culture* (Bloomington: Indiana University Press, 1988), 167–206.

98. Nancy Shields Kollmann, "The Seclusion of Elite Muscovite Women," *Russian History* 10 (1983): 170–87; Ostrowskii, *Muscovy and the Mongols*, 64–84; Marshall Poe, "The Public Face of Private Life: The Family-Presentation Ritual in Muscovite Russia," in Marker et al., *Everyday Life in Russian History*, 5–21.

99. Sandra Levy, "Women and the Control of Property in Sixteenth-Century Muscovy," *Russian History* 10 (1983): 201–12; Nataliya L. Pushkariova, "The Russian woman and her property and legal status: Was the XVI century a turning point?" in *La Donna Nell'Economia secc. XIII-XVIII*, ed. Simonetta Cavaciocchi (Florence: Le Monnier, 1990), 597–604.

100. George G. Weickhardt, "Legal Rights of Women in Russia, 1100–1750," *Slavic Review* 55 (1996): 1–23; Janet Martin, "The *Pomest'e* System as a Means of Support for Women in Sixteenth-Century Muscovy," in *Novye napravleniia i rezul'taty v rusistike / New Directions and Results in Russistics*, ed. Gyula Szvák (Budapest: Magyar Ruszisztika Intézet, 2005), 61–73; Daniel H. Kaiser, "*Pomest'e prozhitki:* Muscovite Patriarchy on the Ground," *Russian History* 42 (2015): 86–89, 95–96.

101. *AI* vol. 1, no. 154, 254–57; *PRP* 4: 534, 562; Pushkariova, "The Russian woman," 603.

102. Igor O. Tiumentsev, "Rossiia i poiavlenie kazachestva na Volge i na Donu v XV—pervoi polovine XVI vv.," *Cahiers du monde russe* 46 (2005): 75–82; *SGGD* vol. 2, no. 44, 62; *Akty otnosiashchiesia k Istorii Voiska Donskogo, sobrannye general-maiorom A. A. Lishinym*, vol. 1 (Novocherkassk: Tipografiia.A. A. Karaseva, 1891), no. 1, no. 2, 1–2.

103. Ekaterina Nikolaevna Kusheva, *Narody Severnogo Kavkaza i ikh sviazi s Rossiei vtoraia polovina XVI-30e gody XVII veka* (Moscow: AN SSSR, 1963), 243; Kusainova, *Russko-nogaiskie otnosheniia i kazachestvo*, 94–116; Catherine Wendy Bracewell, *The Uskoks of Senj: Piracy, Banditry, and Holy War in the Sixteenth-Century Adriatic* (Ithaca: Cornell University Press, 1992); Gunther Erich Rothenberg, *The Austrian Military Border in Croatia, 1522–1747* (Urbana: University of Illinois Press, 1960).

104. Shane O'Rourke, *The Cossacks* (Manchester: Manchester University Press, 2007), 47–55; Tiumentsev, "Rossiia i poiavlenie kazachestva," 81.

105. *Dokumenty Livonskoi voiny*, 56–57, 59–60, 60–62, 91–92, 92–93, 99–100,

108–9, 110–11, 187–89, 205–7, 227, 229–30; Baranov, "Zapisnaia kniga Polotskogo pokhoda," 126–27; Ankhimiuk, "Rospisi Kazanskogo zimnego pokhoda," 183, 184; Charles J. Halperin, "Ivan IV's State Cossacks," *Journal of Military History* 82 (2018): 357–71.

106. *Posol'skaia kniga po sviaziam Rossii s Nogaiskoi Ordoi (1576 g.)*, 29, 32, 34, 35; Kusainova, *Russko-nogaiskie otnosheniia i kazachestvo*, 80, 81.

107. Bychkova, *Rodoslovnye knig*, 190–93; Kollmann, *By Honor Bound*, 29, 31–33, 146, 248.

108. Kollmann, "Muscovite Russia 1450–1598," 53.

109. Staden, *The Land and Government of Muscovy*, 17–18, 18n19; *Tsar' Ivan Groznyi* (St. Petersburg: Izdatel'skaia gruppa "Azbuka-klassika," 2010), 71–77, 92–94; M. N. Tikhomirov, "Novye material ob Ivane Groznom," *TODRL* 14 (1958): 251, 254.

110. Stone, *The Crisis of the Aristocracy*, 20–21, 108–24; Ariès, *Centuries of Child-hood*, 258–61; Kivelson, "Merciful Father," 656; Kollmann, *By Honor Bound*, 103; A.V. Mashtafarov, "Iavochnye chelobitnye 1568–1612 godov iz arkhiva Suzdal'skogo Pokrovskogo Devich'ego monastryia," *Russkii diplomatarii* 9 (2003): 1–20.

111. Diefendorf, *Beneath the Cross*; Jouanna, *The Saint Bartholomew's Day Massacre*.

112. Janos Bak, ed., *The German Peasant War of 1525* (London: Frank Cass, 1976); Bob Scribner and Gerhard Benecke, ed., *The German Peasant War 1525—New Viewpoints* (London: George Allen & Unwin, 1979); Peter Blickle, *The Revolution of 1525: The German Peasants' War From a New Perspective*, trans. Thomas A. Brady Jr. and H. C. Erik Midelfort (Baltimore: Johns Hopkins University Press, 1981); Thomas A Brady Jr., "German Burghers and Peasants in the Reformation and the Peasants' War," in Charles J. Parker and Jerry H. Bentley, *Between the Middle Ages and Modernity: Individual and Community in the Early Modern World* (Lanham: Rowman and Littlefield Publishers, Inc., 2007), 33–51.

113. Nicholas P. Canny, *The Elizabethan Conquest of Ireland: A Pattern Es-tablished, 1565–76* (New York: Barnes & Noble, 1976); McGurk, *The Elizabethan Conquest of Ireland*; Parker, *The Dutch Revolt*; Deiss, *Captains of Fortune*; Kamen, *Philip II of Spain*, 130–31.

114. Charles J. Halperin, "The Scourge of God: The Mongols and Violence in Russian History," in *Times of Trouble: Violence in Russian Literature and Culture*, ed. Tatyana Novikov and Marcus C. Levitt (Madison: University of Wisconsin Press, 2007), 23–29.

115. Perry Anderson, *Lineages of the Absolutist State* (London: NLB, 1974), 121; Greenblatt, *Renaissance Self-Fashioning*, 139; Kamen, *Philip II of Spain*, 83; William G. Naphy and Penny Roberts, ed., *Fear in Early Modern Society* (Manchester: Manchester University Press, 1997).

Chapter 17. Muscovy, 1572–1584

1. Salmon, *Society in Crisis*, 196, 206–16; Koretskii, *Zakreposhchenie krest'ian*, 93–94; Grekov, *Krest'iane na Rusi*, 784–807; Richard Hoyle, "War and Public Finance," in MacCulloch, *The Reign of Henry VIII*, 89.

2. Zlotnik, "Muscovite Fiscal Policy: 1462–1584," 243–58; Janet Martin, "Economic Development in the Varzuga Fishing *volost'* during the Reign of Ivan IV," *Russian History* 14 (1987): 317; Turchyn and Nefedov, *Secular Cycles*, 252–54, 259.

3. "Puteshestvie v Rossiiu datskogo poslannika Iakova Ul'fel'da v 1575 g. v perevod XVIII veka," *Chteniia* (1883): bk. 1, 12, 14, 24, 25; Smith, *Peasant Farming in Muscovy*, 234, 238; Pavlov-Sil'vanskii, *Pistsovye knigi Rossii XVI v.*, 46; Janet Martin, "Economic Survival in the Novgorod Lands in the 1580s," in *New Perspectives on Muscovite History: Selected Papers from the Fourth World Congress for Soviet and East European Studies, Harrogate, 1990*, ed. Lindsey Hughes (New York: St. Martin's Press, 1990), 101–28.

4. S. M. Kashtanov, "Evoliutsiia velikokniazheskogo i tsarskogo titula v gramotakh Afonskim monastyriam XVI v.," *Rossiia i khristianskii vostok* 1 (1997): 105–34.

5. Fekhner, *Torgovlia Russkogo Gosudarstva*, 5–6, 75–76; Khodarkovsky, *Russia's Steppe Frontier*, 26–28.

6. *PDSDR* vol. 1, 481–764; *PDSDR* vol. 10, 5–386; *Posol'skaia kniga po sviazam Rossii s Pol'shei (1575–1576 gg.)*; B. N. Floria, *Russko-pol'skie otnosheniia i politicheskoe razvitie Vostochnoi Evropy vo vtoroi polovine XVI–nachale XVII v.* (Moscow: Nauka, 1978), 32–119.

7. *RIB* vol. 6, no. 28, 103–6; no. 29, 105–10.

8. Iuzefovich, *"Kak v posl'skikh obychaiakh vedetsia,"* 146.

9. Koroliuk, *Livonskaia voina*, 54; Ia. S. Lur'e, "Stateinyi spisok Konstantina Skobel'tsyna (1573–1574 gg)," *Arkheograficheskii ezhegodnik za 1979* (1981): 308–10.

10. *SGGD* vol. 5 (Moscow: Tipografiia E. Lissnera and Iu. Romana, 1894), no. 124, 155–56; no. 125, 157–59.

11. Lynch, *Spain, 1516–1598*, 482–85; Kamen, *Philip II of Spain*, 156.

12. Hoyle, "War and Public Finance," 99; Roberts, *The Early Vasas*, 264.

13. Valerii Vladimirovich Lepakhin, "Dva poslaniia Ivana Groznogo Stefanu Batoriiu," in Szvák, *Mesto Rossii v Evrazii*, 130–38; Malyshev, *Povest' o prikhozhdenii*.

14. *The Moscovia of Antonio Possevino, S. J.*; *PDSRD* vol. 1, 765–906; Jan Joseph Santich, O.S.B., *Missio Moscovitica: The Role of the Jesuits in the Westernization of Russia, 1582–1689* (New York: Peter Lang, 1995), 85–111; *DRV* vol. 12, 194–225.

15. Filjushkin, *Ivan the Terrible: A Military History*, 259–60, 265.

16. Dmitrii Volodikhin, *Ivan IV Groznyi* (Moscow: Veche, 2010), 151–55.

17. Donnert, *Die Livländische Ordensritterschaft*, 62.

Chapter 18. Ivan, 1572–1584

1. *DDG* no. 104, 426–44 (on the *oprichnina*, 444); Robert Craig Howes, *The Testaments of the Grand Princes of Moscow* (Ithaca: Cornell University Press, 1967), no. 13, 307–60 (on the oprichnina, 360); *Poslaniia Ivana Groznogo*, 162–92.

2. Charles J. Halperin, "Ivan IV's 1572 Testament as a Literary 'Mystification,'" *Palaeoslavica* 22 (2014), 199–219; Iurganov, *Kategorii russkoi srednevekovoi kul'tury*, 122–44; Cornelia Soldat, *Das Testament Ivans des Schrecklichen von 1572: Eine Kritische Aufklärung* (Lewiston, Queenstown, Lampeter: Edwin Mellen Press, 2013).

3. Howes, *The Testaments*, 305; Soldat, *Das Testament*, 55–66.

4. "Piskarevskii letopisets," 81–82, *PSRL* 34, 226–27; Donald Ostrowski, "Simeon Bekbulatovich's Remarkable Career as Tatar Khan, Grand Prince of All Rus,' and Monastic Elder," *Russian History* 39 (2012): 269–99; Ostrowski, "Response," *Russian History* 39 (2012): 339–45; Alexander Filjushkin, "The Mystery of a Political Masquerade (Concerning the Article of Donald Ostrowski)," *Russian History* 39 (2012): 301–5; Janet Martin, "Simeon Bekbulatovich and Steppe Politics: Some Thoughts on Donald Ostrowski's Interpretation of the Tsar's Remarkable Career," *Russian History* 39 (2012): 331–38; Charles J. Halperin, "Simeon Bekbulatovich and the Mongol Influence on Ivan IV's Muscovy," *Russian History* 39 (2012): 306–30.

5. *AAE* vol. 1, no. 292, 356–67; *Akty sluzhilykh zemlevladel'tsev*, vol. 3, no. 417, 341–42; *DRV* vol. 14, 293–94; *Razriadnaia kniga 1475–1605*, vol. 2, pt. 2, 391, 402; *Razriadnaia kniga 1475–1598 gg*, 259.

6. Shmidt, "Neizvestnye dokumenty," 4, 150, 155–57.

7. S. M. Kashtanov, "O vnutrennoi politike Ivana Groznogo v period 'velikogo kiazheniia' Simeona Bekbulatovicha," *Trudy Moskovkogo gosudarstvennogo istoriko-arkhivogo instituta* 16 (1961): 427–62; V. I. Koretskii, "Zemskii sobor 1575 g. i chastichnoe vozrozhdenie oprichniny," *Voprosy istorii* (1967) no. 5, 42.

8. *Zakonodatel'nye akty*, 1, no. 39, 57, 2: 60; K. V. Baranov, "Zhalovannaia gramota velikogo kniazia Simeona Bekbulatovicha Suzdal'skomu Aleksandrovichu devich'iu monastyriu 1576 g.," *Russkii diplomatarii* 1 (1997): 38–41; Kashtanov, *Ocherki russkoi diplomatiki*, 159.

9. "Dela po mestnichestvu," *Russkii istoricheskii sbornik* 5 (1838), 1–36.

10. *Poslaniia Ivana Groznogo*, 195–96.

11. *Akty sluzhilykh zemlevladel'tsev*, vol. 4, no. 28, 23–24; no. 129, 94–95.

12. Koretskii, "Materialy po istorii Zemskogo Sobora 1575 g.," no. 5, 298, 303; *PSRL* 34, 226.

13. Philip Longworth, *Russia's Empires, Their Rise and Fall: From Prehistory to Putin* (London: John Murray, 2006), 105n33, 114; Filiushkin, *Tituly russkikh gosudarei*, 95; Iuzefovich, *"Kak v posl'skikh obychaiakh vedetsia,"* 110; Hugh F. Graham, ed., "Paul Juusten's Mission to Muscovy," *Russian History* 13 (1986): 84, 87.

14. "Akty Kopengagenskago arkhiva, otnosiashchiesia k russkoi istorii," pt. 2: "1570–1576," no. 182, 32–35; *PSRL* 34, 226; Panchenko and Uspenskii, "Ivan Groznyi i Petr Velikii," 60; Skrynnikov, *Tsarstvo terrora*, 430–31, 433; Martin, *A Bride for the Tsar*, 143–44.

15. Pavlov-Sil'vanskii, *Gosudarevy sluzhilye liudi*, 78–82; Koretskii, "Zemskii sobor 1575 g.," 42; R. G. Skrynnikov, "'Kniazhenie' Simeon Bekbulatovicha i vozrozhdenie oprichniny v 1575–1576," *Istoricheskie zapiski* 87 (1971): 178, 203, 218; Pavlov and Perrie, *Ivan the Terrible*, 172–77.

16. *PSRL* 30, 161; *Pskovskie letopisi*, 2: 262; Shaposhnik, *Tserkovno-gosudarstvennye otnosheniia*, 362–82; *Opis' arkhiva Posol'skogo prikaza 1626 goda*, pt. 1, 258.

17. Wooding, *Henry VIII*, 268–71; Mordovina and Stanislavskii, "Sostav osobogo dvora," 160; Floria, *Ivan Groznyi*, 309–16.

18. Greenblatt, *Renaissance Self-Fashioning*, 162, 167.

19. Graham, "*A Brief Account*," 225–27; Pokrovskii, *Izbrannye proizvedeniia*, bk. 1, 322; Cherniavsky, "Russia," 134; Kobrin, *Ivan Groznyi*, 126–27; Ivanov, *Holy Fools*, 287–89.

20. Halperin, "*Stepennaia kniga*," 67–69; Martin, *A Bride for the Tsar*, 121–22; *The Correspondence of Prince A. M. Kurbsky and Tsar Ivan IV*, 192–93; Wooding, *Henry VIII*, 51; Filiushkin, *Andrei Mikhailovich Kurbskii*, 543–45.

21. *Puteshestviia russkikh poslov*, 150.

22. M. N. Speranskii, "Russkie poddelki rukopisei v nachale XIX veka (Bardin i Sulakadzev)," *Problemy istochnikovedeniia* 5 (1956): 62–74, 99–101; I. P. Smirnov, "O poddelkakh A. I. Sulakadzevym drevnerusskikh pamiatnikov (mesto mistifikatsii v istorii kul'tury)," *TODRL* 34 (1979): 200–19; Martin, *A Bride for the Tsar*, 112–66; Martin, "Truth and Fiction in A. I. Sulakadzev's *Chronograph of the Marriages of Tsar Ivan Vasil'evich*," *Canadian-American Slavic Studies* 47 (2013): 436–58.

23. Martin, "Truth and Fiction," 456; Isolde Thyrêt, "The Royal Women of Ivan IV's Family and the Meaning of Forced Tonsure," in *Servants of the Dynasty: Women in World History*, ed. Anne Walthall (Berkeley: University of California Press, 2008), 159–71.

24. Martin, *A Bride for the Tsar*, 72, 138–39; Daniel H. Kaiser, "'Whose Wife Will She Be at the Resurrection?' Marriage and Remarriage in Early Modern Russia," *Slavic Review* 62 (2003): 302–23; Morozova and Morozov, *Ivan Groznyi i ego zheny*, 166, 170, 173.

25. *AAE* vol. 1, no. 284, 329–32; William Craft Brumfield, *Gold in Azure: One Thousand Years of Russian Architecture* (Boston: David R. Godine Publisher, 1983), 146; Morozova and Morozov, *Ivan Groznyi i ego zheny*, 176–203.

26. Morozova and Morozov, *Ivan Groznyi i ego zheny*, 204–43; Martin, *A Bride for the Tsar*, 149; *SRIO* 38, 3–8, quote: 6; *Puteshestviia russkikh poslov*, 52, 153; Karamzin, *Istoriia gosudarstva Rossiiskago*, vol. 9, 266.

27. Wooding, *Henry VIII*, 230; Martin, *A Bride for the Tsar*, 52, 53; Bogatyrev, "Reinventing the Russian Monarchy in the 1550s," 277–78; *SRIO* 38, 3–64, 71–133.

28. Edward L. Keenan, "Ivan the Terrible and His Women," *Russian History* 37 (2010): 342; Keenan, "The Privy Domain of Ivan Vasil'evich," 87; Kollmann, "Muscovite Russia 1450–1598," 33.

29. *Razriadnaia kniga 1550–1636*, 339; *Razriadnaia kniga 1475–1605 gg*, vol. 3, pt. 1, 212.

30. *The Moscovia of Antonio Possevino, S. J.*, 12–13.

31. Viacheslav Maniagin, *Pravda Ivana Groznogo* (Moscow: "Algoritm" "Eksmo," 2006), 77–87; Pouncy, *The Domostroi*, 143–44; Frank Kämpfer, "*Dikaniki-on-posox*," 9–19.

32. Keenan, "Vita: Ivan Vasil'evich. Terrible Czar: 1530–84"; Keenan, "The Privy Domain of Ivan Vasil'evich," 87; Keenan, "Ivan the Terrible and His Women," 342; Alain Besançon, *Le Tsarévich Immolé: La symbolique de la loi dans la culture russe* (Paris: Librairie Plan, 1967), 77–87, 96- 102, 106.

33. Paul Bushkovitch, "Possevino and the Death of Tsarevich Ivan Ivanovich," *Cahiers du monde russe* 55 (2014): 119–34.

34. Kamen, *Philip II of Spain*, 120–23.

35. Martin, *A Bride for the Tsar*, 148; Tikhomirov, *Rossiiskoe gosudarstvo*, 82.

36. Hellie, "What Happened?" 215; Skrynnikov, *Tsarstvo terrora*, 430, 433, 494–95.

37. Floria, *Ivan Groznyi*, 372–73; Platt, *Terror and Greatness*, 100n43; *PSRL* 13, 142; *PSRL* 32 (Moscow: Nauka, 1975), 125; Graham, "*A Brief Account*," 230; Buganov and Rogozhin, "Kratkii Moskovskii letopisets," 563–64; Filiushkin, *Andrei Mikhailovich Kurbskii*, 422.

38. A. D. Sedel'nikov, "Dve zametki po epokhe Ivana Groznogo," in *Sbornik statei k sorokaletiiu uchenoi deiatel'nosti Akademika A. S. Orlova* (Leningrad: AN SSSR, 1934), 168–69; Elena Aleksandrovna Ryzhova, *Antonievo-Siiskii monastyr'. Zhitie Antoniia Siiskogo. Knizhnye tsentry russkogo severa* (Syktyvkar: Izdatel'stvo Syktyvkarskogo universiteta, 2000), 79.

39. Wooding, *Henry VIII*, 55; *Povest' o Petre i Fevronii*, 75–78; Ryzhova, *Antonievo-Siiskii monastyr'*, 49–96; Natal'ia Vasil'eva Ramazanova, *Moskovskoe tsarstvo v tserkovno-pevcheskom iskusstve XVI-XVII vekov* (St. Petersburg: Dmitrii Bulanin, 2001), 102, 151–67, 206–21, 272–73; Nikolai Tupikov, "Literaturnaia deiatel'nost' tsarevicha Ivana Ivanovicha," in Fomin, *Groznyi Tsar' Ioann Vasil'evich*, 149–62; Makarii, Bishop of Archangel and Kholmogory, "Istoricheskiia svedeniia ob Antonievom Siiskom monastyre," *Chteniia* 106 (1878), bk. 3, 25–26; *Biblioteka literatury drevnei Rusi*, vol. 13, 668–77.

40. Johann von Gardner, "War Zar Johann IV. (1533–1584) auch ein Melode?" *Die Welt der Slaven* 23 (1978): 42–57; von Gardner, *Russian Church Singing*, vol. 2,

History from the Origins to Mid 17th Century, trans. Vladimir Morosan (Crestwood: St. Vladimir's Seminary Press, 2000), 259–71; Claudia R. Jensen, *Musical Cultures in Seventeenth-Century Russia* (Bloomington: Indiana University Press, 2009), 3, 5, 27, 30, 40.

41. Gail Lenhoff, "The 'Stikhiri Ivana Groznogo' as a Cultural Myth," in *Poetika istoriia literatura lingvistika. Sbornik k 70-letiiu Viacheslava Vsevolodicha Ivanova* (Moscow: OGI, 1999), 45–54; Marchalis, *Liutor "izhe liut,"* 8–12; Sergei Fomin, *Pravda o pervom russkom tsare. Kto i pochemu iskazhaet obraz gosudaria Ioanna Vasil'evicha (Groznogo)* (Moscow: Russkii izdatel'skii tsentr, 2010), 31–41.

42. Ryzhova, *Antonievo-Siiskii monastyr'*, 217–18; Pettegree, *Europe in the Sixteenth Century*, 278.

43. *Pskovskie letopisi*, vol. 2, 263; Skrynnikov, *Ivan the Terrible*, 194; Petrei di Erlezunda, "Istoriia o velikom kniazhestve Moskovskom," 153–57. I wish to express my sincerest appreciation to David Savignac for consultation on the translation of *ostnem pokolol* (personal communication, January 31, 2019).

44. Tsepkov, *Reinol'd Geidenshtein*, 285, 288; *Salomon Henning's* Chronicle *of Courland and Livonia*, trans. Jerry Smith et al. (Dubuque: Kendall/Hunt Publishing, 1992), 148; *RIB*, vol. 13, 280; *Vremmenik Ivana Timofeeva*, 19.

45. Perevezentsev, "Gosudar' Ivan IV Vasil'evich Groznyi," 46–47; Miller; "The Orthodox Church," 282–83; E. A. Gordienko, *Novgorod v XVI veke i ego dukhovnaia zhizn'* (St. Petersburg: Dmitrii Bulanin, 2001), 383, 397–98; Steindorff, "Vklady tsaria Ivana Groznogo," 100; Bulychev, *Mezhdu sviatymi i demonami*, 35, 38, 177–79.

46. Zimin, *V kanun groznykh potriasenii*, 95.

47. V. I. Buganov, "K izucheniiu Sinodika opal'nykh tsaria' Ivana Groznogo 1583 g.," *Arkhiv russkoi istorii* 3 (1993): 145–60; Iu. D. Rykov, "Zapis' v sinodike moskovskogo kremlevskogo Arkhangel'skogo Sobora—novyi istochnik po istorii oprichniny tsaria Ivana Groznogo," in *Mir istochnikovedeniia (sbornik v chest' Sigurda Ottovicha Shmidta)*, ed. A. D. Zaitsev et al. (Moscow-Penza: Rossiisskii gosudarstvennyi gumanitaryni universitet, Istoriko-arkhivnyi institut. Penzenskaia oblastnaia administratsiia, Department kul'tury, 1994), 47–57; Ludwig Steindorff, "Equality under Reserve: Men and Women in Donations and Commemoration in Muscovite Russia," trans. Barbara Hegels, *Canadian-American Slavic Studies* 49 (2015): 194–95.

48. *Akty Rossiiskogo gosudarstva*, no. 3, 19–20; Bulychev, *Mezhdu sviatymi i demonami*, 35; Goldfrank, "The Deep Origins of *Tsar'-Muchitel'*," 354.

49. H. W. Dewey and A. M. Kleimola, "Old Muscovite Amnesties: Theory and Practice," *Russian History* 3 (1976): 49–60; Kleimola, "The Muscovite Autocracy at Work," 45.

50. Bulychev, *Mezhdu sviatymi i demonami*, 11–41.

51. Steindorff, "Vklady tsaria Ivana Groznogo," 97.

52. Veselovskii, *Issledovaniia po istorii oprichniny*, 323–478; Skrynnikov, *Oprichnyi Terror*, 249–65; Skrynnikov, *Tsarstvo terrora*, 10–18, appendix, 529–44.

53. Skrynnikov, *Vasilii III. Ivan Groznyi*, 378.

54. Diefendorf, *Beneath the Cross*, 177; Jouanna, *The Saint Bartholomew's Day Massacre*, 3; Salmon, *Society in Crisis*, 186–87; Richardson, *Renaissance Monarchy*, 138; Jürgen Bücking, "The Peasant War in the Habsburg Lands as a Social Systems-Conflict," in *The German Peasant War 1525—New Viewpoints*, 172; Salmon, *Society in Crisis*, 276–91.

55. *PSRL* 13, 404; D. N. Al'shits, "Neizvestnye poslaniia Ivana Groznogo," *TODRL* 12 (1956): 429; V. B. Kobrin, "Novaia tsarskaia gramota 1571 o bor'be s chumoi," *TODRL* 14 (1958): 26–27; Hindle, *The State and Social Change*, 169–71.

56. *RIB* 16, no. 51, 209–12.

57. Graham, "Paul Juusten's Mission to Muscovy," 81; Kobrin, *Ivan Groznyi*, 133; Pettegree, *Europe in the Sixteenth Century*, 129; Wooding, *Henry VIII*, 267; Plowden, *Elizabeth I*, 68; Kamen, *Philip II of Spain*, 301–16.

58. W. F. Ryan, "Ivan the Terrible's Malady and its Magical Cure," *Incantatio* 2 (2012): 23–32.

59. *PSRL* 34, 229; *RIB* 13, 275, 449; *Vremmenik Ivana Timofeeva*, 15; Mikhail Mikhailovich Gerasimov, *The Face Finder*, trans. Alan Houghton Brodrick (London: Hutchinson and Co., 1971), 184–89.

60. Edward Keenan, "Ivan IV and the 'King's Evil': *Ni Maka li to Budet?*" *Russian History* 20 (1993): 10–11; Bogatyrev, "Ivan IV (1533–84)," 252.

61. *Vremmenik Ivana Timofeeva*, 15.

62. *PSRL* 34, 229; Anna Feliksovna Litvina and Fedor Borisovich Uspenskii, *Vybor imeni u russkikh kniazei v X–XVI vv. Dinasticheskaia istoriia skvoz' prizmu antroponimiki* (Moscow: Indrik, 2006), 553; V. I. Koretskii, "Smert' Groznogo tsaria," *Voprosy istorii*, no. 9 (1979): 93–103; Koretskii, *Istoriia russkogo letopisaniia*, 48–70.

Conclusion

1. Dmitry Likhachev, *The Great Inheritance: The Classical Literature of Old Rus*, trans. Doris Bradbury (Moscow: Progress Publishers, 1981), 151, 152, 282–303; Kalugin, "Tsar' Ivan Groznyi: Stili khudozhestvennogo myshleniia," 183–210, especially 186–87, 191.

2. Solov'ev, *Istoriia Rossii*, bk. 3, vol. 6, 702–14, bk. 4, vol. 7, 141; Keenan, "How Ivan Became 'Terrible,'" 521; Kobrin, "Ivan Groznyi," 127–62.

3. Kliuchevskii, *Lektsii po russkoi istorii*, 355–78; Kliuchevskii, *Sochineniia*, vol. 2, 187–99.

4. Marchalis, *Liutor "izhe liut,"* 167; Mikhailova, *I zdes' soshlis' vse tsarstva*, 167, 203; Nørretranders, *The Shaping of Czardom*, 64n85.

5. Jules Menken, "Ivan the Terrible," *History Today*, no. 3 (1953): 173.

6. Wooding, *Henry VIII*, 179–80, 238–43; Kamen, *Philip II of Spain*, 225, 222; Richardson, *Renaissance Monarchy*, 195–98; Roberts, *The Early Vasas*, 198; Wooding, *Henry VIII*, 278–89.

7. Kleimola, "'In Accordance with the Canons,'" 228–89; Isolde Thyrêt, "Women and the Orthodox Faith in Muscovite Russia: Spiritual Experience and Practice," in Kivelson and Greene, *Orthodox Russia*, 159; Charles J. Halperin, "A Comparative Approach to Kievan Rus'," *Russian History* 42, no. 2 (2015): 149–57.

8. Gyula Szvák (Diula Svak), "Russkii Samson? (K voprosu ob otsenke istoricheskoi roli Ivana IV)," *Otechestvennaia istoriia*, no. 5 (1999): 174–80.

9. Mut'ia, *Ivan Groznyi*, 31–32; Aleksandr Ianov, *Rossiia: U istokov tragedii 1462–1584. Zametki o prirode i proiskhozhdenii russkoi gosudarstvennosti* (Moscow: Progress-Traditsiia, 2001), 372.

10. Norman W. Ingham, "The *Groza* of Ivan Groznyi in Russian Folklore," *Russian History* 14 (1987): 225–45; Maureen Perrie, *The Image of Ivan the Terrible in Russian Folklore* (Cambridge: Cambridge University Press, 1987).

11. Karamzin, *Istoriia gosudarstva Rossiiskago*, vol. 9, 274–77.

12. Kappeler, *Ivan Groznyi*, 77–81.

13. Kollmann, "Muscovite Russia 1450–1598," 60–62.

14. V. D. Nazarov, "Gosudarstvo, sosloviia i reformy serediny XVI v. v Rossii," in *Reformy i reformatory v istorii Rossii: Sbornik statei* (Moscow: IRI, RAN, 1996), 10–22.

15. Bogatyrev, "Ivan IV (1533–84)," 262–63.

16. Charles J. Halperin, "Ivan the Terrible and Muscovite Political Culture," in Kivelson et al., *Seeing Muscovy Anew*, 49–65.

17. Karavashkin, *Russkaia srednevekovaia publististika*, 159n67; Thyrêt, "The Royal Women of Ivan IV's Family," 166; Pavlov, *Gosudarev dvor*, 79; Weickhardt, "Due Process and Equal Justice," 13, 24; Korogodina, "Penitential Texts," 388.

18. *Poslaniia Ivana Groznogo*, 520.

19. *RIB* 13, 270–87, 448–49, 521, 561–63, 619–20, 629; Cherniavsky, *Tsar and People*, 53–59; Bushkovitch, *Peter the Great*, 38.

20. Sergei Bogatyrev, "Lestnitsa v nebesa. Simvolika vlasti Ivana Groznogo," *Rodina*, no. 12 (2004): 9 (color illustration); Bogatyrev, "Bronze Tsars," 48–61.

21. Ekaterina Sergeevna Ovchinnikova, *Portret v russkom iskusstve XVII veka: Materialy i issledovaniia* (Moscow: Iskusstvo, 1955), 62–65; Kämpfer, *Das Russische Herrscherbild*, 172–55; Kämpfer, "Die 'parsuna' Ivans IV. in Kopenhagen—Originalporträt oder historisches Bild?" in Waugh, *Essays in Honor of A. A. Zimin*, 187–204; M. M. Krasilen, "Portret tsaria Ivana Groznogo: vek XVII ili vek XX?," in *Prostranstva zhizni. K 85-letiiu akademika B. V. Raushenbakha* (Moscow: Nauka, 1999), 503–13.

22. Kämpfer, *Das Russische Herrscherbild*, 175–98; N. Golovin and L. M. Vol'f, ed., *Tsar' Ioann Groznyi. Ego tsarstvovanie, ego deiania, ego zhizn', sovremenniki i deiateli v portretakh, graviurakh, zhivopisi, skul'pture, pamiatnikakh zodchestva i pr. i pr.* (Moscow: Izdanie Postavshchikov Ego Imperatorskago Velichestva Tovarishchestva Tipografiia M. O. Vol'f, 1904); Cherniavsky, *Tsar and People*, between 50 and 51: no. 1, 3, 4, 14, 17; Gerasimov, *The Face Finder*, illustration 16 (between 160 and 161).

23. Gerasimov, *The Face Finder*, 284–89; 5' 10", according to Hellie, "In Search of Ivan the Terrible," xxiv. Tsarevich Fedor was 5' 3".

24. Cited by Allen Mikaelian, in *Perspectives on History: The Newsmagazine of the American Historical Association* 52, no. 9 (2014): 45.

Index